Linguistic Variation in the Shakespeare Corpus

Pragmatics & Beyond New Series

Volume 106

Linguistic Variation in the Shakespeare Corpus: Morpho-syntactic variability of second person pronouns
by Ulrich Busse

Linguistic Variation in the Shakespeare Corpus

Morpho-syntactic variability of second person pronouns

Ulrich Busse

Martin-Luther-University Halle-Wittenberg

John Benjamins Publishing Company
Amsterdam / Philadelphia

∞ ™ The paper used in this publication meets the minimum requirements of American National Standard for Information Sciences – Permanence of Paper for Printed Library Materials, ANSI Z39.48-1984.

Library of Congress Cataloging-in-Publication Data

Busse, Ulrich
    Linguistic variation in the Shakespeare corpus : morpho-syntactic variability of second person pronouns / Ulrich Busse.
       p. cm. (Pragmatics & Beyond, New Series, ISSN 0922-842X ; v. 106)
    Includes bibliographical references (p.) and indexes.
       1. Shakespeare, William, 1564–1616--Language. 2. English language--Early modern, 1500–1700--Pronoun. 3. English language--Early modern, 1500–1700--Variation. I. Title. II. Series.

PR3081.B87   2002
822.3'3-dc21   2002026159
ISBN 90 272 5346 3 (Eur.) / 1 58811 280 2 (US) (Hb; alk. paper)

John Benjamins Publishing Co. · P.O. Box 36224 · 1020 ME Amsterdam · The Netherlands
John Benjamins North America · P.O. Box 27519 · Philadelphia PA 19118-0519 · USA

For Daniela and my parents

Table of contents

CHAPTER 10
"Stand, sir, and throw us that you have about ye":
The syntactic, pragmatic and social implications of the pronoun *ye*   249

CHAPTER 11
Summary and conclusion   283

Preface and acknowledgements

The present study is a revised and updated version of my *Habilitationsschrift*, which was accepted by the faculty of languages and literature of Osnabrück University in the winter term 2000/01. The main bulk of the manuscript was written between 1996 and 2000 and revised for publication in 2001. Last additions to the bibliography were made at the stage of proof-reading in the summer of 2002. Norman Blake's Shakespeare Grammar, which had appeared earlier this year, came too late for inclusion in the book. For this reason it is only mentioned very briefly and does not get the attention that it truly deserves.

After this rather matter-of-fact report it is my duty and pleasure to say a few words of thanks to various people who in some form or other have helped me in getting this work done.

First of all, my thanks go to Oliver Grannis, my *Habilitationsvater*. He gave me all the personal freedom to pursue my way of studies. I greatly appreciate that he never acted the boss during all those years and was always willing to read through the various stages of the work and to supply helpful comments. Over the years he has not only been a mentor but turned into a friend.

For various helpful suggestions I would also like to thank Prof. David Reibel and the discussants at the national and international conferences I attended between 1996 and 2000 to introduce pilot versions of some chapters of this book. I also greatly profited from the work of many colleagues whom I did not meet in person but whose publications were inspiring. All remaining errors or shortcomings are, of course, my own.

Special thanks also go to Prof. Andreas H. Jucker and the anonymous reviewers for accepting the manuscript for publication in the series Pragmatics & Beyond.

Finally, I would like to express my thanks to Isja Conen and the whole production team of John Benjamins Publishing Company for their swift and efficient management of producing this book.

Halle (Saale) July 2002   Ulrich Busse

Abbreviations

1. Sigils used for reference to Shakespeare's works (following the conventions of citation in Marvin Spevack's concordances 1968–1980)

ADO	*Much Ado About Nothing*	LUC	*The Rape of Lucrece*
ANT	*Antony and Cleopatra*	MAC	*Macbeth*
AWW	*All's Well That Ends Well*	MM	*Measure for Measure*
AYL	*As You Like It*	MND	*A Midsummer Night's Dream*
COR	*Coriolanus*	MV	*The Merchant of Venice*
CYM	*Cymbeline*	OTH	*Othello*
ERR	*The Comedy of Errors*	PER	*Pericles*
1H4	*The First Part of King Henry The Fourth*	PHT	*The Phoenix and Turtle*
		PP	*The Passionate Pilgrim*
2H4	*The Second Part of King Henry The Fourth*	R2	*King Richard The Second*
		R3	*King Richard The Third*
H5	*King Henry The Fifth*	ROM	*Romeo and Juliet*
1H6	*The First Part of King Henry The Sixth*	SHR	*The Taming of the Shrew*
		SON	*The Sonnets*
2H6	*The Second Part of King Henry The Sixth*	STM	*Sir Thomas More*
		TGV	*The Two Gentlemen of Verona*
3H6	*The Third Part of King Henry The Sixth*	TIM	*Timon of Athens*
		TIT	*Titus Andronicus*
H8	*King Henry The Eighth*	TMP	*The Tempest*
HAM	*Hamlet*	TN	*Twelfth Night*
JC	*Julius Caesar*	TNK	*The Two Noble Kinsmen*
JN	*King John*	TRO	*Troilus and Cressida*
LC	*A Lover's Complaint*	VEN	*Venus and Adonis*
LLL	*Love's Labor's Lost*	WIV	*The Merry Wives of Windsor*
LR	*King Lear*	WT	*The Winter's Tale*

2. General abbreviations

Parts of speech, cases, tenses and other "traditional grammatical terms" are referred to by their usual abbreviations.

CEEC Helsinki Corpus of Early English Correspondence
EModE Early Modern English
FTA Face Threatening Act
ME Middle English
ModE Modern English
OE Old English
T *thou, thee, thy, thine*, etc.; also: from Latin *tu*, familiar pronoun in any language
V from Latin *vos*, polite pronoun in any language
Y *you, ye, your*, etc.

3. Symbols

>	becomes ... (etymology); larger than ... (statistics)
<	derived from ... (etymology); smaller than ... (statistics)
*	ungrammatical
?	usage questionable
⟨ ⟩	grapheme
[ ]	pronunciation
/ /	phoneme
{ }	morpheme
Ø	zero
'...'	meaning
/	end of a verse line in citations from Shakespeare's works

CHAPTER 1

General introduction

1.1 Scope and objectives of the study

In view of recent work on diachronic historical corpora of the English language such as the *Helsinki Corpus of English Texts*,[1] the *Helsinki Corpus of Early English Correspondence*,[2] the *Lampeter Corpus*,[3] the *Archer Corpus*,[4] or the most recent one, the *Corpus of English Dialogues*, one might ask why write yet another study on the well-ploughed field of address forms in drama, and, on top of that, on the basis of Shakespeare?

However, in accord with many textbooks, Crystal (1988) maintains that for the final decades of the Renaissance the works of William Shakespeare (1564–1616) and the King James Bible (the *Authorized Version*) of 1611 are the dominating influences:

> Dominate, that is, from a linguistic point of view. The question of their literary brilliance and significance is not an issue for this book. Our question is much simpler yet more far-reaching: what was their effect on the language? (Crystal 1988: 196)

As far as Shakespeare is concerned, the present study pursues basically the same objectives. Spevack (1972) also supports this claim when he states that

> indeed, our picture of English as a whole will be improved by a detailed study of all of Shakespeare's language not only because Shakespeare, we will agree, may be the greatest practitioner of English but certainly because he accounts for about 40 per cent of the recorded English of his time. (Spevack 1972: 108)

Depending upon one's definition of *word*, different results concerning the total size of the Shakespeare Corpus may be obtained. If the word count of the Spevack concordances (1968–1980) is taken as a reliable basis, the sum total of words used in the 38 Shakespeare plays amounts to 835,419 (see Table 1).

When, for example, the Shakespeare Corpus is compared to the Early Modern English section of the Helsinki Corpus, which largely excludes drama as a text type,[5] this enormous output more than matches the entire subcorpus. In the *Helsinki Corpus of English Texts* the period of Early Modern English (1500–1710) is sub-divided into three subperiods of 70 years each. According to Kytö (1996: 2) the words in the first subperiod EModE I (1500–1570) amount to 190,160. EModE II

Table 1. The overall size of the Shakespeare Corpus

Complete works	884,647	words
	118,406	lines
38 plays	835,419	words
	112,230	lines

(1570–1640), into which falls Shakespearean drama, comprises 189,800 words, and the final subperiod EModE III (1640–1710) accounts for 171,040 words, so that the entire EModE part of the corpus with its 551,000 words is far smaller than the Shakespeare Corpus.

The *Corpus of English Dialogues* (1560–1760), which is being jointly compiled at Uppsala and Lancaster Universities, includes comedies in corpus design, but it is not yet complete. The word count is currently approaching 700,000 words of running text. Once finished, the corpus will contain about 1,300,000 words from two major categories: authentic dialogues (trials and witness depositions) and constructed dialogues (comedy drama and handbooks), for the entire 200 year time-span.[6]

Despite, or rather because of these corpora, there are several convincing reasons for carrying out a completely new, corpus-based study on the factors that (can) influence the selection of second person pronouns in Shakespearean drama:

Even though the above-mentioned electronic corpora do not concentrate primarily on dramatic texts they provide invaluable databases that allow for comparisons with the Shakespeare Corpus. The advances in corpus linguistics over the past decade now make it possible to investigate synchronic and diachronic linguistic variation on a larger scale. In this way stylistic variation can be studied and sociolinguistic questions can be addressed. In the past, it was impossible to do so systematically.

As regards the Shakespeare Corpus, there are a number of mostly shorter works that deal with various aspects of Shakespeare's use of language, yet many of these studies are mainly oriented towards literary criticism rather than towards modern linguistics. The extant works on forms of address are scattered, and partly atomistic in scope, as they usually consider aspects of pronoun use in individual plays.

Many of the older works are based on the Brown and Gilman (1960) model of power and solidarity, which tries to elucidate the selection of the pronouns in a sociological approach. On the other hand, studies within the tradition of structuralist linguistics treat the choice and fluctuation of address pronouns primarily in terms of markedness.[7]

More recently, pragmatically-oriented approaches on the basis of Brown and Levinson's (1987) politeness theory have come to the fore, which, however, regard the choice of address pronouns as irrelevant, because within the framework of their theory pronoun usage is viewed as being socially predictable and thus does not add to the politeness of an utterance.

For these reasons a study that tries to incorporate the different approaches of earlier research into a comprehensive, empirically grounded description and explanation of usage on the basis of a large corpus is still wanting: only an approach such as this will allow us to draw the more general conclusions that are still needed.

1.2   Morpho-syntactic variation of second person pronouns — A working definition

Although linguistic change is a continual process, for reasons of accountability boundaries between periods have been somewhat arbitrarily established. Conventionally, the EModE period is dated from roughly 1500 to 1700.[8] Thus, Shakespeare's writing career (1589–1613) falls approximately in the middle of this period. Table 2 below shows the inventory of forms for the personal pronouns and pronoun-determiners in EModE.[9] At the beginning of the period in 1500 there is an overlap in function between second person singular and plural forms but also between individual T forms (*thy* and *thine*) and Y forms (*ye* and *you*). At the end of the period, about 1700, the only forms left over in Standard English are *you* and *your*.[10] Görlach gives a concise summary of the various processes:

> The loss of *thou/thee* and the rise of *ye/you* which left ModE with the single form *you* to express case and number is partly a syntactic phenomenon, but mainly a matter of pragmatics. [...] While the motivation of the change [to *you*] was mainly social, the choice of *thou* involved, in the decisive period between 1550 and 1620, various stylistic aspects, all of which survived only in peripheral form after 1620. (Görlach 1999a: 10f.)

Schematically, the development of the pronoun system in EModE can be represented by three isolectal stages as shown in Table 2. The personal pronouns make distinctions for gender, number and case (subjective, objective, possessive). The table presents an idealised picture, because it omits the various spellings that coexisted. Recessive variants have been put in brackets.

The table illustrates the fact that there is synchronic and diachronic morpho-syntactic variation[11] between *thou* and *you*, *ye* and *you* and between *thy* and *thine*. The variant forms are conditioned by various intra- and extra-linguistic factors. Thus, sociolinguistically *thou* and *you* can, in a loose sense of the term, be seen as being in complementary distribution in the first two stages of the period. However, a glance at the OED immediately proves that this is a gross simplification, because for Shakespeare's time a number of senses are documented that defy this neat

Table 2. Second person pronouns, absolute possessives and pronoun-determiners in EModE from 1500 to 1700

	Sg.	Pl.
1500		
Subjective	*thou*	*ye*
Objective	*thee*	*you*
Possessive	*thine*	*yours*
Determiner	*thy, thine*	*your*
1600		
Subjective	*thou*	*you (ye)*
Objective	*thee*	*you (ye)*
Possessive	*thine*	*yours*
Determiner	*thy (thine)*	*your*
1700		
Subjective	*you*	
Objective	*you*	
Possessive	*yours*	
Determiner	*your*	

(Table mine, based on Barber 1997: 148, 152, 157)

dichotomy and prove that *you* could perform a number of syntactic and social functions. Its role as polite second-person singular address pronoun is perhaps the most conspicuous in comparison to the rarer ones attested in the OED:

5. a. *Nominative*, replacing thou. Always constructed with plural verb, except in the collocation *you was*, prevalent in 17th and 18th centuries.[12]
1588 Shakes. *L.L.L.* i. i. 53 You swore to that Berowne, and to the rest.
a 1596 *Sir T. More* i. ii. 194 Well, Maister Moore, you are a merie man.

b. As *vocative*, chiefly in apposition with a noun following; in reproach or contempt often repeated after the noun (cf. thou 1 b).
1590 Shakes. *Mids. N.* iii. ii. 288 Fie, fie, you counterfeit, you puppet, you.

c. Phrase *you and your* —: a contemptuous, impatient, or good-natured dismissal of the thing or person mentioned. *colloquial.*
1607 Shakes. *Coriolanus* iv. vi. 97 You haue made good worke, You and your Apron men.

6. Denoting any hearer or reader; hence as an indefinite personal pronoun: One, any one.
1577 Googe *Heresbach's Husb.* ii. (1586) 87 You shall sometime have one branch more gallant than his fellowes.

7. Used with no definite meaning as indirect object ('ethical dative'). Cf. <u>me</u> 2 c. *archaic.*

1590 <u>Shakes</u>. *Mids. N.* i. ii. 84, I will roare you as gently as any Sucking Doue; I will roare and 'twere any Nightingale.

1602 — *Ham.* v. i. 183 If he be not rotten before he die..., he will last you some eight yeare, or nine yeare. A Tanner will last you nine yeare.

As regards the second person plural forms *you* and *ye*, there is a huge discrepancy in frequency between them in Shakespeare's time, because earlier on, *you* had already largely encroached on the former territory of *ye* as a subjective pronoun. Hence, *ye* is only marginally attested in the Shakespeare Corpus and occurs mostly in postverbal position, which can be explained by a combination of syntactic and pragmatic factors:

> When *you* had usurped the place of *ye* as a nominative, *ye* came to be used (in the 15th century), vice versa, as an objective singular and plural (= 'thee' and 'you').
>
> Now (in all uses) only *dialectal, archaic,* or *poetic*; in ordinary use replaced by <u>you</u> (OED).

In contrast to this, the choice between *thy* and *thine* is often explained in terms of a phonological constraint, in that by 1600 *thy* occurs before consonants, while before vowels both can be used:

> *Thy*: [Early ME. *þī* reduced form of *þīn* <u>thine</u>, used in ME. before consonants except *h*, but occurring before vowels in 15th century, and ultimately universal in prose use as the possessive adjective preceding its noun, = German *dein, deine*, French *ton, ta, tes*.] (OED).
>
> *Thine*: 2. *Attributively* (= German *dein*, French *ton*). Now *archaic* or *poetic* before a vowel or *h*, or when following the noun: otherwise superseded by <u>thy</u> (OED).[13]

It should be added that in analogy to *you* (cf. OED sense 6 above) the pronoun *your* also had two different functions in Shakespeare's time. So that one could establish two pronouns *your*[1] ('direct address' to one or more persons) and *your*[2] ('generic reference'):

[2] a. as possessive plural, referring to a number of persons addressed.

1591 <u>Shakes</u>. *1 Hen. VI*, ii. iv. 26 In dumbe significants proclayme your thoughts.

b. as possessive singular, referring to one person addressed (originally as a mark of respect, later generally: cf. <u>you</u> II.): replacing <u>thy</u>.

1613 <u>Shakes</u>. *Hen. VIII*, v. i. 167 Sir, your Queen Desires your Visitation.

[5] b. Used with no definite meaning, or vaguely implying 'that you know of', corresponding to the 'ethical dative' *you* (you 7): often expressing contempt.
1590 Shakes. *Mids. N.* iii. i. 33 There is not a more fearefull wilde foule then your Lyon liuing.
1602 — *Ham.* v. i. 188 Your water is a sore Decayer of your horson dead body (OED).

Since Wales has repeatedly (1985, 1995)[14] reported on the two different functions of *your* in detail, it will be left out from the present study. In summary she has found that the generalising-possessive, or generic-deictic *your²*, as in the examples cited above from the OED [sense 5.b], originated in the 1550s and that it has continued in use until the present day. The indefinite use of *your²* rose by means of extension from the possessive sense, combining "features relevant both to its referential (generic) and discourse (deictic) meaning, features which are themselves interdependent" (1995:310).

This use enjoyed particular popularity in 17th century drama and showed a significant increase between the years 1603 and 1608. But only certain playwrights and certain types of play prominently feature this usage:

> (I) 1598–1605: the satirical comedies of chiefly Jonson and also Chapman: mostly witty academic plays arising out of the so-called 'War of the Theatres'

> (II) 1603–1608: the satirical city comedies and tragicomedies chiefly written in collaboration and popular with the rising middle class. (Wales 1995:319)

In the Shakespeare Corpus it is also those plays which were written between 1603 and 1608 that testify to this dramatic fashion (cf. MND, ANT, AWW, MM and HAM). The instances of *your²* can be related to "fashionable and satirical dramatic speech acts" (ibid.). As an instructive case in point HAM (4, 3) can be mentioned. In this scene Claudius asks Hamlet where Polonius is. In his answer Hamlet gives a sententious and cynical comment on Polonius's death. He reiterates *your²* no less than four times in quick succession. *Your* is used to reinforce the self-assumed superiority of the speaker in particular areas of competence.

> (1) King: Now, Hamlet, where's Polonius?
> Hamlet: At supper.
> King: At supper? where?
> Hamlet: Not where he eats, but where 'a is eaten; a certain convocation of politic worms are e'en at him. *Your* worm is *your* only emperor for diet: we fat all creatures else to fat us, and we fat ourselves for maggots; *your* fat king and *your* lean beggar is but variable service, two dishes, but to one table — that's the end. (HAM 4, 3, 16–25, my emphasis)[15]

The ambivalence makes the pronoun very useful for the dramatist, as it simultaneously supports the illusion of the dramatic world by the speaker-addressee-bond, but also goes beyond it by incorporating the audience and by appealing to their knowledge (cf. Wales 1985: 21 f.).

1.2.1   Variation vs. choice

Change in language is caused by a deep psychological need to conform, i.e. to identify with the norms of the power elements in a social complex. There are literally thousands of possible reasons for the initial impetus for what *may* develop into an accepted change. The present study subscribes to the variationist approach as developed by the "Helsinki School":

> The variationist approach focuses on existing variation in the linguistic usage at any given time and sets out to explore the factors conditioning alternative ways of expressing (near-)synonymy. Both linguistic and external factors are commonly assessed. Studies based on this methodology are empirically highly demanding and therefore tend to operate at the level of individual changes and their textual embedding rather than social variation at large.
> (Nevalainen 1996a: 4)

Rissanen mentions that "according to Samuels [1972], change in language is caused, firstly, by variation due to inertia and differences in style, secondly, by systemic regulation, and, thirdly, by contact and extralinguistic factors" (1986: 97). In this context he introduces the term *variant field* that can also be put to use for the variability of second person pronouns:[16]

> A variant field is the pattern formed by the variants expressing one and the same meaning or relationship, and it should be defined not only by enumerating the variants and giving information on their proportion of occurrence, but also by discussing the factors, both internal and external, which affect the choice of the variant. (Rissanen 1986: 97)

Applied to the choice of second person pronouns in EModE, the variant field can quite easily be delimited by taking into account the dyads of *thou* vs. *you, ye* vs. *you*, and *thy* vs. *thine* as simple two-member fields. The individual changes will be dealt with in a synchronic and diachronic form-to-function mapping by outlining the variants in the Shakespeare Corpus and by then tracing their historical development (cf. Jacobs and Jucker 1995: 13 ff.).

In this respect, *variation* in the present study shall be defined in the following way: in the course of linguistic performance a meaningful choice between two (or more) discrete alternatives has been made. Synchronically, this choice may have been influenced by a number of factors "such as features in the phonological environment, the syntactic context, discursive function of the utterance, topic, style, interactional situation or personal or sociodemographic characteristics of the speaker or other participants" (Sankoff 1988:984).[17] In the diachronic perspective, these choices may affect the shape of the variant field; i.e. the field members may change their status by becoming marked, obsolescent, etc. leading, in the case of the English system of pronominal address, to a restructuring of the paradigm.

If two linguistic forms in a specific language co-occur at a given time it is from the point of view of economy in language very likely that they are not semantically identical — at least in their connotations, or since we deal with a set of closed-class elements that acquire meaning through their capacity of anaphoric reference or their pragmatic value we may assume that they are neither in free variation nor in complementary distribution — to borrow two terms from structural phonology — but that there is a certain overlap in function in that they should not be viewed as if in a clear-cut binary division, but as if on a sliding-scale.

Schulze (1998:7ff.) states that there is a considerable overlap between the concepts of *variation* and that of *choice*. He argues that to use a language expressively and communicatively involves cognitive processes which take place in a social world with a variety of linguistic or extralinguistic constraints. For the mechanisms and motivations behind the choices he draws on the four basic distinct properties of language as put forward by Verschueren (1995:14ff.), viz.: intersubjectivity, variability, negotiability and adaptability, of which the last two deserve special emphasis in the framework of the present study, because the pronoun choices are by no means totally mechanical and thus predictable, but flexible, which allows language users to make meaningful choices.

1.3   Theoretical foundations and methodology of the study

Wales has pointed out that the topic of address pronouns is "one of the most interesting of the grammatical changes that have taken place in English over the centuries" (1983:107). Despite the fact that its major developments have been outlined in a number of classical accounts she is of the opinion that there is still space for new research. More recently, she has reaffirmed her claim that "even material that is well known from this period (e.g. Shakespeare's plays) has not itself been probed in sufficient depth from the kind of broader perspectives and context-ualisations" (1995:310) of discourse analysis, sociolinguistics and pragmatics and their bearing on linguistics and English grammar.

Thus, the present study will try to bring some of these aspects to fruition by being multifarious, i.e. it will try to integrate different research methods, in particular those of:

1.   corpus linguistics,[18]
2.   socio-historical linguistics and
3.   historical pragmatics.

1. The study is strictly empirical and corpus-based. In contrast to earlier research which concentrated on individual plays, the whole of Shakespearean drama will be investigated by making use of Spevack's concordances and new electronic media such as the *Oxford Electronic Shakespeare*.[19] By means of investigating a corpus with its total accountability rather than a selection of texts according to hermeneutic principles, the results can be put on a basis that is statistically representative. Earlier research on Shakespeare was clearly marred by the non-availability of a complete corpus and modern (electronic) retrieval facilities:

> Twentieth-century studies tended to think small, and in small pieces. Selected phenomena were analyzed on the basis of small and representative samples, although, lacking the yardstick of completeness and an easy access to the complete Shakespeare, we could never really say just how small or large, representative or unrepresentative, the samples or for that matter the phenomena were. (Spevack 1972: 107)

With the completion of the concordances, Spevack could indeed study single phenomena or combinations "against the background of Shakespeare's total usage" (1972: 108). Thirty years later, with the publication of the above-mentioned diachronic corpora it is not only possible to account completely for the distribution of items in the Shakespeare Corpus and come to linguistically relevant conclusions (cf. Stein 1974: 2) but also to extend and project the findings by comparing them with data from other recently assembled corpora or other related studies in order to answer, for example, questions such as whether pronoun usage in drama resembled that of contemporary society or was rather conventionalised.[20]

In the past there have been objections to corpus studies, especially from theoretically minded scholars working within the field of generative transformational grammar.[21] First and foremost, the limitations of a corpus, especially its selectiveness and its accidental nature, were objected to, as they will only allow for the analysis of those forms or features that are present in the corpus, and that it cannot be verified which of the data should be ascribed to performance, but not to competence.

This is of course not true for historical linguistics. Svartvik (1992: 8–10) points out ten reasons in support of corpus linguistics, among which, for the present investigation, the aspects of verifiability and the absence of native speakers in historical studies are the most important ones.

Adding to this, the Shakespeare Corpus is a special case of a closed and complete set of data allowing "the possibility of total accountability of linguistic features" (Svartvik 1992: 9). Stein in his analysis of inflections in the Shakespeare Corpus also draws attention to the special nature of the corpus. In his opinion the Shakespeare Corpus poses two major problems which are closely connected. Firstly, it is a literary corpus, and, secondly, there are a number of uncertainties in its textual transmission. Both features give rise to a dialectics of grammatical description and literary interpretation (cf. Stein 1974: 7).

2. It has often been noted that in the period of EModE apart from the pronoun system a number of other important morpho-syntactic changes were underway, as e.g. the inflections of the third person singular -*th*/-*s*, the auxiliaries *will*/*shall*, the relative pronouns *which*/*the which* etc., use or non-use of *do*, etc. In Shakespeare's time all of these were viable alternatives, however, they could quite purposefully be used as means for social, stylistic, rhetorical, etc. variation, and we can positively assume that Shakespeare was keenly aware of the effects of this variability.

Despite the varied history of transmission for individual plays, many of these variants are textually stable and cannot simply be attributed to the hands of different scribes or compositors.[22] For this reason, they can be accounted for in the framework of socio-historical linguistics. Romaine (1982), Milroy (1992) and others have provided the theoretical basis to transpose modern techniques employed in sociolinguistics for explaining language variation and change into the domain of historical linguistics.[23]

On the one hand, this implies of course that modern methods of socio-linguistics (e.g. Labov 1994) based on socio-economic factors cannot immediately be transferred to Early Modern England, with its rank system representing an intermediate stage between medieval society with its three estates and the modern class society (cf. Laslett 1983, Wrightson 1991, Burke 1992, Leith 1997).

On the other hand, such approaches to explain linguistic variation by establishing correlations between intra- and extralinguistic factors presuppose that stable relations obtain between factors like regional background, socio-economic status of speakers, situation, text type etc. with linguistic features. For the Late Medieval and Early Modern society in England, which was still hierarchically structured and only at the brink of the modern upwardly mobile society, such a relationship may with some confidence be assumed.[24]

The substitution of *thou* by *you* in the course of some 500 years is an interesting case in point. The S-curve model of linguistic change (cf. Aitcheson 1991: 83 ff., Labov 1994: 65 ff., Ogura and Wang 1996) accounts for the frequencies of incoming and recessive variants during language change. The replacement of *thou* by *you* starts very slowly in the 13th century, reaches its peak in the 16th and 17th centuries, and then slowly recedes from the 18th century onwards, except in special genres and registers. Hope notes that

> the important point here is that during the exponential phase, an early Modern English speaker's frequency of use of 'thou' will be determined by a number of factors. We know that in-coming prestige variants like 'you' are used more frequently by younger, more educated, more urban members of the speech community. (Hope 1994b: 7)

Applied to the context of Shakespeare's plays, socio-historical linguistic tools will, on the level of macro analysis, allow for the objective measurement of usage frequencies that might be attributed to language change as Shakespeare was progressing through his writing career, and on the other hand, on the micro level, discourse (dyads) of the fictional characters can reveal patterns in the socially and pragmatically motivated choices that speakers make in communication.

3. As mentioned above, historical pragmatics is to serve as a third theoretical foothold of the present study. In their conceptual outline of the discipline, Jacobs and Jucker concede that "it might be argued that historical pragmatics is just a new label for a range of research efforts that have existed for a long time" (1995:4) but, nonetheless, they deem the new label justified because it "will give these research efforts a focus that has been lacking so far". In their state-of-the-art report they distinguish between two different approaches within this broad framework, i.e. synchronic/diachronic pragmatics and pragmaphilology. The two domains of historically oriented pragmatics are characterised as follows:

1. the description and the understanding of conventions of language use in communities that once existed and that are no longer accessible for direct observation, and

2. the description and the explanation of the development of speech conventions in the course of time. [...] However, historical pragmatics can also be used as a philological tool to explain literary artefacts from the past.
    (Jacobs and Jucker 1995:6)

In his description of the Shakespeare hypertext, Neuhaus (1990:81) gives an outline of the contributions of linguistics to Shakespeare studies and deplores that it has hitherto played only a marginal role and that many of its efforts still belong to the older conception of linguistics. On the basis of the hypertext, he sees possibilities in the immediate future for applied informatics and linguistics in the fields of quantitative stylistics and the study of linguistic variation.

Stein (1987) and Rissanen (1990) also comment "on the happy reunion of English philology and historical linguistics" after a period of benign neglect in the 1960s. Among the factors that have helped to end "this unfortunate breakdown in communication between historical linguists and philologists" (354) Rissanen mentions:

– the rapid increase of sociolinguistic studies

– growing interest in language variation

– focused interest on performance, i.e. the communication situation, and the members of the speech community linked especially to the works of Labov (1966, 1994), Samuels (1972), Bailey (1973), Romaine (1982) and Milroy and Milroy (1985).

In a graph, he explains the relationship between philology and linguistics in historical studies of the English language as follows: for the periods of OE and ME, philology takes up a large part in studies which demand "a great deal of solid philological knowledge on the background of texts" (361). This focus shifts rapidly with the emergence of EModE texts, about which a lot of background information is known. For these texts (socio-)linguistic studies become possible.

For Rissanen the new approach to historical language studies, to which I would like to subscribe whole-heartedly, should combine the following strong points of both disciplines:

> From philology it should inherit an "ear for the language of the past", based on extensive reading of texts, an interest in the finest nuances of expression, a solid textual basis for research, and a focus on cultural, historical, educational, and personal aspects in analysing the language of a text. The contribution of linguistics should be a solid theoretical background to encourage disciplined generalizations, a vision of language as a simultaneously individual and social phenomenon, an interest in not only written but also spoken expression, and more powerful methodological and technological tools for collecting and handling linguistic data. (Rissanen 1990: 366)

Methodologically, the study will be inductive and data-driven by incorporating quantitative and qualitative features. McEnery and Wilson summarise the difference between these two ways of analysis as follows: "in qualitative research no attempt is made to assign frequencies to the linguistic features which are identified in the data. Whereas in quantitative research we classify features, count them, and even construct more complex statistical models in an attempt to explain what is observed [...]" (1996: 62f).

The intention to combine the three different strands of linguistic research as outlined above and their methodologies is twofold:

on the one hand, to bridge the gap between empirical and theoretical linguistics by evaluating the data in the light of recent advances in theoretical linguistics in terms of language change, grammaticalization, etc. and, especially to shed light on some of the sociolinguistic patterns governing variation as postulated by Weinreich et al. (1968), namely constraints, transition, embedding, evaluation and actuation by linking the results of the corpus study to research on other diachronic corpora, and thus contribute to a better understanding of a crucial period of language change in the English system of pronominal address, from 1500 to 1700, that has led to a complete restructuring of the pronoun paradigm, and,

on the other hand, to contribute to Shakespeare studies, which for a long time have been preoccupied with the interpretation of individual plays, characters, or the explanation of difficult text passages in the sense of "crux-busting" by drawing attention to phenomena of corpus-internal developments that are, putatively, also of importance for the literary appreciation and interpretation of characters, plays, genres, dates of composition, authorship studies etc.

1.4   Outline of the study

While there is an overall structure to the arrangement of chapters in the book leading from primarily quantitative to qualitative corpus investigations of related aspects, the individual chapters are self-contained entities.

The chapters of the book usually begin with a working hypothesis on the items of variation under scrutiny, followed by a critical discussion of seminal previous work in the field that will then serve as a backdrop for the empirical corpus studies. The data are categorised and analysed by applying the basic methods as outlined in Chapter 1.3. The findings of each chapter are summarised in a short conclusion.

For this reason, readers are not forced to stick to the pre-arranged order of chapters but can feel free to create an order of their own choice. Very impatient readers may find it desirable to start at the far end and take the final summary and conclusion as an introduction to the topic that puts everything that has gone before into a clearer, more concise perspective.

Previous research on the use of personal pronouns in Early Modern English with special reference to Shakespeare's plays

2.1 Introduction

Rudanko says that "to write on Shakespeare today poses many challenges, including that of familiarity. Whatever one may want to say may have been said before and not only said before, but rebutted twice over" (1993: 1). His solution to the problem is "to avoid rehearsing old arguments" and to employ new tools for inquiry. However, to do this in the field of the second person pronouns implies basically two things: firstly, to prepare a comprehensive study to review the vast amount of work which has already been done, and, secondly, once the critical literature has been brought up to date, to decide what still needs to be done and how it should be carried out.

Critical surveys of the works published on forms of address in the Shakespeare Corpus show that the complex problem of personal pronouns has attracted a great number of scholars from the late nineteenth century onwards. For the reason that these works have been outlined before (cf. Wales 1983, Busse 1998a and Stein forthc.) only those texts that can be considered as cornerstones for our topic shall be presented here in this overview chapter. This is not to say that the texts not mentioned are considered to be of less value or importance. There are a number of mostly shorter works that cover the topic of address forms in Shakespeare, but these usually investigate the use of personal pronouns in individual plays or deal with specific issues connected to pronoun use. These works will be discussed in the following chapters in the light of specific research questions.

2.2 Classics in the field

In the late nineteenth century we find general reference works and dictionaries that list and describe linguistic peculiarities of Shakespeare's language use, including the personal pronouns. The first comprehensive, and in many respects, classical account of the function of the address pronouns in Shakespeare's works is to be found in Abbott's *Shakespearian Grammar* ([1870] 1972). The book may be old-fashioned, but it contains useful material (cf. Barber 1997: 182). In §§231–235, pp. 153–159, Abbott deals with "Thou and You". Despite this heading he mostly concentrates on *thou*. In §231 (p. 154) he describes the four basic functions of *thou* as follows:

1. affection towards friends,
2. good-humoured superiority to servants,
3. contempt or anger to strangers,
4. in the higher poetic style and in the language of solemn prayer.

Due to the fact that *thou* had largely fallen into disuse in Shakespeare's time, it was usually regarded as archaic and thus often readily adopted in usages as listed under (4). To these functions he adds "that this use is modified sometimes by euphony [...] and sometimes by fluctuations of feeling" (154). The various uses are illustrated by numerous examples. Unfortunately, he does not provide a similar outline for *you*. Thus, we have to infer its use *ex negativo* from the functions of *thou* as listed above.

In form of an alphabetically organised dictionary, Schmidt and Sarrazin ([1874/75] 1962) also give a short outline of the major (social) functions of the two pronouns:

> Thou [...] being the customary address from superiors to inferiors, and expressive, besides, of any excitement of sensibility; of familiar tenderness as well as of anger; of reverence as well as of contempt.
> (Schmidt and Sarrazin [1875] 1962: 1214)

> You [...] the usual address to one as well as to several persons [...]. Used indefinitely, = one, they: *in these times you stand on distance*, Wiv. II, 1, 233.
> (Schmidt and Sarrazin [1875] 1962: 1407 f.)

In addition to further information on the use after imperatives, the exchange of *thou* for *thee* and *you* as ethical dative, they also point to the frequent fluctuation of the pronouns. All of these uses are amply illustrated by quotations.

Franz (1898/99) follows in this tradition. In the fourth edition of his book ([1939] 1986) in §§289–306 (pp. 257–278) he gives an even more detailed description of the social and emotive functions of the two address pronouns, again by providing quotations and philological interpretations of specific pronoun usages. The (proto-)typical functions of the pronouns as outlined by these three classics in the field still hold until the present day, although, despite their pioneering character and philological precision, these early treatments can be criticised for paying too much attention to detail and of not allowing comparisons in distribution. For instance, Stein (1974: 2 f.) deplores that the older studies, including Franz, did not try to account for total distributions of variant forms and that in this way they do not make statements that are linguistically relevant.

For reasons of fairness and historical justice it needs to be mentioned that these scholars were excellent and widely-read philologists. However, this older strand of research had to rely on gathering data by extensive reading and collecting them by means of citation slips. But the drawer-cum-slip-method hardly allows for quantitative comparisons between authors, epochs, etc.

Byrne ([1936] 1970) provides a detailed treatment of the use and functions of the address pronouns in Shakespeare's works. After a historical outline of the development of pronoun use from the 13th century onwards, she discusses the significance of pronoun usage as a means for characterisation. She subdivides Shakespeare's work chronologically into four periods and treats all plays with the exception of TNK. She concludes her thesis by providing a summary of pronoun usage by the chief character types in the plays and by giving evidence on the motivation of pronoun choices. For instance, in her summary of *you/thou*-usage in LR, she gives the following usage patterns for the two pronouns:

> *thou* is used by father to daughters; in respect; in appeal; in anger; in love; in apostrophe; in confidence; to self; to an inferior, servant or messenger; to a fool in privileged language; in affection; in sympathy; to the absent; in appeal; in companionship; in excitement; in contempt; by lower class equals; in reverence; in intimacy; in tenderness; in surprise; in contempt; in threat; in gratitude; to a spirit; to the dead.

> *you* is used in courtly intercourse; by sisters ordinarily; to a steward as a gentleman servant; to a superior or master; to a parent; by a parent to children of rank. (Byrne [1936] 1970:114)

2.3   Brown and Gilman's concept of power and solidarity semantics

In the more recent past the (inter-)social functions of the second-person pronouns have often been discussed within the framework of the model introduced by Gilman and Brown (1958), Brown and Gilman (1960) and Brown and Ford (1961),[1] who wrote three consecutive articles on the development of the forms of pronominal and nominal address in European languages. In their first paper, Gilman and Brown (1958) trace the difference of pronominal address back to the Roman Empire of the 4th century, when the pronoun *vos* appears as a reflex of the *nos pluralis majestatis* of the emperor. From then on, they show the spread of the plural form and the development on two planes: a vertical dimension of status which yields the polite plural pronoun as a deferential address to superiors, and the singular pronoun as an address form for social inferiors, and on the horizontal level a reciprocal exchange of plural pronouns among social equals when not intimate or well acquainted, and the singular pronoun as a sign of intimacy. In their 1960 article they introduce the term *power semantics*, which is characterised by a non-reciprocality of the forms of address between members of different social strata. Wales

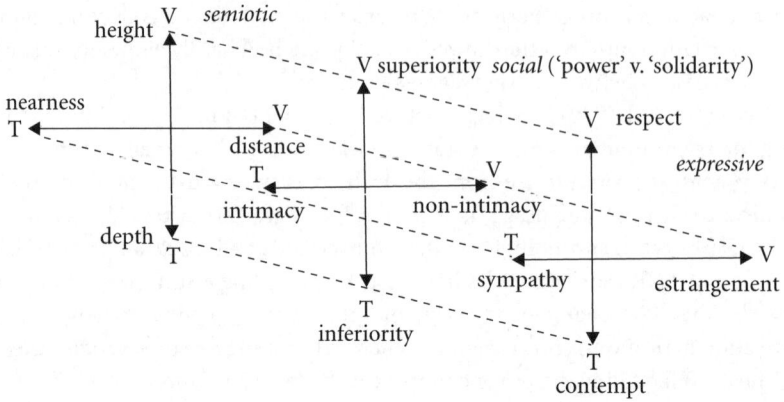

Figure 1. The planes of Brown and Gilman's power and solidarity semantics.

(1983:110) neatly summarises the dichotomies of power and solidarity in form of a figure.

In Figure 1 T and V stand as generic language independent designators for the simple or intimate second person singular pronoun of address (T) and the polite and more distant second person plural pronoun (V). The symbols have been introduced by Brown and Gilman (1960) and the abbreviations refer to the putative origin in Latin *tu* and *vos*.

Brown and Gilman relate this scheme to static and hierarchical societies in Europe from the Middle Ages well into the 19th century. Although not precisely dated, but allegedly operational in EModE society, Brown and Gilman see the development of a new scheme which they term *solidarity semantics* and which does not operate on hierarchical class distinctions but on notions of intimacy and like-mindedness, and which results in a reciprocal exchange of pronouns; the choice of singular or plural forms depending on whether the addressee is regarded as closely related to the speaker or not. Brown and Gilman attribute the emergence of this category to a change in the social structure of European societies that led to "social mobility and an equalitarian ideology" ([1960] 1972:117).

In so doing they construct a close link between changes in society and those in language, or to put it more directly — the choice of the pronouns of address would then be the immediate corollary of social change. I would subscribe to the criticism put forward by Wales, where she refutes the "direct connection between social structure, group ideology, and linguistic features, i.e. pronouns" (1983:123) in favour of a mere relatability.

By providing typical relational pairs, Hope (1994b) has formalised the reciprocal and non-reciprocal exchange of T/V pronouns in form of a table.

He has applied this model to the gender variable finding that "there is a general tendency towards the predicted weighting of V forms from women to men, and that

Table 1. T/V choice and social relationship

1. *T forms* non-reciprocal (unequal power relationship) used by superior to inferior, e.g.:
    husband to wife; parent to child
    master or mistress to servant
    monarch to subject
    male to female

2. reciprocal (equal power relationship/solidarity) used to signal equality of social power (lower class) or shared concern/interest, e.g.:
    between lower class members
    between siblings
    between lovers
    between close friends

3. *V forms* non-reciprocal (unequal power relationship) used by inferior to superior, e.g.:
    wife to husband
    child to parent
    servant to master or mistress
    subject to monarch
    female to male

4. reciprocal (equal power relationship, neutral or uncertain power relationship), e.g.:
    between upper class members
    as a neutral form to strangers
    and increasingly as the general second person singular pronoun

(Table from Hope 1994b: 57, slightly edited)

this is more marked in Fletcher than in Shakespeare" (1994b: 60), but he also admits that due to a general lack of female characters in the plays a particular "thouful" male speech can skew the statistics. Mazzon confirms that in HAM, LR and OTH "men do tend to use more *thou* than women" (1992: 133).[2]

For the usefulness of the Brown and Gilman model to explain pronominal variation in EModE, Wales comes to the conclusion that

> BG's model is 'powerful' and therefore attractive, because it formulates sociolinguistic universals. But the danger is with such models that the potentiality for individual variation and development on the part of specific speech communities is under-estimated, or backgrounded; and that other potential universals are not considered. (Wales 1983: 122)

The main difficulties within the Brown and Gilman approach to the English language, and to EModE in particular, lie in the facts that the overlay of social and affective usages of *thou* are often difficult or impossible to distinguish, and, furthermore, in Shakespearean English there is often momentary fluctuation in

Table 2. The stages of the development of T and V in Europe

	Stage 1		Stage 2		Stage 3		Stage 4	
	S	NS	S	NS	S	NS	S	NS
a. I P → I P	T	T	V	V	T	V	T	V
b. − P → − P	T	T	T	T	T	V	T	V
c. + P → − P	T	T	T	T	T	*T*	T	V
d. − P → + P	T	T	V	V	*V*	V	T	V

Stage 1: original situation, only singular and plural distinguished
Stage 2: introduction of the power factor, non-reciprocal usage between c) and d)
Stage 3: introduction of the solidarity factor, points of conflict of the two factors italicized
Stage 4: resolution today of the conflict in favour of the solidarity factor

(Table from Wales 1983:112)
Abbreviations: P = Power; S = Solidarity; NS = no solidarity

pronoun usage among two interlocutors which cannot be explained by a model assuming rather static social hierarchies.

Brown and Gilman's model is further flawed for some linguists by the fact that the solidarity factor and the power factor come into conflict, especially when in in-group situations e.g. among relatives or friends of unequal social status the socially inferior speaker can choose between the *thou* of in-group solidarity or the deferential *you* of power semantics.

With reference to Trudgill (1974:107) Wales has tabulated the various stages of the introduction of power and solidarity semantics in Europe. In Table 2 the areas of conflict in stage 3 have been highlighted.

Many European languages other than English have resolved this problem by resorting to the T pronoun for solidarity and the V pronoun for non-solidarity. This is, however, somewhat oversimplified. There is in fact a definite hierarchy of factors, so that someone may use V to an older person although there is a strong element of solidarity in the relationship. For instance, in German *Sie* is frequently used to soften or avoid a conflict situation. In English, however, this did not happen, as *you* eventually (except in dialectal use) pushed *thou* out of the system.

In this respect, Lutz argues that the "Modern English paradigm is exceptional not only in comparison with that of the immediately preceding stages of the language and with that of the other Germanic and Indo-European languages [...], but also compared to many entirely unrelated languages" (1998:190). Table 3 illustrates that the person systems of the world's languages consist of four, five or six members.

The OE, ME and EModE 6-person system is the most frequent among the world languages. It occurs in 19 of the 60 languages investigated by Ingram (1978:216). "By contrast, the system distinguishing only five forms, as exemplified

Table 3. Person systems in the languages of the world

6-person system e.g.: OE, ME, EMode		5-person system e.g.: ModE		4-person system e.g.: Korean, Kamanugu	
Sing.	Plur.	Sing.	Plur.	Sing.	Plur.
I	we	I	we	I	we
thou	you		you	thou	
he	they	he	they	he	

(Combination of Tables from Lutz 1998: 191 and Yong-Lin 1988: 159 f.; slightly edited)

by Modern English [...] is not recorded by Ingram for any other language of his sample" (Lutz 1998: 191).

Yong-Lin (1988: 159) states that there are 150 languages exhibiting at least two separate forms to indicate number variation in second person pronouns. He points out that in addition to English, Korean and Kamanugu lack the singular–non-singular distinction for the second person. In fact, these two languages do not have a plural form for the third person either.

Apart from these two languages, the notion of markedness may be evoked here, saying that according to Greenberg's (1966) "universal implication law" a language that has the item A, necessarily also has the item B, but not vice versa. In this dyad A is regarded as the marked element and B the unmarked one. This can also be applied to the two pronouns *thou* and *you*. Head has shown that any language that has a second person singular pronoun also possesses a second person plural pronoun, but not the other way around. In his study 90 languages make use of number variation "with second person pronouns as a means for showing degrees of respect or social distance" (1978: 157).

Given basically the same social background as France and Germany, why did the English pronominal system develop so differently? Following Wales (1983), Mühlhäusler and Harré and also Leith think that unlike Brown and Gilman's assumption there was not an "equalitarian ideology" or "an egalitarian ethic" operating in 16/17th century England. Leith believes that, quite to the contrary, the pronominal change is "a reflex of middle-class insecurity" (1997: 107), particularly in the London urban society, which would also explain the "Elizabethan obsession" with titles. Mühlhäusler and Harré also subscribe to this point of view in that they interpret *you* as an urban status marker which was "simply bound to become more and more widely used" (1990: 153).[3] However, Mausch (1993) suggests that the pronominal system collapsed for morphological rather than sociological reasons.

These questions are not dealt with satisfactorily in the concept of Brown and Gilman. Owing to this, it has been criticised as being too rigid and too deterministic, as it does not readily lend itself to account for variation as a rule rather than an exception, although — from the present-day point of view — the intricate nature of pronoun variation makes it difficult to include it in any theoretical concept. Our knowledge of 16th and 17th century society is still very incomplete. For example, Hope (1994b) finds the factors governing EModE pronoun usage quite confusing, "with at least three competing systems — a social system, an emotional/politeness-based system, and a system in which 'you' is the only available form — all open to use by speakers" (1994b: 58). From these he only expects the last subsystem to show "socio-historical linguistic patterning consistently", because the social and emotional subsystems "would be expected to disrupt it" (ibid.). With respect to the demise of the T forms during the EModE period it must be added that "*you* is polite only as long as it is opposed to *thou*. When *thou* loses frequency, the polite connotation of *you* is worn out to the same extent" (Braun 1988: 59).

In a third influential paper, Brown and Ford (1961) examine the nominal forms of "Address in American English". They contrast usages of first names/last names and (honorific) titles with the result that in the vast majority of cases first names are exchanged reciprocally and last names and titles occur only at the beginning of an acquaintanceship. The relationship is symmetrical and the choice is governed by factors of intimacy and distance. Non-reciprocal exchange is put down to differences in age or professional status. The progression from formal to less formal forms of nominal address in the course of a relationship is usually initiated by the older and/or socially superior speaker.

Despite the dictum of Brown and Ford that Modern English nominal forms of address are reasonably well described by the binary contrast of First Name vs. Title and Last Name, it should have become clear that in a hierarchically structured society as in Early Modern England the forms of nominal and pronominal address do not work as separate systems but in unison, and they should hence not be reduced to a dichotomy. Blake, for instance, has pointed out that the incorporation of "all forms of address used in a play [could] help to provide some guidance for the correct interpretation of the social and emotional context of a given scene so that its pragmatics can be properly assessed" (1990: 68). Thus, a study on pronoun choices in Shakespeare's plays, especially those where pronoun switching is difficult to assess or seems to be unmotivated, could possibly be made firmer by analysing all forms of address together with the register of the whole utterance in respect of ordinary or ornate vocabulary and/or syntax, etc.

2.4   Politeness theory applied to Shakespearean drama

After this criticism of their earlier theories it is interesting to discuss the Brown and Gilman (1989) approach to Shakespearean drama in the concept of politeness theory as proposed by Brown and Levinson (1987).[4] In this article, Brown and Gilman investigate the four tragedies of HAM, LR, MAC and OTH.

The four plays were systematically searched for pairs of minimally contrasting discourse dyads where the dimensions of contrast were *power*, *distance*, and the *intrinsic extremity* of the Face Threatening Act (cf. Brown and Gilman 1989: 161). The dimensions of social power and horizontal social distance (earlier termed *solidarity*) are the same as those put forward in Brown and Gilman (1960). But in addition to these two parameters concerned with the interpersonal relationship between speaker and addressee, a third dimension is taken into account — the intrinsic extremity of the speech act, i.e. "how great a thing is requested" (ibid.) accounts for what is being communicated. Politeness theory, which makes use of speech act theory, pragmatics, and discourse analysis goes far beyond the immediate scope of pronoun variation in that it claims that the three above-mentioned variables are universal.

Within this larger framework, the forms of address, and, in particular the personal pronouns, play only a minor role. For each of the four plays stretches of discourse between two characters have been selected that differ in only one of the three variables above. Factors that are taken into account when the degree of politeness of an utterance is evaluated are, among others, the use of names and titles as indicators of deference.

Apart from this, the authors note the affective usages of the pronouns. Although they refer to Jespersen ([1946] 1972), who "believed that English *thou* and *you* in Shakespeare's time were more often shifted to express mood and tone than were the cognate pronouns in continental languages" (1989: 177), Brown and Gilman pay very little attention to this phenomenon "very unusual among world languages" (178) in their theory. Even if they grant that the two principles of status and expressive values alone cannot explain the full usage of the pronouns in Shakespeare, they leave the aspect of fluctuation largely aside and "assign complications to context" (ibid.).

Despite his criticism of the theory in the first part of his study, Kopytko (1993a, 1995)[5] has also carried out research in the theoretical framework of Brown and Levinson. He has investigated linguistic politeness strategies in four of Shakespeare's comedies, and four of his tragedies. Explicitly excluded from his study were all the forms of address, e.g. names, titles and pronouns. In contrast to Brown and Gilman, who subdivided social distance into the two independent variables of *interactive intimacy* and *affect*, Kopytko offers a more complex set of factors, such as *affect*, *cunning*, *importance*, and *intimacy*. He regards this set of components by no means as final and exhaustive. Methodologically, he differs from Brown and Gilman in that his version of politeness theory is indeterministic.

He has found that in his sample of eight plays positive politeness strategies prevail over strategies of negative politeness. The tendency is more clearly marked though in the tragedies with 338 cases of positive politeness prevailing over only 80 cases of negative politeness (4.2:1). This contrast is not so clearly borne out in the comedies with only 162 instances of positive politeness compared to 57 of negative politeness (2.8:1). Kopytko says that the question of why there are more instances of politeness in tragedies than in comedies cannot easily be explained without resorting to guessing or making such trivial statements "because the exigency of plot, or a character delineation etc., require it so" (1993a:110). He thinks that the question of how this happened is much more interesting than why this happened in the first place, suggesting that the more frequent use of politeness in tragedies in comparison to comedies "is closely associated with the numerical increase of some social/psychological variables correlated with particular strategies of politeness in tragedies" (1993a:111).

In summary, he tentatively concludes that "the interactional style or 'ethos' of British society has evolved from the dominating positive politeness culture in the 16th c. towards the modern negative politeness culture" (1993a:110), if it can rightly be assumed that the strategies depicted by Shakespeare bear resemblance to those prevalent in Elizabethan society around him.

Magnusson has also applied the Brown and Levinson model to Shakespearean drama. She has analysed directives in H8, but was unaware of Brown and Gilman's paper while writing her article. Nonetheless, she comes to the same conclusion regarding terms of address by referring to the predictive force of Brown and Levinson's politeness theory: "if Brown and Levinson's politeness theory has predictive force for Elizabethan usage, then we should expect to find increased frequencies of vocative titles in the contexts of 'face-threatening acts'. A brief survey shows that this is true at least of *Henry VIII*, I, 1. This scene contains twelve such vocatives [...]" (1992:399).

More recently, she has elaborated her study on H8, finding that "much of the complicated eloquence of characters like Katherine and Wolsey in *Henry VIII* arises not as a matter of their individual expression but instead out of the contexts of their interactions — both out of the immediate relations of their dialogue and out of their long-term, habituated speech positions" (Magnusson 1999:11). From this she concludes that a character's speech habits are more constrained by factors of social politeness than by matters of personality or by Shakespeare's personal style (34).

Rudanko (1993) also applies various pragmatic approaches to Shakespeare. He investigates OTH in terms of discourse analysis and case grammar, COR in the framework of a Searlian speech act analysis, and, more importantly for our present purpose, TIM in the light of the above-mentioned theories of Brown and Levinson and their extension and special application to Shakespeare by Brown and Gilman. While he grants that Brown and Levinson's model is pioneering and impressive, he is of the opinion that it is incomplete and thus in need of addition. He argues that politeness theory rests basically upon two notions, viz. *face* and *rationality*. In Rudanko's opinion, these concepts do not automatically lead to linguistic politeness:

> Even if rationality is accepted as a principle guiding human behavior, it is still perfectly possible to hold that it does not always lead to politeness. Even a perfectly rational human being is capable of acting in a way other than politely, for any number of reasons. (Rudanko 1993: 167)

Because "acting in a way other than politely [is not] necessarily the same as the absence of politeness", Rudanko introduces the concept of *nastiness*. "Nastiness consists in adding something gratuitously to offend the hearer" (167). Holding this assumption to be true, then entails the formulation of a sixth super strategy for doing FTAs. "Given the scale from 1 to 5 […] with 1 being 'Do the FTA on record without redressive action, baldly', this new strategy may be numbered = and labeled [as the 0-strategy] 'Do the FTA on record with aggravating action employing nastiness'". Against the background of the substrategies of negative and positive politeness, Rudanko develops a fully-fledged inventory of substrategies for nastiness (168–171) and then applies this apparatus to the analysis of TIM.

Some of the substrategies of nastiness have a direct bearing upon the forms of address, because they affect the choice of pronouns and/or vocatives, e.g. substrategy 4 of positive nastiness: "use markers denoting lack of identity and emphasizing difference of group" by inappropriately addressing interlocutors as *sir* or *boy* in order to express "disrespect, contempt or some similar negative attitude" (168); or, substrategy 5 of positive nastiness: "exclude expressions of deference. Instead demand obsequious deference from the hearer, for instance, in the form of terms of address such as *sir*" (170).

The application of the "0-strategy" in a conversation shows that the speaker tries to achieve a "turning the knife in the wound"-effect by aggravating unpleasant matters through the means of nastiness. This can be illustrated by many speeches in Shakespeare's plays. As an example, the exchange between Duke Frederick and his niece Rosalind in AYL that leads to her banishment from his court shall be discussed briefly:

(1) Duke Frederick: *Mistress*, dispatch *you* with your safest haste, / And get *you* from *our* court.

(2) Rosalind: Me, *uncle*?

(3) Duke Frederick: *You, cousin.* / Within these ten days if that *thou* beest found / So near *our* public court as twenty miles, / *Thou* diest for it.

(4) Rosalind: I do beseech *your Grace* / Let me the knowledge of my fault bear with me: / If with myself I hold intelligence, / Or have acquaintance with mine own desires; / If that I do not dream, or be not frantic / (As I do trust I am not), then, *dear uncle*, / Never so much as in a thought unborn / Did I offend *your Highness*.

(5) Duke Frederick: Thus do all *traitors*: / If their purgation did consist in words, / They are as innocent as grace itself. / Let it suffice *thee* that I trust *thee* not. (AYL 1, 3, 41–55, my emphasis)

In (1) Duke Frederick addresses his niece formally and respectfully as *mistress*, a title of honour[6] and with the corresponding pronoun *you*. He distances himself by resorting to the royal *our*, by which he stresses his independence and authority. In Rosalind's short question (2), the vocative *uncle* seeks to assert common ground by stressing their family relationship with a familiar form of address which functions as an in-group identity marker in speech. However, the effect of Rosalind's strategy does not last long. Her familiarity has only upset the duke momentarily, when he (in 3) takes up the relational vocative with *you, cousin*, but then immediately stresses power and distance by resorting to *thou* and royal *our*, bluntly maximising the imposition: "thou diest for it". Rosalind in turn (4) gives him deference by calling him *your Grace* and *your Highness* and asks for reasons for his behaviour, but he does not comply with the conversational maxim of co-operativeness and simply ignores her wants. Instead (5), he uses a number of substrategies of negative and positive nastiness, because he does not hedge, is deadly serious, asserts lack of common ground, excludes all expressions of deference, personalises the hearer by means of *thee*, thus stating that the FTA applies to the hearer in particular, and not to others.

As another step forward, Culpeper (1996, 1998) has developed a theory of impoliteness and has, among other areas, explored its role in dramatic dialogue. As an example for impoliteness in drama dialogue, he (1996:364ff.) discusses the banquet scene in MAC (3, 4, 57–73) after the murder of Banquo, during which Macbeth loses his nerve at the appearance of Banquo's ghost and upon which his wife uses impoliteness to attack Macbeth's face "Are you a man?" (3, 4, 57). Her tactics seem to succeed because Macbeth regains his composure and returns to the banquet table.

Culpeper states that "in drama, impoliteness is not thrown in haphazardly for audience entertainment: it serves other purposes. Conflict in interaction appears either as a symptom, or as a cause of, social disharmony, and where there are tensions between characters we are more likely to see developments in character and plot" (1998:86).[7]

2.5   The problem of standard use and its implications for Shakespeare studies

It is a truth acknowledged in many studies that the choice of the pronouns of address is not only a grammatical problem, but that it constitutes a meaningful choice in terms of sociolinguistics. For example, Grannis points out that "the use of *thou* rather than *you*, or the other way around, obviously has an important communicative function, although it is not always clear to us what this function is" (1990:109). For this reason he suggests the approach of micro-sociolinguistics, which investigates language "at the individual and small-group-level" (ibid.).

While on the one hand it is correct to advise critics that we must not assume that Shakespeare's usage of the pronouns of address is an exact mirror-image of that of society around him, it seems on the other hand indispensable to have a knowledge of the communicative value of the "language-coins", i.e. the pronominal system and its social grammar in the historical context at large. In a situation characterised by the absence of linguistic records other than written texts and, in addition, without the possibility of using native speaker intuition, historically interested sociolinguists are in the dilemma of being at the mercy of their corpus, so we must be careful not to draw circular conclusions, and, as Labov once put it, make the best of bad data and let the data speak for themselves.

The difference between the language of drama and 'authentic' language has been stressed by various scholars in the recent past. Barber, for example, says: "it would be perfectly possible for *Thou* to play a relatively small role in real life, while in drama, because of its concentration of emotional tension and its tendency to present scenes of confrontation, *Thou* appeared much more frequently" (1981:287).

Rissanen maintains that the language of drama can be useful to reconstruct spoken language: "Imitated dialogue differs from actual speech in many respects, but it contains a number of features with which an author hopes to create an illusion of spoken idiom. If these features can be defined by comparing variant fields, the results can be used for drawing inferences about spoken language" (1986:99).

Brown and Gilman justify their selection of plays "because there is nothing else" (1989:170). Apart from the alleged scarcity of evidence they subscribe to Salmon's point of view that "the more skilful the dramatist, the more skilful he will be, if presenting the normal life of his time, in authenticating the action by an acceptable version of contemporary speech" (1965:105). Some pages further on they state that "Shakespeare surely used *thou* and *you* with a confident intuition that mirrored general Elizabethan usage" (179). In so doing they themselves take a confident intuition as a working hypothesis.

Walker (forthc.) is also of the opinion that drama texts do not provide an accurate picture of EModE language use, because often the language is exaggerated for artistic purposes. For this reason, the aspect of the density of language use in a drama will no doubt contribute to a false understanding of the significance of the contrastive use of pronominal forms if simply compared to other forms of language use outside drama without due consideration of genre constraints.

2.6   The concept of markedness

Scheler (1982:40f.) points out that in Shakespeare's time *you* was the common pronoun of social exchange among the middle classes, but that the final loss of *thou,* with the exceptions of dialects, the archaising language of poetry and ecclesiastical usage, took place in the 17th and 18th centuries.

He adds that in the Shakespeare Corpus a count of all the singular and plural forms of pronouns results in a ratio of 2:5 in favour of *you*. The original nominative form *ye* has mostly been replaced by the former oblique form *you*. *Ye*, however, prevails in the *Authorized Version* of the Bible (1611),[8] generally acknowledged to show very conservative usage, but has apparently become archaic elsewhere. He regards the pronoun *thou* as stylistically marked in relation to unmarked *you*:

> Während *you* bei Sh.[akespeare] als respektvolle Anrede gegenüber Höherstehenden und als wertneutrale Anredeform unter Standesgleichen (häufig bereits unter Vertretern der niederen Schichten) gebraucht wird, dient *thou* zur sozialen Distanzierung nach unten und zum Ausdruck des Affekts. Es ist die stilistisch "markierte" Form gegenüber "unmarkiertem" *you*. (Scheler 1982:41)

Since stylistic variation is responsible for the choice of pronoun forms, the labeling of pronoun forms outside of such a context, does not make much sense. Quirk quite rightly points out that it is indeed an oversimplification to say that by 1600 "*you* was polite, formal usage but *thou* was familiar or insulting" (1974:50). Instead he suggests treating them in terms of markedness.[9] "*You* is usually the stylistically unmarked form: it is not so much 'polite' as 'not impolite'; it is not so much 'formal' as 'not informal'" (ibid.).

Although *you* is taken as "the general unmarked form beside which the use of *thou* is conspicuous" (51), the concept of the mutual expectancy of the unmarked pronoun usage also implies the reverse in that "where *thou* is expected, *you* can likewise be in contrast and conspicuous" (ibid.). He refers to the following discourse samples from LR, acts 1 and 2:

(6)   Lear: Know that *we* have divided / In three our kingdom; and 'tis our fast intent / To shake all cares and business from our age, / Conferring them on younger strengths, [...] (LR 1, 1, 37–40)

(7)   Lear: To *thee* and *thine* hereditary ever / Remain this ample third of our fair kingdom, / [...]. Now, our joy, / [...] what can *you* say to draw / A third more opulent than *your* sisters'? Speak. (LR 1, 1, 79–86)

(8)   Cordelia: Nothing, my lord [...] I love your Majesty / According to by bond, no more nor less (LR 1, 1, 85–93)

(9)   Lear: But goes *thy* heart with this?

(10) Cordelia: Ay, my good lord.

(11) Lear: So young, and so untender?

(12) Cordelia: So young, my lord, and true.

(13) Lear: Let it be so: *thy* truth then be *thy* dow'r! (LR 1, 1, 104–108)

(14) Lear: Are *you* our daughter?

(15) Goneril: I would you would make use of your good wisdom (LR 1, 4, 218–219)

(16) Lear: *Your* name, fair gentlewoman?

(17) Goneril: This admiration, sir, is much o' th' savor / Of other your new pranks
       (LR 1, 4, 236–238)

(18) Lear: Beloved Regan, / *Thy* sister's naught. O Regan […]

(19) Regan: I pray you, sir, take patience (LR 2, 4, 133–137, my emphasis)

Quirk interprets these sequences of dialogues as follows:

> Lear addresses Goneril and Regan as *thou*, and again — from father to daugh-
> ter — this is what we should expect. Against this background of perfect
> decorum and the fully expected, it should no doubt come as a surprise to us
> that Lear addresses Cordelia at first as *you* [in (7)]. […]. When, however, he is
> shocked by what he takes to be her lack of love, he uses *thou* — not now the
> *thou* of father to daughter but the *thou* of anger. [in (9) and (13)]. […] Lear
> grows cool to Goneril and the change is reflected in the use of *you* [in (16)].
> […], and he turns to Regan with his customary affectionate paternal *thou* [in
> (18)]. (Quirk 1974: 51 f.)

These examples reveal, however, that the two forms, and *thou* in particular, convey
several communicative functions, which in some cases show a certain amount of
overlap. One could even go a step further and ask if Quirk is justified in calling such
uses "conspicuous" when they are simply doing that which is the principal difference between the use of these forms: they indicate a subtle change in the attitude
and communicative intention of the speaker.[10] Aers and Kress are also of the
opinion that

> throughout the play the use of personal pronouns is a precise indicator of self-
> assessment and assessment of others by the characters. Lear's use of the royal
> 'we' of himself contrasts with the slighting 'thou' to Goneril and Regan. His use
> of the honorific 'you' to Cordelia serves to highlight the distinction he had
> drawn between her and her sisters; and it accentuates his abrupt switch to
> 'thou' when she refuses to accede to his demands. (Aers and Kress 1981: 79)

Whereas Ilson (1971: 65 f.) is of the opinion that the theory of markedness is of only
limited value for the studies of Elizabethan drama, Mulholland also takes up the
term *markedness*. On a contextual or attitudinal basis the marked term in this dyad
is taken as an affective index. Thus, in order to meet the requirements of linguistic
decorum (in Shakespeare's plays) in a given situation depending mostly on the
intersocial relationship of the characters, one form of address almost triggers or
elicits its expected response. In this sense of a mutual expectancy the unmarked
form can be fully predicted. She draws our attention to the fact that "with regard to
the expected/affective forms, the majority forms must be established before the

force of the 'marked' term can be recognised and used for character study" (1967:36). With reference to McIntosh's (1963a) paper on AYL, where he takes *thou* as the unmarked form and *you* as the marked, Mulholland shows that such grammatical clues to character may be quite misleading if the system works the other way around.[11] For this reason she is right in demanding "that the norms must be established before the problem can be adequately dealt with" (41). As already pointed out earlier, these norms of the micro-cosmos of Shakespearean plays need not necessarily be a true picture of English-language usage around 1600.

As regards the evaluative norms within Shakespeare's plays Mulholland, who based her findings on an analysis of ADO and LR, and Barber, working on R3, come to different results in terms of the usualness of *you* as the "generally accepted majority form of the pronoun in use in the upper classes, except from father to daughter, and, possibly, from women to their female servants" (Mulholland 1967:42). While Barber concedes that also for R3, *you* can be regarded as the normal, stylistically unmarked form among the upper classes the statistical material brings some counter-evidence. For the exchanges between characters of noble rank in R3 the examples of "*Thou* in fact outnumber examples of singular *You* in the ratio of about 54 to 46" (1981:286). He counts 568 examples of *thou* and 491 instances of singular *you*.

According to Barber the overall figures for the whole body of Shakespeare's works are as follows: there are 14,410 examples of T pronouns, and 22,767 examples of Y pronouns (1981:287). Barber gathers, however, that quite a number of these *you* forms must be plural and for this reason comes to the conclusion: "it can by no means be said, therefore, that in Shakespeare's works as a whole the usual form is *You*, and *Thou* merely an occasional variant used on special occasions" (ibid.).

In this respect it seems useful to distinguish between descriptive (statistical) norms — the majority form — and evaluative (correctness) norms. It seems conceivable that the *thou* vs. *you* distinction might be exploited for a number of purposes, and the data would reflect more than one dimension of variation. *Thou*, in particular, might signal archaising usage in (some) historical plays. To have this value, the *thou* form would not have to be used consistently as long as it occurred in pragmatically prominent contexts (cf. Busse 2001).

Such context-independent counts of pronoun usage in individual plays do not bring us very far. If, for example, we have a play with a very high proportion of formal scenes and another with a much higher rate of quasi-intimate scenes, it is obvious that the language structures will also be different. Furthermore, we are completely unaware today of the archaising or possibly humorous or other effects of particular pronominal forms on the audience of around 1600.

Hope (1994a) also doubts that *thou* is to be considered as the marked form in Elizabethan drama at the turn of the 16th century. By investigating depositions from the ecclesiastical court of Durham from the 1560s, he challenges both arguments of Brown and Gilman, viz. paucity of evidence and the claim of drama to mirror 'real' usage of the pronouns of address. His work on the court records indicates that there *thou* is clearly the marked form, and that as early as 1560. But by drawing on Barber (1981) and his own work on Marlowe's usages he questions whether *thou* can be regarded as the marked form in drama: "so as late as the 1590s in drama, it is possible to find writers who do not seem to have 'marked' one of the forms over the other" (1994a: 148). If this observation is correct, then it is not only a matter of chronology but it would have the further semantic-pragmatic implications "that Shakespeare's dramatic usage, if it bears any relation to 'real' Early Modern [English] usage at all, preserves modes of usage which have long disappeared from everyday speech" (ibid.). But as regards the authenticity of depositions, Görlach (1994: 9f.) is sceptical, because even in trial transcripts it is possible that editing has taken place.

2.7   Shifts in pronominal address

It has frequently been noted (cf. Abbott 1870, Byrne 1936) that in Shakespeare and other EModE authors quite a number of sudden shifts in pronominal usage occur. Often these are interpreted as affective overtones, regarded as erratic, or dismissed completely.

For instance, Eagleson treats such shifts in pronoun usage in terms of the theory of markedness: "*you* had become the unmarked or neutral form, while *thou* was the marked form, being used to register any important shift not simply in rank but especially in emotion, be it love or anger, respect or contempt" (1971: 13). He provides us with a striking example taken from LR (first mentioned in Abbott ([1870] 1972: 158):

(20)   Goneril [to Edmund]: Decline *your* head: this kiss, if it durst speak, / Would stretch *thy* spirits up into the air. (LR 4, 2, 22–23, my emphasis)

In trying to win him over for her plans, Goneril tries to deceive Edmund in making him believe that she is in love with him. She subtly achieves this effect by first addressing him with *you*, and after the bestowal of the kiss passionately *thou*ing him. Mazzon points out that pronoun switches which mark the turning points in the plotting of alliance between characters are conditioned by "social network density" (1992: 134). With respect to the above example, she comments that even nowadays "a kiss is still interpreted as a switching point between T/V pronouns in many films and books, in languages which still have the pronoun distinction" (ibid.).

Another striking example is the first encounter between Romeo and Juliet (in ROM 1, 4, 93–109). In this scene Romeo likens himself to a profane pilgrim and compares Juliet to a saint. As soon as he feels assured that his feelings are shared, he moves to *thou*:

(21)   Romeo: O then, dear saint, let lips do what hands do, / They pray — grant *thou*, lest faith turn to despair.
Juliet: Saints do not move, though grant for prayers' sake.
Romeo: Then move not while my prayer's effect I / take.
[Kissing her.] / Thus from my lips, by thine, my sin is purg'd.
(ROM 1, 5, 103–107, my emphasis)

Hope points out that such "rapidly modulating forms addressed to the same person" (1993:85) have hitherto been explained as being affectively marked deviations from the forms expected on a social basis according to the Brown and Gilman model of power and solidarity. Yet his work on depositions would suggest that such shifts should, moreover, be interpreted on a micro-pragmatic level. Therefore Hope has divided conversations into "'address', where only one of the participants uses a pronoun form, and 'exchange', where they both do" (1993:94). In a small sample of 89 instances, a clear imbalance with 32% of exchanges shifting against only 2% of addresses was marked. These figures indicate that shifting is far more common in interactive dyadic exchange than in address. The reason the author gives for this is the following: first, addresses are shorter than exchanges, and thus provide less space for shifts, but, more importantly, this indicates "the way in which micro-pragmatic factors come more into play as a conversation develops. A probable explanation for this imbalance is that conversations tend to begin with socially pragmatic usages [...], and move on into non-socially pragmatic usages" (95). In accord with Calvo (1992a), Hope concludes that in contrast to the norm/ deviant model a macro/micro, or social/non-social model would free both forms as potential carriers of meaning.

Calvo rightly criticises that one of the greatest shortcomings of Brown and Gilman's (1960, 1989) theory is that it does not give a satisfactory explanation for pronominal shifts in a dyad when the interlocutors remain constant. While accepting the marked/unmarked dichotomy of the two pronouns, Calvo is of the opinion that this approach has to be supplemented in order to explain frequent shifting. Halliday's (1978) theory of ideational, interpersonal and textual meaning is then taken as a theoretical foothold. In contrast to Brown and Gilman's (1989) rather static model of social station or rank as a permanent feature, the concept of social identity which has to be negotiated between speakers, and which, further-more, allows the selection of more than one social identity at the same time in the course of one single interaction (cf. Goodenough 1965:5) has the advantage that in this case, shifting pronouns can be interpreted as indirect social markers in their function of in- or out-group markers.

In describing the inherent features of (dramatic) dialogue, Salmon has argued that interlocutors will "choose the exponents of those features which express their attitudes towards all aspects of the situation and to one another" (1967:40). These exponents may then either be attributable to permanent relationships (which can be explained by the sociological model of Brown and Gilman), or temporary attitudes [= social identities, my addition] such as "politeness, formality, anger or dislike, which often overlap both with one another and with the permanent attitudes" (40f.); a point that cannot be stressed enough.

In addition to this, Calvo (1992a: 22f.) suggests further that when the marked/ unmarked dichotomy of *thou* and *you*, and their interpretation as social markers both fail to account for a sudden shifting, this could also be due to the textual function of the pronouns as pragmatic markers in a wider sense signalling discourse boundaries. Pronoun changes of this kind are often accompanied by changes in topics, conversational mood, and in deixis.

This is also borne out by Lass' investigation of letters. Especially at the later stages of EModE — he refers to the 1660s — "the *you* v. *thou* contrast finally became a deictic one: *you* is the distal (distant from the speaker) pronoun, *thou* the proximal (speaker-oriented). The general tendency is to use *thou* when the topic is within the 'charmed circle' of a relationship, and restricted to an immediate, factual or real present" (1999: 153).

As a conclusion of her threefold (marked/unmarked, social markers, and pragmatic markers) re-analysis of pronominal use in AYL Calvo states

> that in some cases it is not the use of one particular pronominal form or another in a precise context that is meaningful but rather the *shift* from one pronoun to the other. The shift, and not each pronominal form *per se*, performs a signalling function in the global organisation of the dramatic dialogue. (Calvo 1992a: 26)

For the above-mentioned reasons the concept of *markedness* seems inadequate for dealing with the subtle shifts of social variety and usage. Calvo's article on the frequent shifting of pronominal address in Shakespeare's plays suggests, moreover, that besides the well-recognised expressive and attitudinal meanings of the pronouns and a Hallidayan interpersonal function of negotiating personal identities they, or their shifting, for that matter, can also mark discourse boundaries by indicating changes in topics. Thus, they can be viewed as pragmatic markers in a wider sense (cf. also Brinton 1996: 22).

In terms of Shakespeare studies the latest accounts of personal pronouns in terms of markedness have been provided by Bruti (2000) and Stein (forthc.). Bruti tries to reconcile the notions of markedness and pronoun shifting. As a textual basis she takes the so-called "Falstaff Plays" (1H4, 2H4, H5 and WIV). She does not look at markedness from a statistical point of view, but concentrates instead on micro-sociolinguistics and pragmatics. She argues that even though unmarked terms have a wider distribution than marked ones, "quantitative results are in fact neither necessary nor sufficient to establish which pronoun is marked and which is unmarked" (2000: 26). By adopting the concept of markedness reversal as developed by Shapiro (1983), she accounts for a number of marked pronoun switches that are situationally bound or determined. She illustrates that in a context previously coloured by *you* a switch to *thou* must be considered as marked, and also the other way around. So that between the same interlocutors it becomes possible to move from social/emotional remoteness to closeness and vice versa. This concept of markedness is then clearly situationally-bound, or, in other words, context-dependent, rather than absolute. This is indeed a step forward from a paradigmatic concept or system to a pragmatic or contextual one.

Stein (forthc.) in his in-depth-study of AYL and LR combines quantitative and qualitative aspects of previous markedness studies. For the micro-cosmos of the two plays he sets out to establish the social norm in a statistical way, because in his opinion corpus-based results "are much more reliable than text-based ones" as carried out by Mazzon (1992, 1995) and Bruti (2000). With reference to Sperber and Wilson's (1995) relevance theory the approach taken is also informationally-based, that is to say "the meaning of the deviating form is weak in intention and has a high share of inferencing. It is clear that the semiotic processes involved can be analysed as implicatures, or accounted for in terms of relevance theory."

His numerous and very detailed findings can only be summarised very sketchily here as follows: Shakespeare's use of unmarked pronouns in these two plays is in keeping with that of the social decorum of EModE society at large. However, due to "the concentrated language and emphatic emotionality typical of plays" in both plays about 30% of pronoun uses are marked. This corresponds to a 1:2 ratio in favour of the unmarked form. In fact, both T pronouns and V pronouns can be used in a marked way. Among social equals it is T that is the unmarked form. "V is used with marked status towards common servants, members of the lower class, and minor-aged children." In line with other studies on the social structure of Early Modern England, Stein has found that in these two plays it is especially the higher classes among themselves and the middle stations of society that have room for a "semiotic exploitation" of pronoun use. By contrast, the pronoun use of the upper and lower class is socially highly predictable, leaving only little space for social or emotional negotiation.

2.8 Special cases of conventionalised pronoun use

Aside, soliloquy and apostrophe have to be regarded as special formulaic cases of pronoun use in EModE drama, because none of these is directed to an addressee who is present on stage. These instances are governed by the use of invariant *thou*.[12] Edmund's invocation of nature is a well-known example of apostrophe:

(22)   Edmund: Thou, Nature, art my goddess, to thy law / My services are bound
        (LR 1, 2, 1–2)

Another example from LR is King Lear's invocation of the elements in his soliloquy during the storm on the heath:

(23)   Lear: Let the great gods, / That keep this dreadful pudder o'er our heads, / Find out their enemies now. Tremble, thou wretch, / That hast within thee undivulged crimes / Unwhipt of justice! Hide thee, thou bloody hand; / Thou perjur'd, and thou simular of virtue / That art incestuous! (LR 3, 2, 49–55)

Wales remarks that the *thou* of invocation and apostrophe reflects the old singular, which is also to be found in the Latin texts. In these special uses *thou* "would become identified with liturgical-*thou*, because of its markedness, and because of their own elevated and 'distancing' effect. [...] The T[hou] of soliloquy and aside has connotations of privacy, intimacy and contempt" (1983:121, footnote). While she states that these usages are not yet well-researched it appears that there are connections with non-literary usages. Finkenstaedt refers to religious singular, oaths, and other pseudo-ritual usages. Under the heading of "various singular usages" (1963:154ff.) he subsumes the *thou* of apostrophe by saying that the singular is used in all those cases where no reply is possible, i.e. in invocations to God(s), imagined people, and address to oneself, to animals and inanimate objects.[13] A famous example for the address to an inanimate object can be found in MAC:

(24)   Macbeth: Is this a dagger which I see before me, / The handle toward my hand? Come, let me clutch thee: / I have thee not, and yet I see thee still. (MAC 2, 1, 33–35)

Yong-Lin takes us a step further. With ten Shakespeare plays as his textual basis, he has investigated the address to supernatural beings such as ghosts, witches, and spirits, concluding that despite a role-governed rule the reasons for Shakespeare's use of *thou* to individual supernatural beings are still opaque. He is not sure whether this pronominal usage has a connection to liturgical *thou*. He believes that it can, moreover, be attributed to the people's great fear of supernatural powers. As a result of which, such beings were linguistically treated with distance, exclusion, and possibly even contempt. This attitude was reinforced by the prevalence of witch-hunting (cf. 1991:258f.).

Stoll briefly mentions that Shakespeare uses the address to oneself for character description and for the depiction of atmosphere of a scene: "Immer aber ist die Selbstanrede Ausdruck der tatsächlichen oder emotionalen Isoliertheit und inneren Einsamkeit der sie verwendenden Person" (1989:7). However, despite the character traits or nuances that are expressed by the address to the self in dramatic mono- logue, these instances do not permit pronoun variation, as for this solemn register a T pronoun is mandatory:

(25)   King Richard: I had forgot myself, am I not king? / Awake, *thou* coward majesty! *thou* sleepest. (R2 3, 2, 83–84)

(26)   King Henry: From Scotland am I stol'n, even of pure love, / To greet mine own
       land with my wishful sight. No, Harry, Harry, 'tis no land of *thine*; / *Thy* place is
       fill'd, *thy* sceptre wrung from *thee*, / *Thy* balm wash'd off wherewith *thou* was
       annointed. (3H6 3, 1, 13–17)

(27)   King Richard: Alas, I rather hate myself / For hateful deeds committed by myself
       / I am a villain; yet I lie, I am not. / Fool of *thyself* speak well; fool do not flatter:
       [...] (R3 5, 3, 189–192)

Common to all these conventionalised usages of the singular pronoun are the highly
affective connotations.[14]

2.9   Summary and conclusion

My critical survey of the works published on the use of second person pronouns in
EModE with special reference to Shakespeare's plays has shown that over the years
a considerable body of critical texts has been assembled. First, there are the philo-
logically oriented 19th century classics in the field of Abbott (1870) and Franz
(1898/99) and older monographs such as Byrne (1936). In contrast to these
extensive and comprehensive works, the authors of the newer studies seem to think
small. The approaches and objectives of these investigations are often quite
different. On the one hand, there are empirical analyses of pronominal usage in
individual plays. These often concentrate on such issues as markedness and
pronoun switching. Some of the papers are related to each other, whereas others
stand alone. On the other hand, there are the more theoretical studies by Brown
and Gilman. Apart from the many repercussions of their seminal papers, much
work is isolated and fragmented. The newer studies carried out in the framework of
politeness theory tend to disregard pronominal variation.

       As suggested in chapter one, it would probably be a step in the right direction
to link up existing theories and methodologies, especially those of corpus linguistics, sociolinguistics and pragmatics, in order to check whether these individual
findings can be verified on a macro level of investigation for the entire corpus, and
also be borne out on a micro level by in-depth-studies of a selected number of
discourse samples etc. Such a combination of both quantitative and qualitative
approaches could yield a more profound basis for assessing the impact of the
personal pronouns in a single scene or play of Shakespeare, in Shakespearean drama
in general, and their relationship to usage in other authors and text types at the turn
of the 16th to the 17th century.

Chapter 3

Thou and *you*

A quantitative analysis

3.1 Working hypothesis and objectives

With reference to Barber (1981) it was reported in Chapter 2.6 that in the complete works of Shakespeare there are 14,410 tokens of T pronouns, and 22,767 tokens of Y pronouns, including Y forms used to address more than one person. From this Barber gathers that it can by no means be maintained that *you* is the usual form and *thou* merely an occasional variant (cf. 1981:287). Thus, the objective of this chapter will be to find out the numerical relationship of the two pronouns and their variants and their development in the course of Shakespeare's writing career. In addition to this, the influence of the dramatic genre on pronoun variation will also be investigated. Once the figures for the Shakespeare Corpus have been established, they will be compared to those of other playwrights and also to data from text types other than drama in order to elucidate whether Shakespeare's use of second person pronouns is in keeping with those of his contemporaries or not.

3.2 The importance of genre and date of composition

It has been argued by Brainerd (1979) and Hope (1994b) that within the Shakespeare Corpus the development of pronominal usage, and pronouns of address in particular, is largely dependent on the correlation of the two parameters of date of composition and genre. In a mathematical approach based on the figures of the Spevack concordances, Brainerd has carried out a statistical analysis of Shakespeare's use of personal pronouns. Due to the fact that Brainerd used a concordance as a database he did not distinguish between the two functions of *you* as a second person singular and/or second person plural pronoun. Thus, it is not clear how this problem was solved.

Nonetheless, Brainerd shows that the use of T pronouns in Shakespeare's plays decreased with time, and he comments that "Shakespeare, in accordance with the general decline in the use of second person singular during the transition from Middle English to Modern English, uses fewer instances of second person singular pronouns as he progresses through his writing career" (1979:7). Almost parallel to the decrease of the T forms is the increase of the Y forms, which "accords with the gradual replacement, as Shakespeare grew older, of second person singular forms by second plural" (ibid.). Still, the use of Y forms differs significantly from genre to genre, with Comedy being distinguished by a higher value of Y forms in comparison to the other genres.

From these findings he concludes that the usage of second person pronouns in Shakespeare is concrete evidence of language change over time. If we follow this argument, the possible socio-grammatical interpretation of the pronouns of address in individual plays of Shakespeare has to take account of date of composition and genre, because these factors can clearly have a bearing on whether the data of individual plays are commensurable or not.

This point could then also serve as one possible explanation why e.g. Mulholland (1967) in her analysis of ADO and LR, and Barber (1981) in his study of R3 come to different conclusions concerning the markedness value of *thou* and *you*, with ADO being a comedy probably composed in 1598–1600, R3 being a history play composed in 1595, and LR being a tragedy, written presumably in 1605–06 (dates according to Schabert 2000: 241 f.).

Hope has also carried out a quantitative analysis of all T forms in Shakespeare's plays. His findings only partly bear out the result of Brainerd. According to Hope, there is, generally speaking, a degree of correlation between genre and relative percentages of T and Y forms in so far as Histories have a high proportion of T forms, whereas Comedies have a lower proportion but, on the other hand, in his opinion the ranges of variation within genres mean that there is no consistent relationship between genre and the number of pronouns: "it looks as though non-fixed factors are in operation here again" (1994b: 63).

However, despite their statistical rigour, the above studies seem to take the variables of date of composition and the subcategorisation of Shakespeare's plays into genres for granted. For this reason once the exact pronoun tallies for each play have been established, different chronologies and subcategorisations of the Shakespeare canon will be compared to each other, for scholars are by no means unanimous in their decisions on the number of dramatic genres and the respective attribution of individual plays to these genres.

3.3   Numerical outline of the second person pronouns

Pronouns belong to the high frequency items in the corpus. Among the 100 most frequent words are the following personal and possessive pronouns in order of decreasing frequency: *I* (3. most frequent word), *you* (7.), *my* (8.), *me* (13.), *it* (15.), *his* (18.), *your* (20.), *he* (21.), *thou* (25.), *him* (27.), *her* (30.), *thy* (31.), *we* (39.), *thee* (40.), *our* (41.), *she* (47.), *they* (51.), *their* (62.), *them* (68.) and *us* (83.); cf. Spevack (1970: 4177 ff.).

On the basis of Spevack (1968–1980) the total figures for the two second person pronouns, their oblique forms and compounds for the 38 plays are as follows: there are 13,186 T forms (1.578%) and 22,400 Y forms (2.681%). In their relative frequencies the two pronouns and their variants differ by 1.103% in favour of *you* (see Tables 1 and 2). In these tables a slash before certain word-forms indicates emendations and additions to the copy-text.[1] Due to the inclusion of these slash-forms, Barber's figures given in Chapter 3.1 are slightly higher than the ones presented in Tables 1 and 2.

Table 1. The number of T forms in the 38 plays and in the complete works of Shakespeare

Type	38 plays	/Tokens + ordinary tokens	Complete works	/Tokens + ordinary tokens
ta = 'thou'	1	1	1	1
th = thou/thee	31	31	33	33
/thee	38		39	
thee	3,110	3,148	3,384	3,423
thee't	1	1	1	1
/thine	4		4	
thine	418	422	494	498
thine's	2	2	2	2
/thou	55		55	
thou	5,366	5,421	5,800	5,855
thou'dst	11	11	11	11
thou'ldst	1	1	1	1
thou'lt	16	16	16	16
thou'rt	20	20	20	20
thou'st	2	2	2	2
thou't	8	8	8	8
/thy	54		69	
thy	3,839	3,893	4,291	4,360
/thyself	3		3	
thyself	206	209	236	239
Total	13,031	13,186	14,300	14,470
% (rel. freq.)	1.560	1.578	1.712	1.732

In his report on Brainerd (1979), Hope has criticised the fact that he did not work out the ratio between the T and the Y forms. This is most likely due to the fact that Brainerd worked with concordance evidence, which does not distinguish singular from plural tokens, and such a ratio, including all the plural tokens, would hence have skewed the ratio in favour of *you*. Barber (1981) has addressed this issue for R3. Kiełkiewicz-Janoviak (1994) takes us a step further when she incorporates

Table 2. The number of Y forms in the 38 plays and in the complete works of Shakespeare

Type	38 plays	/Tokens + ordinary tokens	Complete works	/Tokens + ordinary tokens
y'	62	62	63	63
y' ave	1	1	1	1
/ye	4		4	
ye	339	343	342	346
/you	106		106	
you	14,116	14,222	14,326	14,432
you'd	4	4	4	4
you'ld	15	15	15	15
you/'ll	1		1	
you'll	163	164	165	166
/your	62		62	
your	6,872	6,934	7,003	7,065
/you're	1		1	
you're	27	28	27	28
you'st	1	1	1	1
/yours	4		4	
yours	259	263	265	269
/yourself			1	
yourself	288	288	299	300
yourself's	1	1	2	2
/yourselves	1		1	
yourselves	73	74	75	76
Total	22,222	22,400	22,588	22,767
% (rel. freq.)	2.660	2.681	2.704	2.725

the data of Mulholland (1967) on ADO and LR and those of Barber (1981) into her analysis of AYL. Her results are shown in Table 3.

From this comparison she draws the rather disconcerting conclusion that there is considerable fluctuation showing no definite direction, and she thus subscribes to Barber's view that in the light of these data it is difficult to accept the idea "that *you* was the unmarked, general address form, while *thou* was only used as an expression of special, marked social relations and emotional states" (1994: 51).

However, what can at least indirectly be gleaned from her data is the ratio of singular to plural Y forms, as in her sample there are 2,833 Y forms altogether, out of which 2,289 (80.80%) are singular and 544 (19.20%) plural. This relativises the high results of Barber for R3 (28.74%).

As neither the paper concordances nor the electronic corpus tell us which of the Y forms are plural, these have to be sorted out manually. Stein (forthc.: 4) emphasises

Table 3. The ratio of T forms and Y forms in ADO, LR, R3 and AYL

	T forms	Y sing.	Y total	T:Y sing.	T:Y total
ADO	220 (219)*	584**	700	0.37	0.31
LR	533 (538)	575	706	0.93	0.75
R3	568 (568)	491	689	1.18	0.82
AYL	313 (296)	639	738	0.46	0.42
Total	**1,634**	**2,289**	**2,833**	**0.71**	**0.58**

(Combination of two tables from Kiełkiewicz-Janoviak (1994: 51), last line my addition)
* The figures in brackets were slightly edited for the comparison with Mulholland, as she excluded pronouns occurring in songs from her analysis.
** My own count of singular Y forms is higher than this; it amounts to 641 singular Y forms (cf. Chapter 4.2.3.2). This changes the T:Y ratio to 0.34.

the importance of establishing the social norm of pronoun usage in a statistical way, but he simultaneously admits that "counting frequencies of all occurrences of the two pronouns even only for selected dyads in two plays is a colossal menial and lowly task." In order to keep this time-consuming and unwieldy effort in proportions manageable for a single scholar, a control corpus with nine plays from different genres and different dates of composition (as illustrated in Table 4) has been set up, which investigates the figures for singular *you* in relation to *thou* and *thee* and also the ratio between singular and plural *you*.

Table 4. The ratio of *thou* and *thee* to singular *you* and plural *you* in selected plays

Play	Thou+Thee = T	Y sing.	%	Y plur.	%
3H6	220+119 = 339	130	67	67	33
R3	207+121 = 328	260	67	128	33
MND	116+ 63 = 179	212	77	63	23
WIV	61+ 52 = 113	498	90	51	10
ADO	86+ 74 = 160	448	91	44	9
AYL	143+ 90 = 233	434	97	15	3
TN	133+ 90 = 223	374	82	84	18
LR	214+143 = 357	139	67	68	33
MAC	96+ 61 = 157	498	90	51	10
Total	**2,089**	**2,993**	**80.9**	**571**	**19.1**

While on the one hand this control corpus reveals that there are indeed considerable discrepancies between singular and plural *you* forms in individual plays, on the other hand, it confirms that the proportion of plural *you* forms amounts to less than 20% on average.

Another indicator pointing towards the overall ratio of singular and plural Y forms is the relationship between the forms *yourself* and *yourselves* (cf. Table 2). The 38 plays exhibit 289 tokens (80%) of *yourself('s)* and 74 tokens of *yourselves* (20%). On the basis of the control corpus the ratio of T:Y sing. is 0.70 in comparison to 0.59 including plural forms (on the authority of Spevack; cf. Tables 1 and 2).

When in the following for the entire Shakespeare Corpus the figures based on concordance evidence are used it has to be borne in mind that the frequencies for the Y forms (including plurals) are, in all likelihood, about 20% too high. These difficulties not withstanding, the T forms are unambiguous and can be interpreted straight away without any reservations. Table 5 lists all the T and Y forms in the chronological order of plays that is given in the *Riverside Shakespeare* (cf. Evans and Tobin 1997: 55–87).

3.4   The sequence and subcategorisation of Shakespeare's plays

As the interpretation of the numerical results depends highly on the assumed sequence and subcategorisation of the plays, some considerations to the chronology of Shakespeare's plays and their attribution to dramatic genres do not seem to be amiss.

The most detailed information on the putative chronology of Shakespeare's plays is to be found in Wells et al. (1987: 69–144; but see also Evans and Tobin 1997: 77–87; Schabert 2000: 237–242). Evans, the editor of the *Riverside Shakespeare*, admits that "any attempt to arrange the plays chronologically is beset with hazards and uncertainties" and that "the undertaking has given rise to differences of opinion among a long line of editors and critics" (1997: 77). The chronology in Evans and Tobin is mainly based on the works of Chambers (1930), McManaway (1950) and special investigations of particular plays.

The evidence for the dating of Shakespeare's plays can generally be drawn from both kinds of internal and external evidence:

> internal evidence [...] is drawn from the texts of the plays [...] and deals for the most part in topical allusions (which if dateable may establish a *terminus a quo*, i.e., a date before which the work cannot have been written), metrical development, kinds and handling of imagery, incidence of rhyme, and vocabulary. External evidence is concerned with rather more concrete matters: dates of actual publication; entry on the Stationers' Register [...] etc.; and allusions to, or imitations of, Shakespeare's plays [...] by contemporary writers whose works can be dated. [...] External evidence can generally establish a *terminus ad quem*, i.e. the date after which the work cannot have been written [...].
> (Evans and Tobin 1997: 77)

Table 5. Synopsis of T and Y forms in relation to date of composition alone

No.	Play	Date	T tokens	Y tokens	rel. freq. T	rel. freq. Y
1	1H6	1589–90*	457	368	2.225	1.791
2	2H6	1590–91	543	399	2.217	1.629
3	3H6	1590–91	575	355	2.465	1.521
4	R3	1592–93	568	689	2.003	2.428
5	ERR	1592–94	274	432	1.903	3.001
6	TIT	1593–94	519	380	2.619	1.919
7	SHR	1593–94	300	718	1.463	3.510
8	TGV	1594	340	513	2.009	3.034
9	LLL	1594–95**	236	534	1.120	2.534
10	JN	1594–96	397	420	2.329	2.056
11	R2	1595	458	295	2.094	1.349
12	ROM	1595–96	605	414	2.528	1.728
13	MND	1595–96	251	409	1.559	2.539
14	MV	1596–97	234	647	1.120	3.091
15	1H4	1596–97	480	492	2.000	2.052
16	WIV	1597***	165	773	0.778	3.654
17	2H4	1598	355	776	1.371	3.015
18	ADO	1598–99	220	700	1.057	3.368
19	H5	1599	251	623	0.978	2.431
20	JC	1599	230	562	1.202	2.938
21	AYL	1599	313	739	1.467	3.464
22	HAM	1600–01	272	821	0.916	2.775
23	TN	1601–02	345	645	1.776	3.321
24	TRO	1601–02	346	586	1.353	2.292
25	AWW	1602–03	291	734	1.287	3.250
26	MM	1604	226	842	1.059	3.953
27	OTH	1604	320	728	1.231	2.806
28	LR	1605	550	709	2.175	2.842
29	MAC	1606	222	339	1.348	2.061
30	ANT	1606–07	422	539	1.775	2.266
31	COR	1607–08	277	986	1.040	3.703
32	TIM	1607–08	513	439	2.886	2.468
33	PER	1607–08	231	568	1.300	3.199
34	CYM	1609–10	406	687	1.512	2.559
35	WT	1610–11	290	767	1.178	3.121
36	TMP	1611	401	329	2.498	2.049
37	H8	1612–13	77	803	0.329	3.769
38	TNK	1613	223	640	0.951	2.731

* According to Evans and Tobin (1997:78) revised 1594–95.
** Revised 1597 for court performance.
*** Revised circa 1600–01.

In the case of Shakespeare's plays, this general classification is complicated by the factors "that Shakespeare reworked an earlier play by another writer (mixed authorship) and the possibility that a play as we now have it represents Shakespeare's reworking of his original version (revision)" (1997: 77) or — a rewriting by the Folio editors. Blake draws attention to the fact that "for example, the second person of the personal pronoun [...] may appear in the singular in Q[uatro] and the plural in F[olio], or vice versa" (2002a: 4).

By applying the method of external evidence, a general dating within the time-span of one or two years can be established for each play. Internal evidence can lead to still finer distinctions, but has to be based on conjecture. Suerbaum (1996: 325) reports that this fine-tuning of the datings of individual plays largely relies on conventions, which in turn mirror our conception about the place of individual plays within the sequence of the whole canon. This way the oeuvre is seen as a long-term artistic development.

On this basis four different suggestions for the chronology of the Shakespeare canon have been compared, i.e. Evans and Tobin (1997), Schabert (1992, 2000) and Wells et al. (1987). Although the chronological sequence of Shakespeare's plays still mainly follows the line-up established by Chambers (1930), editorial scholars have recently cast some doubts on the dates of individual plays of the early dramas.

As established by Suerbaum (1996: 325f.), the three parts of H6 cause the most problems, with some critics moving it forward to 1587–88, and others assuming a date as late as 1592. Additionally, special difficulties are connected with ERR, which some believe to have been written about 1590, and also with JN and TN. JN is difficult to date exactly, but it was definitely written before 1598. Brainerd (1980: 229) suggests a date later than that given in the *Riverside Shakespeare* (1594–1596). TN may have been written earlier than 1601–02. Uhlig's (1968) antedating of TIT, which would move this play to the very beginning of the Shakespeare canon, has been abandoned by most editors.

When the four sequences are compared to each other it becomes evident that, minor problems set apart, there seems to be less reason for doubt concerning the sequence of plays from LLL onwards. The relative frequencies outlined in Table 5 reveal that the date of composition alone does not provide a clear-cut rise or fall of the T pronouns over time, so that the two factors of *date* and *genre* need to be combined.

Apart from their putative order, the assignment of plays to literary genres is also a hazardous stumbling block, because from the publication of the *First Folio* (1623) onwards scholars have argued about the number of genres and the genre assignment of certain plays.

In the *First Folio* the compilers subdivided the plays into the three genres of Comedy, History and Tragedy. Since then, many attempts have been made to categorise Shakespeare's plays. In modern times a fourth genre Romance, has become widely accepted. Other subgenres such as Roman Plays and Late/Problem

Plays have been proposed and partly rejected again (cf. Craig 1991, Schabert 2000: 324–574 and Suerbaum 1996: 169–209).

For this reason it needs to be established whether different subcategorisations of the Shakespeare canon lead to significantly different results concerning second person pronouns. When the arithmetical means for the T forms per genre of a three-, four- or fivefold division of the canon are compared to each other, there are only differences in degree rather than in kind, as it is always the Histories that exhibit the highest degree of T forms, with a relative frequency of about 2%. At the other end of the spectrum we find the Comedies. Depending upon the fact which and how many plays are included in this category the relative frequency of the T forms is about 1.4%. In-between there are the subgenres of Roman Plays, Romances and Late/Problem Plays in declining order of '*thou*fulness'. This result shows that in the Histories there are on average 20 tokens of T forms in 1,000 words of running text as opposed to only 14 in the Comedies.

For the reason that there are no large discrepancies between the above sub-categorisations and that, in addition, the categories of Roman Plays, Romances and Late/Problem Plays are rather small and not universally accepted, the threefold division of the *First Folio* will be further analysed.

3.5 Interpretation of the numerical results

The different approaches for subcategorising Shakespeare's plays into genres unanimously confirm that the Histories as early plays (1590–1599, excepting H8) feature the highest numbers of T forms as opposed to the group of Comedies, which show the lowest rates (see Graphs 3–5 in the appendix to this chapter).

With Brown and Gilman's (1960) theory and the rules for linguistic decorum in Elizabethan England in mind, this result is quite contrary to the hypothesis that in Comedies with personnel mostly from the medium or lower social strata, a majority of T forms could have been expected.

The scores obtained for Tragedy, Romance and Roman Plays are too similar to base any major differences of pronominal usage in relation to these genres. However, in their use of second person pronouns the Tragedies bear more similarities to the History Plays than to the Comedies. Furthermore, the date-figures indicate a fairly clear-cut caesura within the Shakespeare Corpus, in that from the turn of the 16th to the 17th century, or more particularly from 1598 (= 2H4) onwards, the ratio of T forms to Y forms is clearly in favour of the latter, even if we have to subtract about 20% plural tokens which are included in the tally. The only plays to pose some numerical counter-evidence to this are: TIM (1607/08, T 513:Y 439) and TMP (1611, T 401:Y 329) with their "unproportionally" high number of T forms and H8 (1612/13), with its exceptionally low score of T forms (T 77:Y 803).

In his socio-historical authorship analyses of the Shakespeare-Fletcher and Shakespeare-Middleton collaborations and the apocryphal plays, Hope (1994b: 100–104) has suggested — although not on the basis of pronoun usage — that there is evidence of TIM being a collaboration between Shakespeare and Middleton, and that H8 and TNK are most likely collaborations with Fletcher. With reference to Holdsworth (1982: 171), Hope states that the high proportion of T forms in TIM "may be due to the excess of accusation in that play (in fact Holdsworth notes that 'over half' of the uses of 'thou' in the play occur in 4.03. 1–457, which contains Timon's most sustained 'invective')" (1994b: 63).

H8 is the play with the lowest score for T pronouns in the whole corpus. Hope has found that the play with its low figures for *thou* and its high figures for *you* is unusual even in terms of Fletcher's use of pronouns: "these figures have obvious implications for the question of authorship [...]. The absence of 'thou' forms, and of modulation, has to be addressed, as does the fact that thirty-five of the eighty-four 'thou' forms in the play occur in one half of one scene (3.02. 203–459), the first half of which contains only one 'thou' form" (1994b: 82).[2]

For the reason that the choice of second person pronouns did not prove a reliable criterion in authorship studies,[3] Hope has applied this analysis only to H8 and not to the other collaborative plays such as TNK. In a mathematical study that analyses lexical, metrical and structural devices that covary with date of composition, Brainerd has found out that in the two collaborative plays H8 and TNK "Fletcher's contribution was either minimal or in a style not too deviant from Shakespeare's. Both plays are predicted significantly earlier than the *Riverside* dates" (1980: 229).

Although not conspicuous in second person pronouns, Hope (1994b: 106–113) has also suggested that the text of PER is likely to be a final draft by Wilkins. For this reason, these plays should perhaps be left out of calculations of the Shakespeare corpus proper.

The figures still calling for an individual explanation are those of TIT (1593/94, T 519:Y 380) with its relatively high number of T forms, ROM (1595/96, T 605:Y 414) and TMP (1611, T 401:Y 329).

In the chronology of Wells et al. (1987), Evans and Tobin (1997) and Schabert (2000), TIT is grouped as play number six. Schabert (1992), on the other hand, regards this as Shakespeare's first play and gives the putative date (1589–90). No matter which date of publication we assume, TIT remains one of the very early plays, as it may have been written between 1590 and 1592. This early date of composition could possibly explain the relatively high number of T forms.

The high proportion of T forms in ROM could possibly be interpreted along the same line. Without a detailed analysis of the play it can be assumed that the high number could be due to its being the earliest Tragedy and that the T forms mostly occur in the frequent exchanges between the two lovers.

However, the two variables of date of composition and genre fail to give an explanation for the unproportionally high number of T forms in TMP, which is a kind of family drama, with a great deal of the dialogue being on an intimate level, and with fairies, monsters, freaks, and jesters, and the familiarity that comes from being imprisoned together so long. Therefore subject-matter and characterisation are extremely important. Hope states that "the high usage of T forms can be ascribed to factors such as Prospero's holding all of the other characters prisoner, and therefore being able to use captor's T, and Ariel's use of the spirit's T (spirits tend to give and receive T forms)" (1994b: 61 f.).

Within the relatively homogeneous group of Histories, 2H4 with its low number of T forms does also not match the overall picture. Hibbard (1977: 8) and Brainerd (1979: 12) are of the opinion that in particular in 2H4 the comical elements outnumber the historical aspects and tragical motives — which would explain its "Comedy-like" behaviour with the relatively high number of Y forms.

The Comedies encompass the largest number of plays and constitute a fairly heterogeneous genre. They nearly span Shakespeare's entire writing career. For this reason, some scholars, as for example Suerbaum (1996: 197 f.), assume a further subclassification of these plays into:

1. Early Comedies: ERR, SHR, TGV, LLL [WIV]   (1592–1595) [1597]
2. Mature Comedies: MND, ADO; AYL, TN   (1595/96; 1601/02)
3. Problem Plays: MV, TRO, AWW, MM   (1596/97–1604)
4. Romantic Comedies: PER, CYM, WT, TMP   (1607/08; 1611)
   (= Romances)

The only play that does not quite fit into this classification is WIV. Although it was written at a later stage (1597), typologically it belongs to the Early Comedies.

The relative frequencies of the second person pronouns in the genre of Comedy also point to a regression of T forms over time if the Early Comedies, the Mature Comedies and the Late/Problems Plays are considered. So, if we take for instance ERR (1592–94) as the earliest comedy with a relative frequency of 1.9% T forms and compare it to MM (1604) with only about 1.1% (see Table 5), this shows that the T forms have almost been halved in the course of time.

On average, the results for these subgenres are as follows. In the Early Comedies the T forms have a relative frequency of 1.624%, in the Mature Comedies this drops to 1.465%, and in the Problem Plays to only 1.204%. Contrary to this are the numbers for the subgenre of Romance, which as the latest set of plays provides counter-evidence with 1.622% of T forms. However, on closer inspection this result can mainly be attributed to TMP, which with its high incidence of T forms skews the statistics. Hence, if TMP is omitted, the average score for the remaining plays drops to 1.330% T forms.

If we accept the prerequisites on genre subdivision made in this chapter, these empirical findings on the use of second person pronouns in the Comedies confirm some of the general statements made by Suerbaum (1996: 200 ff.) on the characteristics of this genre, and its respective subgenres.

Suerbaum attributes the inhomogeneity of the Comedies to the fact that the 17 plays, having been composed between 1592 and 1611, stretch over almost the entire period of Shakespeare's writing career. Nonetheless, the different subgenres can be set apart from each other by factors such as setting, *dramatis personae*, and plot structure. For example, the personnel of the Early Comedies is lower in social rank than that of the later Comedies. This, together with their early date of composition could account for the highest frequency of T forms. If WIV with its low frequency of T forms were to be included in the calculation, the T score in the Early Comedies would drop slightly, or if it is grouped alternatively among the Mature Comedies the rate there would drop, too.

For the second group of Mature Comedies, Suerbaum concludes that the cast of characters is of high social status, because the plays are mostly set at royal courts. The lower frequency of T forms in comparison to the results of the Early Comedies could possibly be attributed to the different social setting. While he acknowledges that the Problem Plays are of a diverging nature, and that in this way the plays bear similarities to other genres, e.g. MV to the Early Comedies, and TRO to the Tragedies, he regards the Romances as a more uniform subgenre characterised by similarities of dramatic structure, plot and characters. He states (1996: 202) that the cast of characters in terms of social hierarchy and in family relationships resembles that of the Tragedies. This statement is borne out by the numbers of T and Y forms, which indeed are fairly similar to those of the Tragedies.

The evidence of exceptional second person pronoun usage in the Romances also ties in with the results of Brainerd on the probability for secondary genre assignment. He has proved by analysing all personal pronouns that it is possible to show for most of the plays a "preferred" second genre, such as Romantic Tragedy, Tragical Romance, and so forth. History and Romance are much tighter genres than Comedy and Tragedy which "appear to be more diffuse in nature" (1979: 11). Brainerd argues further "that History Plays (excepting *Henry IV. Part 2*) are assigned the secondary genre Tragedy [...] objectifies a not unexpected generic affinity. That the Romances are assigned a secondary genre, Tragedy, is also in accord with our intuition" (1979: 13).

In his study on the nature of replies, Ilsemann (1998: 263–275) has also tried to work out typological contrasts between the four genres of History, Comedy, Tragedy and Romance in the Shakespeare Corpus, finding that there are indeed typological differences and also similarities between them. He states that there is only a gradual difference to be found between Comedy and Romance, whereas there is a stark contrast between Comedy and History. Tragedy and History share many features, but only Tragedy exhibits a large amount of focalisation and concentration on the main characters.

3.6   Comparison of the findings to other corpora

3.6.1   Mitchell's Corpus of British Drama (1580–1780)

In order to decide whether the surprisingly low turnout of T forms in all of Shakespeare's comedies in contrast to the tragedies and histories is merely accidental, an idiosyncratic feature of personal style, or, moreover, a structural, genre-specific phenomenon that can be corroborated by evidence from other authors, my findings on the correlation between pronoun and genre shall be compared to the usage of second person pronouns of Shakespeare's contemporaries and later dramatists.

To my knowledge, there are two monographs that deal with address pronouns in Elizabethan, Jacobean, Restoration and 18th century drama. Bock's dissertation (1938) on "Der stilistische Gebrauch des englischen Personalpronomens der 2. Person im volkstümlichen Dialog der älteren englischen Komödie" covers the period ranging from 1497 to 1775/79. His study is based on a total of 36 comedies (for authors and titles cf. Chapter 10.3.3.1). Appended to his investigation is a 36 page (unnumbered) detailed breakdown of pronoun occurrences in each of the plays grouped according to number and case. Unfortunately, Bock's corpus is made up entirely of comedies. Owing to this, it can serve only partly the purpose of an ancillary corpus for further evidence on pronoun use and genre.

Mitchell (1971) has also analysed a corpus of British drama spanning the two-hundred year period from 1580 to 1780. Her corpus includes sixty-two plays by twenty-nine dramatists and is subdivided into fifty-year-, ten-year- and also one year time-spans. In so doing, she has investigated a grand total of 57,580 occurrences of second person pronouns.[4] She has analysed this set of plays in various directions: chronologically for each of the subperiods, according to individual dramatists, genre, and to differences between individual pronoun usages. Her detailed statistical analysis shall here only be summarised to such an extent as is needed for the confirmation or refutation of my initial hypothesis.

When Shakespeare's use of the second person pronouns is compared to that of his fellow playwrights in terms of numbers (see Table 6), the following figures can be gathered from Mitchell's corpus. It should be added though that the selection of dramatists from the period in which Shakespeare wrote is imbalanced due to the inclusion of ten Shakespeare plays, compared to only two each from Marlowe, Jonson and Ford.

For Shakespeare's contemporaries, Mitchell explains that "with the exception of Jonson, the percentages of *th* to *y* forms follow chronological order rather closely" (1971:45). Of the four playwrights, Marlowe uses the highest percentages of T forms in his two blank verse tragedies. For Shakespeare she has investigated five history plays, three tragedies, and two comedies. The two plays by Ford are blank verse tragedies, and Jonson is represented by two blank verse comedies. From this

Table 6. T forms and Y forms in Elizabethan dramatists

Dramatist	T forms	%	Y forms	%
Marlowe	624	56	482	44
Shakespeare	4,139	44	5,369	56
Ford	576	43	775	57
Jonson	442	18	2,021	82

(Table based on Mitchell 1971:55)

set-up it is difficult to work out whether birthdate, place of birth, date of play, type of play or even further factors play an important role in the usage of address pronouns. When Mitchell in her year-by-year-analysis of plays, compares Jonson's *Volpone* and *Every Man in His Humor* to Shakespeare's H5 and JC, all composed in 1598, she explains Jonson's low incidence of T forms (18%) with his "concern for purity of language [which] could very well explain the small percentage of *th* pronouns, already becoming archaic in his own time" (1971:66). However, with all the wealth of statistical information that is provided in her diachronic breakdown of figures, I would assume that the high incidence of Y forms in Jonson should rather be attributed to the fact that these plays are comedies.[5] On the other hand, Jonson is also the one to make least use of *ye* in comparison to *you* (cf. Chapter 10.3.3.2, Table 2), which would indicate a preference for up-to-date variants over recessive ones. A diachronic analysis of the data irrespective of usage differences between individual authors and drama types for the two-hundred-year-time-span looks as shown in Table 7.

When these data are arranged in form of a graph (see Graph 1), it becomes apparent that the demise of the T forms and the subsequent rise of the Y forms illustrates the typical S-curve of linguistic change (cf. Chapter 1.3) with a rapid inception, a period of stabilisation, and eventually, an acceleration of the attrition. "Therefore, these four periods, beginning in the sixteenth century with the *th* forms already showing a decline over the *y* forms, point to the virtual disappearance of the *th* forms in the latter half of the eighteenth century" (Mitchell 1971:54).

Table 7. T and Y forms in English drama from 1580 to 1780

	T forms	%	Y forms	%	Total
Period I (1580–1630)	5,781	40	8,647	60	14,428
Period II (1630–1680)	3,014	19	12,645	81	15,659
Period III (1680–1730)	2,962	18	13,184	82	16,146
Period IV (1730–1780)	1,130	10	10,217	90	11,347
Total	**12,887**		**44,693**		**57,580**

(Table mine, based on Mitchell 1971:43–54, especially page 54)

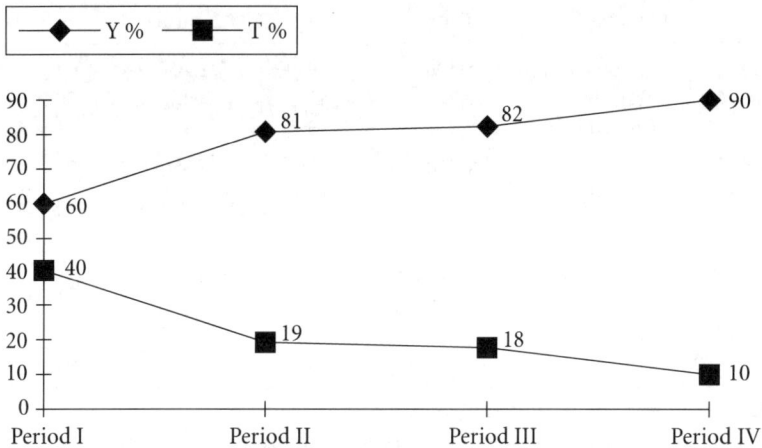

Graph 1. The percentage of T and Y forms in all plays from 1580 to 1780.

This result was to be expected and basically confirms the findings of Bock (1938), to whose work Mitchell did not have access. On the basis of Bock's quantitative evidence, Finkenstaedt (1963) gives the following qualitative explanation of the development. Until well after Shakespeare's time, the same types of pronominal address are to be found in drama and authentic colloquial speech, although not in the same proportions. The higher frequency of T forms in drama can be attributed to the exigencies of plot, which demand a condensation of both action and language. This would e.g. explain the high frequency of the affective singular in drama. In his opinion, Restoration drama shows less contact to colloquial speech than the previous period. The T forms become conventionalised for affective usage and to add pathos to grand speeches (cf. 1963:159f.). While for the 17th century he still sees a connection between the language of drama and colloquial speech as regards address pronouns, he maintains that from the 18th century onwards the use of T forms in literature has become a mere traditional device (cf. 1963:227).

When Mitchell's data on the four periods are broken down according to drama types, a pattern emerges that supports the findings on the correlation of pronoun usage and genre as put forward for the Shakespeare Corpus.

Put on a cline, the five Chronicle Plays in Period I (= five History Plays by Shakespeare) contain the highest percentage of T forms, thus supporting my results for the Shakespeare Corpus. The 49% even surpasses the 41% of the Tragedies. As the instances of Heroic Drama, Farce and Pantomime are restricted to one play each, these can be neglected for the diachronic analysis.

Mitchell offers only a partial explanation for the high number of T forms in the Tragedies, and the corresponding low figures in the Comedies. An additional test

Table 8. T and Y forms from 1580 to 1780 according to genres

	Drama Type	T forms	%	Y forms	%
Period I	Chronicle	2,306	49	2,401	51
(1580–1630)	Tragedy	2,259	41	3,279	59
	Comedy	1,216	29	2,967	71
Period II	Tragedy	1,460	23	4,850	77
(1630–1680)	Comedy	1,433	17	6,976	83
	Heroic Drama	121	13	819	87*
Period III	Tragedy	1,939	43	2,547	57
(1680–1730)	Comedy	1,023	9	10,637	91
Period IV	Tragedy	617	32	1,327	68
(1730–1780)	Comedy	513	5	8,890	95**

(Table mine, mainly based on Mitchell 1971:56)

* The category contains only one play, namely Dryden's *Conquest* (1631).
** The figures given for Comedy are the aggregate figures from Farce, Comedy and Pantomime. Because the categories of Farce and Pantomime contain only one play each, *The Lying Varlet* (1741) and *Harlekin's Invasion* (1759) both by David Garrick, Mitchell (1971:53) has suggested to treat them jointly.

carried out by her has revealed that the high incidence of T forms in Tragedy can possibly be ascribed to their use in apostrophe. "71% of the occurrences appear in tragedy and 81% of the occurrences are *th* forms" (1971:56). For the low performance of T forms in the Comedies she assumes that this has to do with imbalances in the corpus due to the increase of this genre in her sample towards the final periods.

If again the data, excepting Chronicle and Heroic Drama, which only occur in one period, are arranged in the form of a graph the frequencies given in per cent reveal a pattern over time (see Graph 2).

3.6.2 Johnson's Corpus of British Drama and Prose (1599–1712)

In an article that is often overlooked, Johnson (1966) has carried out quantitative research on "The pronoun of address in seventeenth-century English" on the basis of a selection of 17 plays ranging from Thomas Dekker, *The Shoemaker's Holiday* (1599) to George Farquhar, *Sir Harry Wilding* (1701), supplemented by "fiction" ranging from Thomas Deloney, *Jacke of Newberrie* (1597) to Joseph Addison and Others, *The Coverley Papers from "The Spectator"* (1711/12).[6]

She presents the well-known tripartite stratification of English society and has assigned the characters from the *dramatis personae* of the comedies and other fictional works to one of the three social divisions of the upper class (gentlemen), the middle class (yeomen, merchants, professionals, lower clergy, etc.) and lower class (cottagers, labourers, artificers, etc.). On this sociological basis she offers the following results as given in Table 9.

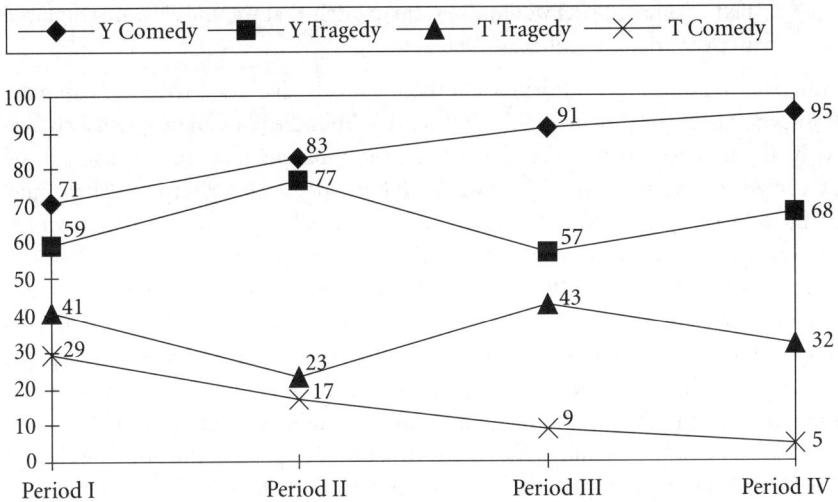

Graph 2. The percentage of T and Y forms from 1580 to 1780 according to genres.

Table 9. Social stratification in 17th century Comedy

	You tokens	*Thou* tokens	*You* %	*Thou* %
1600–1649				
Upper Class	5,851	2,664	64.36	35.64
Middle Class	2,807	629	81.40	18.60
Lower Class	2,385	470	83.47	16.53
Total	**11,043**	**3,763**		
1650–1699				
Upper Class	10,853	2,353	81.40	18.60
Middle Class	3,145	574	81.77	18.23
Lower Class	2,849	317	88.32	11.68
Total	**16,847**	**3,244**		

(Table from Johnson 1966:265)

The conclusions Johnson draws, to my mind, do not fully exploit her data. She states that

> the three classes employ the pronouns of address with relative frequencies that are extremely erratic; their variability immediately suggests that the distinction between *you* and *thou* had become meaningless in the seventeenth century. [...] This maintenance of the distinction between the two pronouns by the

better educated [...] would also seem to imply that *you* and *thou* are employed in free variation. (Johnson 1966:265)

However, quite to the contrary, when these data are discussed within a Labovian framework of correlational sociolinguistics that links the place of origin of a change with the direction of its diffusion it becomes apparent that this change can be described as coming from below.[7] Among other aspects, changes from below "may be introduced by any social class, although no cases have been recorded in which the highest-status social group acts as the innovating group" (Labov 1994:78). These findings also contradict Taavitsainen's statement on fiction (cf. 3.6.3) and support my claim that in Shakespearean and later Comedy *you* is the usual (un-marked) form of exchange even among the lower social orders. Johnson's figures even suggest that the lower and middle ranks as depicted in 17th century drama have initiated the change and the upper class maintains an older distinction.

The data for the second half of the 17th century imply that the ongoing change has lost some of its impetus for the lower and middle classes. The differences between the three social groups are much less marked, but the fall of *thou* by 17% in the upper class is decisive.

Johnson breaks down her data according to whether the pronouns are ex-changed among social equals or in uneven power constellations (see Table 10).

By making use of the categorisation of address forms as put forward by Trudgill (1974:107; cf. Chapter 2.3, Table 2), the data from Tables 10a) and b) can be interpreted in the following way: for the first half of the 17th century the middle class in equal power relationships is in the lead as *you*-users, followed at equal distance by the upper and the lower class. These figures contradict the predictions of Brown and Gilman's power and solidarity model with Y being the predominant form, almost regardless of social rank. This is even more so for the latter half of the

Table 10a. The sociolinguistic distribution of T forms and Y forms 1600–1649

1600–1649		You tokens	Thou tokens	You %	Thou %
+power ↔ +power	Upper Class to Upper Class	4,310	1,609	74.26	25.74
↔	Middle Class to Middle Class	1,129	231	83.14	16.86
−power ↔ −power	Lower Class to Lower Class	617	370	62.32	37.68
+power → −power	Upper Class to Middle Class	899	395	69.69	30.31
	Upper Class to Lower Class	642	660	49.84	50.16
	Middle Class to Lower Class	282	248	53.22	46.78
−power → +power	Middle Class to Upper Class	1,396	150	90.40	9.60
	Lower Class to Middle Class	432	27	94.14	5.86
	Lower Class to Upper Class	1,336	73	94.89	5.11

17th century when among social equals of the three estates the figures amount to 84 or 85% Y as opposed to 14 to 15% of T.

For the situation of discourse between persons categorised as +POWER to those ranked as −POWER the choice of address pronouns for the first half of the century is about 70% Y from upper to middle class and about 50% Y from both upper and middle class to lower class speakers. For the second half of the century this distinction gets levelled, as in more than two thirds of all cases Y is employed as pronoun, which again defies the explanation given by Brown and Gilman.

The most clear-cut cases which do not show a very significant development over this 100-year period are dyads involving speakers of −POWER addressing +POWER speakers. Following the predictions of theory, these cases amount to about 90% Y throughout the period of observation.

3.6.3   The Helsinki Corpus (1500–1710)

Having found that quite a considerable difference in the use of address pronouns exists between the genres of Tragedy and Comedy, it is tempting to put these results into a wider perspective of literary versus non-literary texts. Due to the pioneering work done by a number of scholars at Helsinki university and elsewhere, it is possible to make such comparisons. The following data have been taken over from Taavitsainen (1997a), who discusses EModE genres and text types under the specific perspective of how personal affect is dealt with linguistically in fiction and adjoining text types.[8] Among the factors tested for personal affect are also the second person pronouns. From a diachronic statistical analysis, Taavitsainen finds that "the difference between the use of the second person singular in fiction and the adjoining genres is significant" (1997a: 239).

Table 10b. The sociolinguistic distribution of T forms and Y forms 1649–1699

1649–1699		You tokens	Thou tokens	You %	Thou %
+power ↔ +power	Upper Class to Upper Class	8,920	1,687	84.14	15.86
↔	Middle Class to Middle Class	1,912	322	85.83	14.17
−power ↔ −power	Lower Class to Lower Class	540	98	84.24	15.76
+power → −power	Upper Class to Middle Class	1,099	304	78.42	21.58
	Upper Class to Lower Class	834	362	69.95	30.05
	Middle Class to Lower Class	293	136	68.31	31.69
−power → +power	Middle Class to Upper Class	940	116	89.10	10.90
	Lower Class to Middle Class	1,112	139	89.02	10.98
	Lower Class to Upper Class	1,197	80	96.00	4.00

(Table from Johnson 1966: 266; first column added, sequence of rows altered)

The figures of Table 11 suggest that Fiction followed at some distance by Autobiography are the only genres to make use of *thou* throughout all phases of EModE. Interestingly, for Fiction the numbers rise with time, and for Autobiography there is a marked drop in EModE 2 followed again by a rise. The "unusual" behaviour of Fiction in EModE 3 can be explained by the fact that all examples found, stem from Aphra Behn's *Penny Merriments* (1685) "a parody with exaggerated emotionality and comical imitation of religious language" (1997a: 241).

The high frequency of *thou* in Fiction is explained by Taavitsainen with reference to Wales (1983: 116) in the following way:

> A possible surge feature available in the language at the time in focus was the use of *thou.* Statistically it proved significant, but a closer consideration revealed that the frequent use of *thou* in fiction is connected with the social classes depicted in these texts: country folk and lower and middle class people among which it was the unmarked pronoun of address. [...] In non-literary texts such as autobiography the use of *thou* to express heightened emotionality is evident. Some instances are found in outbursts of accusation and contempt, and in one example it is used in a solemn and affective speech. (Taavitsainen 1997a: 256 f.)

These observations tie in only partly with my results obtained for Shakespearean drama, because most of the T forms occur in the History Plays, which feature mostly characters of noble rank. While it seems to be true that many instances of *thou* in the Tragedies are used for means of personal affect and due to genre conventions, e.g. in apostrophe, it cannot be maintained that in (Shakespearean) Comedy the characters come from the lower classes. Except for the early Comedies, the characters in the Mature Comedies have the same high social background as those in the Tragedies. The low incidence of T forms in Comedies in general — see for instance Jonson with only 18% of T forms in Table 6 — can possibly be explained by the difference in setting, plot and subject matter and a generally less intense atmosphere that does not so often call for means to highlight personal affect.

Table 11. Absolute occurrences of second person singular in the Helsinki Corpus

	Total	EModE 1 (1500–1570)	EModE 2 (1570–1640)	EModE 3 (1640–1710)
Fiction	102	20	29	53
Autobiography	23	9	4	10
History	2	0	0	2
Biography	1	0	1	0
Diary	3	0	0	3
Travelogue	0	0	0	0

(Table from Taavitsainen 1997a: 239; years for periods added)

3.6.4   The Corpus of English Dialogues (1560–1720)

Walker (forthc.) reports on her ongoing research on pronoun usage on the basis of the *Corpus of English Dialogues (1560–1720)*. As this corpus is still under compilation at Lancaster and Uppsala Universities she uses a preliminary version that consists of approximately 200,000 words of running text. The study compares the use of the second person pronouns in the two text categories of Authentic Dialogue as represented by the text types of Trials and Depositions as opposed to the Constructed Dialogue of Comedy drama and Handbooks for the periods of 1560–1600 and 1680–1720, with the aim of investigating the importance of the two extra-linguistic factors of text type and gender on the use of the second person pronouns.

Table 12. The ratio of *thou* to *you* by text type in the Corpus of English Dialogues

1560–1600	*Thou*	*You*	1680–1720	*Thou*	*You*
Trials	64 (9.8%)	590 (90.2%)		234 (26%)	667 (74%)
Depositions	150 (44.2%)	189 (55.8%)		11 (20%)	44 (80%)
Comedies	331 (26.4%)	924 (73.6%)		106 (8.6%)	1,128 (91.4%)
Handbooks	29 (6.2%)	439 (93.8%)		137 (17.4%)	651 (82.6%)
Total	574 (21.1%)	2,142 (78.9%)		488 (16.4%)	2,490 (83.6%)

(Combinations of Walker's tables 2, 3 and 4)

As Walker gives detailed commentaries and reasonings on the pronoun frequencies with respect to each text category and type, these shall here only be briefly summarised. The rate of *thou* at 26.4% for the Comedies in the period 1560–1600 (cf. Table 12) is still fairly high when compared to that for Trials (9.8%) and Handbooks (6.2%). The considerable drop to only 8.6% in the period 1680–1720 is in keeping with the findings from the other corpora on British drama, which all show a similar decrease over time. In comparison to the aggregate results of the text type, the figures for the individual dramatists[9] confirm the general trend, but again, not surprisingly, show usage differences from author to author. The rise of *thou* in the period 1680–1720 in the Trials and Handbooks can be attributed to the special circumstances of individual texts, but not to a general tendency.

3.7   Conclusion

The results of this mainly numerical approach to the function of variability in the second person pronouns *thou* and *you* and their variants in the Shakespeare Corpus have shown that the difference in frequency between T forms with a relative frequency of 1.578% and Y forms with 2.681% evidenced by the concordances through the incorporation of the plural Y forms needs to be relativised. On the basis of the control corpus it can be positively assumed that about 20% of the Y tokens are plural. This leaves about 18,000 Y singular forms, and hence reduces their relative frequency to ca. 2% in the corpus, so that the margin between the 13,186 T forms and the 22,400 Y forms would be narrowed down to a "surplus" of only 5,000 Y forms instead of 9,000 (see Tables 1 and 2). The ratio of the T forms in relation to the singular Y forms then drops to 0.70 instead of 0.59 with the inclusion of plural forms.

The high proportion of T forms proves that *thou* is indeed much more than "an occasional variant used on special occasions" (Barber 1981: 287). However, Hope's findings that "as late as the 1590s in drama, it is possible to find writers who do not seem to have 'marked' one of the forms over the other" (1994a: 148) seems to apply only to Shakespeare's History Plays and to his early Tragedies and to the plays of Christopher Marlowe (see Table 6).

Contrary to the sceptical opinions of Barber (1981) and Kiełkiewicz-Janoviak (1994), who could not find a definite preference for either of the forms in their limited material, my data suggest the following: in terms of second person pronouns the Shakespeare Corpus can be divided into two parts – an early part leading up to 1600, or more precisely 1598, and a later part after 1600. With the only exceptions of TIM (1607–08) and TMP (1611) all the plays showing more T than Y forms are early History Plays; viz.: 1–3H6, R3, JN, R2 and, if a share of putative plural Y tokens is subtracted, also 1H4, and the early Tragedies, namely TIT and ROM.[10]

While Hope is of the opinion that "the ranges of variation within genres mean that no consistent relationship can be made between genre and the number of forms. It looks as though non-fixed factors are in operation here again" (1994b: 63), Brainerd (1979: 7) has proved that for the T forms the two factors of genre and date taken together provide a statistically highly significant result.[11]

The differences between Tragedy, Roman Plays and Romance are not very significant. Surprisingly, and quite contrary to what could be expected according to the body of critical literature as presented in Chapter 2, is the extremely low frequency of T forms in the Comedies, which exhibit the lowest rates of all genres. This result has been confirmed by an additional test carried out on the basis of Mitchell's (1971) corpus. Throughout the two-hundred-year time-span from 1580 to 1780, and despite considerable vacillation among individual authors, there is a constant "surplus" of Y forms in Comedy in comparison to Tragedy. A comparison of drama to other non-literary text types based on Taavitsainen (1997a) has proved that in the genres of Fiction and Autobiography the use of *thou* lingers on through all phases of EModE, while in History, Biography, Diary and Travelogue it has been a marginal form from the very beginning of the period.

The lower degree of T forms in the Comedies in comparison to the Tragedies could probably be attributed to the fact that even among middle or lower class speakers, which constitute the majority of the personnel of the Comedies, the normal form of exchange was *you* and not *thou,* as Wales (1983: 116) and Taavit-sainen (1997a: 256f.) seem to suggest for social equals of the lower class when they regard *thou* as the unmarked pronoun of address among these speakers. This hypothesis is strongly confirmed by the incorporation of Johnson's (1966) data from 17th century fiction, which corroborates that in Comedy the middle and lower class speakers make more use of *you* than do the upper class speakers. Johnson finds that on the whole women "employ the *you*-singular more frequently than men" that in moments of feeling *thou* "persists in the dialogue of men and women of every station" (1966: 268f.) and that, although less frequently, *thou* is used in soliloquy, by an insane person, in address to a supernatural creature, in the speech of the devil and in aside.

For this reason it can be argued with some confidence that the relatively higher percentage of T forms in the Tragedies is not, or presumably not in the first place, the T of vertical social distance used by superiors to pull rank but rather the emotive T used to express feelings of anger and/or affection, which would be in accordance with the finding that the interactional style in Comedies differs from that expressed in Tragedies with their large amount of emotional intensity. This hypothesis is supported by Mitchell's findings that Tragedies contain a higher degree of apostrophe, for which *thou* is the characteristic pronoun.

For the reason that such a quantitative approach allows one to look only for general tendencies or directions of development from a bird's eye view by backgrounding content matter, it will be supplemented by further detailed quantitative and qualitative investigations which also incorporate the dramatic medium, the context of the utterance, and the nominal forms of address.

Appendix: Graphs showing the frequencies of T and Y forms in the Shakespeare Corpus according to genre

Graphs 3–5 visualise the relative percentages of the T and Y forms for the three genres of History, Tragedy and Comedy, each in chronological order. For the sake of graphic clearness one per cent appears as 1000.[12]

□ T forms □ Y forms

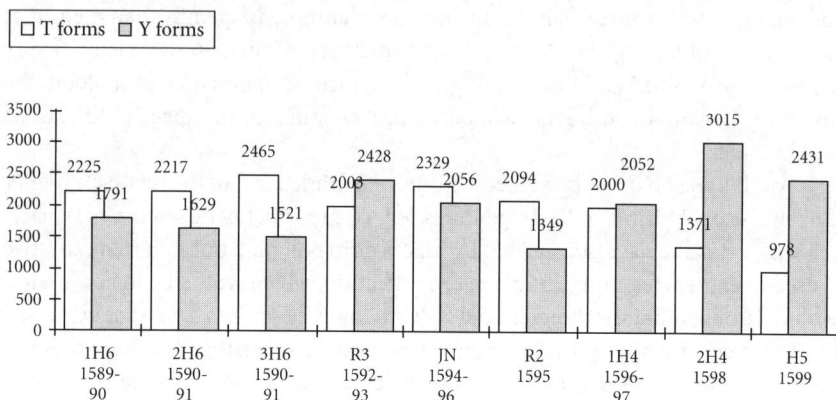

Graph 3. T and Y forms in the Histories.

□ T forms □ Y forms

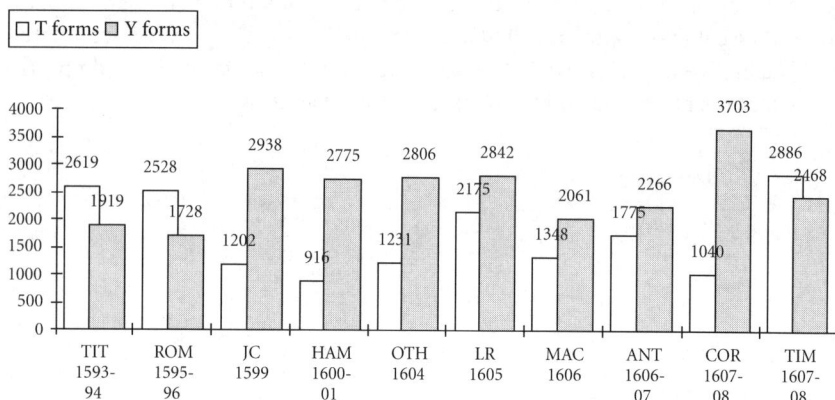

Graph 4. T and Y forms in the Tragedies.

□ T forms □ Y forms

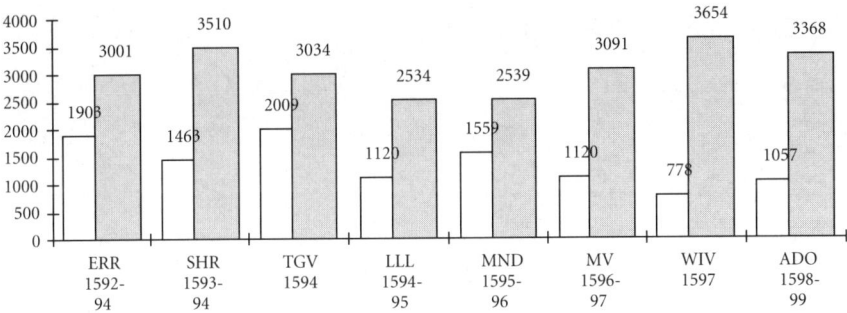

Graph 5a. T and Y forms in the Comedies.

□ T forms □ Y forms

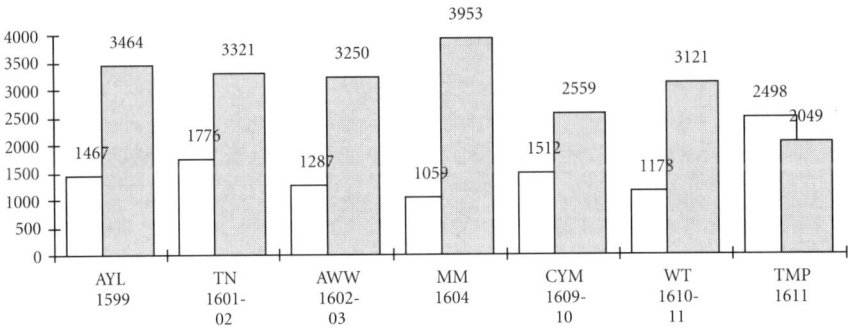

Graph 5b. T and Y forms in the Comedies (continued).

CHAPTER 4

The distribution of *thou* and *you* and their variants in verse and prose

4.1 Working hypothesis and objective

The previous chapter has shown that — at least to a certain extent — pronoun use correlates with genre, so that, put on a scale, History and Tragedy employ more T forms than Comedy does. As the different dramatic genres make use of the media verse and prose to different extents, it seems imperative to investigate whether the two media show a different affinity towards T- or Y forms.

The problem of the characteristics and the distribution of the two dramatic media of verse and prose has, especially in the late 19th and earlier 20th centuries, resulted in quite a number of studies trying to account for this phenomenon from various perspectives. Tschopp's dissertation (1956:4–12) and the annotated bibliography in Crane (1951:214–216) both give a balanced summary of the older works. Despite the various facets of verse and prose that have been looked into, it seems surprising that apparently nobody has so far linked the social implications of verse and prose to the address pronouns being used.

The fact that in Elizabethan drama blank verse constitutes a linguistic and literary norm has often been pointed out (cf. Borinski 1955, 1969, Crane 1951, Vickers 1968). For this reason the poetic device of blank verse is, among other things, a stylistic means for social characterisation. In this tradition, persons of rank speak in blank verse in normal speech situations. If verse thus constitutes a norm, a switch to prose indicates a deviation from this norm. Persons speaking in prose, whether constantly or only temporarily, are either not capable, because of their inferior social status, or not willing to comply with this norm.

On the other hand, rhymed passages with couplets, often at the end of a scene, also mark a deviation from the norm. In some of Shakespeare's early plays, whole scenes are written in verse, e.g. the exchange between Romeo and Juliet in ROM (1, 5, 93–106) has the form of a sonnet. In MND a number of rhyming couplets are to be found, e.g. Hero to Lysander in 1, 1, 171–178, a fairy to Puck in 2, 1, 2–13 or Oberon to Puck in 2, 1, 249–268.

> (1)   Hero: My good Lysander,
>   I swear to thee, by Cupid's strongest bow,
>   By his best arrow with the golden head,

> By the simplicity of Venus' doves,
> By that which knitteth souls and prospers loves,
> And by that fire which burn'd the Carthage queen
> When the false Troyan under sail was seen, [...]. (MND 1, 1, 169–174)

Finkenstaedt comments on the use of rhymes, couplets, split couplets, etc. by saying that the only overall characteristic of rhymes is that of an intensifier (1954: 87ff.). In analysing the interplay between form and content, the position of a personal pronoun within a versed line may also be of importance, i.e. whether it appears in a stressed or an unstressed position.

As regards the factors that govern the overall distribution and the dramatic function of verse and prose, the study of Tschopp (1956) offers valuable insights. In her opinion the distribution of the two media largely depends on the factors below:

1. The change of the medium serves the function in the general organisation of the drama in order to expound opposites in character, actions, forms, existence, etc.
2. By a change a scenic effect can be achieved or highlighted such as dissimulation, intrigue, private vs. official communication, etc.
3. Certain groups of characters may be linked exclusively to one of the media, irrespective of their environment (cf. Tschopp 1956: 115–118).

It would be rather simplistic to assume that the two media are directly tied to certain (groups of) persons or *vice versa*. Although there are speakers who only converse in one medium, there are others who speak predominantly in prose or verse or in a mixture of both, depending on the circumstances. General reference works on Shakespeare and case studies such as Tschopp (1956) state that lower class characters, in particular peasants, artisans, soldiers, etc. speak exclusively in prose, which in turn can be interpreted as an indicator of social class. The servants of noblemen, on the other hand, usually speak in verse, e.g. Oswald in LR. The porter in MAC is an exception, for he is intended to indicate drunkenness. Children and fools normally also speak in prose. Noblemen temporarily turn to prose under exceptional circumstances in situations of extreme stress or strain, e.g. the mad King Lear on the heath, Ophelia while mentally deranged, or the somnambulant Lady Macbeth. Furthermore, prose can also be used in asides where the speeches are given off record and are not normally expected to be overheard by those just talked about, e.g. the dialogue between Kent and Gloucester in the opening scene of LR, where the bastardy of Edmund is revealed.

With the only exceptions of H8 and TNK Tschopp has categorised all the characters of the other plays according to the parameters of whether they speak entirely or predominantly in verse or prose or in a mixture of both, and comes to the conclusion (1956: 22 f.) that a clear boundary between verse and prose speakers cannot be drawn. Nonetheless, the following tendencies become apparent: the court and the aristocrats are among the verse speakers, whereas the lower class speakers converse in prose. There are, however, exceptions to this rule.

Among the characters who speak entirely in blank verse are:

1. the chorus,
2. allegoric persons,
3. manifestations of the supernatural: gods, elves, witches, ghosts, apparitions, etc.
4. mediators between the realm of the supernatural and the real world: priests, soothsayers, sorcerers, prophets, etc.
5. official persons embodying stately power.

Among the characters who speak entirely in prose are:

1. clowns, fools, jesters (with few exceptions),
2. actors, musicians, dancers, whores, etc.
3. inn keepers, servants, butlers, chambermaids, etc.
4. foreigners (also non-Englishmen such as Irish, Welsh and Scottish persons),
5. persons characterised by "telling" names such as *Abhorson, Andrew Aguecheek, Toby Belch, Pompey Bum, Dogberry, Doll Tearsheet, Martext, Shallow, Silence, Slender, Touchstone,* etc. or by typical epithets such as "a drunken butler", "a rogue", etc.

The alternation of verse and prose could then, in the broadest sense of the term, be interpreted as a discourse or textual marker. A switch between these two dramatic media can convey a change of mood or attitude, topic of discourse, social setting etc. as outlined above.

With due attention to the fact that there are different layers of prose styles and that prose fulfils different dramatic functions in Comedy and Tragedy and, in addition, that an artistic development of Shakespeare throughout his writing career took place, the following working hypothesis could be formulated: it can be generalised that prose is usually an indicator of social inferiority or some other deviation from a norm. On the basis of this, it can further be assumed that this social division of the two dramatic media has a bearing on the forms of address that are being exchanged.

However, the expectation that the T forms would prevail in the Comedies with their typical lower class personnel and a higher degree of prose passages has been refuted in the previous chapter. In the Comedies the T forms are clearly outnumbered by the Y forms.

Thus, it will be the objective of this chapter either to validate or to falsify the hypothesis that one of the two pronouns is stylistically marked or socially restricted and thus dominates in verse or prose by means of a statistically significant deviation.[1]

4.2   Corpus study

4.2.1   Methodology

The analysis of the data will proceed on two different levels. In order to find out, from the beginning, the general development, concordance data shall serve, as before, as a basis. With the help of Spevack all incidences of T and Y forms will be added up and accounted for, whether they appear in verse or in prose. As this result will still include plural Y forms, more detailed investigations will be carried out for selected plays which have proved in the first analysis to be suitable candidates for more extensive qualitative investigations.

4.2.2   Quantitative outline of pronoun distribution in verse and prose

Table 1 provides the data on the absolute and relative frequencies of words, lines and speeches appearing in a verse or prose context in the Shakespeare Corpus. Not surprisingly, a high correlation was found to exist between the percentages of lines and words in both verse and prose, differing by less than 1%. The percentage of entire speeches in verse or prose is often considerably lower than the lines/words percentage. For the 38 plays as a whole, the ratio between words occurring in a verse or prose context is: 75.65% verse and 24.35% prose.

Table 1. The overall size of the Shakespeare Corpus and its division in verse and prose

		Total	Verse	%	Prose	%	split lines
Compl. works	words	884,647	680,755	76.95	203,892	23.05	
	lines	118,406	91,464	77.25	26,942	22.75	5,572
38 plays	words	835,419	631,968	75.65	203,451	24.35	5,536
	lines	112,230	85,339	76.04	26,891	23.96	
	speeches	31,959	21,726	67.98	10,026	31.37	171

Table 2 shows the aggregate data of pronoun occurrence in a verse or prose context for the three genres of History, Tragedy and Comedy.

As regards the second person pronouns, 10,473 T forms (79.44%) occur in a verse context, and only 2,711 (20.56%) in a prose context. In comparison to these numbers, the Y forms feature more prominently in prose contexts, viz. 15,731 Y forms (70.23%) in verse as opposed to 6,669 (29.77%) in prose; the margin being 9.21%.

However, one has to consider that the overall proportions of verse and prose vary quite considerably from genre to genre. While the Histories feature the highest percentage of verse, and the Tragedies exhibit a range from 99% to 73%, the

Table 2. Frequencies of second person pronouns in verse and prose per genre

	T Verse	%	T Prose	%	Y Verse	%	Y Prose	%
Hist	3,469	83.36	692	16.63	4,106	75.12	1,114	24.88
Trag	3,377	85.93	553	14.07	4,675	79.00	1,242	21.00
Com	3,627	69.17	1,466	30.83	6,950	58.55	4,313	41.45
Total	10,473	79.44	2,711	20.56	15,731	70.23	6,669	29.77

Comedies, not surprisingly, differ sharply from these as they show the lowest ratio of verse in the corpus.

Tables 3–5 demonstrate that there is considerable vacillation in the ratio of verse and prose between the individual plays.

Table 3. The distribution of T and Y forms in verse and prose in the History Plays

Play	Verse %	Prose %	T Verse	%	T Prose	%	Y Verse	%	Y Prose	%
1H6	99.70	0.30	457	100	0	0.00	366	99.46	2	0.54
2H6	84.48	15.52	472	86.92	71	13.08	338	84.71	61	15.29
3H6	99.92	0.08	575	100	0	0.00	355	100	0	0.00
R3	98.42	1.58	556	97.89	12	2.11	687	99.71	2	0.29
JN	100	0.00	397	100	0	0.00	420	100	0	0.00
R2	100	0.00	458	100	0	0.00	295	100	0	0.00
1H4	54.54	45.64	171	35.63	309	64.37	280	56.90	212	43.10
2H4	48.19	51.81	149	41.97	206	58.03	301	38.79	475	61.25
H5	58.17	41.83	158	62.95	93	37.05	276	44.30	347	55.70
H8	97.50	2.50	76	98.70	1	1.30	788	98.13	15	1.87

Unfortunately, the History Plays are a rather unsuitable starting point to demonstrate the distribution of the second person pronouns in the media of verse and prose, because many of them are written entirely or predominantly in verse and thus occupy an exceptional status in the canon of Shakespeare's plays.

As a genre, the Histories comprise ten plays (including H8), two of which, namely JN and R2, are written exclusively, and 1H6, 3H6, R3 and H8 almost entirely in verse, with the figures ranging between 98% and 100%. This leaves only four plays for further consideration.

While in 2H6 the distribution of *thou* and *you* between verse and prose is fairly similar, 1H4, 2H4 and H5 show a marked difference with 2H4 and H5 exhibiting the expected preponderance of *you* in prose and with 1H4 providing counter-evidence.

Although the mere figures defy a socio-historical explanation, some interesting connections to previous research can be drawn. With reference to the titles of the Quartos, Tschopp draws attention to the implicit duality of spheres in the two parts of H4: "dass schon die Titel [...] die Verteilung von Vers und Prosa in diesen beiden Dramen implicite charakterisieren, indem nämlich die 'history', das Leben und der Tod Heinrichs IV., in Versen, die 'humorous conceits' dagegen in Prosa erscheinen" (1956: 34f.).[2] She goes on to say that verse is basically restricted to the domain of the court and the historical plot, whereas prose is linked to the comic episodes in inns, on the road and in the rural, petit bourgeois milieu.

Table 4. The distribution of T and Y forms in verse and prose in the Tragedies

Play	Verse %	Prose %	T Verse	%	T Prose	%	Y Verse	%	Y Prose	%
TIT	98.64	1.36	519	100	0	0.00	365	96.05	15	3.95
ROM	86.97	13.03	543	89.75	62	10.25	307	74.15	107	25.85
JC	92.45	7.55	225	97.83	5	2.17	524	93.24	38	6.76
HAM	72.53	27.47	217	79.78	55	20.22	508	61.87	313	38.13
OTH	81.01	18.99	252	78.75	68	21.25	564	77.47	164	22.53
LR	74.95	25.05	400	72.73	150	27.27	533	75.16	176	24.82
MAC	93.36	6.64	213	95.95	9	4.05	315	92.92	24	7.08
ANT	91.72	8.28	417	98.82	5	1.18	479	88.87	60	11.13
COR	78.00	22.00	247	89.17	30	10.83	738	74.85	248	25.15
TIM	77.48	22.52	344	67.06	169	32.94	342	77.90	97	22.10

According to this grouping, the Tragedies comprise ten plays. Similarly to most of the History Plays, there are a number of plays that are also mostly written in blank verse, namely TIT, JC, MAC and ANT.

Eight out of the ten plays show a preponderance of *thou* in verse and of *you* in prose. With varying degrees of statistical significance[3] this holds for ROM, HAM, ANT and COR. That is to say, there are more *thou*s to be found in verse than there should be, theoretically speaking, if according to the null hypothesis their distribution were the product of pure chance. The only play to counteract this tendency is TIM, because it shows a clear deviation of the *thou* forms to the other side; to a much lesser extent the same also holds true for LR.

The overall development of the verse-prose ratio in the Comedies is uneven. In the first set of Early Comedies, comprising ERR, SHR, TGV and LLL, the ratio of verse declines from 88% to 68%. With the exception of MND with its 80% verse, the other Mature Comedies show a much lower degree of verse ranging between 28% in ADO to 43% in AYL. With only 13%, WIV features the lowest percentage of verse in the entire corpus. In the Problem Plays and even more so in the Romances the proportion of verse rises again, reaching its maximum with 85% in CYM.

Concerning the distribution of the second person pronouns in verse and prose, 15 out of the 18 comedies show a "surplus" of T forms and a "lack" of Y forms in verse. In this respect the result seems to suggest the following interpretation: with the only exceptions of the "untypical" behaviour of the T forms in SHR, LLL and

Table 5. The distribution of T and Y forms in verse and prose in the Comedies

Play	Verse %	Prose %	T Verse	%	T Prose	%	Y Verse	%	Y Prose	%
ERR	88.47	11.53	256	93.43	18	6.57	396	91.67	36	8.33
SHR	82.00	18.00	243	81.00	57	19.00	627	87.33	91	12.67
TGV	75.18	24.82	256	75.29	84	24.71	351	68.42	162	31.58
LLL	67.88	32.12	122	51.69	114	48.31	393	73.60	141	26.40
MND	79.93	20.07	244	97.21	7	2.79	290	70.90	119	29.10
MV	77.28	22.72	207	88.09	28	11.91	490	75.73	157	24.27
WIV	12.53	87.47	37	22.42	128	77.58	55	7.12	718	92.88
ADO	27.68	72.32	88	40.00	132	60.00	153	21.86	547	78.14
AYL	42.63	57.37	160	51.12	153	48.88	280	37.89	459	62.11
TN	38.28	61.72	128	37.10	217	62.90	232	35.97	413	64.03
TRO	70.34	29.66	239	69.08	107	30.92	361	61.60	225	38.40
AWW	53.20	46.80	168	57.73	123	42.27	380	51.77	354	48.23
MM	61.48	38.52	154	68.14	72	31.86	462	54.87	380	45.13
PER	82.60	17.40	195	84.42	36	15.58	446	78.52	122	21.48
CYM	85.43	14.56	368	90.64	38	9.36	529	77.00	158	23.00
WT	72.49	27.51	204	70.34	86	29.66	635	82.79	132	17.21
TMP	79.90	20.10	335	83.54	66	16.46	253	76.90	76	23.10
TNK	94.27	5.73	223	100	0	0.00	617	96.41	23	3.59

WT, where they were found to be "over represented" in prose, in all the other plays which have yielded statistically significant results the T forms have a higher incidence in verse.

Tschopp (1956: 100–114) gives a detailed analysis of the distribution of verse and prose in WT that could perhaps also account for the deviance of the pronouns. While prose encompasses about two fifths of the play, it is remarkable that the first part of the play is almost entirely in verse, with prose mainly occupying the second half of the play. In her opinion, the second half of the play bears many characteristics of comedy. In form of a simplification, WT can then be characterised as a combination of a tragedy and a comedy, in which the caesura in plot away from tragedy coincides with a transition from verse to prose.

However, these results have to be taken into consideration with care, because the assumed dichotomy of verse and prose is complicated by the frequent use of doggerel in ERR and in LLL, which with its loose and irregular measure occupies an intermediate position between verse and prose and deserves special attention in a case study. Crane is of the opinion that "the use of prose for comic matter appears to have grown out of doggerel or 'tumbling verse', which was confused with — and — eventually became prose" (1951: 189).

Nonetheless, the numerical analysis on the basis of the concordances has proved that for 32 of the 38 plays there is indeed a more or less marked "surplus" of T forms to be encountered in verse and a corresponding "lack" of Y forms. For the reason that this result is still flawed by the incorporation of the plural Y forms, at this point no further-reaching conclusions should be drawn from these preliminary observations, but on the basis of these "rough" data more systematic fine-tuning can be done than in any random choice of plays.

4.2.3   Qualitative analysis of selected plays

The statistical data reveal that a number of plays show a marked difference (of 10% or more) in the distribution of the second person pronouns in verse and prose. For the Histories this goes in particular for H5 (18.65%). In the group of Tragedies the following four plays exhibit a marked deviation: ROM (15.60%), HAM (17.91%), COR (14.32%), ANT (9.95%), and among the Comedies, MND (26.31%), MV (12.86%), WIV (15.30%), ADO (18.40%), AYL (13.23%), MM (13.27%) and CYM (13.64%). Because the group of the so-called Mature Comedies features strongly among these plays, two of them shall be further analysed. MND and ADO show the greatest deviation, and, in addition, both have characters of high aristocratic rank as well as simple workmen, which should allow for certain sociolinguistic observations.

4.2.3.1   *Pronoun distribution in verse and prose in MND*
In MND about 80% of the lines or words occur in verse, but only 68% of the speeches. In contrast to this, the pronouns, and in particular the T pronouns with more than 97% verse and less than 3% prose, show a very extreme distribution. With the removal of the plural tokens, the tally for the Y forms shows 318 probable singular forms, out of which 235 (73%) occur in verse lines and 83 (26.1%) in prose.[4] These corrected figures change the original margin by some 3% in favour of verse.

A look at the settings and the characters of the play reveals that there are three completely different groups of people:

1.   The aristocratic world of Athens is represented by Theseus, the Duke of Athens; Hippolyta, who is betrothed to Theseus; the nobleman Egeus and his daughter Hermia. Her father forces Hermia to marry Demetrius, even though she is in love with Lysander. To complicate matters, Helena, an Athenian maid, is in love with Demetrius. All of these characters speak entirely in verse up to 5, 1 when by means of scenic contrast, they comment in prose upon the mechanicals' play.
2.   The workmen Quince, Snug, Bottom, Flute, Snout and Starveling introduced in 1, 2, speak in prose, except when they rehearse or perform their play. In those scenes (3, 1 and 5, 1) their language differs markedly from their colloquial language in terms of style and medium, as they declaim mostly in iambic pentameters.
3.   The last group consists of Oberon, the King of the fairies, and his wife Titania with their retinue of elves and fairies. They too converse entirely in verse. It has to be added though that in stylistic terms the verse of the Athenian aristocrats is very different from that employed by the spirits.

The relatively small number of seven T forms occurring in prose can be accounted for individually, as all are related to the group of workmen and their play. In act 1, scene 2 the mechanicals rehearse their play, "The most lamentable comedy and most cruel death of Pyramus and Thisby", in the woods. When Quince summons his fellow players each by name and role he speaks prose and says *you* to them, and only when Bottom quotes from the play and impersonates Thisby does he switch to *thou* and prose rhymes:

(2)   Quince: Flute, you must take Thisby on you. [...]
Flute: Nay, faith; let not me play a woman; I have a beard coming.
Quince: That's all one; you shall play it in a mask, and you may speak as small as you will.
Bottom: And I may hide my face, let me play Thisby too. I'll speak in a monstrous little voice, "Thisne! Thisne! Ah, Pyramus, my lover dear! thy Thisby dear, and lady dear!"
Quince: No, no, you must play Pyramus; and, Flute, you Thisby. (1, 2, 44–56)

The other T forms in prose occur as a reaction to Puck's enchantment of Bottom when he appears with an ass's head. The normal pronoun of rapport between the workmen being *you*, they switch to *thou* on his transformation:

(3)   Snout: O Bottom, thou art chang'd! What do I see on thee?
Bottom: What do you see? You see an ass-head of your own, do you? [*Exit Snout.*]
Quince: Bless thee, Bottom, bless thee! Thou art translated. (3, 1, 114–119)

Later on, Puck ironically comments upon his sport: "When they him spy, / As wild geese that the creeping fowler eye, [...] Sever themselves and madly sweep the sky, / So, at his sight, away his fellows fly" (3, 2, 19–24). This intended reaction is also signalled by the unusual use of T forms in prose, because apart from these occasions all the other T forms in the entire play occur in verse lines.

That the workmen's world of prose and the tragi-comical realm of acting and the world of the fairies intersect but do not come together is also clearly signalled by pronoun use.

In 3, 1 the craftsmen converse in prose and use *you* as their normal pronoun of rapport. It is only when they begin with the rehearsal of their play that they switch to verse and *thou*. Normal conventions indicated by a switch back to prose and to *you* are at work again when the blunders are corrected:

(4)   Flute: Must I speak now?
Quince: Ay, marry, must you; for you must understand he goes but to see a noise that he heard, and is to come again.
Flute: "Most radiant Pyramus, most lily-white of hue,
Of color like the red rose on triumphant brier,
Most brisky juvenal, and eke most lovely Jew,

> As true as truest horse, that yet would never tire,
> I'll meet thee, Pyramus, at Ninny's tomb."
> Quince: "Ninus' tomb", man. Why, you must not speak that yet. That you
> answer to Pyramus. You speak all your part at once, cues and all. (3, 1, 89–100)

There is an exact parallel to this scene when the actors perform their play before Duke Theseus in 5, 1. The change from the verse of the play to the ordinary prose of the actors is again highlighted by pronoun switching from *thou* to *you* when they make blunders or miss their cues. As a reaction to the stilted verse of the players the aristocrats do not comment upon the achievement of the "hard-handed men that work in Athens here, / Which never labor'd in their minds till now" (5, 1, 72–73) in their ordinary medium of verse, but in prose. They do not alter their pronoun use. With the beginning of the dance, the Bergomask (206ff.), they move back to verse.

As mentioned above, there are also two scenes in which the world of the workmen intersects with the realm of the fairies. After Oberon has cast a spell upon his wife "What thou seest when thou dost wake, / Do it for thy true-love take" (2, 2, 27–28) she sets her eyes upon Bottom with his ass's head and accordingly addresses him in lyrical verses. She "thous" him passionately and dotes on him, upon which he replies "prosaicly" by sticking to his normal workman's diction:

(5)   Titania: I pray thee, gentle mortal, sing again.
       Mine ear is much enarmored of thy note;
       So is mine eye enthralled to thy shape;
       And thy fair virtue's force (perforce) doth move me
       On the first view to say, to swear, I love thee.
       Bottom: Methinks, mistress, you should have little reason for that. And yet, to
       say the truth, reason and love keep little company together now-a-days.
       (3, 1, 137–145)

Again, this scene has a parallel later on in the play (4, 1, 1–45) which makes use of the same structural devices. However, Bottom's nominal addresses to the fairies signal a slight accommodation to the new "exotic" environment as he now addresses the fairies as *(good) mounsieur.*

(6)   Bottom: Give me your neaf, Mounsieur Mustardseed. Pray you, leave your
       curtsy, good mounsieur. (4, 1, 19–20)

By contrast, in 3, 1, he addresses them as if they were Elizabethan labourers:

(7)   Bottom: I pray you commend me to Mistress Squash, your mother, and to
       Master Peascod, your father. Good Master Peaseblossom, I shall desire you of
       more acquaintance too. (3, 1, 186–189)

The title *mo(u)nsieur* normally applied to Frenchmen and other foreigners could assume that it has dawned on him that he is in some foreign land, even so he concludes on waking up: "Methought I was — there is no man can tell what" (4, 1, 207–208).

Of course there are a large number of pronouns that do not act as a structural device, but which signal shifts in emotional attitude, as e.g. between Oberon and Titania or after Puck has erroneously applied the love drops to Lysander's eyes instead of Demetrius' and both woo Helena passionately, upon which she feels scorned and Hermia spurned. So there are a number of pronoun switches that indicate either true or rejected feelings.

In contrast to this, all the examples discussed above, clearly evidence that as far as the players are concerned, pronoun usage exactly correlates with that of the dramatic medium, so that a shift in either signals a topical shift and acts as a textual marker.

4.2.3.2   *Pronoun distribution in verse and prose in ADO*

In ADO verse occupies only about one quarter of the text — depending on whether speeches (22.88%), lines (27.52%) or words (27.68%) are taken as reference points. Once the plural Y forms are removed from the analysis, the ratio looks like this: 88 T forms (40%) appear in verse and 132 (60%) in prose as opposed to 127 Y forms occurring in a verse context (19.81%) and 514 Y forms in prose (80.19%). This narrows the original margin of 26.31% with the inclusion of the plural Y forms to 20.19%.

In order to prove whether a link exists between the dramatic medium and pronoun usage, in the following a brief plot outline will be given for the play, combined with information on the dramatic medium and pronoun usage. As it can be expected that there are a number of pronoun switches within a scene, not each pronominal form *per se*, but rather a switch is considered as "a signalling function in the global organisation of the dramatic dialogue" (Calvo 1992a: 26; cf. Chapter 2.7). Greiner (1983) also provides us with a detailed analysis of the discourse organising functions of the pronouns in ADO, but he does not correlate pronoun use, and in particular pronoun switching, to the dramatic media of verse and prose. He dismisses the issue by saying that Shakespeare's prose has been analysed in all its facets (cf. 1983: 136).[5]

In the synopsis appended to this chapter, isolated pronoun switches from the normal pronoun of rapport between interlocutors have been omitted, as e.g. in 2, 1, 18–19 when Leonato and Beatrice say *you* to each other throughout the scene, but not when Leonato comments upon her cheekiness: "By my troth, niece, thou wilt never get thee a husband, if thou be so shrewd of thy tongue."

The synopsis illustrates that the two media clearly serve different textual functions. From the point of view of textual criticism, Wilson points out: "since three-quarters of the received text is in prose and the verse-scenes are almost entirely concerned with the Hero and Claudio plot, we infer that the 1598–9 revision was a prose one and that the verse belongs to the older play" (1923: 103f.). Tschopp (1956: 75–88) takes up this point from the perspective of stylistics and argues that verse and prose act as textual markers that separate the main plot (represented by the two lovers Claudio and Hero and by Leonato) from the subplot[6] (Beatrice and Benedick). In the main plot almost all of the verse parts are connected with serious and emotional scenes, which are concerned with the destiny of Claudio, Hero and Leonato, e.g. in 1, 1, 290ff.: as soon as Benedick has left, Claudio continues his conversation with Don Pedro in verse. The prose parts are linked to Don John's intrigue, but only to its inception, execution and discovery (not to the personal consequences for the persons involved; these are described in verse), the comic dialogues between Dogberry, Verges, the watch and those lightweight comic exchanges in which Beatrice and Benedick have a considerable share and which show an overlap with the subplot.

The tabular overview also shows that, not surprisingly, a number of pronoun switches have to be attributed to the intersocial function of the pronouns in those cases in which they signal vertical social distance, sudden changes of emotion, etc. But, on the other hand, a fair share of pronouns document what Calvo (1992a) has described as their function of textual markers in the organisation of dramatic dialogue when the pronouns indicate topical shifts.

In addition to these findings, the detailed synopsis of plot structure, dramatic medium and pronoun use has revealed that a correlation between pronoun use and dramatic medium holds.

For instance, a comparison of act 2, scene 1 and 5, 1 provides a striking contrast. In both of these scenes Leonato talks to his brother Antonio. In 2, 1 they talk about the rumour that the Prince is in love with Hero in prose and say *you* to each other, by contrast in 5, 1, where Leonato expresses his grief about the loss of his child, the serious emotional subject matter is expressed in verse and Leonato uses T forms.

The parallelism in the two eavesdropping scenes, which serve the purpose of making Benedick and Beatrice believe that the other one is madly in love, is countered by a chiasm of prose and verse. The prose monologue (2, 3, 220–247) does not make use of address pronouns, but Beatrice expresses her true feelings in heroic couplets (107–116) by employing no less than five T forms. In public she remains much more distanced and recalcitrant. In her bantering with Benedick, which is given in prose, she says *you* to him until the very end of the play: "I would not deny you" (5, 4, 94).

Act 4, scene 1, 23ff. is another case in point. The remark on Claudio's hesitation and his circumlocutions at the wedding ceremony leads to a change from prose to verse. In the following verse passage there are some Y forms, but characteristically accusations and lamentations are signalled by T forms.

The final act, which is dominated by verse scenes, does not show such a stringent correlation between medium and pronoun use, but a short and also very striking example is provided in 5, 1, 246–252. Up to Borachio's remorseful confession the conversation between Don Pedro and Claudio has been conducted in prose by a mutual exchange of Y forms. However, after the confession, which has run like iron through their blood, both continue in verse and switch over to T forms. Another fitting example for the correlation of T forms with the medium of verse is Hero's burial scene.

It would clearly be amiss to assume that Shakespeare somehow doggedly adhered to this pattern, but both the quantitative analysis and the foregone qualitative investigation have given ample proof that a number of crucial turning points in the play are linked to a change of the dramatic medium, which in many cases is tied up with a shift in pronoun use, so that a preponderance of T forms in verse and of Y forms in prose can positively be established for ADO.

4.3   Conclusion

It has been the objective of this chapter to prove or to disprove the existence of a correlation between the two address pronouns and their distribution in verse and prose. The data seem to suggest the following interpretation: in the majority of cases, with only a few counter-examples, the T pronouns usually show a higher incidence in verse than would be the case given the null hypothesis of a merely random distribution. Simultaneously, the Y forms display a significant cline in the other direction, viz. an "over representation" in prose. Surprisingly, these figures hold despite the vast differences between genres, dates of composition and the extremely different overall proportions of verse and prose, and also regardless of the number and predominance of either *thou* or *you* forms in a given play.

In this respect, the initial working hypothesis that there exists a correlation between *you* or *thou* as the statistically more or less probable form in either of the media has been confirmed. However, the preponderance of *you* in the genre of Comedy (cf. Chapter 3) and its higher incidence in the medium of prose do not immediately support the claim that prose is an indicator of social inferiority in Shakespeare's plays. Quite to the contrary, in ADO prose is the dominant medium; there are the two layers of aristocratic prose (represented by Beatrice and Benedick) and the "clowns' prose" of the constables. Both groups use *you* as their normal pronoun form, which is also true for the mechanicals in MND. This result should be interpreted as a clear sign that even before the turn of the 16th century *you* was the ordinary form of address, even among the lower social orders (as depicted in Shakespeare's plays cf. Chapter 3.6.2). Owing to this, further studies on the variation of verse and prose should take into account the pronouns as a concomitant factor and *vice versa*. This is of course not to say that the choice of pronominal address immediately depends on whether a certain passage is in verse or prose; rather the other way around, due to the social position of a speaker and the intended illocutionary force of the utterance a dramatic medium of verse/prose and communicatively appropriate address forms are chosen.

In Chapter 2.6 the advantages and disadvantages of treating the two pronouns in terms of markedness have been critically appraised. Recently, Andersen (2001) has shown that in contemporary linguistics the term *markedness* is used in a number of different ways, thus losing much of its earlier terminological precision. Nonetheless, the concept may, among many other areas, be fruitfully applied to linguistic change by assuming that the actualization of linguistic change can be understood as being governed by the principle of markedness agreement:

> If so, we should be able to observe, in the progression of such changes, that as a linguistic innovation gains currency and is generalized in a language, the process of actualization conforms to the Principle of Markedness Agreement in that the innovated element is favored first of all in marked environments, if the innovated element is marked, but in unmarked environments if it is unmarked. (Andersen 2001:31)

In an earlier paper on the notion and direction of drift in the sense developed by Sapir, Hjelmslev and Coseriu, Andersen has shown that "certain elements of the theory of drift make it understandable why markedness relations in language would structure the actuation of linguistic change" (1990:13). As examples he lists a number of correlations that hold between morphological categories such as present tense vs. preterite, grounding distinctions such as main clauses vs. subordinate clauses, genre categories, as for example prose vs. poetry, spoken vs. written media, casual vs. formal style, etc., in which the first category in each dyad is described as being "more compatible with innovation" than the latter (cf. Chapter 5.2, Table 1).

In his most recent paper he has extended his research on the Principle of Markedness Agreement to phonology, morphophonology, morphosyntax, grounding structures of narrative discourse, text structures, and ritual behaviour, finding that the principle "provides a basis for making systematic observations of details in the actualization of linguistic change of all kinds" (2001:52).

When this model is applied to the problem of the distribution of the two address pronouns in the media of verse and prose, the higher incidence of the Y forms in prose can then be accounted for. So, if the *yous* in Shakespearean drama occur with a higher frequency in prose than in verse this could be an indicator of them being the unmarked form correlating with prose as the unmarked genre (in contrast to poetry). Due to its unmarked status it is more compatible with innovation.

Stein in his study on the discourse marking functions of *-s/-th* and the use of *do*, in EModE has found similar evidence. With recourse to Halliday, he attributes to the endings a textual function in the global organisation of discourse "in the sense of differentiating between two different media of narrating and reporting" (1985a:284) with the result that the contrast "is functionalised as a broad denominator for a broad range of heterogeneous functions, depending on the specific type of context of that text type or genre" (1985a:294).

Earlier on, it has been suggested that in a very broad sense of the term the two media of verse and prose can also be regarded as discourse or textual markers. That is to say, the choice or change of one medium (verse or prose) has a textual "dramatic" function but also an interpersonal one. It is not only to be realised by the listener/reader, but also by the fictional interlocutors. Thus, if fully realised, the medium works both ways in that the speeches are directed at the fellow players, but simultaneously at the audience.

It would be too simplistic and overdone to conclude with McLuhan's aphorism that "the medium is the message", but since a correlation between the medium and the distribution of the pronouns has been confirmed, it seems to be rewarding when trying to account for the often unexpected changes in address pronouns (cf. Chapter 2.7) to investigate them together with the textual or interpersonal function of the respective medium.

Appendix: Synopsis of the correlation between plot, medium and pronouns in ADO

Act	Plot	Medium	Pron
1, 1, 1–161	Exposition	prose	Y
1, 162–203	Claudio tells Benedick that he is in love with Hero and is ridiculed by him [Claudio: T — Benedick: Y].	prose	mixed
1, 204–289	Benedick reveals to Don Pedro that Claudio is in love with Hero. Claudio is too shy in love matters and asks Don Pedro's advice: "My liege, your Highness now may do me good" (290).	prose	mixed
1, 290–328	Once Benedick has left, Claudio continues in verse and entreats Don Pedro to assist him to woo Hero in his place. Don Pedro: "I will assume thy part in some disguise, / And tell fair Hero I am Claudio" (321–322). [Don Pedro: T — Claudio: Y; vertical social distance]	verse	mixed
2, 1–27	Leonato and his brother Antonio talk about the rumour that Don Pedro is in love with Hero.	prose	Y
3, 1–40	Don John tells Conrade about his sadness.	prose	Y
3, 41–75	Don John, Conrade, and Borachio plan the intrigue against Hero and Claudio. [Don John: T — Conrade: Y; vertical social distance; Y forms are plurals: "You are both sure, and will assist me?" (68–69).	prose	mixed
2, 1, 1–85	Leonato, Antonio and Beatrice talk about marriage.	prose	Y

1, 86–154	Conversation at the masked ball between: Don Pedro — Hero; Borachio — Margaret; Beatrice — Benedick. She characterises him as "the Prince's jester, a very dull fool" (137–138). Don John insinuates to Claudio that Don Pedro, his half-brother, is in love with Hero and is slandering her: "Signior, you are very near my brother in his love. He is enamor'd on Hero. I pray you dissuade him from her, she is no equal for his birth" (163–165).	prose	Y
1, 172–182	The masked ball: Claudio laments that "the Prince woos for himself" (174).	verse	–
1, 183–210	Benedick tells Claudio about the Prince's alleged intentions and ridicules Claudio: "Alas, poor hurt fowl" (202).	prose	Y
1, 211–261	Benedick and Don Pedro talk light-heartedly about Claudio's affliction and about Benedick's relationship to Beatrice.	prose	Y
1, 262–387	Engagement of Hero and Claudio in the presence of Don Pedro, Leonato and Beatrice; fixing of the wedding day [mostly Y, except: Don Pedro: "Name the day of marriage, and God give thee joy!" (300–301).	prose	Y
2, 1–57	Don John and Borachio plan the intrigue against Hero and Claudio. [Don John: T — Borachio: Y; vertical social distance]. Don John: "Be cunning in the working this, and thy fee is a thousand ducats." Borachio: "Be you constant in the accusation" (52–54).	prose	mixed
3, 1–36	Benedick's monologue on love	prose	–
3, 37–76	Don Pedro, Claudio, Balthasar about the song; song [Don Pedro: T — Balthasar Y; vertical social distance].	verse	mixed
3, 76–264	After the song the scene continues in prose. Don Pedro, Leonato and Claudio plan the intrigue for Benedick to make him believe that Beatrice is in love with him. He overhears their conversation and comments: "This can be no trick" (220) [cf. 3, 1, 107–116].	prose	Y
3, 1, 1–106	Hero and her two gentlewomen want to make Beatrice believe that Benedick is in love with her and want her to eavesdrop on their conversation: "My talk to thee must be how Benedick / Is sick in love with Beatrice" (20–21) [Hero: T — maids Y; vertical social distance].	verse	mixed

1, 107–116	Beatrice confesses to herself her love for Benedick in heroic couplets: "And, Benedick, love on, I will requite thee, / Taming my wild heart to thy loving hand" (111–112) [cf. 2, 3, 220–246].	verse	T
2, 1–79	Don Pedro, Claudio and Leonato ridicule Benedick's love-sickness [cf. 3, 4, 39–99].	prose	Y
2, 80–134	Don John slanders Hero: "I came hither to tell you [...] the lady is disloyal" (102–104). His success is signalled by pronoun switching. Don Pedro: "And as I woo'd for thee to obtain her, I will join with thee to disgrace her" (126–127).	prose	Y
3, 1–94	Dogberry and Verges instruct the watch [some of the Y forms may be plural].	prose	Y
3, 95–163	Borachio and Conrade talk about their plot.	prose	T
3, 164–180	The watch arrests them. [The Y forms are most likely plurals.]	prose	[Y]
4, 1–38	Hero and her maids discuss matters of dress. [Hero: T — maids: Y; vertical social distance].	prose	mixed
4, 39–99	They ridicule Beatrice's love-sickness [Y, excepting the 2 T forms to the attendants; cf. 3, 2, 1–79].	prose	Y
5, 1–64	Dogberry and Verges indict the culprits without success.	prose	Y
4, 1, 1–22	Wedding ceremony of Hero and Claudio	prose	Y
1, 23–143	Benedick ironically comments upon Claudio's allusions to Hero's alleged unfaithfulness with a somewhat displaced quote from Lily's grammar on the function of interjections: "How now! interjections?" (21) which leads over to a change from prose to verse. Claudio: "Stand thee by, friar. Father, by your leave…" (23). [Mixed pronoun use, but accusations and lamentations are indicated by a switch to *thou*]:* Claudio: "Out on thee seeming!" (56). Leonato: "I charge thee do so, as thou art my child" (76). Claudio: "O Hero! what a Hero hadst thou been" (100). [Hero swoons]. Leonato: "Do not live, Hero, do not ope thine eyes" (123).	verse	mixed
1, 144–254	Lamenting and counselling among Heros friends	verse	mostly Y

1, 255–336	Beatrice and Benedick mourn Hero. "Lady Beatrice, have you wept all this while?" (255). A change of topic, when Benedick confesses his love, brings about a pronoun switch to *thou*: "By my sword, Beatrice, thou lovest me" (274). She remains distant and wants proof for his love: "Kill Claudio" (289).	prose	mixed
2, 1–87	Dogberry and Verges interrogate Borachio and Conrade. The constables say *you* to each other. In the course of the interrogation they move from (insincere) friendly vocatives: "What is your name, friend"; "yours, sirrah" to abusive vocatives: "Pray thee, fellow, peace"; O villain! thou wilt be condemn'd"; "Thou naughty varlet!"	prose	mixed
5, 1, 1–44	Leonato laments his grief to his brother Antonio. Antonio: "If you go on thus, you will kill yourself" (1). Leonato: "I pray thee cease thy counsel" (3). [Antonio: Y — Leonato: T; contrast to 1, 2, 1–27]	verse	mixed
1, 45–109	Leonato and Antonio accuse Claudio and challenge him to a duell. Leonato: "Thou hast kill'd my child. If thou kill'st me, boy, thou shalt kill a man" (78–79). Antonio: "Sir boy, I'll whip you from your foining fence" (84) brings about a pronoun switch to *you*.**	verse	mixed
1, 110–200	Benedick challenges Claudio and is ridiculed by Don Pedro and Claudio. Don Pedro: "And hath challeng'd thee?" Claudio: "Most sincerely." Don Pedro: "What a pretty thing man is when he goes in his doublet and hose and leaves off his wit!" (197–200).	prose	mixed
1, 201–245	Claudio and Don Pedro meet Dogberry and Verges with their prisoners. [Y throughout, except]: Don Pedro: "First, I ask thee what they have done; thirdly, I ask thee what's their offense; sixt and lastly, why they are committed; and to conclude, what you lay to their charge" (220–223). On Borachio's remorseful confession Don Pedro says: "Runs not this speech like iron through your blood?" (245).	prose	Y
1, 246–252	Claudio's answer to this is accompanied by a simultaneous change of medium and pronoun. Claudio: "Sweet Hero, now thy image doth appear / In the rare semblance that I lov'd first" (251–252).	verse	T
1, 253–258	Dogberry gives further instructions to the watch	prose	–

1, 259–303	Leonato interrogates Borachio: "Art thou the slave that with thy breath hast kill'd / Mine innocent child?" (263) and asks Don Pedro to "Hang her an epitaph upon her tomb" (284) and to atone for his part in the plot Claudio has to agree to marry his niece [= Hero, disguised]: "Give her the right you should have giv'n her cousin, / And so dies my revenge" (291–292). ·	verse	mixed
1, 304–326	Dogberry in a ponderous and long-winded manner utters more accusations [Y ↔ T of vertical social distance].	prose	mixed
1, 327–332	Parting scene; instructions to the watch. [One pronoun certainly plural.]	verse	[Y]
2, 1–41	Benedick asks Margaret to give Beatrice bucklers [Y ↔ T of vertical social distance].	prose	mixed
2, 42–94	Benedick tells Beatrice that "Claudio undergoes my challenge, and either I must shortly hear from him, or I will subscribe him a coward" (57–59). His confession that he loves her against his will is still coldly countered by: "In spite of your heart" (68).	prose	mixed
2, 95–104	Ursula tells them that the intrigue against Hero has been discovered [Y ↔ T of vertical social distance].	prose	mixed
3, 1–33	Hero's burial ceremony; epitaph, song Claudio: "Now, unto thy bones good night! Yearly will I do this rite" (22–23).	verse	T
4, 1–33	Leonato, Antonio, Benedick and the Friar discuss the happy ending. Antonio: "Well, I am glad that all things sorts so well" (7).	verse	Y
4, 34–51	Greetings; banter between Don Pedro and Benedick. Don Pedro: "Good morrow, Benedick. Why, what's the matter, / That you have such a February face" (39–41).	verse	mixed
4, 51–73	Hero is unmasked and recognised by Claudio.	verse	Y
4, 74–97	Beatrice finally gives in to Benedick's wooing with played magnanimity: "I yield upon great persuasion, and partly to save your life, for I was told you were in a consumption" (95–97).	prose	mixed
4, 98–124	dance	prose	T
4, 125–129	A messenger reports Don John's imprisonment [Y ↔ T of vertical social distance].	verse/ prose	mixed

(Table mine, based on Tschopp 1956: 77–78)

* Pronoun switching in this scene could also be linked to the vocatives used; *father* being much more formal than *friar*.

** Again, the formality of the accompanying vocative is important. *Sir*, even though ironic, necessitates a switch to *you*.

"A woman's face with Nature's own hand painted / Hast thou, the master mistress of my passion"

Address pronouns in Shakespeare's *Sonnets* and other Elizabethan poetry

5.1 Introduction[1]

Having found so far that for the use of second person pronouns in Shakespeare's plays the factors date of composition and genre — or rather their correlation — and the distribution of the pronouns in verse or prose contexts are of considerable importance, it would be tempting to test whether all, or at least some of these factors could possibly be attributed to the use of pronouns in his non-dramatic works. For this reason, Shakespeare's usage in the sonnets and his other poems shall be examined next.

5.2 Working hypothesis and objective

In the previous chapter the predominance of the second-person plural pronoun *you* in the prose parts of Shakespeare's plays was interpreted with recourse to the theory of drift and, as propounded by Andersen (1990, 2001), the concept of markedness. Battistella's monograph sums up the numerous definitions of the concept of markedness since the 1930s. He traces "how both structuralist and generative theories have expanded markedness as a way of characterizing linguistic constructs and as part of a theory of language" (1996:4).[2] However, Battistella also points out that the word *markedness* has lost much of its terminological status because the notion of "markedness has been applied to a wide variety of data [...]. The earliest applications of markedness analyzed phonological correlations [...] and grammatical opposites [...]. Others have extended markedness to connect grammar and discourse categories as well" (1996:16). As an example for the incorporation of discourse categories, Givón (1990) can be mentioned. In his opinion three major criteria can be used to distinguish the marked from the unmarked category in a binary contrast:

a. **Structural complexity:** The marked structure tends to be more complex — or larger — than the corresponding unmarked one.
b. **Frequency distribution:** The marked category (figure) tends to be less frequent, thus cognitively more salient, than the corresponding unmarked one (ground).
c. **Cognitive complexity:** The marked category tends to be cognitively more complex — in terms of *attention, mental effort* or *processing time* — than the unmarked one.
(Givón 1990: 947)

In Table 1 below, Andersen (1990, 2001) links different morpho-syntactic, pragmatic and stylistic categories with their respective openness to linguistic innovation. This table sums up his work on observed chronological differences in a language-particular (Polish) long-term change of the enclitic auxiliary verb *to be* into bound person-and-number markers — first investigated by Teodozja Rittel — and which may have begun around 1300 and still is far from being completed. He has found out that "agglutination of these markers to verb stems occurred earlier in the present tense [...] than in the preterite [...], earlier in the (present or preterite) indicative than in the conditional mood" (2001: 32), and so forth.

The table shows that each category forms a binary contrast or opposition in markedness, "with the unmarked term of each pair in the left-hand column and the

Table 1. Linguistic categories and their openness towards innovation

	More compatible with innovation: [unmarked]	Less compatible with innovation: [marked]
Morphological categories	present tense indicative mood singular number plural number third person first person	preterite conditional plural dual other persons second person
Grounding distinctions	main clauses asyndetic clauses initial lexical noun	subordinate clauses syndetic clauses initial pronoun
Genre categories	prose expository prose secular content	poetry artistic prose religious content
Media	spoken	written
Styles	casual	formal

(Table from Andersen 1990: 10; cf. also 2001: 32)

marked term to the right. The table, in short, attests to a strong correlation, in this development, between the markedness of different conceptual, grammatical and textual contexts, and their compatibility with innovation" (1990: 12). What is interesting, though, is the fact that any indications of sociolinguistic variation are absent from the table. This is due to the fact that they were not shown in the data on which Andersen reports, as writing, for most of the 600-year long progression of this change was a privilege of the Polish elite, which was probably too small to be sociolinguistically differentiated. In this particular case "one might guess that in a society where there is no particular use for sociolinguistic indexes, variation rules simply make reference to more central linguistic categories" (1990: 18).

In light of the findings of the last chapters it seems nonetheless worthwhile to put the theory and its predictive force to the test in the case of the sociolinguistically determined variation of pronominal address. Thus, we shall investigate pronominal usage in Elizabethan poetry and compare it to the findings on pronoun distribution in verse and prose contexts in Shakespeare's plays. According to the interconnection of unmarked linguistic categories and their openness to innovation it should be the case that in Shakespeare's sonnets, with poetry being a marked category, the pronoun *thou* as the marked one in the dyad should prevail. For this reason a short glance will be taken at Shakespeare's sonnets, other Elizabethan sonnets, and poems other than sonnets as a control corpus to see if Andersen's model holds true for the distribution of *thou* and *you* in Elizabethan poetry. However, it has to be acknowledged that blank verse in drama and verse in poetry belong to different literary genres found in completely different contexts.

5.3   Corpus study: Pronominal usage in Elizabethan poetry

5.3.1   Quantitative evidence from Shakespeare's non-dramatic writings

In the Shakespeare Corpus the figures for the T forms and Y forms in the 38 plays and in his poems considered together are as shown in Table 2.

The difference between the plays and the non-dramatic works in their use of the two forms is highly significant, as the plays exhibit a ratio of T:Y of 0.589 as

Table 2. T- and Y forms in the Shakespeare Corpus

	T forms	%	Y forms	%	T:Y
38 plays*	13,186	37.05	22,400	62.95	0.589
poems	1,094	74.12	382	25.88	2.864

* If the additions of Shakespeare to STM are added to the 38 plays, the figures then amount to 13,190 T forms and 22,479 Y forms.

Table 3. T- and Y forms in Shakespeare's non-dramatic works

	Date	T forms	%	Y forms	%
VEN	1592/93	173	85.64	29	14.36
LUC	1593/94	210	95.02	11	4.98
PP	1599	22	91.66	2	8.33
PHT	c. 1601	6	100	–	0
SON	1593–1609	676	67.87	320	33.03
LC	1602/08	7	25.93	20	74.07
Total		1,094	74.12	382	25.88

opposed to 2.864 for the non-dramatic works. This extreme difference in distribution tells us that the two forms have a rather different status in drama and in poetry. The breakdown of figures for each of the works, or cycle in case of the sonnets is given in Table 3.[3]

Table 3 clearly reveals that except LC all the other poems or poem cycles definitely favour T forms, however, with a cline ranging from 95% in LUC to only 68% in the sonnets. As the sonnets constitute the largest group they shall be investigated more closely. For a quantitative analysis of the sonnets the studies of Jones (1981) and Gurr (1982) provide further data on the number and distribution of the pronouns. The figures for pronoun usage in Shakespeare's sonnets are provided by Table 4.

It should be added that if the pronoun *ye*, which is employed in sonnets 42 (at the side of *thou*) and 111 (next to *you*), is also taken into consideration, there are two more sonnets showing mixed pronoun usage. Among other conspicuous pronoun changes from *thou* to *you* and vice versa, the use of *ye* will be analysed in 5.3.2.1.

5.3.2   Qualitative analysis of pronoun distribution in Shakespeare's Sonnets

In respect to the address pronouns it is clear that the *thou* sonnets are much more numerous than the *you* sonnets. As for the structure of the sequence as a whole, there remain some uncertainties about the chronological and structural order (cf. Arden Shakespeare 1997: 97ff.) W. H. Auden, himself a distinguished poet, dramatist, essayist and literary scholar, writes in his introduction to the Signet edition of the sonnets that

> they are not in any kind of planned sequence. The only semblance of order is a division into two unequal heaps — Sonnets 1 to 126 are addressed to a young man, assuming, which is probable but not certain, that there is only one young man addressed, and Sonnets 127–154 are addressed to a dark-haired woman.

Table 4. Pronoun distribution in Shakespeare's Sonnets, by number

Thou	You	He/she	Zero	Mixed
1–4			5	
6–12	13			
14	15–17			
18		19		
20			21	
22			23	
				24
			25	
26–32		33		
34–51	52–55		56	
	57–59			
60–62		63	64–66	
		67–68		
69–70	71–72			
73–74	75–76			
77–79	80–81			
82	83–86			
87–93			94	
95–97	98			
99				100
		101		
	102–104		105	105
	106			
107–110	111–115		116	116
	117–118		119	119
	120		121	121
122			123–124	123–124
125–126				
		127		
128			129	
		130		
131–136			137	
		138		
139–143		144–145	146	
147			148	
149–152			153–154	

(Table from Jones 1981:84)

In both heaps, a triangle situation [cf. sonnets 40, 42 and 144, 152] is referred to in which Shakespeare's friend and his mistress betray him by having an affair together, which proves that the order is not chronological. (Auden 1965:xxi)

The main reason Auden offers against a chronological order is a psychological one. He argues that it seems psychologically implausible that Shakespeare would have written either sonnet 53 or 105 after the experiences described in sonnets 40–42 (cf. 1965:xxii).

At any rate, the two different parts outlined by the citation above can also be recognised in terms of pronoun use: "in the sonnets to the fair youth [1–126] the dominant pronoun is *thou*, occurring in 69 of the 126 sonnets (54.75%); but *you* also appears in 34 sonnets (27%)" (Jones 1981:80). On the other hand, in the sonnets addressed to the dark mistress or to the conventionally-termed dark lady [127–154], which form a less coherent group, *you* is never used to address the dark lady. In the whole sequence there are 86 *thou* poems as opposed to only 34 *you* poems. The *thou* poems also clearly outnumber those in which the young man and the dark lady are addressed indirectly by using a third person pronoun.

Schabert (1992:662) also remarks that the vicissitudes in the relationship between the speaker and the young man are underlined by a skilful play with the forms of address, in which the speaker differentiates between an intimate and comradely *thou*, a reverently-submissive *you*, and a distanced *he*.

This puzzling use of *you* and *thou* has been at the centre of a number of articles, but as far as I can see, these have mostly focussed on the seeming (ir-)regularities of pronoun switching, rather than on broader genre-typical considerations, or aspects of linguistic change, which will serve as a point of departure for my investigation.

Some critics have indeed been puzzled by the frequent use of *thou* in the sonnets, e.g. Gurr considers the shifts in the 126 sonnets to the young man as a "remarkable display of inconsistency" (1982:12), and wonders why in the first twelve sonnets the young man is constantly addressed with *thou*. In the notes to his article, he mentions that "the anomalous use of the pronouns" (1982:25) was first noted by the German scholar Karl Goedeke in 1877, and that from then on a number of inconclusive speculations about the reasons for the pronoun switching followed. For instance, Archer (1936:544) has tried to account for these changes in terms of rhyme and euphony. While Finkenstaedt (1958:456) also considers these factors as important, Jones (1981:80) and Gurr (1982:12f.) regard them as supplementary factors at best. Berry asks the question:

> What is the difference in poetic result between a 'thou' sonnet and a 'you' sonnet? […] We can, in other words, expect some significance in the fact that one sonnet may be built around an 'I–thou' relationship, while another sonnet centres around an 'I–you' relationship.
> (Berry 1958b:138; 140; cf. also 1958a:42; 81)

He states that in his sonnets, Shakespeare uses *thou* for more distanced relationships between the lyrical *I* and the addressee, whereas *you* is being used for closer personal relationships, from which he draws the somewhat surprising conclusion that

'You' is, then, more intimate, 'thou' more formal — the opposite of what might be expected according to some imaginary Elizabethan Fowler of Correct Usage. (Berry 1958b: 143)

Finkenstaedt criticises this viewpoint by remarking that "it is dangerous to make statements about the emotional value of *you* and *thou* in Shakespeare's Sonnets without reference to Elizabethan prose usage" (1958: 456). In reply to this, Berry (1959) defends his results by refuting the idea that pronoun usage of other contemporary writers or different genres could falsify his thesis on Shakespeare's pronoun usage:

It is precisely my belief that poets do or, at least, can use a language in a way other than it is used by writers or speakers of prose [...] personal pronouns — it follows that these are, or can be, apprehended and used in a poetic way. [...] 'each existence has its own idiom'. (Berry 1959: 196)

Finkenstaedt (1963: 166 f., footnote) epitomises their controversy on pronoun use in poetry by dismissing Berry's claim of poets' individual language use as a "Humpty-Dumpty-Theory"[4] of literature.

These contradictory statements could possibly be reconciled if we assign the genres of poetry and prose different degrees of openness towards innovations. By adopting this stance it would be perfectly normal to have two different "Elizabethan Fowlers of Correct Usage" at the same time, one for poetry, and another for prose styles. This is of course not to say that the emotional content of the pronouns varies from genre to genre. It seems indeed out of the way to assume that *you* functions simultaneously as a marker of nearness in one genre and as a marker of distance in another.

In his analysis of the sonnets, Jones regards "the pronoun used by the speaker to designate another person" as "one of the principal signals of rhetorical distance" (1981: 73). In his pronoun usage Shakespeare is very consistent in that "of the 126 poems addressed to the fair youth and the 28 addressed to the dark mistress, only one (24) fails to maintain pronominal consistency" (1981: 79). Similar to Finkenstaedt, Jones is also of the opinion that Berry's findings of *thou* being more formal and *you* more intimate are too simplistic, because they are neither supported by evidence from other Elizabethan sonneteers nor by Shakespeare's own usage: "if anything, the reverse is closer to the truth. [...] In Shakespeare's Sonnets there does not appear to be any direct and consistent correlation, such as Berry suggests, between degree of intimacy and the use of either *thou* or *you*" (1981: 80).

5.3.2.1   Model analyses of pronoun use in selected sonnets
In order to highlight the difference in rhetorical distance and effect between a *thou* sonnet and a *you* sonnet, sonnets 10 and 13 shall be analysed in more detail. These sonnets belong to the so-called procreation sonnets addressed to the young man beloved by the poet. The poet urges the youth to marry and to beget children. The

young man is "of superior beauty and rank but of somewhat questionable morals and constancy [...]. The attitude of the poet toward the friend is one of love and admiration, deference and positiveness, but it is not at all a sexual passion" (Smith 1997: 1839f.).

In all of the first twelve sonnets the young man is addressed with a singular pronoun. Sonnet 13 marks a change to *you*. Sonnet 14 moves back to *thou* and numbers 15, 16, and 17 switch back to *you*. Sonnet 10 is the first in which the poet indicates his own devotion to the young man.[5]

Sonnet 10
1   For shame deny that *thou* bear'st love to any,
     Who for *thyself* art so unprovident.
     Grant, if *thou* wilt, *thou* art belov'd of many,
     But that *thou* none lov'st is most evident;
5   For *thou* art so possess'd with murd'rous hate,
     That 'gainst thyself *thou* stick'st not to conspire,
     Seeking that beauteous roof to ruinate
     Which to repair should be *thy* chief desire.
     O, change *thy* thought, that I may change my mind!
10   Shall hate be fairer lodg'd than gentle love?
     Be as *thy* presence is gracious and kind,
     Or to *thyself* at least kind-hearted prove:
     Make *thee* another self for love of me,
     That beauty still may live in *thine* or *thee*.

Sonnet 13
1   O that *you* were *yourself*! But, love, *you* are
     No longer *yours*, than *you yourself* here live:
     Against this coming end *you* should prepare,
     And *your* sweet semblance to some other give.
5   So should that beauty which *you* hold in lease
     Find no determination; then *you* were
     [*Yourself*] again after *yourself*'s decease,
     When *your* sweet issue *your* sweet form should bear.
     Who lets so fair a house fall to decay,
10   Which husbandry in honor might uphold
     Against the stormy gusts of winter's day
     And barren rage of death's eternal cold?
     O, none but unthrifts: dear my love, *you* know
     You had a father, let *your* son say so.

In his attempt to explain the changes in pronoun use in Shakespeare's sonnets, Gurr, as other scholars before him, also stresses the importance of protocol and decorum in Elizabethan society for the choice of the appropriate address forms and finds the shifts in Shakespeare's sonnets and especially the *thou* to the young man rather surprising. In his explanation of the pronoun switches he concentrates on the first seventeen sonnets on the theme of marriage and procreation for the reasons that there is least argument about their sequence, and "secondly, because it is the first switch, and therefore the one over which we might expect the poet to be most self-conscious" (1982: 14).

He rejects the earlier explanations in terms of rhyme and euphony and "the idea that the sonnets as printed in the 1609 quarto are seriously disarranged" (1982: 13). In his opinion the first 12 sonnets "are all elegant, forceful, witty, and literary in form, matching the 'literary' use of 'thou' which we find in so many of the sonnet sequences by other poets in the 1590s" (1982: 14).

In comparison to these, the switch to *you* in sonnet 13 is interpreted to mark "the change from formal, 'literary', possibly even commissioned poems, written on someone else's behalf, to a wholly personal appeal, in the intimacy and urgency of a loving relationship" (1982: 16).

Auden also believes that the first 17 sonnets, in which the friend is urged to marry, belong together, "though even here, 15 seems not to belong, for marriage is not mentioned in it" (1965: xxi).

Gurr interprets the opening lines of sonnet 13 so that in comparison to the first twelve sonnets a change is being indicated. "And the prime reason for the change is surely signalled chiefly in the very first line by that intrusive vocative [*love*]" (1982: 15).

The latest and also the most comprehensive work on Shakespeare's sonnets by Vendler, does not really touch upon the role of the address pronouns from a structural point of view, but provides detailed and insightful interpretations for each of the 154 sonnets. In her interpretation of sonnet 13, Vendler does not comment on the pronoun switch, but she does draw attention to the fact that "this poem marks the momentous instant in which the speaker first uses vocatives of love: he addresses the young man as *love* and *my dear love*. [...] this poem sets a new tone of personal intensity with respect to an envisaged loss" (1997: 102).

Sonnet 13 takes up the theme of personal affection between the poet and the youth, introduced in sonnet 10, and develops it further to a new degree of intimacy, where the other is seen as a real flesh and blood person rather than an elevated and formal literary convention. This view is supported by Vendler's remark that this

> is the first of many "reply-sonnets", poems which respond to an implied anterior utterance from the young man. We are to imagine that the young man has said, in response to earlier reproaches, "I am myself, sufficient to myself." The speaker replies, as the sonnet opens, "Oh that that were true! [...].
> (Vendler 1997: 103)

The first sonnet to show mixed forms of second person pronouns is sonnet 24:

1   Mine eye hath play'd the painter and hath [stell'd]
    Thy beauty's form in table of my heart;
    My body is the frame wherein 'tis held,
    And perspective it is best painter's art.
5   For through the painter must *you* see his skill,
    To find where *your* true image pictur'd lies,
    Which in my busom's shop is hanging still,
    That hath his windows glazed with *thine* eyes.
    Now see what good turns eyes for eyes have done:
10 Mine eyes have drawn *thy* shape, and *thine* for me
    Are windows to my breast, wherethrough the sun
    Delights to peep, to gaze therein on *thee*.
    Yet eyes this cunning want to grace their art,
    They draw but what they see, know not the heart.

The first four lines put forward the idea that similar to a painter, or rather an engraver, the eyes of the poet have made a permanent image of the young man and that simultaneously they serve as a mirror for the youth, through which he can see a perfect image of himself, because if one looks into somebody else's eyes a small upside-down mirror image of oneself is reflected in the other's pupil. However, through this virtual picture the young man does not see how much the poet loves him.

For the next two lines Shakespeare switches to *you*. The Arden edition of Shakespeare's sonnets glosses line 5 as "both by means of the painter and, more literally, *through* the painter-poet, whose eye is transparent" (1997:158). To my mind the use of *you* in these lines could probably be attributed to its polyfunctionality in that it acts either as a direct address (as in Sonnet 13) or, as these lines express a universal truth, that the pronoun has generic, indefinite reference denoting any hearer or reader.

Sonnet 42 — an early betrayal sonnet — is a poem built around the triangular relationship between the poet (*I*), the friend (*thou*) and the mistress (*she/her*). Apart from 111 it is the only one to make use of *ye*.

1   That *thou* hast her, it is not all my grief,
    And yet it may be said I lov'd her dearly;
    That she hath *thee* is of my wailing chief,
    A loss in love that touches me more nearly.
5   Loving offenders, thus I will excuse *ye*:
    Thou dost love her because *thou* know'st I love her,
    And for my sake even so doth she abuse me,
    Suff'ring my friend for my sake to approve her.
    If I lose *thee*, my loss is my love's gain,
10 And losing her, my friend hath found that loss;
    Both find each other, and I lose both twain,
    And both for my sake lay on me this cross.

> But here's the joy, my friend and I are one;
> Sweet flattery! then she loves but me alone.

In this sonnet, in which the poet laments both the loss of his young friend and of his mistress, with whom the young man has fallen in love, but grieves more strongly for the loss of the youth, the changing relationships between the three people are expressed by a number of pronoun switches. The mistress is usually referred to in the third person (*she/her*) and until line 9 the young man is directly addressed with *thou*. But from then on he is also referred to in the third person. "By this midway change of address, the speaker demonstrates that he is no longer in a 'thou' relation to the young man. The speaker is excluded from the relation between friend and mistress; they become *my friend* and *she*, not *thou* and *she*" (Vendler 1997: 217). In the end the friend is again implicitly addressed directly (*me*) when speaker and friend finally reunite and the mistress stays outside.

In line 5 the reference of *ye* is ambiguous, because syntactically it could be interpreted as singular (with reference to the young man) or plural to include both lovers — the young man and the mistress. Vendler is of the opinion that "the attempt to magnetize her into the circle of the speaker's affection fails" (1997: 217). The Arden Shakespeare glosses this line as: "although he appears to address both A lovers at this point, subsequent lines make it clear that the youth alone is the poet's true concern, the woman being referred to in the third person" (1997: 194).

In this quatrain Wright sees another ambiguity: "'Loving offenders' can be a form of address, 'loving' being a verbal used to modify 'offenders'. And the phrase can also mean that the persona forgives the two offenders because he loves them" (1993: 124).

Syntactically speaking, *you* could have served the same purpose as *ye*, but a look at the rhyme structure with the feminine rhymes in lines 5–8 *excuse ye, love her, abuse me* and *approve her* makes it obvious that *ye*, which only occurs twice in the entire sonnets, has been adopted for metrical reasons, as seems to have been the case in the final couplet of sonnet 111:[6]

> Pity me then, dear friend, and I assure *ye*,
> Even that your pity is enough to cure me.

These short analyses of how distance and perspective can be manipulated by subtle shifts in pronoun usage should illustrate that one can arrive at less speculative and emotional postulates on pronoun use in poetry as, for example, Berry did.

However, to my mind Finkenstaedt (1963) is right when he argues that relegating the problem of pronoun usage to the individual level is important but not enough.

5.3.3   Other Elizabethan sonneteers

As the investigation of pronoun usage in Shakespeare's sonnets only makes sense on a broader scale when it is compared to that of his contemporaries, the previous findings will be put into the larger perspective of other Elizabethan sonneteers to answer Finkenstaedt's question:

> Wie weit setzt sich im Englischen die alte Konvention der Sg.-Anrede im Gedicht fort, in welchem Umfang erscheint das *you* der täglichen Rede, und wie weit entspricht die Pronomenverwendung der Dichtung jener der Umgangssprache? (Finkenstaedt 1963: 166)

In so doing, some similarities but also differences between Shakespeare's pronoun usage and that of his contemporaries, as illustrated by Table 5, become apparent.

Table 5. Pronoun distribution in Elizabethan sonnet sequences

		Thou	You	She	Zero	Mixed
Anon.	*Zepheria*	33	–	1	3	3
Barnes	*Parthenophil*	36	1	33	17	17
Constable	*Diana*	30	5	18	11	11
Daniel	*Delia*	15	–	31	5	4
Drayton	*Idea*	19	–	16	14	2
Fletcher	*Licia*	6	9	17	5	16
Griffin	*Fidessa*	3	–	33	24	2
Linche	*Diella*	11	2	15	10	1
Lodge	*Phillis*	3	–	16	13	6
Percy	*Coelia*	4	–	8	2	6
Sidney	*Astrophel*	12	3	39	45	9
Smith	*Chloris*	5	–	22	10	10
Spencer	*Amoretti*	–	16	50	13	9
Tofte	*Laura*	35	7	43	27	8
Watson	*Tears of fancy*	3	–	22	27	1
Shakespeare	*Fair youth*	69	34	6	15	1
Shakespeare	*Dark mistress*	17	–	5	5	–
Total: 1089		296	78	371	238	106
%		27.18	7.16	34.08	21.85	9.73

(Table from Jones 1981: 83; last two lines my addition)

If these figures for the other Elizabethan sonneteers are compared to those of Shakespeare, the first point of departure is that Shakespeare's contemporaries prefer the third-person pronoun (360 cases) as the usual form of indirect address of the mistress rather than direct address by means of second person pronouns. "This indirect approach has the general effect of turning the Mistress into an object for contemplation, analysis and commentary, rather than her appearing to be a mute partner in a dramatic dialogue" (Jones 1981: 74).

In addition to this, the two different modes of direct dramatic address (*you/thou*)

and indirect reference (*he/she*) are often functionalised within a single sonnet for textlinguistic purposes. Jones has found out that, for example, Fletcher and Spenser often build sonnets around the following contrast: for the first twelve lines, which are devoted to narrative description, they use third person pronouns, but they then switch to direct address of the Mistress in the final couplets (1981:76). It has been noted earlier (cf. Chapter 4.3) that Stein (1985a, 1990b, 1992) has found similar evidence for the discourse marker functions of the different third-person endings *-s/-th* in texts from the turn of the 16th century: "the *th/s* contrast, then, appears to have a discourse function in the sense of differentiating between two different and alternating modes of narrating and reporting" (1985a:284).

Another interesting divergence between Shakespeare and his contemporaries is the fact that he is much more aware of avoiding pronominal inconsistency in one poem. The ratio of 296 *thous*:78 *yous* clearly shows that in Elizabethan sonnets *thou* is the majority form in those cases where the Mistress is addressed directly. The fact that *you* is absent in quite a number of sonnets cannot be an instance of chance. Jones attributes the numerical dominance of *thou* in Elizabethan sonnets to a number of factors. If in following Jones (1981:76ff.) the intersocial and textual functions of the pronouns at the end of the 16th century are grouped under keywords the following binary categories may be established for EModE literature (see Table 6).

Thus, *thou* "is the 'high' term of invocation and it is also the emotive and familiar term. With *thou* the poet can shift from adulation to familiarity to insult with the same pronoun, depending on the emotional context established" (Jones

Table 6. The function of *thou* and *you* in EModE literature

Thou	You
– in elevated utterances as the pronoun of poetic convention	– neutral, prosaic and unemotive form
– as an archaic and poetic mode	– as socially polite pronoun signalling greater politeness or deference
– private pronoun: prayer, intimate and familial relationships	– pronoun of public address
– old-fashioned in non-poetic usage	– normal social intercourse
– becoming restricted to ritualistic and poetic contexts (invocation)	– conversational and prosaic pronoun signalling a less elevated poetic manner
– in emotive utterances	– neutral, unemotive form
– conventional literary pronoun	– realistic (more usual) pronoun
– (Sonnets): individual addressed as a fictive convenience, often in the context of make-believe emotions	– (Sonnets): addressed to some patron/ mistress or affecting to be addressed to some flesh-and blood woman

Table mine, based on Jones 1981:76–78)

1981:77). This double function of *thou* has also been recognised by Finkenstaedt (1963:169), who establishes a *thou*[1] as an impersonal conventional pronoun in poetry and an intimate *thou*[2]. Yet, on the other hand, matters are even more complicated, because *you* can also be used in a double-bind function as the neutral default and as socially polite pronoun.

In his appraisal of the communicative functions of the two pronouns, Jones offers the following convincing conclusions why *you* is generally avoided as pronoun of address in Elizabethan sonnets other than Shakespeare's. In his opinion, *you* is "the neutral, prosaic and unemotive form. [...] This emotional and social neutrality appears to be the major reason why most sonneteers, writing consciously in an elevated manner and ostensibly *not for the public ear*, avoid *you*, the prosaic term reminiscent of normal social intercourse" (1981:77, my emphasis).

5.3.4   Elizabethan poems other than sonnets

For this type of poetry I can offer only random evidence from secondary sources, especially Finkenstaedt (1963) and Jones (1981). Patchy as the data may be, a tentative conclusion may, nonetheless, be drawn. In my opinion, future analyses of Elizabethan poetry should take into account socio-pragmatic genre constraints as developed by Biber and Finegan (1992), who in their diachronic study of text types compare written 'literate' genres such as essays, fiction and personal letters to speech based 'oral' genres, e.g. dialogue from plays and from fiction, because the different degrees of privacy and/or orality and literate/formal, i.e. more "written", could, among other things, also trigger the selection of address pronouns.

For instance, Jones (1981:78) states that Drayton, who avoids *you* in his sonnets, uses it in his odes and elegies, and Daniel does similarly in many of his poetic epistles. Finkenstaedt, (1963) in his discussion of Harington's epigrams, comes to the following numerical distribution of the second person pronouns: 257 of his epigrams contain 32 real plural addresses, including those to the reader/s where it is not clear whether a single reader or the reading public in general is meant, 108 contain only *thou*, 73 only *you*, and 44 show a change. For Donne he concludes that his pronoun use is highly conventionalised and that metre in contrast to rhyme is not an important factor. A case in point for the dichotomy of private (more oral) vs. public (more written) seems to be the following:

> In allen Widmungsgedichten steht *you*; in den *Letters to Several Personages* steht *you* bei allen mit vollem Namen genannten Personen. Bei den nur mit den Anfangsbuchstaben des Namens adressierten poetischen Episteln steht fast nur *thou*. (Finkenstaedt 1963:170)

Thus, the avoidance of *you* in the sonnet sequences (other than Shakespeare's) could then be attributed to their more private nature as opposed to more overtly public poems such as odes, epistles and epigrams which, quite to the contrary, feature *you* more strongly.

Finkenstaedt is right in demanding that any study trying to scrutinise pronominal usage in poetry, and pronoun switches in particular, must try to determine whether the addressee remains the same, and/or content matters (literary conventions) demand a shift, or whether formal criteria such as rhyme, metre and euphony necessitate a change. In the more recently developed framework of pragmaphilology, this implies that all "the contextual aspects of historical texts, including addressers and addressees, their social and personal relationship, the physical and social setting of text production and textreception, and the goal(s) of the text" (Jacobs and Jucker 1995:11) have to be taken into account.

5.4   Conclusion

From the data on Shakespeare's sonnets and those by his contemporaries the following conclusions on the correlation between pronoun use in poetry and markedness may be drawn:

1. Following the putative dating of their composition, the distribution of second person pronouns in the Shakespeare Corpus does not reflect a change over time from one variant to the other as did the pronoun use in drama, which clearly pointed towards a change in the ratio of the two forms and towards a corpus-internal variation, splitting the corpus into two halves with a divide around 1600.

2. In contrast to drama, where *you* can be established as the majority form, in the sonnets it proved to be the other way around. When Shakespeare's usage of second person pronouns in the sonnets is compared to that of this fellow poets, it becomes apparent that he shows a greater preference for *thou*. In contrast to this, the other sonneteers favour indirect address in the third person and often switch to direct address in the final couplets.

3. In comparison to drama, where pronoun switches in dialogue involving the same speakers are frequent and can, depending on a number of circumstantial factors, be interpreted as the rule rather than the exception, pronoun use in Shakespeare's sonnets is much more consistent. The only ones showing mixed pronoun use are sonnets no. 24, 100, 105, 116, 119, 121, 123 and 124. These changes can be attributed to shifting personae, real and/or imagined social contexts, etc.

4. While Battistella (1996), Andersen (2001) and others admit that the notion of markedness has never been clearly defined and developed in a number of different directions, quantitative evidence has proved that it is difficult to conceive of the stylistically marked category as the less frequent one, as *thou* was found to be the minority form in drama as opposed to poetry. Owing to

this, frequency and stylistic value are relative criteria depending on the regulari-
ties and necessities of different text types. In both cases *thou* is the stylistically
marked pronoun in the dyad. Thus, it would be useful to distinguish between
descriptive (statistical) norms in terms of frequency, and evaluative norms in
terms of correctness or appropriateness.

5.   In the explanation of language change, markedness not only plays an important
role in the progression of change, but also on the synchronic level. In the case
of EModE second person pronouns, sociolinguistic and textlinguistic factors
have to be taken into account to accomodate pronoun shifts in a society keenly
aware of social indexes.

The evidence presented in this chapter and the arguments of the previous studies
seem to validate the initial hypothesis on the direction of drift, in that it could be
proved that despite vacillation between individual authors the stylistically marked
pronoun of the dyad (*thou*) prevails numerically in poetry as the form of direct
address. As a genre, poetry, with its preference for more traditional address forms,
seems to be more restricted to literary conventions than e.g. the different text types
of prose writing, or non-literary colloquial usage. Within the genre of poetry a cline
from more overtly public, colloquial "written orality" — preferring *you* — to more
private, artistic, conventionalised and formal "truly written" kind of writing —
preferring *thou* — could be shown to exist. This cline could account for the
appropriateness of pronouns in terms of genre conventions, distance between
author and addressee, etc. For this reason, pronoun use in Elizabethan poetry
corroborates the dichotomies as put forward by Anderson in Table 1, because three
of the variables, namely genre categories, media and styles, provide supporting
evidence. On the other hand, it seems unfounded to maintain (as Berry did) that in
terms of distance the two pronouns function antagonistically in poetry and in prose
writing or colloquial language.

Despite the differences that exist between blank verse in drama and poetry, as
primarily exemplified by the sonnets, their similarity in the preference for the
pronoun *thou* "in the higher poetic style" (Abbott [1870] 1972:154) has been
confirmed.

CHAPTER 6

"You beastly knave, know you no reverence?"

The co-occurrence of second person pronouns and nominal forms of address

6.1 Introduction and objective[1]

The point of the social implications of address behaviour in Shakespeare's plays could be enhanced by not only taking into account the variance of the T and Y pronouns but by extending the scope of investigation to all the forms of address in a play. But to my knowledge, so far nobody has combined the two aspects of pronominal and nominal address in a large-scale study.

It can be hypothesised that the second person pronouns used together with nominal forms of address to a certain extent mirror the social or relational position expressed by the vocative. Thus, the more reverential and deferential vocatives, e.g. the titles of courtesy, should attract a Y pronoun, and the more intimate vocatives and the terms of abuse should show a preponderance of T forms, with an area of overlap in-between.

The objective of this chapter will be to investigate the co-occurrence between the second person pronouns *thou* and *you* and their variants with nominal forms of address in order to validate or refute the claim made by Brown and Gilman that the pronoun of address generally follows the status rule and is therefore a predictable obligatory part of speech that "is automatic and ever-present and so does not function to redress an FTA" (1989: 197).

6.2 Previous research

While many articles have been devoted to the pronouns of address, work on nominal address is still scarce. In the context of Shakespeare studies, Böhm (1936) provides an older book-length account on the use of titles. Replogle (1967, 1973) emphasises the importance of honorific titles in Elizabethan England and their representation in Shakespeare's plays. She states that despite "abundant evidence that the Elizabethans were punctilious in their use of titles and forms of address to strangers, friends, even members of their families in private life as well as public" (1973:180) the significance of this indicator of social or political hierarchy has been largely neglected. Since then the subject has only been taken up again twice: firstly, by Breuer (1983), who concentrates on social ranks and titles in Tudor and Stuart England and their importance for a proper literary assessment of Shakespeare's figures and their social relationships, and secondly by Stoll, who has investigated non-pronominal address in Shakespeare. She describes the objective of her study as follows:

> Ziel und Aufgabe dieser Arbeit ist es, die von Shakespeare in seinen Dramen verwendeten nicht-pronominalen Anreden zu erfassen, zu ordnen und die hinter ihnen stehenden spezifischen sozio-kulturellen Regeln und Normen zu definieren. Besondere Bedeutung gilt dabei Abweichungen von diesen Normen [...]. (Stoll 1989:3f.)

More recently, in the Helsinki project on EModE, a number of studies have been devoted to titles (cf. Nevalainen 1994), social stratification in Tudor English (cf. Nevalainen and Raumolin-Brunberg 1996a) and to address formulae in early English correspondence (cf. Nevalainen and Raumolin-Brunberg 1995, Nevala forthc.). For instance, Nevalainen and Raumolin-Brunberg (1995) use the *Helsinki Corpus of Early English Correspondence* ranging from 1420 to 1680 in their socio-pragmatic study of "the form of address used in the salutation at the beginning of a letter" (1995:541). They state that despite their conventionalised form and their social motivation, the address forms used in letter openings are by no means totally predictable as Brown and Gilman claim them to be.

Regarding Shakespeare's works, a first step towards combining the two factors of nominal and pronominal address has been undertaken by Barber when he in his scrutiny of *you* and *thou* in R3 examines the interplay of the pronouns with nominal forms of address, in particular respectful or disrespectful vocative expressions. Thus, for instance, respectful vocatives containing the word *lord* exclusively collocate with *you*, and so do *madam*, *sir*, and *brother*, whereas *cousin* and *lady* are rather indiscriminate of collocators. Abusive vocatives, such as *beggar, cacodemon, coward, dissembler, devil, dog, fool, hag, hedgehog, homicide, knave, slave, villain* and *witch* always collocate with *thou*, never with *you*. He finds that "throughout the play there is a clear correlation between the vocative expression used and the choice of pronoun" (1981:284). His results for R3 are given in Table 1.

However, the results from a single play do not lead us very far, because the data can be skewed or biased in a certain way, and, what is even more important, a mere computer-assisted study or a glance at concordance lines will not suffice, as in some cases a *you* followed by a reverential address may be ironical or mock-polite. Therefore, the situational context of an utterance and its illocutionary force have to be taken into account.

Table 1. Collocates of *you* and *thou* in R3

Collocating with:	You	Thou
madam	17	0
sir	4	0
brother	5	0
cousin	5	4
lady	3	3
fellow	0	4

(Table from Barber 1981:285)

For these reasons Mazzon criticises former approaches to this topic as being "either extremely specific, discussing pronoun choices in single plays or single scenes and overlooking the rest, or disappointingly vague" (1995:23). She goes a step further by analysing "pronouns and, marginally, terms of address in their role as markers of socio-affective relationships" (1995:20) in LR, OTH and HAM. She focuses on dyadic symmetrical or asymmetric relationships such as *husband – wife, parent – child, brother – brother*, etc.

B. Busse (1997)[2] basically works along the same lines when she scrutinises vocatives, and to a lesser degree also second person pronouns in HAM and ADO as linguistic indications of attitude in the language of Shakespeare. She has investigated vocative usage, and placed special emphasis on changes that occur in "pairs" such as Gertrude and Claudius, Gertrude and Hamlet, Ophelia and Hamlet and Beatrice and Benedick in ADO, finding that throughout the categories there are genre differences, as the comedy shows a higher correlation of Y forms with vocatives than the tragedy. However, she refutes the sweeping idea that "the vocative determines the form of the pronoun or vice versa" (1997:38) and rather suggests that the forms be analysed individually in their context. Her statistical data for the two plays are shown in Table 2.

In contrast to the above-mentioned studies, investigations carried out in the framework of politeness theory tend to disregard the relationship of pronominal and nominal address. Brown and Gilman in their analysis of HAM, LR, MAC and OTH say that "in the four tragedies, more than 100 different forms of address are used, aside from Christian names and pronouns" (1989:175). In order to work out the deference expressed by the names and titles, these are categorised according to whether they are adorned, or unadorned, as shown in Table 3.

What Brown and Gilman deliberately do not take into account systematically is the interplay between pronominal and nominal forms of address, because in their opinion "*thou* and *you* are not very important in scoring speech for politeness" (1989:179). They only deal with a small number of unusual personal pronoun uses.

Kopytko in his pragmatic study of eight Shakespearean plays says that "the

Table 2. *Thou/you* and vocative occurrence in HAM and ADO

	HAM		ADO	
	you	*thou*	*you*	*thou*
personal names	27	24	14	15
titles of respect	69	0	60	2
terms of endearment	2	5	3	2
terms of abuse	0	2	0	4
terms of family relationship	10	2	17	1
terms of address — soliloquies	5	4	0	1
generic names	0	1	1	0
markers of status	7	4	32	3
mocking terms of address	1	4	0	0
Total	**121**	**46**	**127**	**28**

(Table from B. Busse 1997:37)

Table 3. Scales of deference

Name	Example	Weighting
name alone	Desdemona, Iago, Macbeth, Laertes	no points for deference
unadorned titles	sir, madam, my lord, signior, your Grace	one point for deference
names with one honorific adjective	worthy Montano, good Hamlet	one point for deference
titles adorned with honorific adjectives	my dread lord, good your Grace, good madam, etc.	two points for deference

(Table mine, based on the data of Brown and Gilman 1989:175)

topic of forms of address in Shakespeare's plays is so vast that so far it has not received any exhaustive treatment" (1993a:52). For reasons of practicability and the assumed futility of the effort to incorporate pronouns for the purposes of his study, he has also decided to neglect them:

> A pedantic analysis of forms of address in Shakespeare's plays [...] would have to go into thousands of instances frequently contextually ambiguous and to some extent dependent on the selection of data (plays) from different periods of his authorship. Predictively, such an analysis would prove inconclusive for the purpose here. (Kopytko 1993a:53)

Obviously, scholarly opinion on the interdependence and predictability of pronominal and nominal address in Shakespeare's plays and in EModE society at large is divided. Thus, it will be a further goal of this chapter to find out which viewpoint is more viable.

6.3 Corpus study

On the basis of Laslett (1983), Breuer (1983) and others, Nevalainen and Raumolin-Brunberg (1996a: 307) present a table of the social stratification in Elizabethan and Jacobean society. When adapted to Shakespeare's dramatic style and supplemented by examples from some of his plays, a slightly modified chart looks like the one given in Table 4.

As outlined in Table 4, the array of names and titles used as direct address in Shakespeare's plays is vast. For this reason the present study is in the dilemma of claiming representativenes of its results and for reasons of practicability of self-imposed restrictions. As a way out of this contradiction, a broad social spectrum of address forms ranging from the most deferential honorifics to terms of abuse will be scrutinised for the whole of Shakespeare's plays. On the other hand, the number of terms investigated, has been arbitrarily limited to 36, which means that an average of six expressions for each of the six categories given in Table 5 will be examined. This number should be large enough to make comparisons and show gradients within each group and between the different categories. The categorisation of address forms basically follows Salmon: "these forms of address [i.e. vocatives] may consist of personal names, terms of family relationship, generic names (*man, boy*), names of occupations, titles of courtesy, endearments and terms of abuse" (1967:50).[3] The personal names (Christian names and/or surnames) have been excluded for the reason that they express personal relationships and attitudes towards a special character in a given play and do not occur in the entire corpus and thus do not allow for considerations of differences in corpus-internal variation as e.g. distribution between genres.

The approach taken consists of a form-to-function mapping (cf. Jacobs and Jucker 1995:13), which means that a linguistic form, in this case a name or title used vocatively, is taken as a starting point, and it will then be investigated whether this form shows a preference for a T or Y pronoun. In addition to this quantitative distributional study, qualitative, and especially sociopragmatic aspects such as the social relationship between the speakers, sentence types and their discourse functions, different settings, etc. will be incorporated.

In any good numerical study, the units to be counted should be clearly defined in order to allow for comparability and repeatability of the results. As a basis for counting the window of collocates from the node will not be limited to an arbitrarily set span of *x* words to the left and to the right, but will be limited to one single uninterrupted utterance by a single speaker.[4]

Table 4. Social ranks and titles in Tudor and Stuart England

Estate	Rank	Title	Form of Address	Example
SOVEREIGN	Royalty: King/Queen, the Prince (heir apparent, Prince of Wales), the royal family		*my lord, sir, madam, your majesty, your highness, your grace, your lordship/your ladyship*	*Your Majesty, Your dear highness, Good my Lord, my Liege, Royal Lear, your highness, sir*
GENTRY nobility	Duke/Duchess	**Lord/Lady**	*1) sir, madam, my lord, your lordship/ your ladyship* *2) your grace*	*My Lord of Burgundy, Right noble Burgundy, your grace (Gloucester to Cornwall)*
	Archbishop			
	Marquess/ Marchioness		1) see above 2) *your honour*	
	Earl (Count/ Countess)			*My Lord of Kent, your Lordship*
	Viscount/Viscountess			
	Baron			
	Bishop			
GENTRY proper	[Baronet (from 1611–)]	**Sir/Lady** **Dame** (obsolete)		
	Knight		Sir + first name (+ surname) *your worship*	*Sir John Falstaff, your worship*
	Esquire (Squire)	**Master/Mistress**		*Robert Shallow, Esquire Master/Mistress Page, Ford*
	Gentleman			
	Clergyman		*your reverence*	*master parson, Sir Hugh Evans*
PROFESSIONS	Army Officer, Government Official, Lawyer, Medical Doctor, Teacher, etc.		Occupational Title: *Captain, Doctor*, etc.	*master lieutenant, master doctor*
NON-GENTRY middle class	*country*: Yeoman, Freeholder, Husbandman Tenant	**Goodman/Goodwife** **Dame**	*Worthy* (obsolete)	
	city: Merchant, Crafts-man, Tradesman	**Master/Mistress** **Dame**	Name of craft: *Carpenter*, etc.	*Robin Starveling, tailor Nicholas Bottom, weaver*
	Artificer			
lower class	Labourer Cottager Pauper	**None**		

(Table mine, based on Breuer 1983, Nevalainen and Raumolin-Brunberg 1995, 1996a)

Table 5. Categorisation of address forms with illustrative examples

Titles of courtesy	Terms of address indicating occupation	Terms of family relationship
*Your Grace**	captain	brother
Your (royal) Highness	doctor	cousin
*Your Honour***	esquire	daughter
Your Ladyship	justice	father
Your Lordship	knight	husband
Your Worship	lieutenant	mother
dame	nurse	sister
goodman	parson	son
goodwife	...	uncle
lady		wife
(my) liege		...
lord		
madam		
master		
mistress		
monsieur		
sir		
sire***		
sirrah		
...		

* *Your Grace* and all the other styles have been italicised, as they are fixed expressions that always co-occur with *your*, excepting cases as in footnote **. For this reason they can be omitted from this study because there is no choice of pronouns to be made.
** For comic purposes these styles can also be used incongruously, as e.g. in TMP when Caliban tries to flatter Stephano by addressing him with: "How does thy honor? Let me lick thy shoe" (3, 2, 23) cf. also Replogle (1967: 140f.).
*** *Sire* can also be excluded because on the authority of Schmidt and Sarrazin it has the meaning 'father', occurs only in verse and is never used as an address; cf. also Spevack (1973).

The nominal forms of address will be organised into formal categories (see Table 5) and within each group, the vocative expressions for men and women appear in alphabetical order in the form of a "standardised" dictionary-type entry that begins by giving the meaning(s) of the term from the *Shakespeare Lexicon* of Schmidt and Sarrazin and, if necessary, the OED, followed by a short socio-historical outline of the address form from the 16th to the 17th century, and, where applicable, additional information from special studies such as Böhm (1936), Replogle (1967), Salmon (1967), Stoll (1989) and others. At the centre of these entries will be the presentation and discussion of illustrative stretches of dialogue from the corpus.

Table 5 continued. Categorisation of address forms with illustrative examples

Generic terms of address	Terms of endearment	Terms of abuse
boy	bully	devil
friend	chuck	dog
gentleman	coz	fool
gentlewoman	heart	hag
lad	joy	knave
maid	love	rascal
man	wag	rogue
woman	...	slave
...		varlet
		villain
		witch
		...

6.3.1   Titles of courtesy

6.3.1.1   *Dame*

Schmidt and Sarrazin give the following sense divisions:

1. mistress,
   a.   a woman who governs
   b.   a woman beloved or courted
2. mother
3. lady
   –   Before names
   –   Used as a term of contemptuous address

These short definitions show that the term covers quite a broad social spectrum in Shakespeare's plays. This not withstanding, its frequency in the corpus, with only 28 tokens in the plays (25 verse and 3 prose), and an additional 8 in the non-dramatic works, is small, especially in comparison to other female titles such as *lady* and *mistress*. Table 6 shows the distribution of co-occurring pronouns in the three genres of Comedies, Histories and Tragedies.[5]

This scarcity can be accounted for. Böhm (1936: 61–64) shows that before the 16th century *dame* could be used in the same way as *lady*, but that from then on the title has undergone a broadening of meaning and a pejoration:

> [Nach dem Baronetspatent von 1611] zeigt sich uns das Bild so, daß lady gesetzmäßig als der höhere Titel angesehen wurde, der nur den Peersfrauen zustand, während die Ritterfrauen Dames waren, aber der Brauch beachtete diese feinen Unterschiede nicht [...] die Anrede dame kam schnell in Verfall, d. h. im 16 Jht. war sie die übliche Anrede der Bürgersfrauen, während sie bis

Table 6. T and Y pronouns co-occurring with *dame*

	T pronoun	Y pronoun	combined
Comedies	–	1	1
Histories	2	2	4
Tragedies	1	2	3
Total	**3**	**5**	**8**

heute (Sweet, Law Dict.) die legale Bezeichnung der Ritters- und Baronetsfrau geblieben ist. (Böhm 1936:63)

Salmon goes even further and states that at the beginning of the 17th century the term had become degraded in meaning to "'old woman', perhaps because of the traditional collocation with *Partlet* [cf. WT 2, 3, 76; 1H4 3, 3, 52]. The name was applied to fussy, scolding women [...]" (1967:53). Stoll (1989:113) also mentions that *dame* carried pejorative undertones when used on its own.

The title occurs most often in the History Plays (15 tokens), which also furnish all examples of *dame* + *(first) name* as reference to women of rank, as *Dame Mortimer* (1H4 2, 4, 110), *Dame Margaret* (2H6 1, 2, 39; 3, 2, 79) or *Dame Eleanor (Cobham)* (2H6 1, 2, 91, 97; 1, 3, 147; 2, 3, 1).

The distribution of the co-occurring pronouns does not at first sight yield a clear-cut picture (see Table 6). There are 5 instances of *you*, as opposed to 3 of *thou*. However, on second sight they reveal that *dame* is most often used in reprimand, but that *you* conveys a larger social distance.

(1) Antipholus of Syracuse [to Luciana]: Plead you to me, fair dame? I know you not [...]. (ERR 2, 2, 147)

(2) Falstaff [to Hostess]: How now, Dame Partlet the hen? have you inquir'd yet who pick'd my pocket?
Hostess: Why, Sir John, what do you think, Sir John? Do you think I keep thieves in my house? (1H4 3, 3, 52–55)

(3) King: Stand forth, Dame Eleanor Cobham, Gloucester's wife: In sight of God and us, your guilt is great [...]. (2H6 2, 3, 1–3)

(4) Messenger [to Lady Macduff]: Bless you, fair dame! I am not to you known [...]. (MAC 4, 2, 65)

(5) Albany [to Goneril]: Shut your mouth, dame, / Or with this paper shall I [stopple] it. LR 5, 3, 155)

In contrast to the above examples, *thou* co-occurs in those instances in which *dame* is used as a contemptuous address. For additional emphasis, negative adjectives are used:

(6)   Charles, Dauphin and afterwards King of France [to Joan de Pucelle]: Is this thy cunning, thou deceitful dame? (1H6 2, 1, 50)

(7)   Gloucester [to his wife, the Duchess]: Nay, Eleanor, then must I chide outright. Presumptuous dame, ill-nurtur'd Eleanor, / Art thou not second woman in the realm? (2H6 1, 2, 41–43)

Very seldom, *thou* is used for the woman beloved or courted when *dame* (in its original sense) functions as a respectful and courtly form of address:

(8)   Antony [to Cleopatra]: Fare thee well, dame, what e'er becomes of me. This is a soldier's kiss; [...]. (ANT 4, 4, 29–30)

6.3.1.2   *Goodman*

Schmidt and Sarrazin give the following definitions:

a familiar appellation =
a.   gaffer
b.   husband

The occurrences of *goodman* in the Shakespeare Corpus are not numerous. There are only 16 tokens to be found, and the usual pronoun to accompany it is *you* (see Table 7).

Table 7. T and Y pronouns co-occurring with *goodman*

	T pronoun	Y pronoun	combined
Comedies	1	2	3
Histories	–	–	–
Tragedies	–	3	3
Total	1	5	6

According to Böhm (1936:51f.) *goodman* was originally a polite form of address among the lower classes. In the 16th century it became the usual form of address among neighbours who belonged to the class of yeomen instead of *master*. It was used as a prefix to the (sur-)name, but did not have any legal status. "When used properly, then, 'goodman' was a form of respect for someone not of gentle or noble birth and who had no other pretensions to gentility yet had credit in the community. It had no pejorative connotations" (Replogle 1967:54).

Stoll (1989:138) says that in Shakespeare's plays *goodman* is used less often than *neighbour* and that it is socially not respectable and constitutes an insult when given to a person of rank.

The examples from the corpus reveal that in most cases the term is not used symmetrically, but from above with a slightly patronising attitude indicated by epithets as *boy* and *bald-pate*. It can also be used ironically to one below the rank of a gentleman as in (5):

(1) Holofernes [to Dull]: Via, goodman Dull! / thou hast spoken no word all this while. Dull: Nor understood none neither, sir. (LLL 5, 1, 149–150)

(2) Tybald: It fits when such a villain is a guest. I'll not endure him. Capulet: He shall be endured. What, goodman boy?[6] I say he shall, go to! Am I the master here, or you? go to! (ROM 1, 5, 75–78)

(3) Edmund: How now, what's the matter? Part! Kent: With you, goodman boy,[7] [and] you please! Come, I'll flesh ye, come on, young master. (LR 2, 2, 45–46)

(4) 2. Clown [to 1. Clown]: Nay, but hear you, goodman delver — (HAM 5, 1, 14)

(5) Lucio [to the Duke in his friar's habit]: 'Tis he, my lord. Come hither, goodman bald-pate, do you know me? (MM 5, 1, 325–326)

In the sense of 'husband' there are two occurrences (MM 5, 1, 326 and SHR Induction 2, 105 where *you* is used as a pronoun:

(6) Sly, a drunken tinker: Are you my wife and will not call me husband? My men should call me "lord"; I am your goodman. Page, dressed as a woman: My husband and my lord, my lord and husband, I am your wife in all obedience. (SHR Induction 2, 103–107)

6.3.1.3 *Goodwife*

Schmidt and Sarrazin say that *goodwife* is "an appellation applied to women as *goodman* to men, gossip"[8] and Replogle adds: "'Goodwife' was [...] also prefixed to the surname of middle-class persons of substance. In this case, as is obvious, the person addressed had to be married" (1967:54). Stoll (1989:139) goes even a step further when she states that the title has sunk to the level of the bourgeoisie or even lower.

In fact, *goodwife* appears only twice in the entire corpus and is not accompanied by any address pronoun. This ties in with Salmon's dictum: "as *mistress* was so widely used in the 16th century for all women, possibly *goodwife*, as a title of address, was slightly derogatory by c. 1600" (1967:53).

(1) Mistress Quickly: Give your worship good morrow. Falstaff: Good morrow, goodwife. Mistress Quickly: Not so, and't please your worship. Falstaff: Good maid then. (WIV 2, 2, 33–36)

(2) Hostess: Did not goodwife Keech, the butcher's wife, come in then and call me gossip Quickly? (2H4 2, 1, 93–94)

6.3.1.4 *Lady*

Schmidt and Sarrazin indicate the following sense divisions:

1. mistress, the woman who presides over an estate or family
   = the mistress of the household
   = my patroness
2. wife to a man of distinction
3. any woman of distinction
   – In compellations
4. any woman, called so in complaisance and courtesy
5. a woman beloved, mistress
6. the holy Virgin
7. the person performing the principal female part in a play
8. a name of dogs
9. the burden of a certain song

Senses 1–5 indicate that *lady* in the Shakespeare Corpus covers a wide social spectrum, ranging from a woman of distinction, often a princess or "the feminine designation corresponding to *lord*" (OED) to a courtesy title given to any woman irrespective of social rank. This usage is in accord with the use of the term in the 16th century. Social rules for the use of the title are e.g. given in the *Book of Precedence*. Böhm (1936: 56–61) gives the following historical outline (cf. also OED):

> Im 16. Jht. ist im Gegensatz zu anderen Titeln die Graderhöhung, die mit der Benennung verbunden war, noch recht streng beachtet worden, [...]. Um die Jahrhundertwende findet sich bei der steigenden Zahl von Rittern der Rangtitel immer häufiger, so daß wohl daraus der Gebrauch der Anrede Lady mit und ohne Namen im Singular und Plural herzuleiten ist, die nun als erste von den strikten Regeln abweicht und sich auch, besonders im Plural, für Frauen findet, die zwar in adliger Umgebung, aber oft nur gentlewomen sind. [...] halb im Spott für einfache Frauen angewendet, dann wird es allmählich zu einem Vorrecht gegenüber den Männern und allgemein üblicher Brauch. Noch ist es aber eine Ausnahme und der Titel das erstrebenswerteste Ziel jeder Frau [...]. (Böhm 1936: 58; 59)

Stoll (1989: 120f.) adds that *lady* instead of the more general *madam* is used especially in situations that are characterised socio-pragmatically by formulaic patterns of speech and comportment such as introducing important messages, greeting and parting formulae, etc. The title gains in respect the larger the social distance between the interlocutors is.

A glance at the female characters who are addressed as *lady*, reveals that this title is usually given vocatively only to women of distinction, e.g. to Silvia, daughter of the Duke of Milan (TGV), Beatrice, niece to Leonato, the Governor of Messina and his daughter Hero (ADO), Rosaline, one of the ladies attending the Princess of France (LLL), Portia, a rich heiress (MV), Olivia, a wealthy lady of Illyria (TN), Julia, daughter to Capulet (ROM), Cressid, daughter of Calchas (TRO), Paulina, lady-in-

Table 8. T and Y pronouns co-occurring with *lady*

	T pronoun	Y pronoun	combined
Comedies	10	55	65
Histories	10	19	29
Tragedies	9	35	44
Total	**29**	**109**	**138**

waiting to Hermione [= Queen to Leontes] (WT), Lady Constance (JN), Regan, daughter of King Lear (LR), Desdemona, wife to Othello (OTH), Cleopatra, Queen of Egypt (ANT) and to Imogen, daughter of Cymbeline, King of Britain (CYM).

The examples from the opposite end of the social scale are fewer. An example to highlight asymmetrical pronoun use and the somewhat unbecoming and ironic use of the title is to be found when in 1H4 Prince Henry addresses Mistress Quickly, the hostess of the Boar's Head Tavern, as *lady*:

(1)   Hostess: O Jesu, my lord the Prince!
      Prince: How now, my lady the hostess! what say'st thou to me?
      Hostess: Marry, my lord, there is a nobleman of the court at door would speak
      with you. (1H4 2, 4, 284–288)

The overall ratio of address pronouns co-occurring with *lady* looks as follows: *Lady* has a total frequency of 650 tokens in the plays (445 verse; 205 prose). Out of the 138 cases in which pronouns co-occur, there are 109 instances of *you* and 29 instances of *thou* (see Table 8). Once again their distribution over genres is not even, as the Comedies show considerably more *you* forms.

Table 8 yields a chi-squared value of 4.44 (2 df<0.10). If H8 with its 8 tokens is omitted from the set, the use of *thou* and *you* in the Histories is almost levelled and the chi-squared value reaches 9.60, which is well above the 0.02 level of confidence.

Quite unsurprisingly, *you* has turned out to be the preferred form in conjunction with *lady*. This shows that *you* is the default pronoun, which is employed either out of respect for the (superior) rank of a woman, or as the neutral form given "to all women above a loosely-defined and variable, but usually not very elevated standard of social position. Often used (*esp.* in 'this lady') as a more courteous synonym for 'woman', without reference to the status of the person spoken of" (OED).

Basically, the instances of *thou* + *lady* can be grouped into two categories; i.e. those conditioned by love and other emotions, especially by suitors in wooing in the sense of: "a woman who is the object of chivalrous devotion; a mistress, 'lady-love'" (OED), and those showing a benignant social superiority as either from husband to wife or from royal father to daughter. Both uses have in common that they are given from male speakers only:

(2) Berowne [to Rosaline]: Here stand I, lady, dart thy skill at me, / Bruise me with scorn, confound me with a flout, [...]. My love to thee is sound, sans crack or flaw. (LLL 5, 2, 396–397; 415)

(3) Prince of Morocco [to Portia]: I tell thee, lady, this aspect of mine / Hath fear'd the valiant; by my love, I swear [...] Yea, mock the lion when 'a roars for prey, / To win [thee], lady. (MV 2, 1, 8–9; 30)

(4) Bottom: And I may hide my face, let me play Thisby too. I'll speak in a monstrous little voice, "Thisne! Thisne! Ah, Piramus, my lover dear! thy Thisby dear, and lady dear!" (MND 1, 2, 51–54)

(5) Gloucester [to Lady Anne]: He that bereft thee, lady, of thy husband, / Did it to help thee to a better husband. [...] Thine eyes, sweet lady, have infected mine. [...] Teach not thy lip such scorn; for it was made / For kissing, lady, not for such contempt. (R3 1, 2, 138; 149; 172)

(6) Antony [to Cleopatra]: Where hast thou been, my heart? Dost thou hear, lady? If from the field I shall return once more / To kiss these lips, [...]. (ANT 3, 13, 172–174)

The second category comprises addresses from husband to wife and from father to daughter:

(7) Lady: But hear you, my lord.
Hotspur: What say'st thou, my lady? (1H4 2, 3, 73–74)

On the other hand, Titania in MND does not reciprocate with an obedient *you* but with *thou* to her husband Oberon because she is angry and jealous:

(8) Oberon: Tarry, rash wanton! Am not I thy lord?
Titania: Then I must be thy lady; but I know / When thou hast stolen away from fairy land, / And in the shape of Corin sat all day, / Playing on pipes of corn, and versing love / To amorous Phillida. (MND 2, 1, 63–68)

(9) Lear [to Regan]: Of all these bounds, even from this line to this, / With shadowy forests and with champains rich'd / With plenteous rivers and wide-skirted meads, / We make thee lady. (LR 1, 1, 63–66)

Sudden changes of feeling vented through pronoun switching are very seldom:

(10) Cornwall: Bind him, I say. [Servants bind him.]
Regan: Hard, hard. O filthy traitor!
Gloucester: Unmerciful lady as you are, I'm none.
Cornwall: To this chair bind him. Villain, thou shalt find — [Regan plucks his beard.]
Gloucester: By the kind gods, 'tis most ignobly done / To pluck me by the beard.
Regan: So white, and such a traitor?
Gloucester: Naughty lady, / These hairs which thou dost ravish from my chin / Will quicken and accuse thee. (LR 3, 7, 32–39)

6.3.1.5 *(My) Liege*

Schmidt and Sarrazin only give the rather short gloss of "lord paramount, sovereign" and Böhm does not provide an entry at all, but the OED offers comprehensive information (including adjective use):

> 1. The characteristic epithet of persons in the relation of feudal superior and vassal.
> a. Of the superior: Entitled to feudal allegiance and service. Now rare exc. in *liege lord*, which is also used *fig*. [1292–1865]
> b. Of the vassal: Bound to render feudal service and allegiance. (See liege man.)
> † Also, owing allegiance *to* (law). [13..–1848]
> † c. *transf.* of persons in other relationships: Entitled and bound to mutual fidelity. *Obs.* [1350–1555]
> ¶ d. Used for: Loyal, faithful. *rare.* [1478–1890]
> 2. Of or pertaining to the bond between superior and vassal. [1399–1818]
> B. *n.* 1. The superior to whom one owes feudal allegiance and service; = *liege lord.* [1400–1837]
> 2. A vassal bound to serve his superior, a liege man. Hence in a wider sense: A loyal subject of the king. [1377–1880]

Stoll (1989: 161) mentions that the use of *liege* characterises the speaker as a loyally devoted follower such as the trusty Kent in LR, the officious Polonius in HAM, the assiduous Talbot in 1H6 and the faithful Westmerland in 1/2H4.

The numerical distribution of *(my) liege* in the corpus is as follows: the absolute frequency of *liege* is 139 tokens (132 verse; 7 prose). Its distribution over the genres shows a clear imbalance, because 31 tokens (22.30%) appear in the Comedies, 94 tokens (67.63%) in the Histories, and only 14 tokens (10.07%) in the Tragedies. Thus, despite many structural similarities between Histories and Tragedies, *(my) liege* features most prominently in the Histories.

As regards the co-occurring address pronouns, Table 9 shows a clear-cut picture, as a Y pronoun occurs 54 times, and a T pronoun only twice.[9] This almost exclusive use of a Y pronoun makes it the default form, which obviously is necessitated by the high social rank of the person so addressed. The only T-forms are the following:

Table 9. T and Y pronouns co-occurring with *(my) liege*

	T pronoun	Y pronoun	combined
Comedies	1	17	18
Histories	1	30	31
Tragedies	–	7	7
Total	2	54	56

(1)   Berowne [to King]: Now step I forth to whip hypocrisy. Ah, good my liege, I
pray thee pardon me! Good heart, what grace hast thou thus to reprove / These
worms for loving, that art most in love? (LLL 4, 3, 149–152)

(2)   The Duke of York knocks at the door and crieth [to King Henry]: York
[Within]: My liege, beware! Look to thyself, / Thou hast a traitor in thy presence
there.
King Henry: Villain, I'll make thee safe. [Draws] (R2 5, 3, 38–41)

In the vast majority of cases, *my liege* is used by social inferiors ranging from the
Queen over nobles to commoners as address to the sovereign, be it a king, or duke
(as in ERR, MM, AYL). Especially in requests and entreaties the utmost deference
is given. For this reason *(my) liege* is mostly preceded by honorific adjectives; the
most frequent combination being *good my liege* with the adjective transposed, *my
good liege* is more seldom. Other combinations are:[10]

my	dear	liege
my	gentle	liege
my	liefest	liege
my	most royal	liege
my	most sovereign	liege
	most dread	liege
	most gracious	liege
	thrice puissant	liege

Sometimes, in addition to their verbal obsequiousness, the supplicants humble, or
even debase themselves by kneeling down before the sovereign:

(3)   Duke: We do enstate and widow you with all, / To buy you a better husband.
Mari: O my dear lord, I crave no other, nor no better man.
Duke: Never crave him, we are definitive.
Mari [kneeling to the Duke]: Gentle my liege —
Duke: You do but lose your labor. Away with him to death! (MM 5, 1, 423–428)

(4)   Duchess: O King, believe not this hard-hearted man! Love loving not itself, none
other can.
York: Thou frantic woman, what dost thou make here? Shall thy old dugs once
more a traitor rear?
Duchess [kneeling]: Sweet York, be patient. Hear me, gentle liege.
(R2 5, 3, 87–91)

In requests, politeness is usually expressed by the impersonal construction *if you
please* (cf. Chapter 7.7) and not by *I pray you* and by using the verb *to beseech*, which
is more deferential than *pray*. In addition, *my liege* is often used in conjunction with
styles.

(5) King: Your oath is pass'd to pass away from these.
     Berowne, a lord attending on the King: Let me say no, my liege, and if you
     please: I only swore to study with your Grace, […]. (LLL 1, 1, 50–51)

(6) Duke Frederick: How now, daughter and cousin? are you crept hither to see the
     wrastling?
     Rosalind: Ay, my liege, so please you give us leave. (AYL 1, 2, 156–157)

(7) King: Why then, young Bertram, take her, she's thy wife.
     Bertram: My wife, my liege? I shall beseech your Highness, / In such a business,
     give me leave to use/ The help of mine own eyes. (AWW 2, 3, 104–108)

(8) King Richard: Why, uncle, what's the matter?
     York: O my liege, / Pardon me, if you please; if not, I, pleas'd / Not to be
     pardoned, am content withal. (R2 2, 1, 186–188)

On the other hand, in compliance to an order from the sovereign that demands
immediate action to be taken, shorter unadorned forms are used as replies. This
also holds for questions from the sovereign seeking information:

(9) King: Let him approach / A stranger, no offender; and inform him / So 'tis our
     will he should.
     Gentleman: I shall, my liege. [Exit.] (AWW 5, 3, 25–27)

(10) King: Cousin, on Wednesday next our Council we / Will hold at Windsor, so
     inform the lords. But come yourself with speed to us again, / For more is to be
     said and to be done / Than out of anger can be uttered.
     Earl of Westmerland: I will, my liege. (1H4 1, 1, 104–108)

(11) King Henry: What treasure, uncle?
     Duke of Exeter, uncle to the King: Tennis-balls, my liege. (H5 1, 2, 257–258)

(12) King Richard: Old John of Gaunt, time-honored Lancaster, / Hast thou,
     according to thy oath and band, / Brought hither Henry Herford thy bold son, […]?
     John of Gaunt, Duke of Lancaster and uncle to the King: I have, my liege.
     (R2 1, 1, 2–7)

Changes in social status are immediately expressed through the appropriate title:

(13) [The King dies. Salisbury to Bastard]: You breathe these dead news in as dead an
     ear. My liege, my lord! but now a king, now thus. (JN 5, 7, 65–66)

6.3.1.6 *Mistress*

Schmidt and Sarrazin show that mistress has a number of different meanings in
Shakespeare's plays:

1. a woman who has command and governs; opposed to servant
   – Used in addressing women
2. a female owner
3. a woman beloved and courted

4. a female teacher
    And = a woman well skilled in a thing
5. = lady
    = partner
6. a term of courtesy used in speaking of or to women (except those of high
    rank), indiscriminately whether they are married or not (comprising the
    modern Madam, Mrs., and Miss)
    — Used with some unkindness or contempt of or to women, from whom
    the affections of the speaker have been estranged.
7. the small ball at the game of bowls, now called the Jack, at which the
    players aim

This usage conforms to the social conventions of 16/17th century England as
expounded by Böhm (1936: 70–74):

> Der frz. Titel bürgerte sich ebenso wie master bald so ein, daß seine Entwick-
> lung zum allgemeinen vorgesetzten Titel schon bei der überaus häufigen
> Anwendung des 16. Jhts. vorauszusehen ist. Die Grenze nach oben ist zu der
> Zeit noch nicht fest [...]. Die Anwendung nach unten ist dagegen noch recht
> beschränkt. Nur Frauen, denen die Bezeichnung Gentlewoman zusteht,
> werden mit der Anrede mistress vor dem Namen geehrt. Ein Unterschied
> zwischen verheirateten Frauen und jungen Mädchen besteht bis ins 17. Jht.
> nicht [...]. Anfang des 17. Jhts. ist eine scharfe Abgrenzung des Titels gegen die
> Nebenbedeutungen nicht erfolgt, lady wie Handwerkersfrau heißen mistress,
> ebenso wie die Geliebte des Ritters [...].
> (Böhm 1936: 71f; cf. also Stoll 1989: 133–135)

The overall frequency with 389 tokens (202 verse; 187 prose) bears out the versatili-
ty of this term. However, despite the broad social and attitudinal range that is
covered, comprising women of rank, e.g. the Queen in CYM and also bawds, such
as Mistress Overdone in MM, the distribution of co-occurring address pronouns is
extremely clear-cut in favour of *you*; the ratio being 72 tokens of *you* and only 6
tokens of *thou* (see Table 10).[11]

Table 10 reveals, not surprisingly, that *mistress* dominates in the Comedies,

Table 10. T and Y pronouns co-occurring with *mistress*

	T pronoun	Y pronoun	combined
Comedies	4	51	55
Histories	2	3	5
Tragedies	–	18	18
Total	6	72	78

while the play to make most use of the term is WIV, where *mistress* is the usual address for Mistress Ford, Mistress Page and her daughter Anne Page. Whereas the elder women are usually addressed as Mistress Ford and Mistress Page, her daughter is called Mistress Anne, often preceded by the adjectives *fair* or *good*.

(1) Shallow: Here comes fair Mistress Anne. Would I were young for your sake, Mistress Anne!
Anne: The dinner is on the table. My father desires your worship's company.
(WIV1, 1, 259–262)

When *mistress* is premodified by adjectives, they are usually positive, e.g. *(most) dear, fair, gentle, good, noble* and *sweet*. As outlined by Table 10, the attitude towards a speaker, message or situation is seldom expressed by pronoun changes but usually by other linguistic devices as the following examples, except those used in courting (see 2–4), illustrate. When Sir Valentine and Sir Proteus, two old friends from Verona, fall in love with Silvia in TGV they play with the meanings of *mistress* and *servant*. Berowne in LLL also makes use of elevated diction when he falls in love with Rosaline. On the other hand, when Falstaff plays court to Mistress Ford the diction indicates his character, the social setting and the degree of intimacy:

(2) Valentine: Welcome, dear Proteus! Mistress I beseech you / Confirm his welcome with some special favor.
Silvia: His worth is warrant for his welcome hither, / If this be he you oft have wish'd to hear from.
Valentine: Mistress, it is: sweet lady, entertain him / To be my fellow-servant to your ladyship.
Silvia: Too low a mistress for so high a servant.
Proteus: Not so, sweet lady, but too mean a servant / To have a look of such a worthy mistress. (TGV 2, 4, 99–108)

(3) Berowne: Studies my lady? Mistress, look on me, / Behold the window of my heart, mine eye, / What humble suit attends thy answer there. Impose some service on me for thy love.
Rosaline: Oft have I heard of you, my Lord Berowne, / Before I saw you; and the world's large tongue / Proclaims you for a man replete with mocks, / Full of comparisons and wounding flouts [...]. (LLL 5, 2, 837–844)

(4) Falstaff: Mistress Ford, I cannot cog, I cannot prate, Mistress Ford. Now shall I sin in my wish: I would thy husband were dead. I'll speak it before the best lord, I would make thee my lady. (WIV 3, 3, 48–51)

However, except from courting, *thou* does not play any significant role in conjunction with *mistress*, clearly shown by the following examples, all given in unkindness or even contempt because of estranged or disappointed feelings by husbands to their wives or by fathers to their daughters. Despite the strong emotions *you* is used as a pronoun:

(5)   Capulet [to Juliet]: How how, how how, chopp'd logic! What is this? "Proud",
       and "I thank you" and "I thank you not", / And yet "not proud", mistress
       minion[12] you? (ROM 3, 5, 149–151)

(6)   Emilia: You told a lie, an odious, damned lie; / Upon my soul, a lie, a wicked lie.
       She false with Cassio? did you say with Cassio?
       Iago: With Cassio, mistress. Go to, charm your tongue. (OTH 5, 2, 180–183)

(7)   Pericles: Then as you are virtuous as fair, / Resolve your angry father [...]
       Simonides [to Thaisa, his daughter]: Yea, mistress, are you so peremptory? [...]
       Therefore hear you, mistress, either frame / Your will to mine — and you, sir,
       hear you — Either be rul'd by me, or I'll make you — Man and wife.
       (PER 2, 5, 67–84)

(8)   Rosalind [to Phebe]: No, faith, proud mistress, hope not after it. 'Tis not your
       inky brows, your black silk hair, / Your bugle eyeballs, nor your cheek of cream /
       That can entame my spirits to your worship. (AYL 3, 5, 45–48)

6.3.1.7 *Monsieur*

According to Schmidt and Sarrazin, *monsieur* is the "French address used to
gentlemen". Stoll (1989: 112) confirms that *monsieur* is used for and by Frenchmen
(with or without pronoun) and that it is not restricted to a particular estate.

Monsieur, with its spelling variants *mounseur* and *mounsieur*, has an overall
frequency of 53 tokens (8 verse; 45 prose) and occurs primarily in the Comedies (45
tokens, Histories 5 tokens and Tragedies 3 tokens), out of which LLL, AYL, AWW
and MND feature most prominently. The pronoun that co-occurs exclusively with
monsieur is *you* (see Table 11).

Table 11. T and Y pronouns co-occurring with *monsieur*

	T pronoun	Y pronoun	combined
Comedies	–	19	19
Histories	–	–	–
Tragedies	–	–	–
Total	–	19	19

The characters addressed in this way are usually Frenchmen, as Boyet in LLL,
a lord attending the Princess of France, Le Beau in AYL, one of Duke Frederick's
courtiers, Jaques, a melancholic lord attending the banished Duke of Burgundy
(AYL) and Parolles, a follower of Bertram (AWW). Alternatively, it is used to
address any foreigner, as in MND 4, 1, 8–24 where Bottom addresses the fairies as
Mounsieur Cobweb and *Mounsieur Mustardseed* and in TMP Caliban is addressed in
this way.

In many cases *monsieur* is used with benevolent irony as *pars pro toto* to describe a character by his (supposedly) most important trait as *Monsieur Monster* (referring to Trinculo in TMP 3, 2, 18), *Monsieur Love* (Claudio in ADO 2, 3, 36), *Monsieur Melancholy* (Jaques in AYL 3, 2, 294), *Monsieur Remorse* (Falstaff in 1H4 1, 2, 113).

Monsieur always occurs with positively connotated adjectives, especially with *good*, and to a lesser degree with *sweet*:

(1) Charles: Good morrow to your worship.
    Oliver: Good Monsieur Charles, what's the new news at the new court?
    (AYL 1, 1, 95–97)

(2) Celia: Call him hither, good Monsieur Le Beau.
    Duke Frederick: Do so; I'll not be by.
    Le Beau: Monsieur the challenger, the princess calls for you. (AYL 1, 2, 163–166)

(3) Bottom [to Cobweb]: Mounsieur Cobweb, good mounsieur, get you your weapons in your hand […]. (MND 4, 1, 10–11)

In the History Plays, which are set in England and not in foreign countries, *monsieur* is used to refer to the French. In (4) the title is translated into English as *master*:

(4) Pistol: Come hither, boy, ask me this slave in French / What is his name.
    Boy: Écoutez: comment êtes-vous appelé?
    French soldier: *Monsieur le Fer.*
    Boy: He says his name is *Master Fer.* (H5 4, 4, 23–27)

6.3.1.8   *Sirrah*

Sirrah is a special case. Although it is not a title of courtesy, it is treated as one in many reference works. The *Shakespeare Lexicon* of Schmidt and Sarrazin provides detailed information about its usage in Shakespeare's works:[13]

1. A compellation used in addressing comparatively inferior persons[14]
2. Resented by one who thinks himself a gentleman
3. Used between equals of low degree
4. a. Implying disrespect when used to persons of note
   b. or at least an unbecoming familiarity
5. Followed by a noun proper or appellative
6. Used as an address to a woman
7. Sometimes forming part of a soliloquy and addressed to an imaginary person or rather to the speaker himself (always preceded by *ah*)

Böhm (1936: 52f.) includes *Sirrah* as the last one in the male titles of courtesy despite the fact that it is not a title of honor for the reason that presumably it was at par with *sir* at an earlier state, but soon turned into a derisive form of address used (seldom also for women) in particular for social inferiors, usually with a scolding, scornful and imperious note:

> Obgleich sirrah kein Ehrentitel ist, muß er auf Grund seiner Häufigkeit als Anrede mit und ohne folgenden Namen hier kurz erwähnt werden. Aus einer vielleicht ursprünglichen Gleichstellung mit sir hat es sich bald zu der spöttischen Anrede entwickelt, die meist für Untergebene gebraucht wurde. Einheitlich ist der Gebrauch im 16. Jht. noch nicht. Beispiele zeigen oft einen fast gleichen Gebrauch von sirrah neben sir [...]. Seit Mitte des 17. Jhts. drücken die zahlreichen Beispiele allerdings meist Spott, Drohung, Herablassung oder Ärger aus [...]. (Böhm 1936:52)

Salmon also includes *sirrah* in the titles of courtesy and gives the following explanation: "It seems to have answered the need for a respectful form of address to a youth not yet old enough to be called *master* [...] if used to anyone other than a boy, or without a title of occupation, [it] denoted either contempt or possibly intimacy" (1967:53; 57). The difficulties connected with the interpretation of *sirrah* can be illustrated by the following dialogue from LR:

(1)   Gloucester [about Edgar]: Abhorred villain! unnatural, detested, brutish villain! worse than brutish! [to Edmund] Go, sirrah, seek him; I'll apprehend him. Abominable villain! Where is he?
Edmund: I do not well know, my lord. (LR 1, 2, 76–79)

Grannis is of the opinion that Gloucester's address to his illegitimate son Edmund "would seem to indicate Gloucester's basic, intuitive rejection of the evil Edmund" (1990:113). In contrast to this, the *Riverside Shakespeare* glosses this use of *sirrah* as "familiar form of address used by parents to children or by masters to servants" (cf. also Stoll 1989:141). It is also possible that the resentful address *sirrah* is brought about by an overspill of verbal outrage against his other son Edgar. Replogle adds that "'sirrah' is often used by parents to their children as a reflection of their authority, usually when telling them to do something" (1967:65).[15]

Corpus evidence for *sirrah* is as follows: it has an absolute frequency of 150 tokens (80 verse; 70 prose) and is used in nearly all of the plays, except in MND, WT and PER. Regarding its distribution over genres, it dominates in the Comedies with 66 tokens (44.00%), followed at equal distance by the Tragedies with 43 tokens (28.67%) and the Histories with 41 tokens (27.33%). The 150 instances of *sirrah* co-occur with 74 Y pronouns and only 23 T pronouns. This leaves 53 occurrences without a pronoun. Most of the Y pronouns occur in the Comedies. When the data are arranged in a contingency table (see Table 12), the result of the chi-squared test with 5.677 and 2 df almost reaches the 0.05 level of confidence.

Despite the above descriptions from the reference works that unanimously stress that *sirrah* is a form of address given to social inferiors it is remarkable that nonetheless the Y pronouns clearly outnumber the T pronouns. From the senses given in Schmidt and Sarrazin, sense 1) "a compellation used in addressing comparatively inferior persons" is by far the largest category. Most of the T forms

Table 12. T and Y pronouns co-occurring with *sirrah*

	T pronoun	Y pronoun	combined
Comedies	6	38	44
Histories	10	16	26
Tragedies	7	20	27
Total	**23**	**74**	**97**

occur in this category of address when a superior addresses a servingman, messenger, boy, etc.:

(2) Servingman: My lord, your son was gone before I came.
York: He was — why, so go all which way it will! The nobles are fled, the commons they are cold, / And will, I fear, revolt on Herford's side. Sirrah, get thee to Plashy, to my sister Gloucester, [...]. (R2 2, 2, 86–90)

(3) Master Gunner: Sirrah, thou know'st how Orleance is besieg'd, / And how the English have the suburbs won.
Boy: Father, I know, and oft have shot at them, / Howe'er unfortunate I miss'd my aim. (1H6 1, 4, 1–4)

(4) Lord Hastings: Go on before, I'll talk with this good fellow. [Exeunt Lord Stanley and Catesby.] How now, sirrah? how goes the world with thee?
Pursuivant: The better that your lordship please to ask.
Lord Hastings: I tell thee, man, 'tis better with me now / Than when thou met'st me last where now we meet. (R3 3, 2, 95–99)

(5) Capulet: Now, fellow, what is there?
1. Servingman: Things for the cook, sir, but I know not what.
Capulet: Make haste, make haste. Sirrah, fetch drier logs. Call Peter, he will show thee where they are. (ROM 4, 4, 14–17)

(6) Messenger: First, madam, he is well.
Cleopatra: Why, there's more gold. But, sirrah, mark, we use / To say the dead are well. Bring it to that, / The gold I give thee will I melt and pour / Down thy ill-uttering throat. (ANT 2, 5, 31–35)

Schmidt and Sarrazin's second category "Resented by one who thinks himself a gentleman" occurs only once in the whole corpus:

(7) Sexton: But which are the offenders that are to be examin'd? Let them come before Master Constable.
Dogberry: Yea, marry, let them come before me. What is your name, friend?
Borachio: Borachio.
Dogberry: Pray write down Borachio. Yours, sirrah?
Conrade: I am a gentleman, sir, and my name is Conrade.
Dogberry: Write down Master Gentleman Conrade. Masters, do you serve God?
Both [Conrade, Borachio]: Yea, sir, we hope. (ADO 4, 2, 7–17)

The third category "Used between equals of low degree" is also not very frequent and can be illustrated by the following examples:

(8)   Launce: Forswear not thyself, sweet youth, for I am not welcome. I reckon this always, that a man is never undone till he be hang'd, nor never welcome to a place till some certain shot be paid and the hostess say "Welcome."
Speed: Come on, madcap, I'll to the alehouse with you presently; where, for one shot of five pence, thou shalt have five thousand welcomes. But, sirrah, how did thy master part with Madam Julia? (TGV 2, 5, 2–11)

(9)   Chamberlain: Good morrow, Master Gadshill. It holds current that I told you yesternight: there's a franklin in the Wild of Kent hath brought three hundred marks with him in gold. [...]
Gadshill: Sirrah, if they meet not with Saint Nicholas' clerks, I'll give thee this neck. (1H4 2, 1, 53–61)

Examples for 4a. "Implying disrespect when used to persons of note" and b. "or at least an unbecoming familiarity" are also scarce:

(10)   Officer: I do arrest you, sir: you hear the suit.
Antipholus of Ephesus: I do obey thee, till I give thee bail. But, sirrah, you shall buy this sport as dear / As all the metal in your shop will answer.
(ERR 4, 1, 79–82)

(11)   Poins [to Prince]: Tut, our horses they shall not see — I'll tie them in the wood; our vizards we will change after we leave them; and, sirrah, I have cases of buckrom for the nonce, to immask our noted outward garments.
(1H4 1, 2, 177–181)

(12)   Falstaff: Therefore, sirrah [stabbing him], with a new wound in your thigh, come you along with me. [He takes up Hotspur on his back.] (1H4 5, 4, 127–128)

A case that calls for special attention is the relationship between King Lear and his fool (LR 1, 4, 97; 110; 115; 171; 181). Here King and fool address each other mutually as *sirrah*, and the fool can take the license to say: "Sirrah, I'll teach thee a speech" with Lear answering simply: "Do."

The instances in which *sirrah* is immediately followed by either a first name (*Sirrah Costard* LLL 3, 1, 120; *Sirrah Grumio* SHR 1, 2, 5 and 5, 2, 95; *Sirrah Biondello* SHR 4, 4, 10 and 5, 2, 86; *Sirrah Jack* 1H4 2, 2, 70; *Sirrah Claudio* JC 4, 3, 299 and *Sirrah Iras* ANT 5, 2, 229) or a name indicating the occupation or another appellative (*Sirrah villain* SHR 1, 2, 19; *Sirrah, young gamester* SHR 2, 1, 400; *Sirrah Beadle* 2H6 2, 1, 145 and *Sirrah Tinker* TNK 3, 5, 82) fall into two subclasses: this form of address is mostly used from master to servant or between equals of lesser rank, e.g. Armado addresses Costard, the clown, as *Sirrah Costard* (LLL 3, 1, 120), or Poins calls Falstaff *Sirrah Jack* (1H4 2, 2, 70). When a pronoun co-occurs, it is *you*, with the only exception in LLL 3, 1, 120. The scene between Petruchio and his man

Grumio is a good case in point, because despite his rising impatience and anger and his use of abusive vocatives, Petruchio keeps strictly to *you*:

(13) Petruchio: [...] Here, sirrah Grumio, knock, I say.
Grumio: Knock, sir? whom should I knock? Is there any man has rebus'd your worship?
Petruchio: Villain, I say, knock me here soundly.
Grumio: Knock you here, sir? Why, sir, what am I, sir, that I should knock you here, sir?
Petruchio: Villain, I say, knock me at this gate, / And rap me well, or I'll knock your knave's pate.
Grumio: My master is grown quarrelsome. I should knock you first, / And then I know after who comes by the worst.
Petruchio: Will it not be? Faith, sirrah, and you'll not knock, I'll ring it. I'll try how you can *sol, fa*, and sing it. [He wrings him by the ears.]
Grumio: Help, [masters], help, my master is mad.
Petruchio: Now knock when I bid you, sirrah villain! (SHR 1, 2, 5–19)

As address to a woman, *sirrah* is only used once when Cleopatra orders her attendant to go: "Sirrah Iras, go" (ANT 5, 2, 229). That no reprimand is involved here becomes clear by Cleopatra's affectionate farewell: "Come then, and take the last warmth of my lips. Farewell, kind Charmian, Iras, long farewell" (5, 2, 290–292).

Although *you* as an address pronoun clearly dominates, as far as the overall politeness of addresses involving *sirrah* is concerned it can be stated that *sirrah* is used predominantly in orders or directives from masters to personnel. These requests are worded directly in form of short imperatives. Imperatives alone account for 61 occurrences of *sirrah*. The verbs most frequently involved are *go* (18 times), *come* (13 times) and *get you/thee gone, be gone* (6 times); as a pronoun *you* occurs usually:

(14) Slender [to his servant Simple]: Go, sirrah, for all you are my man, go wait upon my cousin Shallow. (WIV 1, 1, 271–272)

(15) Dogberry [to Borachio]: Come you hither, sirrah; a word in your ear, sir. (ADO 4, 2, 26–27)

(16) Shylock [to Launcelot, a clown, servant to Shylock]: Go you before me, sirrah, / Say I will come. (MV 2, 5, 38–39)

(17) Countess [to clown]: What does this knave here? Get you gone, sirrah! (AWW 1, 3, 8–9)

Even more directly are verbless imperatives which despite their brusqueness also often make use of *you:*

(18) Cornwall: Peace, sirrah! You beastly knave, know you no reverence?
Kent: Yes, sir, but anger hath a privilege. (LR 2, 2, 68–70)

6.3.1.9   *Summary: Titles of courtesy*

On the basis of the contingency Tables 6–12, a ratio for the co-occurring pronouns has been computed in order to categorise the address forms as "*you* words" or as "*thou* words".The results are shown in Graph 1.[16]

The diagram shows that all the titles of courtesy have a large surplus of Y pronouns. This result was to be expected on the basis of the extant secondary literature. However, the above terms also show a gradient of "*you*fulness". Out of the titles investigated, *liege* is the title that shows the least variation in the use of co-occurring pronouns at all, the T pronouns being outnumbered by Y pronouns at a ratio of 1:27. This almost exclusive use of Y pronouns can be attributed to the exposed social rank of the persons who are addressed in this way. The address *(my) liege*, often preceded by honorific adjectives is reserved for the sovereign, which implies that all his subjects from the queen to commoners have to give deference.[17]

Williams provides a convincing explanation why T pronouns do not occur in the company of titles. Before the distinction between *you* and *thou* became fully operational in the fourteenth century "a speaker who addressed a single person as *Master* or *sir* would not use *you* to that person, because the grammatically correct form would have been *thou*. And in a situation that called for a plain first name (e.g., *Hob*), the speaker would of course have used the same *thou*" (1992:92). In the course of time the use of a respectful title almost automatically triggered the usage of the polite pronoun *you*, and as *you* was gaining ground against *thou*, titles like "*sir* and *Master* were increasingly used to address speakers at all social levels, so would the use of the respectful *you* increase, particularly because respectful titles eventually 'conditioned' the form of the pronoun." Williams claims that for instance the correlation between *you* and *sir* finally became so strong that despite the fact that "in a context previously colored by *thou* there appeared a *sir*, that *sir* momentarily elicited a following *you*, but once past that *sir*, the text would then return to *thou*." (ibid.).

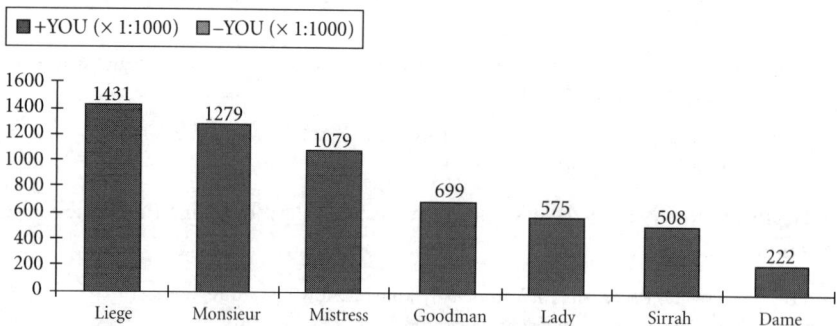

Graph 1. Titles of courtesy.

1H4 1, 2 is an impressive case in point. The pronoun of rapport between Falstaff and the Prince of Wales has been *thou* throughout when the following dialogue takes place:

> Falstaff: But, Hal, I *prithee* trouble me no more with vanity; I would to God *thou* and I knew where a commodity of good names were to be bought. An old lord of the council rated me the other day in the street about *you, sir,* but I marked him not, [...].
> Prince: *Thou* didst well, for wisdom cries out in the streets, and no man regards it.
> Falstaff: O, *thou* hast damnable iteration, and art indeed able to corrupt a saint.
> (1H4 1, 2, 81–91)

In comparison to *liege, monsieur* is a fairly infrequent title of courtesy that is almost exclusively given to foreigners. Probably due to their foreignness, or, in the case of the fairies in MND and Caliban in TMP, their outlandishness, and the resulting social distance, *you* is the pronoun that co-occurs without exception.

Out of the four female titles of courtesy (*mistress, lady, goodwife* and *dame*), *mistress* is the one that attracts the most Y forms. This result is slightly surprising because the term covers a broader social spectrum than *lady*. The range of *mistress* reaches from queen to bawd. This not withstanding, the ratio of *you:thou* is 12:1. From this we can conclude that *mistress* as a title of courtesy is applied to almost any woman irrespective of her social rank, and as a consequence of this, *you* as a pronoun has moved down the social ladder and has become the default pronoun in conjunction with *mistress.*

In contrast to this, *lady* is still a little more restricted in its usage, as it is usually given as address only to women of some social standing. The examples pertaining to women of a lower social rank are fewer and can also imply an ironic stance. The instances of *lady* + *thou* fall into the two categories of wooing and courting and those exposing male social superiority from husband to wife or from father to daughter.

As a title of courtesy, *dame* is almost negligible. Although *de jure* it still was a courtesy title for a knight's wife at the beginning of the 17th century, it had undergone a broadening of meaning accompanied by pejoration, as it could be used almost as a contemptuous address to scolding women. This precarious state is also borne out by the use of co-occurring pronouns: the 3 T pronouns and the 5 Y pronouns are well balanced.

Goodwife is even rarer, for it only appears twice in the entire corpus as a form of address for middle-class women and is not accompanied by personal pronouns. Its male counterpart, *goodman* is also not frequent. The ratio of *you:thou* is 5:1. The instances in the corpus indicate that the term is not only the usual form of address among middle-class neighbours, but that it is also used from above with an ironic or slightly patronising attitude.

The most problematic title in this set is *sirrah*, because when given to grown-ups it usually expresses contempt, reprimand, or some other negative attitude. Despite these facts it is usually treated as a title of courtesy, perhaps for its connection to *sir*.[18] These usually negative emotions on the part of the speaker notwithstanding, *you* clearly predominates as co-occurring address pronoun, with a ratio of more than 3:1. This use of pronouns probably justifies its inclusion in the category of courtesy titles, because in comparison to the terms of abuse (cf. 6.3.6) it shows a marked difference in the use of co-occurring pronouns.

6.3.2   Terms of address indicating occupation

6.3.2.1   *Doctor*

Schmidt and Sarrazin gloss the meaning of *doctor* in Shakespeare's works as follows: "one who has passed the degrees of a faculty, a learned man. [...] Especially a physician." Replogle mentions that physicians appear in only five of the plays and that they have only minor roles. "Medicine was thought less suitable than law as fit employment for gentlemen, but it was generally considered acceptable" (1967:41).

In the corpus *doctor* has an overall frequency of 71 tokens (42 verse; 29 prose). In 29 of these instances *doctor* is used as an address, and the pronoun that co-occurs most often is *you*, with 17 instances. There are only 3 cases of *thou* (see Table 13).

Table 13. T and Y pronouns co-occurring with *doctor*

	T pronoun	Y pronoun	combined
Comedies	–	10	10
Histories	–	–	–
Tragedies	3	7	10
Total	**3**	**17**	**20**

As a term of address, *doctor* most prominently features in the Comedies, especially in WIV, where it functions as address to the French physician Dr. Caius. In this genre it co-occurs exclusively with *you* (10 times). Furthermore, as the other appellations in this set, *doctor* is often preceded by the adjective *good* and the title of honour *master*. In the Histories it is not applied as an address at all. In the Tragedies, MAC and CYM show some interesting cases of pronoun switching:

(1)   Shallow: [God] save you, Master Doctor Caius!
      Page: Now, good Master Doctor!
      Slender: Give you good morrow, sir. (WIV 2, 3, 18–21)

(2)   Macbeth: How does your patient, doctor?
      Doctor: Not so sick, my lord, / As she is troubled with thick-coming fancies, /

That keep her from her rest. [...]
Macbeth: Throw physic to the dogs, I'll none of it. [...] If thou couldst, doctor, cast / The water of my land, find her disease [...]. (MAC 5, 3, 37–51)

(3) Queen: Now, master doctor, have you brought those drugs?
Cornelius: Pleaseth your Highness, ay. Here they are, madam. [Presenting a small box.] But I beseech your Grace, without offense (My conscience bids me ask), wherefore you have / Commanded of me these most poisonous compounds, [...].
Queen: I wonder, doctor, / Thou ask'st me such a question / Have I not been thy pupil long? [...]. Doctor, your service for this time is ended, / Take your own way. [...]
Cornelius: [Aside]: I do not like her. [...].
Queen: No further service, doctor, / Until I send for thee.
Cornelius: I humbly take my leave. (CYM 1, 5, 4–45)

While the use of *master* and *you* in WIV indicates that the speakers are on the same footing, the exchanges between Macbeth and the Doctor and between the Queen and the Physician show asymmetrical usage of pronouns. The answers of the doctors to their sovereigns are very deferential, only in an aside does Cornelius voice his true opinion: "I do not like her". The sovereigns begin their dialogues by the more distanced *you* and switch over to *thou*, or in the case of the Queen back to *you* in order to signal the end of the conversation and, eventually, as Cornelius does not make haste to be gone (he is still on stage giving his aside) she resumes with an irritable *thee*.

6.3.2.2 *Esquire*

On the authority of Schmidt and Sarrazin, *esquire* has the meaning: "a title of dignity, next in degree below a knight."[19] Stoll (1989: 107) mentions that in the 16th and 17th centuries, *esquire* and *gentleman* are predominantly used in written documents as titles following a name. In spoken language they are never used in address; there *master* is used instead.

In the corpus it only has a frequency of 7 tokens (3 verse; 4 prose) and it does not occur as address at all, only as a term of self-reference (used exclusively by Shallow, a country justice, in WIV and 2H4) or in reports (about Sir Alexander Iden in 2H6). By adding *esquire* to his surname, Robert Shallow wants to emphasise his social position as a country justice, for whom *esquire* is the appropriate address. Furthermore, he is indignant about the presumptuous "Sir John Falstaff" and wants to sue him for his offences. In WIV "only Falstaff, and possibly (though improbably) Fenton, would have outranked him" (Replogle 1967: 39).

(1) Shallow: [...] I will make a Star Chamber matter of it. If he were twenty Sir John Falstaffs, he shall not abuse Robert Shallow, esquire. [...] Believe me, Robert Shallow, esquire, saith he is wrong'd. (WIV 1, 1, 1–4; 106–107)

(2)   Bardolph: I beseech you, which is Justice Shallow?
Shallow: I am Robert Shallow, sir, a poor esquire of this country, and one of the
King's justices of the peace. What is your good pleasure with me?
Bardolph: My captain, sir, commends him to you [...].[20] (2H4 3, 2, 56–60)

6.3.2.3   *Justice*

Despite its overall frequency with 172 tokens (146 verse; 26 prose) *justice* is used
rather seldom as a term of address in Shakespeare's plays, as there are only 6
instances of this use. Out of these 6 tokens only 2 co-occur with address pronouns.
In WIV, the Host calls Justice Shallow good-humouredly and ironically "Cavaleiro
Justice", the others address him as *master*. In 2H4, the Lord Chief Justice is also
addressed as either *My Lord Chief Justice* or plainly as *justice*:

(1)   Host: How now, bully-rook? thou'rt a gentleman. Cavaleiro Justice, I say! [...]
Tell him, Cavaleiro Justice; tell him, bully-rook. (WIV 2, 1, 194; 198)

(2)   Warwick: How now, my Lord Chief Justice, whither away? (2H4 5, 2, 1)

(3)   Prince: You are right justice, and you weigh this well, [...]. (2H4 5, 2, 102)

6.3.2.4   *Lieutenant*

Schmidt and Sarrazin give the following meaning: "an officer who supplies the place
of a superior in his absence."[21]

Lieutenant has an absolute frequency of 43 tokens (23 verse; 20 prose), and is
used as an address 26 times, out of which it co-occurs 11 times with *you* and 3 times
with *thou* (see Table 14).

Table 14. T and Y pronouns co-occurring with *lieutenant*

	T pronoun	Y pronoun	combined
Comedies	–	–	–
Histories	2	2	4
Tragedies	1	9	10
Total	3	11	14

Like other forms of address out of this category, *lieutenant* also occurs only in
a limited number of plays, viz.: TMP, the History Plays, ANT, and especially in
OTH, where it is employed by various characters to address Cassio, "an honorable
gentleman". Additionally, the term is very often accompanied by the adjective *good*
and is also used in the combination *Master Lieutenant* (see examples (4)–(5)).

Apart from the social rank of the person addressed, the choice of pronoun
seems to mirror the social distance and the emotive state and type of discourse

between the interlocutors, for in OTH Montano, Iago and also Emilia all address Cassio as *(you)* ... *(good) lieutenant*:

(1) Iago [to Cassio]: You are in the right. Good night, lieutenant, I must to the watch. (OTH 2, 3, 333)

(2) Emilia [to Cassio]: Good morrow, good lieutenant. I am sorry / For your displeasure; but all will sure be well. (OTH 3, 1, 41–42)

If these ritualised instances of greeting formulae are contrasted with the highly emotive speech of Othello to Iago, after the latter has carefully insinuated that there may be something going on between Othello's wife Desdemona and his lieutenant Michael Cassio when he points out that he has seen a handkerchief, once given by Othello to his wife and now "see[n] Cassio wipe his beard with", the impact of the use of *thou* becomes clear:

(3) Othello: Damn her, lewd minx! O, damn her, damn her! Come go with me apart, I will withdraw / To furnish me with some swift means of death / For the fair devil. Now art thou my lieutenant.
Iago: I am your own for ever. (OTH 3, 3, 475–479)

Another set of contrastive examples can be taken from the Histories, where in 3H6 the sovereign addresses his subject in an emotive speech as *thou*, whereas Queen Elizabeth in R3 adds politeness markers to her question and says *you* to Lieutenant Brakenbury and addresses him as *master*. Despite the fact that "the person holding the office is of a higher social degree than that correspondent to the title of the office [...] no insult is intended as has been thought; the queen is merely referring to Sir Robert's official capacity" (Replogle 1967: 45):

(4) Queen Elizabeth: Master Lieutenant, pray you, by your leave, / How doth the Prince and my young son of York?
Lieutenant Brakenbury: Right well, dear madam. (R3 4, 1, 13–15)

(5) King Henry: Master Lieutenant, now that God and friends / Have shaken Edward from the regal seat, / And turn'd my captive state to liberty, / My fear to hope, my sorrows unto joys, / At our enlargement what are thy due fees?
Lieutenant: Subjects may challenge nothing of their sov'reigns, / But if an humble prayer may prevail, / I then crave pardon of your Majesty. (3H6 4, 6, 1–8)

6.3.2.5 *Nurse*

Schmidt and Sarrazin give the following meanings:

1. a woman that suckles or tends an infant
2. one who brings up, or takes a motherly care of another
3. Metaphorically, that which brings up, nourishes, or causes to grow

Nurse has an absolute frequency of 88 tokens (78 verse; 10 prose). Out of the above three meanings it is employed as address only in the sense of 'female attendant, confidante'. Apart from ROM, this sense is restricted to two other occurrences in TIT (4, 2, 83; 86). In these two plays *nurse* is used 34 times as address and it occurs 14 times with *thou* and only once with *you* (see Table 15).

Table 15. T and Y pronouns co-occurring with *nurse*

	T pronoun	Y pronoun	combined
Comedies	–	–	–
Histories	–	–	–
Tragedies	14	1	15
Total	**14**	**1**	**15**

In ROM, the nurse to Juliet, whose name is not given, is always addressed in this way (*nurse* + *thou*) by everyone, with just one exception when Juliet addresses her in the presence of her parents and not in the intimacy of private dialogue (see example (4)). The nurse's status as servant to Capulet and his wife is mirrored in the sentence structure which consists predominantly of (verbless) imperatives using motion verbs such as *come*, *give* and *go* (see examples (1)–(2)). However, the relationship between the nurse and Romeo and Juliet is closer and more amicable, as she acts as a go-between for them and carries secret messages. Linguistically, this is indicated by the adjectives *good* and *sweet*, e.g. in 2, 5, 18–54 when Juliet gets more and more impatient to hear news from Romeo and the old woman just tells her about her weariness, Juliet adorns her imperatives by polite discourse markers and positive adjectives (see example (1)):

(1)   Juliet: O honey nurse, what news? [...] Now, good sweet nurse — O Lord, why lookest thou sad? [...] Nay, come, I pray thee speak, good, good nurse, speak. [...] Sweet, sweet, sweet nurse, tell me, what says my love? (ROM 2, 5, 18–54)

(2)   Lady Capulet: [...] Nurse, give leave a while, / We must talk in secret. Nurse, come back again, I have rememb'red me, thou s' hear our counsel. (ROM 1, 3, 6–9)

(3)   Capulet: Nurse! Wife! What ho! What, nurse, I say! (ROM 4, 4, 24)

(4)   Juliet: Nurse, will you go with me into my closet / To help me sort such needful ornaments / As you think fit to furnish me tomorrow? (ROM 4, 2, 33–35)

6.3.2.6   *Parson*

Neither Schmidt and Sarrazin nor Böhm (1936) make any mention of *parson*; it has an absolute frequency of 15 tokens (0 verse; 15 prose). As address it occurs 6 times and collocates 3 times with *you* and only once with *thou* (see Table 16), the remaining 2 cases being without a pronoun. Furthermore, its usage is very restricted, as it appears only in three of the Comedies, namely WIV, AWW and TN.

Table 16. T and Y pronouns co-occurring with *parson*

	T pronoun	Y pronoun	combined
Comedies	1	3	4
Histories	–	–	–
Tragedies	–	–	–
Total	1	3	4

The term is never used on its own, but only in combination with other titles and names, viz. almost exclusively in the combination *master parson* (10 times), or together with the first name, as in "Parson Hugh" (WIV 1, 4, 77).

In WIV, the term is used as address to Sir Hugh Evans, a Welsh parson, and appears mostly in formulaic discourse of greeting, enquiring about the welfare of the speaker, etc.:

(1) Shallow: How now, Master Parson? Good morrow, good Sir Hugh. Keep a gamester from the dice, and a good student from his book, and it is wonderful.
Slender: [Aside.]: Ah, sweet Anne Page!
Page: [God] save you, good Sir Hugh!
Evans: [God] pless you from his mercy sake, all of you!
Shallow: What? the sword and the word? Do you study them both, Master Parson? (WIV 3, 1, 36–45)

6.3.2.7   Summary: Terms of address indicating occupation

According to Stoll (1989: 167f.) in Elizabethan drama all occupational titles, viz. "Berufs-, Amts- und Funktionsbezeichnungen", have the prime function of additional information for the spectators. Within a given play, they are usually directed at the carrier of a function that is essential to drive the plot forward. In terms of politeness theory "the professional or occupational titles [...] are not far from the negative extreme" (Nevalainen and Raumolin-Brunberg 1995: 557), and Kopytko states that "titles such as *captain, general* or *lieutenant* only count as deferential when used by a person of lower social rank" (1993a: 53).

If the preceding six forms of address indicating occupation constitute a valid sample for the different walks of life in the medical profession, among the lower gentry, the army, domestic service and the lower clergy as depicted in Shakespeare's plays, the first observation that comes to mind when this set is compared to the titles of courtesy is that all these forms of address are not very frequent. This is due to the fact that the characters representing these professions only appear in a limited number of plays for specific, and often slightly comic purposes, at least in the case of *esquire*, which is not used as address at all, and also to a certain degree of *justice* when it pertains to Master Shallow.

Apart from the nurse in ROM, who is almost exclusively addressed as *thou*, either as a menial from above, or confidentially by Juliet, and which can be explained by the relatively small social distance that exists between mistress and confidante, all the other vocatives indicating occupation fall into a different category. They show a greater social distance and appear in emotionally and psychologically 'neutral' situations. As a result of this, *you* prevails as co-occurring pronoun. Thus, with the only exception of *nurse*, all the other vocatives *doctor, justice, lieutenant* and *parson* can be classified as "*you* words". Depending on the majority form of normal rapport between interlocutors, the other pronoun in the dyad, i.e. *you* in the case of *nurse* and *thou* in all the other cases, is employed to signal a deviation from the "norm" which can be induced by the situation, the message, or momentary shifts in (mutual) attitude. Graph 2 shows the "*you*fulness" of the vocatives in declining order.

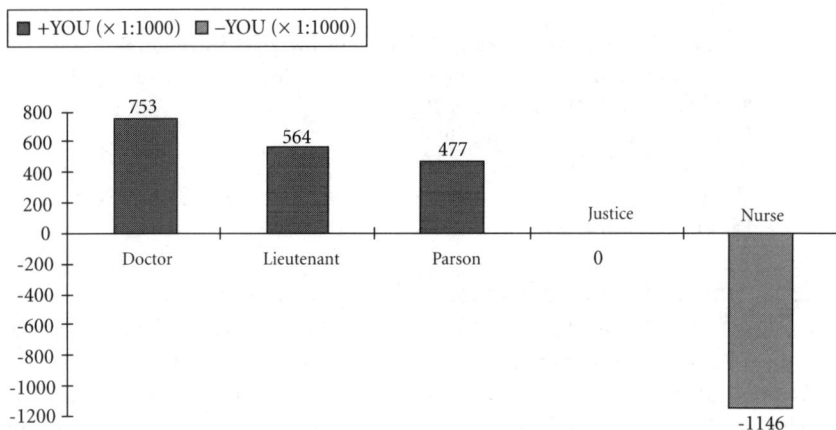

Graph 2. Terms of address indicating occupation.

6.3.3   Terms of family relationship

6.3.3.1   *Brother*
According to Schmidt and Sarrazin *brother* is used in various senses:

1.   one born of the same father and mother
     b. = half-brother

2. = brother-in-law
3. term of endearment for friends
4. fellow-creature
5. associate, colleague [...]. Especially kings calling each other *brothers*
6. a member of a religious order

Brother has an absolute frequency of 537 tokens (450 verse; 87 prose). As address it occurs 73 times in combination with pronouns, in fact 21 times with *thou* and 52 times with *you*. The distribution of pronouns among genres is as shown in Table 17.

Table 17. T and Y pronouns co-occurring with *brother*

	T pronoun	Y pronoun	combined
Comedies	2	17	19
Histories	11	22	33
Tragedies	8	13	21
Total	21	52	73

The Comedies show the smallest numbers of *thous*. The chi-square value for the distribution among the genres is 4.337 (<0.10 with 2 df). The communicative function of *brother* becomes clear by looking at the sentence types and situations in which the term occurs. Very often *brother* is used in formulaic discourse of greeting and parting:

(1) Don John [the bastard]:[22] My lord and brother, God save you!
Don Pedro, Prince of Aragon: Good den, brother. (ADO 3, 2, 80–81)

(2) Rosalind: God save you, brother.
Oliver: And you, fair sister. (AYL 5, 2, 17–18)

(3) Montague [to York]: Brother, I go; I'll win them, fear it not. And thus most humbly I do take my leave. (3H6 1, 2, 60–61)

(4) Cassius: Good night, my lord.
Brutus: Good night, good brother.
Titinius, Messenger: Good night, Lord Brutus. (JC 4, 3, 236–238)

(5) Caesar [to Pompey]: [...] Pompey, good night. Good brother, / Let me request you [off], our graver business / Frowns at this levity. (ANT 2, 7, 119–121)

In these cases differences in social standing are not expressed by pronouns but by showing deference through the choice of the appropriate title. The immediate force of commands is often redressed by positive adjectives. In fact, *brother* always co-occurs with positive adjectives, e.g. *(my) dear, gentle, good, noble, (most) royal, sweet* and *worthy*.

As mentioned above, *thou* is clearly the minority form in the Comedies. It can indicate contempt, as in AYL when Orlando and Oliver have been quarrelling and Orlando feels insulted:

(6)   Orlando: [...] I have as much of my father in me as you, albeit I confess your coming before me is nearer to his reverence.
Oliver: What, boy! [Strikes him.]
Orlando: Come, come, elder brother, you are too young in this. [Collaring him.]
Oliver: Wilt thou lay hands on me, villain?
Orlando: I am no villain; I am the youngest son of Sir Rowland de Boys. He was my father, and he is thrice a villain that says such a father begot villains. Wert thou not my brother, I would not take this hand from thy throat till this other had pull'd out thy tongue for saying so. Thou hast rail'd on thyself.
(AYL 1, 1, 49–62)[23]

In the Histories, the only play that shows a very mixed picture of pronoun usage is 3H6 with 8 instances of *thou* and 9 of *you*. This could possibly be attributed to the fact that pronoun usage is implemented to convey the different attitudes and allegiances of the four sons of Richard Plantagenet, Duke of York and the Marquess of Montague and his older brother the Earl of Warwick. In stark contrast to the above example of an angry *thou*, the *thous* exchanged in 3H6 are clearly a token of intimacy:

(7)   Richard: Father, tear the crown from the usurper's head.
Edward: Sweet father, do so, set it on your head.
Montague: Good brother, as thou lov'st and honorest arms, / Let's fight it out, and not stand cavilling thus.
Richard: Sound drums and trumpets, and the King will fly.
York: Sons, peace! (3H6 1, 1, 114–118)

The address pronoun exchanged between "fellow kings" is *you(r)* or royal *our:*

(8)   King Philip of France [to King John]: Brother of England, you blaspheme in this. (JN 3, 1, 161)

(9)   King Henry: Unto our brother France, and to our sister, Health and fair time of day; [...]
French King: Right joyous are we to behold your face, / Most worthy brother England, fairly met! (H5 5, 2, 2–10)

In the Tragedies, *thou* performs a similar function as in the Histories, because the normal pronoun mutually exchanged between brothers is *you*, e.g. between Edgar and Edmund in LR. The only play to make use of *thou* for mutual exchange between brothers on close terms with each other is TIT, as Titus and Marcus Andronicus and Titus' sons Martius and Quintus address each other with *thou*.[24] Apart from this, *thou* is used sparingly, probably for the dramatic effect of heightened, almost solemn emotions at the catastrophe in the final scenes of ROM when the enemies are reconciled:

(10) Prince: Where be these enemies? Capulet! Montague! See what scourge is laid
upon your hate, [...] All are punish'd.
Capulet: O brother Montague, give me thy hand. This is my daughter's jointure,
for no more / Can I demand.[25]
Montague: But I can give thee more, For I will [raise] her statue in pure gold,
[...]. (ROM 5, 3, 291–299)

This analysis shows that the normal pronoun of rapport between brothers is *you*.
Again, there are genre differences in pronoun use, as *thou* is hardly used at all in the
Comedies. In the Histories and Tragedies the use of *thou* is concentrated on two
plays, namely 3H6 and TIT, both early plays. In ROM *thou* expresses exalted
feelings of grief in the final scene of the play.

6.3.3.2 *Cousin*

Cousin is used as address not only to cousins proper, but for various other relations
as well. Schmidt and Sarrazin give the following sense divisions:

1. the son or daughter of an uncle or aunt
   a. masc.
   b. femin.
2. any kinsman or kinswoman
   = nephew
   = niece
   = uncle
   = brother-in-law
   = grandchild
3. a title given by princes to other princes and distinguished noblemen

Stoll (1989: 184) mentions that especially in the Histories and in MAC, *cousin* is
employed to signal intimacy, friendship or familiarity, however, in contrast to *coz*
it is the more formalised, "official" term.

With 310 tokens (235 verse; 75 prose) the full form is by far more frequent than
its abbreviation *coz*. The ratio between *you* and *thou* is 80 *you* tokens in comparison
to only 34 *thou* tokens (see Table 18). The distribution of the address pronouns
again shows a marked deviance from genre to genre.[26]

This distribution reveals that *you* almost unanimously co-occurs with *cousin* in
the Comedies. The only "couple" to switch back and forth between *you* and *thou* are
Rosalind and Celia in AYL. Otherwise, irrespective of the meaning of *cousin*, *you* is
used consistently, as e.g. mutually between the cousins Shallow and Slender in WIV.
However, different degrees of politeness are expressed by adorning the vocative
expression with various epithets. In most cases the vocative stands alone or is
followed by first and/or surname:

Table 18. T and Y pronouns co-occurring with *cousin*

	T pronoun	Y pronoun	combined
Comedies	2	16	18
Histories	17	41	58
Tragedies	15	23	38
Total	**34**	**80**	**114**

(1)   Shallow: Ay, cousin Slender, and *Custa-lorum.* (WIV 1, 1, 7)
      Slender: Where's Simple, my man? can you tell, cousin? (WIV 1, 1, 134–135)
      Shallow: Cousin Abraham Slender, can you love her? (WIV 1, 1, 232)

On the other hand, *cousin* given as a title by princes to other princes shows deference by means of positive adjectives:

(2)   Duke [to Escalus, an ancient lord]: And you, my noble and well-warranted
      cousin, / Whom it concerns to hear this matter forth, […]. (MM 5, 1, 254–255)

As can be inferred from Table 18, the Histories and Tragedies present a more mingled
picture. The first difference to be noted is that apart from the second person
pronouns, plural *our* is given from the sovereign to relations or other princes:

(3)   King Richard [to Bullinbrook]: What doth our cousin lay to Mowbray's charge?
      (R2, 1, 1, 84; cf. also R2 1, 2, 46; 1, 4, 10; 5, 3, 24, 29; H5 1, 2, 235; 5, 2, 4; R3 3, 1, 101)

In HAM, King Claudius addresses Hamlet in this way:

(4)   King: How fares our cousin Hamlet? (HAM 3, 2, 92)[27]

In the History Plays, the vocative *cousin* is often followed by a reference to the duke-
or earldom in the form of *cousin (of) N* [name of duke- or earldom]:

(5)   King Richard [to Bullinbrook]: Cousin of Herford, what dost thou object /
      Against the Duke of Norfolk, Thomas Mowbray? (R2 1, 1, 28–29)

(6)   Lancaster: Come, cousin Westmerland, […]. (1H4 5, 4, 15)

(7)   King Henry: Follow, good cousin Warwick. (H5 4, 7, 175)

(8)   King: Cousin of York, / We here discharge your Grace from being Regent / I' th'
      parts of France, […]. (2H6 1, 1, 65–66)

(9)   King Henry: Ah, cousin York, would thy best friends did know / How it doth
      grieve me that thy head is here! (3H6 2, 2, 54–55)

As being related to each other is a permanent social feature, changes in address
pronouns between two cousins signal shifts in emotional attitudes. This can be
illustrated by the relationship that holds between King Richard the Second, Henry
Bullinbrook, Duke of Herford and the Duke of Aumerle, cousin of Richard II,

whom he supports against his other cousin Bullinbrook in R2. The shifts in attitude are indicated by the combination of address pronouns and adjectives in the way that positive adjectives such as *(my) fair, gentle, good* and *noble* co-occur with *you*, whereas negative adjectives such as *discomfortable* and those expressing pity or compassion co-occur with *thou*:

(10)   Bullinbrook: My loving lord, I take my leave of you; / Of you, my noble cousin, Lord Aumerle; […]. (R2 1, 3, 63–64)

(11)   King Richard: Aumerle, thou weep'st, my tender-hearted cousin! (R2 3, 3, 160)

(12)   King Richard [to Bullinbrook]: Fair cousin, you debase your princely knee / To make the base earth proud with kissing it. (R2 3, 3, 190–191)

The same tendency can be observed in TNK as regards the shifts in the relationship between the two cousins Palamon and Arcite, who are at first devoted friends and then turn into deadly enemies because of their love to Emilia.[28]

(13)   Palamon: How do you, noble cousin? (TNK 2, 2, 1)

(14)   Palamon: […] falsest cousin / That ever blood made kin, call'st thou her thine? (TNK 3, 1, 37–38)

(15)   Arcite: We shall find / Too many hours to die in, gentle cousin. If you be seen, you perish instantly / For breaking prison, […]. (TNK 3, 6, 112–113)

(16)   Palamon: Know, weak cousin, I love Emilia, and in that I'll bury / Thee and all crosses else. (TNK 3, 6, 125–126)

A further indicator of mutual attitudes between interlocutors is the use of exclamations. In the context of *cousin* there are a number of exclamatives to be found that indicate an emotive reaction of the speaker in relation to the message or the situation; the most frequent being *O* that occurs in the context of *thou*:

(17)   King John [to Bastard]: O my gentle cousin, / Hear'st thou the news abroad, who are arriv'd? (JN 4, 2, 159–160)

(18)   King John [to Bastard]: O cousin, thou art come to set mine eye. (JN 5, 7, 51)

(19)   King Duncan [to Macbeth]: O worthiest cousin! The sin of my ingratitude even now / Was heavy on me. Thou art so far before, / That swiftest wing of recompense is slow / To overtake thee. (MAC 1, 4, 14–18)

Thus, pronoun usage in connection with *cousin* shows structural and genre specificities in that again the Comedies clearly favour *you* as co-occurring pronoun. When given as a title from princes to other princes, *you* is also employed. As a royal prerogative, *our cousin* is given as address in the Histories. (Mutual) changes of attitude are expressed by exclamations, adjectives and pronoun switches.

6.3.3.3   Coz

Schmidt and Sarrazin say that *coz* is "a contraction of *cousin*". Similar to the full form *cousin* it is used loosely in various senses:

= uncle
= nephew
= brother-in-law
Used as a title given by princes to other princes and noblemen

In contrast to the "official" term *cousin*, Stoll (1989: 184) characterises *coz* as an intimate address used in private atmosphere. Yet as far as pronoun use is concerned, such a difference in principle cannot be made out, only one in frequency. With its 44 occurrences (24 verse; 20 prose) in the corpus it is far less frequent than the full form *cousin*. When used as address, *coz* appears 14 times with *you*, 8 times with *thou*, and 14 times without a pronoun (see Table 19).

Table 19. T and Y pronouns co-occurring with *coz*

	T pronoun	Y pronoun	combined
Comedies	2	7	9
Histories	3	2	5
Tragedies	3	5	8
Total	**8**	**14**	**22**

Independently from pronoun use, *coz* collocates exclusively with positive adjectives such as *dear(est), fair, gentle, pretty* and *sweet*. For means of emphasis in states of agitation it is often repeated to stress impatience of the speaker and the importance of the news to be broken:

(1) Shallow [to Slender]: Come, coz, come, coz, we stay for you. A word with you, coz; marry, this, coz [...]. (WIV 1, 1, 206–207)

(2) Rosalind [to Celia]: O coz, coz, coz, my pretty little coz, that thou didst know how many fathom deep I am in love! (AYL 4, 1, 205–207)

(3) Arcite [to Palamon]: My coz, my coz, you have been well advertis'd / How much I dare; [...]. (TNK 3, 1, 58–59)

Among cousins, *coz* is exchanged mutually between Shallow and Slender (WIV 1, 1, 206–243), who use *you* exclusively. The exchanges between Celia and Rosalind (AYL) are characterised by pronoun switching (cf. McIntosh 1963a). Romeo and Benvolio use *thou* (ROM 1, 1, 183–207), and Palamon and Arcite, both nephews to King Creon of Thebes, have eight exchanges, in which they use five times *you* and one time *thee* in TNK.

In the sense of brother-in-law, *coz* occurs only once:

(4)   Mortimer [to Hotspur when they discuss the division of the kingdom in three
      parts]: [...] and, dear coz, to you / The remnant northward lying off from Trent.
      (1H4 3, 1, 77–78)

There are only two instances in which *coz* is used from uncle to nephew:

(5)   King John [to his nephew Arthur]: Coz, farewell. (JN 3, 3, 17)

(6)   Tybald: 'Tis he, that villain Romeo.
      Capulet: Content thee, gentle coz, let him alone, [...]. (ROM 1, 5, 64–65)

On the other hand, the cases of asymmetrical use, i.e. when used from "above",
seem to demand a friendly *thou* as in (7) from King Henry to his devoted follower
Westmerland:

(7)   Earl of Westmerland: O that we now had here / But one ten thousand of those
      men in England / That do no work to-day!
      King Henry: What's he that wishes so? My cousin Westmerland? No, my fair
      cousin. [...] No faith, my coz, wish not a man from England. [...]
      King Henry: Thou dost not wish more help from England, coz?
      Westmerland: God's will, my liege, would you and I alone, / Without more help,
      could fight this royal battle! (H5 4, 3, 17–30; 72–75)

6.3.3.4   *Husband*

According to Schmidt and Sarrazin, *husband* is used in the following senses:

1. one who keeps house
2. one careful and economical
3. a husbandman, a tiller of the ground
4. the correlative to wife, a man contracted or married to a woman

In SHR, towards the end of the play the reformed shrew Katherina succinctly
summarises a wife's duties to her husband: "Such duty as the subject owes the
prince, / Even such a woman oweth to her husband" (5, 2, 155–156).[29] Although the
word has an overall frequency of 293 tokens (213 verse; 80 prose), *husband* is not
used very often vocatively, as the 17 tokens clearly reveal. The ratio of address
pronouns is balanced (see Table 20).

Schmidt and Sarrazin's statement that *husband* as the correlative to *wife* is
"often used vocatively [...] but not, it should seem, among persons of rank [...]
except to give the speech a tone of peculiar tenderness and affection" is not entirely
borne out by the corpus data, as Table 20 proves that its use as vocative is rather
limited. Furthermore, when employed vocatively, *husband* is used in all social
classes, e.g. by Mistress Ford to her husband (WIV), Adriana to Antipholus of
Ephesus/Syracuse (ERR), Katherina to Petruchio (SHR), Blanch to Lewis, the

Table 20. T and Y pronouns co-occurring with *husband*

	T pronoun	Y pronoun	combined
Comedies	3	8	11
Histories	4	–	4
Tragedies	1	1	2
Total	**8**	**9**	**17**

Dauphin (JN), the Duchess of York to the Duke of York (R2), Hostess to Pistol (H5), Virgilia to Coriolanus (COR), Lady Macbeth to her husband (MAC), Emilia to Iago (OTH) and by Imogen to Posthumus (CYM).

The attitude towards the partner can be signalled in different ways. When unadorned by adjectives, *husband* can be taken neutrally and usually implies that one is on good terms with one another. In many cases positive adjectives such as *dear(est)*, *gentle*, *good* and *(honey-)sweet* indicate deep and sincere emotions:

(1) Imogen: My dearest husband, I something fear my father's wrath [...]. You must be gone, / And I shall here abide the hourly shot / Of angry eyes, not comforted to live, / But that there is this jewel in the world / That I may see again.
Posthumus: My queen, my mistress! O lady, weep no more, lest I give cause / To be suspected of more tenderness / Than doth become a man. (CYM 1, 1, 85–92)

(2) Hostess: Good husband, come home presently. (H5 2, 1, 88–89)
Hostess: Prithee, honey-sweet husband, let me bring thee to Staines.
Pistol: No; for my manly heart doth ern. (H5 2, 3, 1–3)

(3) Emilia [to Iago]: Alas, what is the matter? What is the matter, husband?
(OTH 5, 1, 111)

That *thou* need not necessarily be a sign of (com-)passion, but also of a relationship turned sour and that "positive adjectives" can be contrived as a strategy of positive politeness is illustrated by the discourse between the Duke and Duchess of York in R2:

(4) Duchess: But now I know thy mind, thou dost suspect / That I have been disloyal to thy bed, / And that he is a bastard, not thy son. Sweet York, sweet husband, be not of that mind, [...].
York: Make way, unruly woman! (R2 5, 2, 104–110)

(5) York: Speak it in French, King, say "*pardonne moy.*"
Duchess: Dost thou teach pardon pardon to destroy? Ah, my sour husband, my hard-hearted lord, / That sets the word itself against the word! (R2 5, 3, 119–122)

Strong emotions can also be expressed by a change of the vocative expression as e.g. when Mistress Ford reacts to the jealousy of her husband: when he searches their bedchamber for the suspected adulterer Falstaff she no longer calls him *husband* but "Master Ford":

(6)   Ford: I cannot find him. May be the knave bragg'd of that he could not compass.
      [...]
      Mrs. Ford: You use me well, Master Ford, do you?
      Ford: Ay, I do so. (WIV 3, 3, 199–203)

The shifting pronoun usage of Adriana, the jealous wife of Antipholus of Ephesus in ERR, who mistakes her husband for his twin brother Antipholus of Syracuse, can be seen as a mirror image to her feelings, which range from reproach and abandonment to forgiveness and loyalty when she is finally reconciled with her true husband once the errors have been resolved.

In SHR, the discourse between Katherina and Petruchio after they have arrived at his country house and when he complains about the food is an example of marital subjugation which illustrates that the former shrew has become an obedient wife:

(7)   Katherina: I pray you, husband, be not so disquiet. The meat was well, if you
      were so contented.
      Petruchio: I tell thee, Kate, 'twas burnt and dried away, / And I expressly am
      forbid to touch it; [...]. (SHR 4, 1, 168–171)

The examples show that pronoun usage in connection with *husband* is again different from genre to genre, with the Comedies showing the highest degree of co-occurring *you* (chi-squared = 6.238; $p > 0.05$ with 2df). Apart from these genre-specific structural differences, *husband* is used vocatively in all social strata, but pronoun use seems to be conditioned by the situation and "negotiable personalities". The overall ratio between *you* and *thou* is well balanced. According to the asymmetrical power relationship between husband and wife this result is quite surprising.

6.3.3.5 *Sister*

Schmidt and Sarrazin give the following meanings:

1. a female born of the same parents
    = sister-in-law
    Term of endearment
2. a female of the same kind or order
    = a nun
    The French queen addressed so by the English king (H5 2, 2, 90)

The OED adds: "5. In the vocative, as a mode of address, chiefly in transferred senses. Also colloq. as a mode of address to an unrelated woman, esp. one whose name is not known."

In the Shakespeare Corpus, *sister* has an absolute frequency of 201 tokens (169 verse, 32 prose). When used as address, it most often co-occurs with *you* (33 times) and only 9 times with *thou* (see Table 21).

These occurrences are not spread evenly over the corpus, for the Comedies and

Table 21. T and Y pronouns co-occurring with *sister*

	T pronoun	Y pronoun	combined
Comedies	1	14	15
Histories	1	5	6
Tragedies	7	14	21
Total	9	33	42

Histories contain only one case each of *thou*, whereas the Tragedies account for 7. However, statistically, this distribution is not significant (chi-squared = 3.782; $p < 0.10$ level of confidence). In addition to that, 2 out of the 7 *thous* in Tragedy occur in the witches' scene in MAC (1, 3), where the three witches address each other in this way:

(1)   1. Witch: Where hast thou been, sister?
      2. Witch: Killing swine.
      3. Witch: Sister, where thou? (MAC 1, 3, 1–3)

Apart from this, *sister* is used:

– from sister to sister, e.g.: Adriana to Luciana (ERR), Bianca to Katherina (SHR), Regan to Goneril (LR), Hippolyta to Emilia (TNK)
– to a sister-in-law, e.g.: Cornwall to Goneril (LR), or King Lewis of France to Bona, sister to the French Queen (3H6), Theseus to Emilia (TNK)
– to a cousin, e.g.: from Rosalind to Celia (AYL)
– from brother to sister, e.g.: Hector to Cassandra (TRO), Laertes to Ophelia (HAM).

These examples illustrate that *sister* is used as an address to a female relation of some social standing. Probably, as a corollary to that, *you* is the normal pronoun of rapport between the interlocutors. Furthermore, *sister* is very often preceded by positive adjectives, especially *beauteous, bounteous, dear(est), fair, good, noble* and *sweet.*

On the other hand, the examples exhibiting *thou* ((2)–(7)), apart from the three parcae in MAC, all occur in scenes of heightened emotion, as in wooing, parting and pleading, when e.g. in (2) Luciana confuses Antipholus of Syracuse with Adriana's husband Antipholus of Ephesus and is distressed when he makes advances to her, or in (3) where the Duchess vainly pleads to Gloucester to take revenge for the murder of her husband.

(2)   Luciana: All this my sister is, or else should be.
      Antipholus of Syracuse: Call thyself sister, sweet, for I am thee: / Thee will I love and with thee lead my life; / Thou hast no husband yet, nor I no wife. Give my thy hand.
      Luciana: O soft, sir, hold you still; I'll fetch my sister to get her good will.
      (ERR 3, 2, 65–70)

(3) Duchess of Gloucester: Farewell, old Gaunt! Thou goest to Coventry, there to be-
     hold / Our cousin Herford and fell Mowbray fight. [...] Farewell, old Gaunt! thy
     sometimes brother's wife / With her companion, grief, must end her life.
     John of Gaunt: Sister, farewell, I must to Coventry. As much good stay with thee *x*
     as go with me! (R2 1, 2, 44–57)

(4) Lucius: Speak, gentle sister, who hath mart'red thee? (TIT 3, 1, 81)

(5) Lucius: Farewell, Lavinia, my noble sister, / O would thou wert as thou tofore
     hast been! But now nor Lucius nor Lavinia lives / But in oblivion and hateful
     griefs. (TIT 3, 1, 292–295)

(6) Caesar: Farewell, my dearest sister, fare thee well, / The elements be kind to thee,
     and make / Thy spirits all of comfort! Fare thee well.
     Octavia: My noble brother! (ANT 3, 2, 39–42)

(7) Laertes: O rose of May! Dear maid, kind sister, sweet Ophelia! O heavens, is't
     possible a young maid's wits / Should be as mortal as [an old] man's life?
     (HAM 4, 5, 158–161)

6.3.3.6 *Wife*

Schmidt and Sarrazin indicate the following sense divisions:

1. any woman of mature age that is or might be married
2. a married woman considered in her relation to her husband

The term has an overall frequency of 466 tokens (352 verse; 114 prose). Similarly to
its relational counterpart *husband, wife* is not often given as an address, as there are
merely 8 instances of *thou*, 9 of *you* and 11 in which no address pronoun co-occurs
(see Table 22).

Corpus evidence illustrates that the term occurs in all social strata, for the range
contains examples of husbands calling their spouses *wife* from all walks of life,
practically from sovereigns to brothel owners, viz.: Masters Page and Ford address
their wives normally in this way (WIV), as do: Antipholus of Ephesus (ERR), the
Duke of York (R2), King Henry VI (2H6), King Edward (R3), Coriolanus (COR),
Capulet (ROM), Brutus (JC), Macbeth (MAC), Posthumus (CYM) and also the
pandar to his wife, the bawd, in PER.

Table 22. T and Y pronouns co-occurring with *wife*

	T pronoun	Y pronoun	combined
Comedies	1	3	4
Histories	4	1	5
Tragedies	3	5	8
Total	8	9	17

The figure of Sly, a drunken tinker in the induction to SHR, comically expresses how a respectable couple should, according to decorum, address each other. In so doing, he serves as a persona to emphasise the importance of correct address in Elizabethan society. But on the other hand, since he is merely under the illusion of being a lord and having a wife (a page dressed as a woman) and attendants, he simultaneously functions as a caricature, because he unwittingly reveals his low social station through his difficulties in coming to terms with his new rank of a lord and the rules of civility:

(1)   Sly: Are you my wife and will not call me husband? My men should call me "lord"; I am your goodman.
Page: My husband and my lord, my lord and husband, I am your wife in all obedience.
Sly: I know it well. What must I call her?
Lord: Madam.
Sly: Al'ce madam, or Joan madam?
Lord: Madam, and nothing else, so lords call ladies.
Sly: Madam wife [...]. (SHR, Induction 2, 103–112)

With reference to the "Falstaff plays", Salmon states that "husbands and wives on good terms call one another by their titles, i.e. *husband* and *wife*, and indicate greater affection by the use of an epithet [...]" (1967:56). In fact, positively connotated adjectives like *gentle, loving* and *sweet* are used rather seldom.

In the Comedies, Master Ford normally calls his spouse *wife + you*, often rather peremptorily in requests (cf. WIV 3, 3, 226; 4, 2, 119). However, when he suspects her of adultery he mock-politely calls her *Mistress Ford*. As a reaction to his unreasonable jealousy she also does not respond with *husband*, but ironically replies: "You use me well, Master Ford, do you?" (WIV 3, 3, 192). When he finally realises his mistake and asks his wife's pardon, Ford switches to *thou*:

(2)   Ford: Come hither, Mistress Ford, Mistress Ford, the honest woman, the modest wife, the virtuous creature, that hath the jealous fool to her husband! I suspect without cause, mistress, do I? (WIV 4, 2, 129–132)

(3)   Ford: Pardon me, wife, henceforth do what thou wilt. I rather will suspect the sun with [cold] / Than thee with wantonness. (WIV 4, 4, 6–7)

Modulation in the use of pronouns according to the message can be illustrated with an example from LLL. When Dumaine, one of the three lords attending upon the King of Navarre, woos Katherine, one of the ladies waiting on the Princess of France, he calls her "you, gentle wife" and when he promises to serve her "true and faithfully" before he can marry her, he switches to an affectionate *thou*:

(4) Dumaine: O, shall I say, I thank you, gentle wife?
Katherine: Not so, my lord, a twelvemonth and a day I'll mark no words that smooth-fac'd wooers say. Come when the King doth to my lady come; / Then if I have much love, I'll give you some.
Dumaine: I'll serve thee true and faithfully till then. (LLL 5, 2, 826–831)

A completely different matrimonial mood is evoked by the dialogue between the Duke and Duchess of York in R2 when the Duchess receives a scornful *thou* and dutifully replies with "my lord" to her husband, she is eventually rebuked by "Peace, foolish woman":

(5) York: Wife, thou art a fool. [...]
Duchess: What is the matter, my lord? [...]
York: Peace, foolish woman. (R2 5, 2, 68–80)

The discourse between Lord and Lady Northumberland in 2H4 shows them a caring couple. First, he affectionately *thous* his wife and she gives him deference by answering with *you*:

(6) Northumberland: I pray thee, loving wife, and gentle daughter, / Give even way unto my rough affairs; / Put not you on the visage of the times, / And be like them to Percy troublesome.
Lady Northumberland: I have given over, I will speak no more; / Do what you will, your wisdom be your guide.
Northumberland: Alas, sweet wife, my honor is at pawn, / And but my going, nothing can redeem it. (2H4 2, 3, 1–8)

That a *you* does not necessarily imply neutrality or even politeness can be shown by the order that the sick King Edward gives to Queen Elizabeth in R3:

(7) King Edward: Madam, yourself is not exempt from this; / Nor you, son Dorset; Buckingham, nor you; / You have been factious one against the other. Wife, love Lord Hastings, let him kiss your hand, / And what you do, do it unfeignedly. (R3 2, 1, 18–22)

Two further examples from R3 reveal that *wife* is not only used as address from husband to wife but also from other persons when the women are defined in terms of being someone's husband:

(8) Duchess: O Harry's wife, triumph not in my woes! God witness with me, I have wept for thine. (R3 4, 4, 59–60)

(9) Queen Margaret: Farewell, York's wife, and queen of sad mischance, [...]. (R3 4, 4, 114)

From the set of Tragedies, ROM is a play to furnish extensive use of *wife*. Normally, Capulet addresses his wife as *wife* + *you* (cf. 3, 4, 15; 3, 5, 137; 141) only when he firmly sets the wedding day for Juliet and takes matters into his own hands he says:

(10)   Capulet: Tush, I will stir about, / And all things shall be well, I warrant thee, wife;
/ Go thou to Juliet, help to deck up her. I'll not to bed to-night; let me alone, I'll
play the huswife for this once. (ROM 4, 2, 39–43)

All the preceding examples of *wife* amply illustrate that the use of co-occurring
pronouns is variable and does not strictly correspond to a fixed pattern, except that
normally the wives deferentially say *you* to their husbands, but that the latter
employ pronouns according to the demands of the pragmatic factors of the
situation. But a wife may also vary between *thou* and *you* when addressing her
husband, for instance: "Lady Percy addresses Hotspur almost always in dialogue
with *you*: but in the higher style of earnest appeal in *I Hen. IV*. ii. 3. 43–67, and in
the familiar 'I'll break *thy* little finger, Harry', *ib*. 90, she uses *thou* throughout. In
the high Roman style, Brutus and Portia use *you*" (Abbott [1870] 1972: 154).

6.3.3.7   Summary: Terms of family relationship

| ■ +YOU (× 1:1000)   ■ –YOU (× 1:1000) |

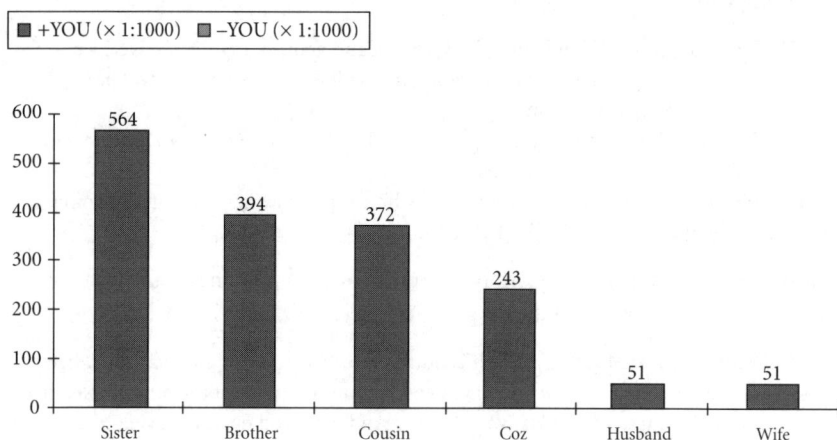

Graph 3. Terms of family relationship.

All the terms of relationship shown in Graph 3 have in common that they exhibit a
higher degree of Y pronouns than T pronouns. However, they can be arranged on
a sliding scale reaching from *brother* and *sister* at the one end to *husband* and *wife* at
the other.

Nevalainen and Raumolin-Brunberg say that "the choice of a relational noun,
which indeed kinship terms and some status nouns are, implies the existence of a
reciprocal relationship, which may either be one of power, and hence of negative
politeness (*father/child, master/servant*), or may express positive reciprocity only
(*sweetheart*)" (1995: 557).

Brother and *sister* show the highest degree of co-occurring *you*; the normal pronoun of rapport between siblings being *you*. Structurally, there are genre differences in the use of *thou*. In both cases, but even more markedly with *brother*, there are hardly any tokens of *thou* to be found in the Comedies. In the other genres, the pronoun *thou* is reserved for situations of deep emotions such as grief and joy or wooing and pleading, often in keynote speeches.

The result that *sister* has turned out to be the most "*you*ful" of the relational nouns differs from the findings of Nevalainen's and Raumolin-Brunberg's investigation of the *Corpus of Early English Correspondence*, in which "it appears that sisters never receive as many deferential forms of address as their brothers" (1995:565). However, they admit that evidence for this in their corpus is scanty.

Cousin is by far the most versatile expression from this set of vocatives because a number of close relatives (first cousins), more distant social equals and also in-laws can be addressed with it. *Cousin* also shows that *thou* hardly ever occurs in the Comedies, and in the Histories and Tragedies its use is practically limited to 3H6 and TIT, both of which are early plays.[30]

In comparison to the full form, abbreviated *coz* shows a slightly lesser degree of co-occurring *you*. Very often, positive feelings are indicated by positive adjectives such as *dear, gentle, pretty* and *sweet*.

Compared to the terms above, *husband* and *wife* are used much less often in direct address. Thus, the scarcity of tokens forbids any genre specific considerations of their distribution. As the use of co-occurring pronouns is almost balanced, both terms allow for what Calvo (1992a) has called "negotiable personalities" which can vary from situation to situation. This hypothesis is supported by the many pronoun switches. On the other hand, this result runs counter to the claim made by power semantics about unequal relationships and to the findings of Finkenstaedt, who claims that in the 16th and 17th centuries husbands so frequently and regularly address their wives with *thou*, but receive a *you* that this pronoun usage can truly be called a "marriage pronoun" (1963:120). However, he did not concentrate on literary sources. Nevalainen and Raumolin-Brunberg (1995:565–568) also stress that the relationship between husband and wife was not an equal one, but add that it was, nonetheless, not as predictable as might be expected.

6.3.4   Generic terms of address

6.3.4.1   *Boy*

Schmidt and Sarrazin outline the main sense divisions as follows:[31]

a male child, a lad
Used as a word of contempt for young men
Familiar term in addressing, or speaking of, grown persons
Often = page, young servant

Corpus evidence shows that *boy* is an address form that is used quite often, as it occurs 352 times (238 verse; 114 prose). However, not all of these instances are forms of direct address. As regards the address pronouns that co-occur with *boy* their distribution is fairly straightforward in favour of *thou* with 82 tokens,[32] and only 18 tokens of *you* (see Table 23). In terms of corpus-internal variation between the different genres no differences are to be made out, as the distribution of T and Y pronouns is even and does not yield any statistically significant deviance:

Table 23. T and Y pronouns co-occurring with *boy*

	T pronoun	Y pronoun	combined
Comedies	21	7	28
Histories	29	4	33
Tragedies	32	7	39
Total	82	18	100

Neither can a clear-cut correlation between the above meanings and pronoun usage be established, because none of the meanings clearly favours one pronoun instead of the other.

As an address to a male child, the intimate *thou* is the most frequent pronoun used by mothers and fathers, for instance in ERR from Egeon to Antipholus of Ephesus, or in 1H6 when Talbot most passionately advises his son to escape imminent death:

(1)   Egeon: But seven years since, in Syracusa, boy, / Thou know'st we parted, but perhaps, my son, / Thou sham'st to acknowledge me in misery. (ERR 5, 1, 321–323)

(2)   Talbot: Now thou art come unto a feast of death, / A terrible and unavoided danger; / Therefore, dear boy, mount on my swiftest horse, / And I'll direct thee how thou shalt escape / By sudden flight. (1H6 4, 5, 7–11)

(3)   Gloucester [to Edmund]: Loyal and natural boy, I'll work the means / To make thee capable. (LR 2, 1, 84–85)

On the other hand, an indirect address accompanied by *thou* can indicate paternal or maternal anger and displeasure:

(4)   Lady Faulconbridge, mother of Robert Faulconbridge and Philip, his half-brother = bastard [to Bastard]: Sir Robert's son! Ay, thou unreverend boy, Sir Robert's son! / Why scorn'st thou at Sir Robert? (JN 1, 1, 227–228)

JN provides more examples that illustrate differences in social distance expressed through different pronouns. For this, Arthur, the nephew to King John with a claim to the throne, is a good case in point. His mother, Constance, *thous* him. Hubert de Burgh, who is ordered by King John to murder the young prince, says *you* to him:

(5) Constance: But thou art fair, and at thy birth, dear boy, / Nature and Fortune join'd to make thee great. (JN 3, 1, 51–52)

(6) Hubert: Come, boy, prepare yourself.
Arthur: Is there no remedy?
Hubert: None, but to lose your eyes. (JN 4, 1, 89–91)

Examples (7)–(8) show that princes even when they are reprimanded are addressed with *boy* accompanied by *you*:

(7) Northumberland [to Harry Percy]: Have you forgot the Duke of [Herford], boy?
Percy: No, my good lord, for that is not forgot / Which ne'er I did remember. (R2 2, 3, 36–37)

(8) King Edward [to Prince]: Peace, willful boy, or I will charm your tongue. *NB*
(3H6 5, 5, 31)

"'Boy' as would seem obvious, was chiefly a chronological appellation, but because of the common Elizabethan practice of keeping a number of adolescents and children as servants and addressing them with this word it acquired an additional connotation of subservience" (Replogle 1967:65). Those cases in which *boy* is used contemptibly, should, according to theory, prefer *thou*. While, generally speaking, this is true (see examples (9)–(11)), there are also some remarkable exceptions, especially when *boy* is preceded by more formal titles such as *sir* and *goodman* as in (12)–(14), which in comparison to the social station of the persons addressed in this way adds to the insult. Being belittled and taunted provokes a violent reaction as in (10):

(9) Hostess [to Dr. Caius]: Thou art a Castalion-King-Urinal! Hector of Greece, my boy! (WIV 2, 3, 33–34)

(10) Coriolanus: Hear'st thou, Mars?
Aufidius: Name not the god, thou boy of tears!
Coriolanus: Ha?
Aufidius: No more.
Coriolanus: Measureless liar, thou hast made my heart / Too great for what contains it. "Boy"? O slave! (COR 5, 6, 99–103)

(11) Plantagenet: Now, by this maiden blossom in my hand, I scorn thee and thy fashion, peevish boy.
Suffolk: Turn not thy scorns this way, Plantagenet. (1H6 2, 4, 75–77)

(12) Claudio: Away, I will not have to do with you.
Leonato: Canst thou so daff me? Thou hast kill'd my child. If thou kill'st me, boy, thou shalt kill a man.
Antonio: He shall kill two of us, and men indeed; But that's no matter, let him kill one first. Win me and wear me, let him answer me. Come follow me, boy;

come, sir boy, come follow me. Sir boy, I'll whip you from your foining fence, /
Nay, as I am a gentleman, I will. (ADO 5, 1, 77–85)

(13)   Tybald: It fits when such a villain is a guest. I'll not endure him.
Capulet: He shall be endured. What, goodman boy? I say he shall, go to! Am I
the master here, or you? go to! (ROM 1, 5, 75–78)[33]

(14)   Edmund: How, now, what's the matter? Part!
Kent: With you, goodman boy, [and] you please! Come, I'll flesh ye, come on,
young master. (LR 2, 2, 44–46)[34]

Examples (15)–(16) illustrate that an appellation formerly used in friendly jest is
resented once the former Prince and consort has become King:

(15)   Prince [playing Falstaff]: The complaints I hear of thee are grievous.
Falstaff [playing the Prince]: 'Sblood, my lord, they are false. — Nay, I'll tickle
ye for a young prince, i' faith.
Prince: Swearest thou, ungracious boy? henceforth ne'er look on me.
(1H4 2, 4, 442–446)

(16)   Falstaff: God save thy Grace, King Hal! my royal Hal! [...] God save thee, my
sweet boy! [...]
Chief Justice: Have you your wits? know you what 'tis you speak?
Falstaff: My King, my Jove! I speak to thee, my heart!
King: I know thee not, old man, fall to thy prayers. (2H4 5, 5, 41–47)

In contrast to these brusque uses, *boy* in the sense of 'young person, page, servant'
is not an unbecoming familiarity. In most cases *thou* is used as a pronoun (ADO 2,
3, 1; LLL 1, 2, 64–122; SHR 4, 1, 41; ROM 5, 3, 1–18; MAC 5, 3, 15). On the other
hand, TGV 2, 1, 79 and WIV 3, 2, 7; 3, 3, 143 feature *you*. While pronoun usage in
these examples is consistent in that there is no switching between address pronouns
there is also one case in which pronoun usage varies:

(17)   Brutus [to Lucius, his boy servant]: Get you to bed again, it is not day. Is not
to-morrow, boy, the [ides] of March? (JC 2, 1, 39–40)

(18)   Brutus [to Lucius, his boy servant]: Bear with me, good boy, I am much
forgetful. Canst thou hold up thy heavy eyes awhile, / And touch thy instrument
a strain or two? (JC 4, 3, 255–257)

All the above examples conform to the rule of "power semantics" in that *boy* is used
asymmetrically when given as an address from a person of a higher social standing
to one of lesser rank and age, but as was the case with *sirrah*, the master-fool-
relationship between King Lear and his fool provides an example in which *boy* (+ a
T-form) is exchanged mutually:

(19)   Fool: How now, nuncle? Would I had two coxcombs and two daughters!
Lear: Why, my boy?
Fool: If I gave them all my living, I'd keep my coxcombs myself. There's mine,

beg another of thy daughters.
Lear: Take heed, sirrah — the whip. [...]
Fool: Can you make no use of nothing, nuncle?
Lear: Why, no, boy, nothing can be made out of nothing. [...]
Fool: Dost know the difference, my boy, between a bitter fool and a sweet one?
Lear: No, lad, teach me. (LR 1, 4, 105–139)

Whether an address involving *boy* is intended to be affectionate, familiar or brusque and insulting can, in addition to pronoun use, be inferred from the adjectives that accompany the address, and which underline its illocutionary force, e.g.: *dear, fair, fond, good, sweet* as positive adjectives, and *foolish, peevish, ungracious, unreverend, willful, wretched* as negative ones. These findings contradict Rudanko's statement that the use of *boy* signals nastiness instead of politeness, because it does "not need any special circumstances to express disrespect, contempt or some similar negative attitude towards the interlocutor" (1993: 168). With the only exception of *willful* (see example (8)) all the above adjectives co-occur with *thou* exclusively, or are not in the immediate vicinity of a pronoun. This underlines the role of *you* as the more distanced and neutral term that is not qualified by any epithets.

6.3.4.2 *Friend*

Friend is used in a number of different senses, as the Shakespeare Lexicon by Schmidt and Sarrazin testifies:

- One joined to another in benevolence and intimacy; masc. [...] fem.
- Used for near relations, particularly parents
- Synonymous to lover, paramour, sweetheart; masc. [...] fem.
- Used as a familiar compellation

Stoll follows the OED and distinguishes between two different senses: "in mutual benevolence and intimacy" (1989: 202–204), which according to her is infrequent (but see e.g. Hamlet and Horatio), and a more general sense of friendly address "to a mere acquaintance, or to a stranger, as a mark of goodwill or kindly condescension on the part of the speaker". In the plural, *friend* is often used by nobles to summon or entreat their peers, especially in the Histories.

In the corpus, both of these senses occur frequently as vocatives. As address for a sweetheart *friend* is rare. *Friend* has an absolute frequency of 423 instances (323 verse; 100 prose), but occurs only 75 times as a vocative in connection with pronouns. The break-down for pronouns and genres is shown in Table 24.

The table illustrates that the use of co-occurring pronouns is fairly balanced between *you* and *thou*. A correlation between genre and pronoun use cannot be worked out. Irrespective of pronoun usage it can be said, however, that *friend* collocates exclusively with a limited set of positive adjectives, viz.: *(my) dear(est), gentle, good, (my) fair(est), (mine) honest, honor'd, noble, (my) old* and *sweet*, out of which *good* is the most commonly used epithet.

Table 24. T and Y pronouns co-occurring with *friend*

	T pronoun	Y pronoun	combined
Comedies	12	15	27
Histories	5	1	6
Tragedies	22	20	42
Total	**39**	**36**	**75**

As already indicated, *friend* can be used in different intersocial relationships. On the one hand, it occurs as address between people who are intimately associated with each other, and on the other hand, as a compellation, it is said to strangers or other fairly distant people, or to subservient persons such as menials, messengers, etc. The first set of examples is to document the exchange of *friend* between persons who are benevolently associated to each other:

(1)　Prospero [to Gonzalo]: First, noble friend, / Let me embrace thine age, whose honor cannot / Be measur'd or confin'd. (TMP 5, 1, 121)

Prospero and Gonzalo are friends. Gonzalo is "an honest old counsillor". In the end Prospero greets him affectionately as "good Gonzalo My true preserver". Another example can be taken from TGV. The two gentlemen, Sir Proteus and Sir Valentine, are old friends from Verona, but now rivals as suitors to Silvia. When Proteus woos Silvia uncivilly "like a soldier, at arm's end", he is addressed reproachfully as *friend* when confronted by Valentine:

(2)　Valentine [Coming forward.]: Ruffian! let go that rude uncivil touch, / Thou friend of an ill fashion!
Proteus: Valentine!
Valentine: Thou common friend, that's without faith or love, / For such is a friend now! treacherous man, Thou hast beguil'd my hopes! [...].
Proteus: My shame and guilt confounds me. Forgive me, Valentine [...].
(TGV 5, 4, 59–64; 73–74)

As address between closely associated women, *friend* is seldom. An example can be found in WIV when Mrs. Page comes to warn Mrs. Ford that her husband is about to search the house for the suspected adulterer. However, the address "my dear friend" could also be interpreted as a punning readoption of *friend* in the sense of 'man friend':

(3)　Mrs. Page: I come before to tell you. If you know yourself clear, why, I am glad of it; but if you have a friend here, convey, convey him out. [...]
Mrs. Ford: What shall I do? There is a gentleman, my dear friend; and I fear not mine own shame so much as his peril. (WIV 3, 3, 115–123)

(4)   Claudio: One word, good friend. Lucio, a word with you.
      Lucio: A hundred! if they'll do you any good. (MM 1, 2, 142–143)

(5)   Duke [to Escalus]: Thanks, good friend Escalus, for thy much goodness, /
      There's more behind that is more gratulate. (MM 5, 1, 528–529)

(6)   Brutus [to Cassius]: What you have said I will consider; what you have to say I
      will with patience hear, and find a time / Both meet to hear and answer such
      high things. Till then, my noble friend, chew upon this: [...]. (JC 1, 2, 167–171)

(7)   Horatio: Hail to your lordship!
      Hamlet: I am glad to see you well. Horatio — or I do forget myself.
      Horatio: The same, my lord, and your poor servant ever.
      Hamlet: Sir, my good friend — I'll change that name with you.
      (HAM 1, 2, 160–164)

Examples (4)–(7) illustrate further instances of *friend*. Although all of these
relationships assume a certain degree of intimacy and benevolence, *you* prevails as
a pronoun. Furthermore, the instances all show some social superiority because
friend is not reciprocated. The answer of Horatio clearly shows deference.

As address for a sweetheart *friend* is quite rare:

(8)   Hermia [to Lysander]: Lysander riddles very prettily. Now much beshrew my
      manners and my pride, / If Hermia meant to say Lysander lied. But, gentle
      friend, for love and courtesy, / Lie further off, in humane modesty; / Such
      separation as may well be said / Becomes a virtuous bachelor and a maid, / So far
      be distant; and good night, sweet friend. Thy love ne'er alter till thy sweet life
      end! (MND 2, 2, 53–61)

(9)   Bianca: 'Save you, friend Cassio!
      Cassio: What make you from home? How is't with you, my most fair Bianca? [I'
      faith], sweet love, I was coming to your house. (OTH 3, 4, 168–171)

The instances of *friend* given as a compellation to strangers and to menials are more
frequent:

(10) Sexton: But which are the offenders that are to be examin'd? Let them come
      before Master Constable.
      Dogberry: Yea, marry, let them come before me. What is your name, friend?
      Borachio: Borachio. (ADO 4, 2, 7–11)

(11) Escalus: Where were you born, friend?
      Froth: Here in Vienna, sir.
      Escalus: Are you of fourscore pounds a year?
      Froth: Yes, and't please you, sir. [...]
      Escalus: Come hither to me, Master Froth. Master Froth, I would not have you
      acquainted with tapsters; they will draw you, Master Froth, and you will hang
      them. Get you gone, and let me hear no more of you.
      Froth: I thank your worship. (MM 2, 1, 193–208)

(12)   1. Fisherman: Come, thou shalt go home, and we'll have flesh for [holidays], fish for fasting-days, and, moreo'er, puddings and flapjacks, and thou shalt be welcome.
Pericles: I thank you, sir.
2. Fisherman: Hark you, my friend. You said you could not beg?
(PER 2, 1, 80–85)

Although the last example (and the whole scene, indeed) shows some pronoun switching, (10)–(12) can be regarded as addresses towards strangers whose social position is not exactly known. In (11) Escalus even inquires directly about Froth's annuity when he warns him not to deal with tapsters like Pompey before he dismisses him. For this reason *you* is chosen and the term *friend* suggests that one does not deal with a person of rank. In (12) Pericles is shipwrecked on the coast of Pentapolis and his armour is saved by fishermen.

On the other hand, a combination of *thou* and *friend* can indicate an (unduly) intimate or condescending attitude triggered by the other's outward appearance or one of sincere friendship and affection:

(13)   Oswald [to Kent in disguise]: Good dawning to thee, friend. Art of this house?
Kent [disguised as Caius]: Ay. (LR 2, 2, 1–2)

(14)   Gloucester: Come hither, friend; where is the King my master?
Kent [disguised as Caius]: Here, sir, but trouble him not — his wits are gone.
Gloucester: Good friend, I prithee take him in thy arms; I have o'erheard a plot of death upon him. (LR 3, 6, 86–89)

(15)   Old Man: O my good lord, I have been your tenant, and your father's tenant, / These fourscore years.
Gloucester: Away, get thee away! Good friend, be gone, / Thy comforts can do me no good at all; / Thee they may hurt. (LR 4, 1, 12–17)

As address for subordinates, *friend* is also quite common. The following dialogues are all characterised by a clear social distance that becomes manifest in the asymmetry of vocatives. The persons addressed as *friend* respond with honorific vocatives such as *sir* or *madam*. A "minimalist" example without pronouns that illustrates "power semantics" by the use of generic terms of address like *friend* and *man* to the subordinate and a reply by a title of courtesy to the superior is the exchange between Enobarbus and Eros, Antony's servant:

(16)   Enobarbus: How now, friend Eros?
Eros: There's strange news come, sir.
Enobarbus: What, man? (ANT 3, 5, 1–3)

(17)   Pandarus: Friend, you! pray you a word. Do you not follow the young Lord Paris?
Servant: Ay, sir, when he goes before me. (TRO 3, 1, 1–3)

After some more exchanges of wordplay in which the servant deliberately misunderstands Pandarus, the latter switches to a slightly irritable *thou*:

(17′)   Pandarus: Friend, we understand not one another; I am too courtly and thou too
         cunning. At whose request do these men play?
         Servant: That's to't indeed, sir. (TRO 3, 1, 27–30)

(18)   King John: Come hither, Hubert. O my gentle Hubert, We owe thee much!
         Within this wall of flesh / There is a soul counts thee her creditor; / And with
         advantage means to pay thy love; / And, my good friend, thy voluntary oath /
         Lives in this bosom, dearly cherished.
         [...]
         Hubert: I am much bounden to your Majesty.
         King John: Good friend, thou hast no cause to say so yet, [...].
         (JN 3, 3, 19–24; 28–30)

(19)   Macduff: Was it so late, friend, ere you went to bed, / That you lie so late?
         Porter: Faith, sir, we were carousing till the second cock; [...].
         (MAC 2, 3, 22–26)

In the next example, due to the bad news the messenger has to break to his mistress,
the friendly *prithee* is changed into an irritable *thee* and a series of invectives. When
Cleopatra regains her composure she momentarily switches to *you*, only to abuse
the messenger physically and verbally upon the confirmation of the bad tidings:

(20)   Cleopatra: Prithee, friend, / Pour out the pack of matter to mine ear, / The good
         and bad together: he's friends with Caesar, / In state of health thou say'st, and
         thou say'st free.
         Messenger: Free, madam, no; I made no such report. He's bound unto Octavia.
         Cleopatra: For what good turn?
         Messenger: For the best turn i' th' bed.
         Cleopatra: I am pale, Charmian.
         Messenger: Madam, he's married to Octavia.
         Cleopatra: The most infectious pestilence upon thee! [Strikes him down.].
         Messenger: Good madam, patience.
         Cleopatra: What say you? [Strikes him.] Hence, / Horrible villain, or I'll spurn
         thine eyes [...]. (ANT 2, 5, 53–63)

6.3.4.3   *Gentleman*

On the authority of Schmidt and Sarrazin, *gentleman* has the following meanings in
Shakespeare's plays (cf. also Stoll 1989: 136f.):

1.   a man of birth, though not a nobleman
2.   a man of honour and good breeding
3.   any man, by way of complaisance
      –   Serving as a compellation[35]
           a.   in the sing.
           b.   oftener in the plur.
4.   attendant of a person of rank
5.   a subordinate officer

These short meaning glosses reveal that the term covered a very broad social spectrum, and that, strictly speaking, meanings (1) and (2) belong rather into the category *titles of honour*. So that only (3) refers to the use of *gentleman* as a generic term of address.

Many dialogues in the plays illustrate the fact that knowledge about a person's rank is of prime importance. However, in many cases it is difficult to differentiate between meanings (1) and (2). Böhm's study (1936: 37–43) confirms this:

> Im Laufe des 16. Jhts., mit dem Aufkommen der bürgerlichen Tendenzen und zugleich mit der wachsenden Wertschätzung von Bildung und Gelehrsamkeit im Gegensatz zu kriegerischen Leistungen und guter Familie, verwischt sich allmählich die Grenze zwischen dem Gentleman = einem Wappeninhaber mit oder ohne Titel auf der einen Seite und dem bloß gelehrten oder bloß reichen oder bloß landbesitzenden, aber nicht waffenfähigen Mann; [...].
> (Böhm 1936: 39)

Gentleman has an absolute frequency of 295 tokens (166 verse; 129 prose), but in many of these cases it is used descriptively and not as an address. There are quite a number of protestations of characters saying: "(As) I am a gentleman ..." (cf. WIV 2, 2, 160; 4, 6, 4; ADO 4, 2, 13; LLL 1, 1, 234; SHR 2, 1, 47, 219; TN 1, 5, 279, 291; R2 3, 1, 27; 2H4 2, 1, 136, 138; 2H6 4, 29):

(1) Petruchio: [...] Good Kate; I am a gentleman —
Katherina: That I'll try. [She strikes him.]
Petruchio: I swear I'll cuff you, if you strike again.
Katherina: So may you lose your arms. If you strike me, you are no gentleman, /
And if no gentleman, why then no arms. (SHR 2, 1, 218–223)

On the other hand, in many cases the interlocutor confirms that his opponent belongs to the class of gentlemen by saying: "Thou art/you are a gentleman ..." (cf. TGV 3, 1, 121; 4, 3, 11; 5, 4, 146; WIV 2, 1, 193; LLL 1, 2, 42; HAM 5, 2, 227):

(2) Silvia: Sir Eglamour, a thousand times good morrow.
Sir Eglamour: As many, worthy lady, to yourself. According to your ladyship's impose, I am thus early come to know what service / It is your pleasure to command me in.
Silvia: O Eglamour, thou art a gentleman — Think not I flatter, for I swear I do not — Valiant, wise, remorseful, well accomplish'd: [...] (TGV 4, 3, 6–13)

(3) Bishop Gardiner [to Sir Thomas Lovell, Chancellor of the Exchequer]: But, sir, sir, Hear me, Sir Thomas, y' are a gentleman / Of mine own way; I know you wise, religious, [...]. (H8 5, 1, 27–28)

Whereas the above are examples for *gentleman* in the sense of "a man of birth" and the broadened meaning of "a man of honour and good breeding", in (4) it is probably not meant very seriously at all, as the other epithets suggest familiarity:

(4) Page: Look where my ranting host of the Garter comes. There is either liquor in his pate, or money in his purse, when he looks so merrily. How, now, mine host? Host: How now, bully-rook? thou'rt a gentleman. Cavaleiro Justice, I say! (WIV 2, 1, 189–194)

Questions as to the state of a person of the type: "Are you/art thou a gentleman?" are used more seldom:

(5) Pistol: Yield, cur!
French soldier: Je pense que vous êtes le gentilhomme de bonne qualité.
Pistol: [...] Art thou a gentleman? What is thy name? Discuss.
French soldier: O Seigneur Dieu!
Pistol: O Signieur Dew should be a gentleman. (H5 4, 4, 2–7)

(6) Theseus: Are you a gentleman?
Arcite: My father said so [...]. (TNK 2, 5, 6–7)

The break-down for *gentleman* used as a form of direct address and the accompanying pronouns is as shown in Table 25. This distribution does not allow for any considerations on corpus-internal variation. Neither can a correlation between the meanings as established by Schmidt and Sarrazin and pronoun usage be drawn.

Table 25. T and Y pronouns co-occurring with *gentleman*

	T pronoun	Y pronoun	combined
Comedies	6	16	22
Histories	1	2	3
Tragedies	4	5	9
Total	11	23	34

When used as a compellation in addressing strangers, *you* is the pronoun normally employed, as e.g. in MV by the old Gobbo, who is purblind, and does not even recognise his son Launcelet, or in COR when a servant enquires about the state of Coriolanus, who is not known to him, or in LR by Edgar in disguise, who takes on the part of a peasant and speaks in Somerset dialect to Oswald:

(7) Gobbo [to Launcelet]: Master young gentleman, I pray you, which is the way to Master Jew's? (MV 2, 2, 39–40)

(8) 3. Servant: What are you?
Coriolanus: A gentleman.
3. Servant: A marv'llous poor one.
Coriolanus: True, so I am.
3. Servant: Pray you, poor gentleman, take up some other station; here's no place for you. (COR 4, 5, 25–30)

(9)   Edgar: Chill not let go, zir, without vurther [cagion].
      Oswald: Let go, slave, or thou di'st!
      Edgar: Good gentleman, go your gait, and let poor voke pass. (LR 4, 6, 235–237)

Usually, there is very little switching between address pronouns, however, one example can be found in TN:

(10)   Sir Toby: 'Save you, gentleman.
       Viola: And you, sir. (TN 3, 1, 69–70)
       Sir Toby: Gentleman, God save thee!
       Viola: And you, sir. (TN 3, 4, 218–219)

Those instances in which *gentleman* co-occurs with *thou* are characterised by emotional intensity, even intimacy between the interlocutors, as e.g. in (11) when Juliet in the "balcony scene" appeals to Romeo's honour as a gentleman, or in reprimand, as in (12) when Iago criticises Rodrigo's ungentlemanly behaviour:

(11)   Juliet [to Romeo]: In truth, fair Montague, I am too fond, / And therefore thou
       mayest think my behavior light, / But trust me, gentleman, I'll prove more true /
       Than those that have [more] coying to be strange. (ROM 2, 2, 98–101)

(12)   Iago: What say'st thou, noble heart?
       Rodrigo [a gull'd gentleman]: What will I do, think'st thou?
       Iago: Why, go to bed and sleep.
       Rodrigo: I will continently drown myself.
       Iago: If thou dost, I shall never love thee after. Why, thou silly gentleman?
       (OTH 1, 3, 302–306)

By and large, *gentleman* is a term that carries very positive connotations which are conveyed through adjectives that characterise superior character, behaviour and appearance, like: *brave, fair, fine, gallant, graceful, good, handsome, honest, honorable, learned, most reverend, noble, smooth-fac'd* and *worthy*. On the other hand, a gentleman who lacks financial means or whose state is to be deplored, is affectionately referred to as *poor gentleman* as in (8).

6.3.4.4   *Gentlewoman*

Schmidt and Sarrazin give the following sense divisions:

1.   a woman of good family
2.   any female person, lady
     –   Used in compellations;
         a.   sing.
         b.   plur.
3.   a female attendant of a lady of high rank

These sense divisions reveal that similar to *gentleman* only the compellative use belongs to the category of generic terms of address.

Stoll (1989: 137 f.) mentions that, unlike *gentleman*, the term is hardly ever used vocatively as address for a woman of honour; in fact only once in Lear's bitter ironic insinuation to the gentle birth of his unthankful daughter.

Böhm (1936: 65–67) gives an historical outline of the development of *gentlewoman*, which has never been a true title but rather a term that was used as an address. For the 16th century she positions the term as follows in the social hierarchy:

> Im 16. Jht. kommt wie für alle Titel das Streben nach Abgrenzung auf, man gibt dem Titel eine bestimmte Stellung in der Rangliste, und zwar unter der Dame als Benennung der Frauen der Esquires, für die es keine weibliche Entsprechung gibt, und für die Frauen der Gentlemen. Schon lange vor dieser Zeit war aus der Gewohnheit der adligen Damen, sich Frauen von guter Abkunft, also Gentlewomen, als Begleiterinnen und Dienerinnen zu halten, eine zweite Anwendung des Wortes geworden: weibliche Begleiterin einer Lady, was allmählich sich von der Ursprungsbedeutung ablöste [...].
> (Böhm 1936: 65)

In contrast to this, Stoll is of the opinion that it did not matter whether the lady in waiting was of gentle birth or not.

In comparison to the frequency of *gentleman*, *gentlewoman* with its 43 tokens (16 verse; 27 prose) occurs much less often. In addition to this, the term clearly prevails in the Comedies (30 tokens) and is used far more sparingly in the History Plays (6 tokens) and in the Tragedies (7 tokens). As a compellation it is used only six times. In all the four cases in which a pronoun co-occurs it is *you* (see Table 26). Twice it is used in ritualised utterances of greeting formulae.[36]

(1) Julia [to Silvia]: Gentlewoman, good day; I pray you be my mean / To bring me where to speak with Madam Silvia. (TGV 4, 4, 108–109)

(2) Nurse: God ye good morrow, gentlemen.
    Mercutio: God ye good den, fair gentlewoman. (ROM 2, 4, 109–110)

The other two instances are:

(3) Prince: You, gentlewoman —
    Doll Tearsheet: What says your Grace?
    Falstaff: His grace says that which his flesh rebels against.[37] (2H4 2, 4, 348–351)

(4) Lear: Your name, fair gentlewoman?
    Goneril: This admiration, sir, is much o' th' savor / Of other your new pranks.
    (LR 1, 4, 236–238)

The tokens illustrate the wide social range of the term outlined by Böhm, because the expression is used for Silvia, the daughter of the Duke of Milan, ironically for Falstaff's mistress, for Juliet's nurse and for a princess in pretended wonderment by her royal father.

Table 26. T and Y pronouns co-occurring with *gentlewoman*

	T pronoun	Y pronoun	combined
Comedies	–	1	1
Histories	–	1	1
Tragedies	–	2	2
Total	–	4	4

6.3.4.5   *Lad*

Schmidt and Sarrazin give the following sense divisions:

1. a boy, a stripling
2. fellow
   – Used as a familiar compellation

Stoll (1989:200f.) regards *lad* as a rarer alternative to *fellow* or *youth*. As a compellation it is used from master to servant, or, more often, as an intimate address among social equals of the middle or lower social orders; especially in informal atmosphere.

When compared to *boy* with 352 tokens, *lad* is used far more sparingly; it has only a total frequency of 28 tokens (16 verse; 12 prose). 14 times is *lad* used as an address to a youth; in 12 instances it co-occurs with *thou*, and only twice with *you* (see Table 27).

Usually, the term is given as an affectionate address by a senior person to a younger, be it a servant, as. e. g. by Lucentio to Tranio in SHR 1, 1, 163; Sir Toby to Fabian, the servant to Olivia, in TN 3, 2, 54; King Henry VI to Henry, Earl of Richmond, a youth in 3H6 4, 6, 70; or from Lear to his fool in LR 1, 4, 139.

In 1H4, *lad* plays a special role and has to be examined on its own. It occurs 9 times and can be said to be *the* term of affection and endearment by which Falstaff addresses the young Prince, because he regards the unruly youth as one of his cronies. Once the Prince also responds in this way to Falstaff and addresses him as "my old lad of the castle" (1H4 1, 2, 41).[38]

Table 27. T and Y pronouns co-occurring with *lad*

	T pronoun	Y pronoun	combined
Comedies	4	–	4
Histories	4	2	6
Tragedies	4	–	4
Total	12	2	14

Whereas all these instances are characterised by a fairly intimate relationship that allows for *thou* as address pronoun, the only cases in which *lad* co-occurs with *you* are marked by greater social distance and a keeping to decorum: Hubert de Burgh, employed by King John to blind Arthur, addresses him with *ye/you*. Poins, although a friend to Prince Henry, does not take the same liberty as Falstaff to *thou* his royal consort:

(1) Hubert [to Arthur, Duke of Britain, and nephew to the King]: Young lad, come forth; I have to say with you. (JN 4, 1, 8)

(2) Prince: [...] shall we be merry?
Poins: As merry as crickets, my lad. But hark ye, what cunning match have you made with this jest of the drawer? (1H4 2, 4, 88–90)

6.3.4.6 *Summary: Generic terms of address*

In this group, *boy* and *lad* share a number of similarities. *Boy* is typically given as an address to a male child from fathers, and more seldom from mothers. In these cases, the pronoun used is normally the intimate *thou*. Greater social distance between the speaker and the person addressed as *boy* is expressed by the choice of *you*. In those cases in which *boy* is said in contempt, *thou* also co-occurs as a pronoun, excepting the few instances in which *boy* is preceded by mock-polite formal titles such as *Sir* or *goodman*.

Although *lad* and *boy* share some sense properties and pragmatic features, in that both are given from a senior person to a younger one, *lad* is often said by a master to his boy-servant. In this social set-up *thou* co-occurs as a pronoun, and the direction of pronoun use is asymmetrical Y → T. However, Falstaff makes it a

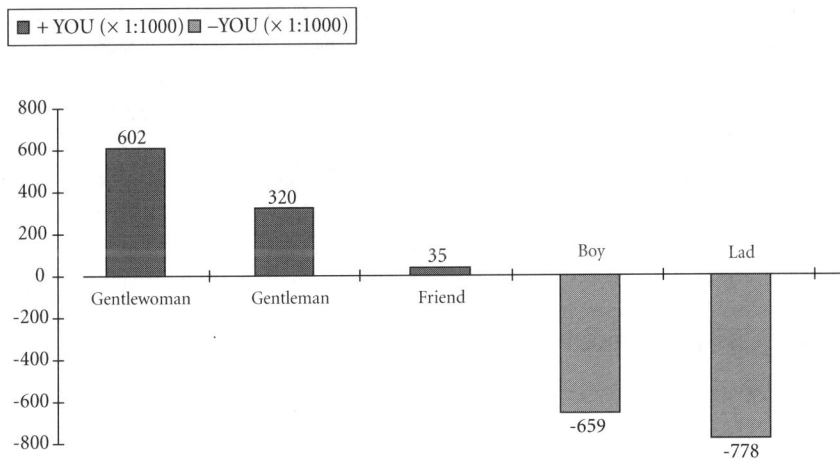

Graph 4. Generic terms of address.

symmetrical T ↔ T one, when he addresses the prince by *lad* and *boy*. In terms of frequency, *boy* is used far more often than *lad*.

Friend shows an equilibrium of pronoun use. It can neither be regarded as a typical "*thou* word" nor as a "*you* word". It stands halfway between *gentleman* and *gentlewoman* on the one hand, and *boy* and *lad* on the other. Although two major uses can be distinguished from each other, viz. as an address to intimate associates and to subordinates, pronoun use does not really differ despite the differences in intimacy and social distance. Whether the *thous* are intended to mean honest affection, condescension, impatience, irritation etc. has to be inferred from the situational context. Nevalainen and Raumolin-Brunberg have found that "apart from members of the nuclear family, it is between close friends that we find the least social distance (D) and its component affect (personal liking) at its greatest" (1995:570).

In the Shakespeare Corpus, *gentleman* performs a number of different functions, as the array of senses outlined in Schmidt and Sarrazin amply documents. On many occasions characters profess that they belong to the social class of gentlemen, and many interlocutors who meet with strangers interrogate them about their rank with questions: "Are you/art thou a gentleman?" This practice underlines the importance of being genteel and as its communicative manifestation the correct address. A failure to do so is met with resentment: "I am a gentleman, sir", replies Conrade in ADO 4, 2, 13 when he is inappropriately addressed by Dogberry as *sirrah*. On the other hand, Dogberry's answer underlines his limited acquaintance with the requirements of social decorum, for he says: "Write down Master Gentleman Conrade."

The adjectives that co-occur with *gentleman* also emphasise its social prestige because the epithets describe superior character traits, behaviour or manners. The distribution of *gentleman* among genres shows that the term predominates in the Comedies. As regards pronoun use, *you* prevails, especially between persons who are not well known to each other. In addition to social distance, appearance, e.g. clothing, is also an important factor influencing vocative address and pronoun choice, as there are "poor but worthy" gentlemen (CYM 1, 1, 7).

In comparison to the ubiquitous *gentleman*, its female counterpart *gentlewoman* plays only a marginal role, as it is very infrequent. The term is mostly used in the Comedies. It co-occurs exclusively with *you*, but its scarcity does not really allow for generalisations. However, its usage documents that the term had serious applications for women of social standing, and could also be given ironically to women of a lower social position such as the Hostess and Doll Tearsheet in 2H4.

6.3.5 Terms of endearment

6.3.5.1 *Bully*

Schmidt and Sarrazin define *bully* as "a brisk, dashing fellow". The OED gives a more precise definition which reveals that originally the term could also be applied to females:

> † 1. a. A term of endearment and familiarity, orig. applied to either sex: sweetheart, darling. Later applied to men only, implying friendly admiration: good friend, fine fellow, 'gallant'. Often prefixed as a sort of title to the name or designation of the person addressed, as in Shaks., 'bully Bottom', 'bully doctor'. *Obs. exc. arch.*

The quotations in the OED range from 1538 to 1754. In Shakespeare's plays, *bully* has a frequency of 12 tokens (1 verse; 11 prose). It also occurs 8 times (all prose) as first part of compounds such as *bully-doctor, bully-knight, bully-monster, bully-rook* and *bully-stale*. Taken together, it is used 19 times as address and once descriptively (H5 4, 1, 48). Out of these cases it co-occurs exclusively with *thou* (see Table 28).

Table 28. T and Y pronouns co-occurring with *bully*

	T pronoun	Y pronoun	combined
Comedies	19	–	19
Histories	–	–	–
Tragedies	–	–	–
Total	19	–	19

Its occurrence is practically limited to WIV, where the "ho[st] is addicted to the use of *bully*, and applies it to everyone, of every rank" (Salmon 1967:58). For instance, Falstaff, Masters Ford and Page and Dr. Caius are addressed by him in this way. Apart from WIV, the term appears in MND, where it is given by Quince and Flute to Bottom.[39] This limitation to plays or scenes in which the life of the lower social classes and artisans is depicted illustrates how these people speak. Such predilections tell us something about group behaviour or even a speaker's idiolect and can be interpreted as clues to character. The host's interpretation of "scholarly and wise" language in (1) has a mock heroic overdrawn air to it. The exclusive use of *thou* indicates familiarity and comradeship.

(1) Falstaff: Mine host of the Garter!
    Host: What says my bully-rook? Speak scholarly and wisely.
    Falstaff: Truly, mine host, I must turn away some of my followers.
    Host: Discard, bully Hercules, cashier; let them wag; trot, trot.

Falstaff: I sit at ten pounds a week.
Host: Thou'rt an emperor — Caesar, Keiser, and Pheazar. I will entertain
Bardolph; he shall draw, he shall tap. Said I well, bully Hector?
Falstaff: Do so, good mine host. (WIV 1, 3, 1–12)

(2)   Quince: What sayest thou, bully Bottom? (MND 3, 1, 8)

(3)   Flute: O sweet bully Bottom! (MND 4, 2, 19)

6.3.5.2   *Chuck*

Schmidt and Sarrazin give the following meaning gloss: "(= *chicken*), a term of
endearment", and Salmon also regards the term as a variant of *chick* that "is not
uncommonly applied to spouses and close friends" (1967:57). Yet, this statement
is somehow contradicted by the infrequency of the item, because its total frequency
amounts to a mere seven tokens in the entire corpus. For this reason the co-
occurrence with three instances of *thou* and only a single one of *you* are of no
statistical significance (see Table 29).

Table 29. T and Y pronouns co-occurring with *chuck*

	T pronoun	Y pronoun	combined
Comedies	1	–	1
Histories	1	–	1
Tragedies	1	1	2
Total	3	1	4

As an exchange between spouses it is used from male to female, as e.g. from
Antony to Cleopatra in ANT 4, 4, 2, from Macbeth to Lady Macbeth, and from
Othello to Desdemona:

(1)   Lady Macbeth: What's to be done?
Macbeth: Be innocent of the knowledge, dearest chuck, / Till thou applaud the
deed. (MAC 3, 2, 44–46)

(2)   Desdemona: My lord, what is your will?
Othello: Pray you, chuck, come hither. (OTH 4, 2, 24–25)

In addition to this, *chuck* is also used between males as a term of affectionate,
masculine respect. In (3) and (4) it occurs next to *bawcock*, an endearing term
which goes back to French *beau coq* 'fine fellow'.

(3)   Pistol [to Fluellen]: Be merciful, great duke, to men of mould. Abate thy rage,
abate thy manly rage, / Abate thy rage, great duke! Good bawcock, bate thy rage;
use lenity, sweet chuck! (H5 3, 2, 21–25)

(4)   Sir Toby [to Malvolio]: Why, how now, my bawcock? How dost thou, chuck?
      Malvolio: Sir! (TN 3, 4, 112–114)

6.3.5.3   Joy

Schmidt and Sarrazin do not list *joy* as a vocative and with reference to the "Falstaff
plays", Salmon says that it was "in all likelihood obsolete by 1623" (1967: 58).[40]
Although the sense of 'darling' is documented in the OED, it is indeed rare in the
Shakespeare Corpus, for there are only eight occurrences in the whole corpus despite
the overall frequency of *joy* with 195 tokens. In three of these cases *joy* is not used as
address (JN 3, 4, 104; 3H6 3, 3, 242; TIT 1, 1, 182). The remaining cases are equally
divided between *thou* and *you* as pronouns (see Table 30), and one instance without
a pronoun (Doll to Falstaff: "Yea, joy, our chains and our jewels." 2H4 2, 4, 47).

Table 30. T and Y pronouns co-occurring with *joy*

	T pronoun	Y pronoun	combined
Comedies	1	–	1
Histories	1	–	1
Tragedies	–	2	2
Total	**2**	**2**	**4**

(1)   Titania [to Bottom with his ass's head]: Come sit thee down upon this flow'ry
      bed, / While I thy amiable cheeks do coy, / And stick musk-roses in thy sleek
      smooth head, / And kiss thy fair large ears, my gentle joy. (MND 4, 1, 1–4)

(2)   Salisbury: Talbot, my life, my joy, again return'd? How wert thou handled, being
      prisoner? [...] Discourse, I prithee, on this turret's top. (1H6 1, 4, 23–24)

(3)   Lear: Now, our joy, / Although our last and least, to whose young love / The
      vines of France and milk of Burgundy / Strive to be interess'd, what can you say
      to draw / A third more opulent than your sisters'? Speak.
      Cordelia: Nothing, my lord. (LR 1, 1, 82–87)[41]

(4)   Desdemona: My dear Othello!
      Othello: It gives me wonder great as my content / To see you here before me. O
      my soul's joy! (OTH 2, 1, 182–184)

The quotations above illustrate that *joy* can be applied for males and females, i.e. for
children and spouses in scenes which are characterised by great affection and/or
emotional intensity. However, the instances are too few to deduct any rules for
pronoun usage.

6.3.5.4 *Love*

In Shakespeare's plays, *love* has a frequency of 1982 tokens (1583 verse; 399 prose) and is used with a number of meanings (cf. Schmidt and Sarrazin). However, as a term of endearing address it is fairly seldom, for there are only 34 occurrences in the corpus, out of which 23 co-occur with *thou*, and 11 with *you* (see Table 31). In addition to these, there are 20 further instances of address without a co-occurring pronoun.

Table 31. T and Y pronouns co-occurring with *love*

	T pronoun	Y pronoun	combined
Comedies	7	4*	11
Histories	5	–	5
Tragedies	11	7	18
Total	**23**	**11**	**34**

* The two tokens of love personified: "Lord love" [Bassanio] in MV 2, 9, 101 and "Good Signior love [Orlando]" in AYL 3, 2, 292 were not taken into account.

When used as a vocative, *love* often collocates with a limited set of positive adjectives like *(my) dear(est), fair, good* and *sweet*, which is also the most frequent one. Typically, *love* is given as an affectionate address from a suitor, lover or spouse to his beloved, e.g. from Ferdinand to Miranda (TMP), Sir Proteus to Silvia (TGV), Lysander to Hermia and Helena (MND), Petruchio to Katherina (SHR), Hotspur to Lady Percy (1H4), Troilus to Cressida (TRO), Romeo to Juliet (ROM), Othello to Desdemona, Cassio to Bianca (OTH) and by Antony to Cleopatra (ANT). This enumeration shows that in most cases the term is not exchanged mutually, but is (about twice as often) given from men to women. This usage is by no means extraordinary, as it is in accord with the findings of the OED: "9. a. A beloved person: esp. a sweetheart; chiefly applied to a female person, but sometimes to a male. (Often used as a term of endearing address.)." The following examples illustrate its use for male persons:

(1)   Portia: O love! dispatch all business and be gone.
      Bassanio: Since I have your good leave to go away, I will make haste; [...].
      (MV 3, 2, 323–325)

(2)   Orlando: For these two hours, Rosalind, I will leave thee.
      Rosalind: Alas, dear love, I cannot lack thee two hours! (AYL 4, 1, 177–178)

(3)   Imogen [to Posthumus, parting]: Look here, love, / This diamond was my mother's. Take it, heart, / But keep it till you woo another wife, / When Imogen is dead. (CYM 1, 1, 111–114)

The only example in which *love* is exchanged mutually is to be found in 2H6 between King Henry the Sixth and Queen Margaret:

(4) King: How now, madam? Still lamenting and mourning for Suffolk's death? I fear me, love, if that I had been dead, / Thou wouldst not have mourn'd so much for me.
Queen: No, my love, I should not mourn, but die for thee. (2H6 4, 4, 23–26)

In this case the pronoun brings about a rhyme with *me*. That considerations of rhyme can also partly influence pronoun choice is borne out by further examples:

(5) Demetrius: O Helen, goddess, nymph, perfect, divine! / To what, my love, shall I compare thine eyne? (MND 3, 2, 137–138)

(6) Othello [to Desdemona]: Come, my dear love, / The purchase made, the fruits are to ensue; / That profit's yet to come 'tween me and you. (OTH 2, 3, 8–10)

There are two plays in which *love* plays a greater role as a vocative, viz.: MND and ROM. In MND Lysander is in love with Hermia. He calls her *love + you*:

(7) Lysander: How now, my love? why is your cheek so pale?
[…]
Lysander: Fair love, you faint with wand'ring in the wood […].
Hermia: Be't so, Lysander. Find you out a bed; / For I upon this bank will rest my head. (MND 1, 1, 128; 2, 2, 35–40)

The application of Puck's magic love-juice to sleeping Lysander's eyes makes him fall in love with Helena when he awakes, and when Hermia protests her love to him he starts to insult her by using *thou* to her and by telling her that he hates her:

(8) Lysander: Hang off, thou cat, thou bur! Vile thing, let loose; / Or I will shake thee from me like a serpent!
Hermia: Why are you grown so rude? What change is this, / Sweet love?
Lysander: Thy love? Out, tawny Tartar, out! Out, loathed med'cine! O hated potion, hence! (MND 3, 2, 259–263)

On the other hand, Titania, the queen of the fairies is also bewitched when Oberon applies magic love-juice to her eyes. When she awakes and falls in love with Bottom, with his ass's head, she calls him *love + thou*. Her affectionate language contrasts with his down to earth working man's style and taste:

(9) Titania: What, wilt thou hear some music, my sweet love?
Bottom: I have a reasonable good ear in music. Let's have the tongs and the bones. [Music. Tongs. Rural music.]
Titania: Or say, sweet love, what thou desirest to eat.
Bottom: Truly, a peck of provender; I could munch your good dry oats.
(MND 4, 1, 27–33)

In ROM, the two lovers often address each other as *love*, especially in the "balcony-scene":

(10) Juliet: Believe me love, it was the nightingale.
Romeo: It was the lark, the herald of the morn, / No nightingale. Look, love, what envious streaks / Do lace the severing clouds in yonder east.
(ROM 3, 5, 5–8)
[…]
Juliet: Art thou gone so, love, lord, ay, husband, friend! / I must hear from thee every day in the hour, […].
Romeo [From below.]: Farewell! I will omit no opportunity / That may convey my greetings, love, to thee. (ROM 3, 5, 43–50)
[…]
Juliet: O God, I have an ill-divining soul! / Methinks I see thee now, thou art so low, / As one dead in the bottom of a tomb. Either my eyesight fails, or thou lookest pale.
Romeo: And trust me, love, in my eye so do you: / Dry sorrow drinks our blood. Adieu, adieu! (ROM 3, 5, 54–59)

These examples from MND and ROM illustrate that such sweeping theories as "power and solidarity semantics" fail to grasp this use of pronouns. Moreover, these instances call for either a micro-sociolinguistic treatment, or perhaps even more appropriately one in terms of textlinguistics that takes into account the peculiarities of the literary corpus with devices such as rhyme, dramatic contrast, and as in (10) even a foreshadowing of the catastrophe with the spatial distance (they cannot see each other clearly any more) emphasised by the more distant pronoun *you*.

6.3.5.5 *Wag*

Schmidt and Sarrazin define the noun *wag* as "a merry droll". Once again, as a term of endearment it is rare. In fact, the only occurrences in the corpus are to be found in 1H4 (1, 2, 16–59; 4, 2, 50) when Falstaff addresses Prince Henry in this way. With reference to 1H4 the OED gives the following meaning: "† 1. A mischievous boy (often as a mother's term of endearment to a baby boy); in wider application, a youth, young man, a 'fellow', 'chap'. *Obs.[olete].*"

Falstaff takes the liberty to call the Prince of Wales and future king as his intimate consort five times: "thou sweet/mad wag"[42] (see Table 32). Replogle comments on this exceptional usage as follows: "it is difficult to recreate the shock that Falstaff's opening words must have given to an Elizabethan audience. He, a man merely knighted on the field, continuously addresses the heir apparent to the throne of England as merely 'Hal' or worse — 'lad', 'boy', 'wag'" (1967:95).

(1) Falstaff: And I prithee, sweet wag, when thou art a king, as, God save thy Grace — Majesty I should say, for grace thou wilt have none — (1H4 1, 2, 16–18)

Table 32. T and Y pronouns co-occurring with *wag*

	T pronoun	Y pronoun	combined
Comedies	–	–	–
Histories	5	–	5
Tragedies	–	–	–
Total	**5**	–	–

6.3.5.6 *Summary: Terms of endearment*

All in all, the terms indicating endearment and affection are fairly infrequent in the corpus. Out of the five vocatives investigated, *love* is the most numerous and, in terms of pronoun usage, the most variable, because unlike the other terms it shows considerable vacillation. What they all share is the fact that they are all "*thou* words", because the ratio of pronouns is clearly in favour of *thou*. However, the gradient of "*thou*fulness" indicates important differences.

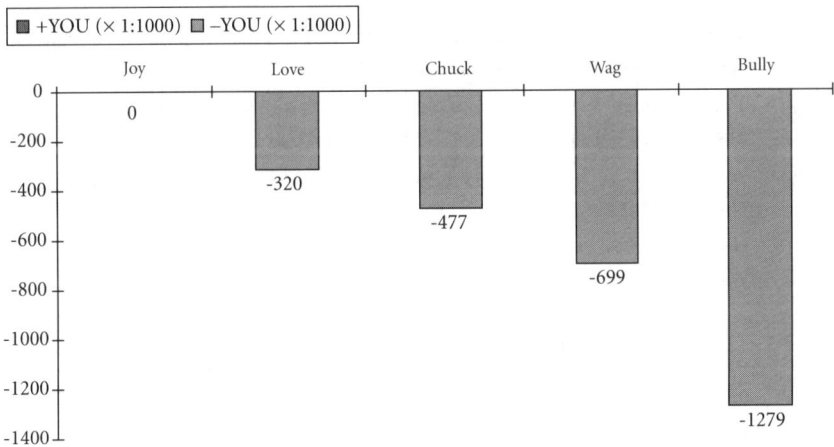

Graph 5. Terms of endearment.

The terms clearly differ in their semantic and pragmatic range, viz. to whom they can be given. *Joy* and *chuck* are used for both men and women. Both are said to loved spouses, children, and *chuck* also to associates. *Love* clearly differs from these, as it is used among lovers, although usually not mutually; men more often address women in this way than the other way around. Stoll also finds that unlike men, women use positive or negative emotional address and also first names less often. She attributes this to the often marginal roles of the female characters in the plays, and more generally to the social role of women in Elizabethan society (cf. 1989:224f.).

Bully and *wag*, on the other hand, are only given from men to men as verbal expressions of male friendship and indicate familiarity in the sense of close fellow- or comradeship or perhaps even bonhomie. Both terms have in common that they practically occur only in a limited number of plays, i.e. the "Falstaff plays" (WIV, 1H4) and are thus instantiations of "Elizabethan colloquial English", as Salmon puts it. As a corollary of this, it is by no means surprising that out of this set *bully* and *wag* are the words that show the highest degree of co-occurring *thou*, because in terms of Brown and Gilman's power and solidarity semantics they fulfil the criteria of nearness, intimacy and sympathy for reciprocal T pronouns.

6.3.6   Terms of abuse

6.3.6.1   *Hag*

Schmidt and Sarrazin give as meaning "an ugly and wicked woman."[43] As a term of contempt *hag* is rather infrequent, as there are only eight tokens (6 verse; 2 prose) in the entire corpus. As address it occurs four times and it collocates three times with *thou* and once with *you* (see Table 33).

(1)   Ford [to Falstaff disguised as Mother Pratt]: Come down, you witch, you hag you, come down, I say! (WIV 4, 2, 178–179)

(2)   Talbot [to Joan de Pucelle]: Foul fiend of France, and hag of all despite, / Encompass'd with thy lustful paramours! (1H6 3, 2, 52–53)

(3)   York [to Joan de Pucelle]: Fell banning hag, enchantress, hold thy tongue! (1H6 5, 3, 42)

(4)   Gloucester [to Queen Mary]: Have done thy charm, thou hateful with'red hag. (R3 1, 3, 214)

Table 33. T and Y pronouns co-occurring with *hag*

	T pronoun	Y pronoun	combined
Comedies	–	1	1
Histories	3	–	3
Tragedies	–	–	–
Total	**3**	**1**	**4**

6.3.6.2   *Knave*

The main sense divisions of *knave* are outlined by Schmidt and Sarrazin as follows (cf. also Stoll 1989: 201):

1. a young fellow, a boy [...]. Often used in compellations, even as a term of endearment
2. a menial
3. rascal, villain

These sense divisions show that the term only partly belongs to the category of abusive vocatives. *Knave* has a total frequency of 167 tokens (50 verse; 117 prose). In most of its occurrences it is used descriptively and not in direct address, e.g. in WIV and in 2H4. As address to an interlocutor, *knave* is used 54 times; i.e. 18 times together with *you*, 29 times together with *thou*, and 7 times without a pronoun (see Table 34).

Apart from the dominance of T forms, the distribution of the pronouns shows a marked difference from genre to genre (chi-squared 4.997 with 2 df; $p > 0.10$ level of confidence).

Table 34. T and Y pronouns co-occurring with *knave*

	T pronoun	Y pronoun	combined
Comedies	9	9	18
Histories	8	7	15
Tragedies	12	2	14
Total	29	18	47

Beside these genre differences which again find the Tragedies "lacking" in Y forms, it is not easy to establish overriding correlations; however, some tendencies can be found in the data. Whether the term is intended to express benign feelings such as endearment or anger or contempt, on the other hand, is clearly signalled by the accompanying adjectives, and at least partly also by pronoun use.

As a compellation or term of endearment, *knave* is preceded by positive adjectives such as *good, gentle* and *pretty* and is used together with an intimate *thou* from the superior:

(1) Berowne: O, my good knave Costard, exceedingly well met!
Costard [a clown]: Pray you, sir, how much carnation ribbon may a man buy for a remuneration? [...]
Berowne: O, stay, slave; I must employ thee. As thou wilt win my favor, good my knave, / Do one thing for me that I shall entreat.
Costard: When would you have it done, sir? (LLL 3, 1, 143–146; 151–154)

(2) Brutus [to Lucius, his boy servant]: What, thou speak'st drowsily? Poor knave, I blame thee not, thou art o'erwatch'd. [...] Gentle knave, good night; I will not do thee so much wrong to wake thee. (JC 4, 3, 240–241; 269–270)

(3)   Lear [to Kent]: Now, my friendly knave, I thank thee, there's earnest of thy
      service. [Giving Kent money.] [...]
      Lear [to Fool]: How now, my pretty knave, how dost thou? (LR 1, 4, 93–96)

(4)   Antony [to Eros, his servant]: My good knave Eros, now thy captain is / Even
      such a body. (ANT 4, 14, 12–13)

In contrast to the above instances, *knave* is mostly preceded by negative adjectives
such as: *arrant, foul-mouth'd, lousy, lying'st, muddy, naughty, scald, scurvy, stubborn,*
etc. when used in the sense of 'menial' or 'rascal'. In these cases, pronoun usage
varies between *thou* and *you;* e.g. the exchanges between Lafeu and Parolles, or
between Lafeu and the clown in AWW show pronoun switching.

In states of aroused emotions, *thou* is preferred when the social distance
between the speakers is relatively small, as in examples (5)–(6). On the other hand,
even in situations of pent-up anger, between relative strangers *you* is used:

(5)   Falstaff: Go, you thing, go.
      Hostess [Mistress Quickly]: Say, what thing? what thing?
      Falstaff: What thing? why, a thing to thank God on.
      Hostess: I am no thing to thank God on, I would thou shouldst know it. I am an
      honest man's wife, and setting thy knighthood aside, thou art a knave to call me
      so. (1H4 3, 3, 115–121)

(6)   Lady Faulconbridge [to Bastard]: Hast thou conspired with thy brother too, /
      That for thine own gain shouldst defend mine honor? What means this scorn,
      thou most untoward knave? (JN 1, 1, 241–243)

When Fluellen quarrels with Pistol in H5, after the latter has insulted him, Fluellen
beats him and abuses him in return and forces him to eat a leek, but uses *you* as
address pronoun, as does Cornwall to Kent, who, having tripped up Goneril's
steward Oswald, is sent to the stocks for his offences:

(7)   Pistol: Quiet thy cudgel, thou dost see I eat.
      Fluellen: Much good do you, scald knave, heartily. (H5 5, 1, 52–53)

(8)   Cornwall: Peace, sirrah! / You beastly knave, know you no reverence? [...] Fetch
      forth the stocks! / You stubborn ancient knave, you reverent braggart, / We'll
      teach you. (LR 2, 2, 68–69; 125–127)

The use of *sir,* be it even in a flippant or ironic way, also "necessitates" a momentary
you, as e.g. when Dromio of Ephesus meets Antipholus of Syracuse and mistakes
him for his master and tells him to come home for dinner, Antipholus beats him
and calls him *sir knave*:

(9)   Antipholus of Syracuse: Where is the gold I gave in charge to thee?
      Dromio of Ephesus: To me, sir? Why, you gave no gold to me.
      Antipholus of Syracuse: Come on, sir knave, have done your foolishness, / And
      tell me how thou hast dispos'd thy charge. [...]

> Dromio of Ephesus: Your worship's wife, my mistress at the Phoenix; / She that doth fast till you come home to dinner; / And prays that you will hie you home to dinner.
> Antipholus of Syracuse: What, wilt thou flout me thus unto my face, / Being forbid? There, take you that, sir knave. [Strikes Dromio.]
> (ERR 1, 2, 70–73; 87–92)

(10) Countess [to clown]: You'll be gone, sir knave, and do as I command you.
(AWW 1, 3, 90–91)

Thus, when *knave* is given from master to servant in the sense of 'menial' no bad character qualities seem to be implied and *you* usually occurs as an address pronoun. Abbott ([1870] 1972: 155) confirms this usage: "*Thou* is generally used by a master to a servant, but not always. Being the appropriate address to a servant, it is used in confidential and good-humoured utterances, but a master finding fault often resorts to the unfamiliar *you*." In so doing, the criticism is reinforced by the more distant pronoun. As a compellation or even as a term of endearment to a boy or a young fellow a benign *thou* is used.

6.3.6.3 *Rascal*

Schmidt and Sarrazin give the following sense divisions:

1. a mean sorry wretch, a scoundrel[44]
2. a lean deer not fit to hunt or kill

Stoll (1989: 216f.) treats *rascal* and *rogue* together, because both terms have in common that they originated as class terms, denoting "the rabble of an army or of the populace; common soldiers or camp-followers; persons of the lowest class" (OED s.v. *rascal*) and "one belonging to a class of idle vagrants or vagabonds" (OED s.v. *rogue*). Later on, both developed into terms of abuse.

In the corpus *rascal* has a frequency of 57 occurrences (19 verse; 38 prose). The distribution of pronouns is as shown in Table 35.

Table 35. T and Y pronouns co-occurring with *rascal*

	T pronoun	Y pronoun	combined
Comedies	1	1	2
Histories	3	5	8
Tragedies	5	6	11
Total	**9**	**12**	**23**

This distribution shows a mixed picture of pronoun use. As an abusive vocative, *rascal* is almost absent from the Comedies. In the Histories, the term is common in the "Falstaff plays", and in the Tragedies, LR is the play that draws extensively on the term. In many cases *rascal* is preceded by negative epithets such as *bald-pated, bottle-ale, cowardly, cutpurse, damn'd tripe-visag'd, dishonest, emboss'd, fat-kidney'd, impudent, lying, muddy, swaggering* and *wide-chopped.* In addition to this, *rascal* is mostly used in exclamatives and (verbless) imperatives.

In 1H4 Prince Henry addresses his crony Falstaff as *rascal* without seriously implying bad character qualities:

(1)   Poins: Come, shelter, shelter! I have remov'd Falstaff's horse, and he frets like a gumm'd velvet.
      Prince: Stand close. [They retire.]
      Falstaff: Poins! Poins, and be hang'd! Poins!
      Prince [Coming forward.]: Peace, ye fat-kidney'd rascal! what a brawling dost thou keep! (1H4 2, 2, 1–6)

On the other hand, when Falstaff has accused the hostess of having picked his pocket and mocked the prince, "I fear thee as I fear the roaring of a lion's whelp", he receives an angry *thou*:

(2)   Prince: Charge an honest woman with picking thy pocket! Why, thou whoreson, impudent, emboss'd rascal, [...]. (1H4 3, 3, 155–157)

When Doll Tearsheet is to be taken to prison for having caused a tavern brawl she quickly switches from a neutral *you* to an angry *thou* to the beadle. In anger Lear also calls Gloucester a "rascal beadle":

(3)   Doll: Nuthook, nuthook, you lie. Come on! I'll tell thee what, thou damn'd tripe-visag'd rascal, and the child I go with do miscarry, thou wert better thou hadst strook thy mother, thou paper-fac'd villain! (2H4 5, 4, 7–10)

(4)   Lear [to Gloucester]: Thou rascal beadle, hold thy bloody hand! (LR 4, 6, 160)

The next quotation illustrates wordplay on the two senses of *rascal*. "Using *rascal* in the sense of 'lean, inferior deer', Falstaff implies that the term is inappropriate for him" (*Riverside Shakespeare*):

(5)   Doll: A pox damn you, you muddy rascal, is that all the comfort you give me?
      Falstaff: You make fat rascals, Mistress Doll. (2H4 2, 4, 39–41)

An interesting case is the lengthy exchange between Kent and Oswald in LR. At first, Kent rails on Oswald with a whole litany of abuse:

(6)   Oswald: What dost thou know me for?
      Kent: A knave, a rascal, an eater of broken meats; a base, proud, shallow, beggarly, three-suited, hundred-pound, filthy worsted-stocking knave; a lily-liver'd, action-taking, whoreson, glass-gazing, superserviceable, finical rogue; one-

trunk-inheriting slave; one that wouldst be a bawd in way of good service, and art nothing but the composition of a knave, beggar, coward, pandar, and the son and heir of a mungril bitch; one whom I will beat into [clamorous] whining, if thou deni'st the least syllable of thy addition. (LR 2, 2, 14–24)

But when he charges him to a duel and asks him to draw (and a duel being one way of settling an affair of honour) he continues to address Oswald with *you*, despite being *thou*d himself. As Oswald does not take up the challenge, he insults him as a coward and switches back to *thou*:

(7) Oswald: Away, I have nothing to do with thee.
Kent: Draw, you rascal! [...] Draw, you rogue, or I'll carbonado your shanks! Draw, you rascal! Come your ways.
Oswald: Help ho! murther, help!
Kent: Strike, you slave! Stand, rogue, stand, you neat slave! Strike! [Beating him.] [...]
Kent: No marvel, you have so bestirr'd your valor. You cowardly rascal, / Nature disclaims in thee: a tailor made thee. (LR 2, 2, 34–43; 53–55)

Thus, the choice of pronoun can depend on the situation, the topic of discourse and also on (mutual) attitudes as well as the meaning of the term, i.e. whether *rascal* is meant as a light term of reproof, punningly or as a serious reproach for character deficiencies.

6.3.6.4 *Rogue*

Schmidt and Sarrazin give the following sense divisions:

a term of reproach, = rascal, knave
Used in pity and tenderness [...]. In this case even a fem. "Alas, poor rogue, I think, [i' faith], she loves me." (OTH 4, 1, 111)

Rogue has a total frequency of 79 tokens (13 verse; 66 prose). The distribution of address pronouns is given in Table 36.

Despite the fact that *rogue* also collocates with negative epithets like *bastardly, blue-bottle, damnable both-sides, finical, glass-gazing, honeyseed* (blunder for

Table 36. T and Y pronouns co-occurring with *rogue*

	T pronoun	Y pronoun	combined
Comedies	1*	10	11
Histories	3	12	15
Tragedies	5	5	10
Total	9	27	36

* There is one further case of *thou* in a letter (TN 3, 4, 162).

homicide), *mechanical salt-butter, mouldy, superserviceable* it shows a higher rate of *you* than *rascal*. The two terms of reproach run parallel in that both abound in exclamatives and imperatives. The cases in which *rogue* collocates with positive adjectives like *sweet little* and *poor rogue hereditary* are fewer.

As Table 36 proves (chi-squared = 5.013; $p > 0.10$ with 2 df), pronoun use is obviously tied up with the genres, as the Comedies again show the highest use of *you*. The only case of *thou* in the Comedies is to be found in WIV 2, 2, 278–281, when Master Ford is being slandered by Falstaff while he visits him under the name of Master Brook.

Pronoun use is also linked to the different meanings of the term. In their competition in misanthropy, Timon and Apemantus slander each other bitterly with abusive vocatives. In this example *rogue* is employed in the sense of "a dishonest, unprincipled person; a rascal" (OED) and co-occurs with a reproachful *thou*:

(1)   Timon: Away, thou issue of a mangy dog! Choler does kill me that thou art alive; I swound to see thee.
Apemantus: Would thou wouldst burst!
Timon: Away, thou tedious rogue! I am sorry I shall lose a stone by thee.
[Throws a stone at him.]
Apemantus: Beast!
Timon: Slave!
Apemantus: Toad!
Timon: Rogue, rogue, rogue! / I am sick of this false world, and will love nought / But even the mere necessities upon't. (TIM 4, 3, 366–376)

This sense sharply contrasts with: "one who is of a mischievous disposition. Common as a playful term of reproof or reproach, and freq. used as a term of endearment by 17th c. dramatists" (OED):

(2)   Falstaff: A rascal! to brave me?
Doll: Ah, you sweet little rogue, you! Alas, poor ape, how thou sweat'st! Come let me wipe thy face. Come on, you whoreson chops. Ah, rogue! i' faith, I love thee. Thou art as valorous as Hector of Troy, worth five of Agamemnon, and ten times better than the Nine Worthies. Ah, villain! (2H4 2, 4, 215–221)

Similar to *rascal*, *rogue* also shows pronoun switching in an utterance:

(3)   Pistol: Didst not thou share? Hadst thou not fifteen pence?
Falstaff: Reason, you rogue, reason; think'st thou I'll endanger my soul gratis? At a word, hang no more about me, I am no gibbet for you. (WIV 2, 2, 14–17)

In addition to these, and in this case comparable to *villain*, *rogue* is also "applied abusively to servants" (OED); this sense predominates in the Comedies and, furthermore, in this sense *you* usually appears as pronoun:

(4)   Berowne [to Moth, page to Armado]: Is this your perfectness? Be gone, you
      rogue! (LLL 5, 2, 174)

(5)   Petruchio [to a servant]: Off with my boots, you rogues! You villains, when? [...]
      / Out, you rogue, you pluck my foot awry. / Take that, and mend the plucking
      [off] the other. [Strikes him.] (SHR 4, 1, 144–148)

The two terms *rascal* and *rogue* show parallels to each other in that both can be used
as a term for serious reproach and even contempt but also in a more light-hearted
way. The difference in pronoun use with a preponderance of *you* in relation with
rogue is brought about mainly by its frequent employment as an abusive term for
servants in the Comedies.

6.3.6.5   *Strumpet*

Schmidt and Sarrazin give only the sense of "a prostitute". The OED adds that the
term can be used figuratively of things personified. *Strumpet* has a total frequency
of 25 tokens (23 verse; 2 prose) in the corpus. In direct address the term is not
frequently used, as there are only 8 occurrences, out of which one token co-occurs
with *you* and 3 with *thou* (see Table 37).[45]

Table 37. T and Y pronouns co-occurring with *strumpet*

	T pronoun	Y pronoun	combined
Comedies	–	–	–
Histories	1	–	1
Tragedies	2	1	3
Total	**3**	**1**	**4**

At first Othello calls his wife "you strumpet" and later switches to *thou*:

(1)   Othello: [Impudent strumpet!]
      Desdemona: By heaven, you do me wrong.
      Othello: Are not you a strumpet?
      Desdemona: No, as I am a Christian. If to preserve this vessel for my lord /
      From any other foul unlawful touch / Be not to be a strumpet, I am none.
      [...]
      Othello: Out, strumpet! weep'st thou for him to my face?
      Desdemona: O, banish me, my lord, but kill me not!
      Othello: Down, strumpet! (OTH 4, 2, 81–85; 5, 2, 77–79)

Bianca resents being called a *strumpet*:

(2)   Emilia: O fie upon thee, strumpet!
       Bianca: I am no strumpet, but of life as honest / As you that thus abuse me.
       (OTH 5, 1, 121–123)

6.3.6.6   Varlet/varlot/varletto

Schmidt and Sarrazin give the following meanings:

1. a servant to a knight
2. a term of reproach, = knave, rascal

In the OED *varlet* is attested from 1456 onwards. Originally it had the meaning of "a man or lad acting as an attendant or servant; a menial, a groom". The term soon developed negative connotations "a person of a low, mean, or knavish disposition; a knave, rogue, rascal". The first quotation in the OED dates from 1555, but the OED also remarks that in later use the bad qualities were often not implied. The first citation as an abusive term of address also goes back to this time (1566).

Salmon says that in comparison to other forms of abuse, *varlet* is "less commonly used in address [in the Falstaff plays], and may be slightly old-fashioned or affected" (1967:59). This statement is also borne out by the data from the complete corpus. *Varlet* together with its spelling variants has a total frequency of 24 tokens (5 verse; 19 prose), and is used both descriptively and in address.

Table 38. T and Y pronouns co-occurring with *varlet*

	T pronoun	Y pronoun	combined
Comedies	6	–	6
Histories	1	–	1
Tragedies	2	–	2
Total	**9**	**–**	**9**

In the sense of 'a servant to a knight' it is only employed descriptively, viz.: Shallow to Falstaff about his servant Davy: "A good varlet, a very good varlet, Sir John" (2H4 5, 3, 13). In 18 cases it is used as address, out of which 9 are accompanied by *thou*, and not a single one by *you* (see Table 38). As address *varlet* is often preceded by adjectives with negative connotations such as *dishonest* (WIV 4, 2, 102), *wicked* (MM 2, 1, 167; 190), *naughty* (ADO 4, 2, 72; 1H4 2, 4, 432).[46]

Varlet is used by Kent and Lear to Oswald (LR 2, 2, 28; 2, 4, 187), Falstaff in imitation of the Prince's father to the Prince in his speech "in King Cambyses' vein" (1H4 2, 4, 432) and by Elbow, a simple constable, in MM:

(1) Pompey: By this hand, sir, his wife is a more respected person than any of us all.
     Elbow: Varlet, thou liest! thou liest, wicked varlet! The time is yet to come that
     she was ever respected with man, woman, or child.
     Pompey: Sir, she was respected with him before he married with her.
     Escalus: Which is the wiser here: Justice or Iniquity? Is this true?
     Elbow: O thou caitiff! O thou varlet! O thou wicked Hannibal!
     (MM 2, 1, 165–175)

6.3.6.7 *Villain*

As indicated by Schmidt and Sarrazin, *villain* is used in the following senses in
Shakespeare's plays:

originally = bondman, slave, servant (cf. AYL 1, 1, 55; TIT 4, 3, 74; LR 3, 7, 78).[47]
But usually as a term of reproach, = a vile and wicked person, a wretch, a rascal.
Sometimes used in a less opprobrious sense, particularly in addresses [...].[48]
Even as a term of endearment. [...] Applied to females: *here comes the little*
v.[illain] (TN 2, 5, 13) (Maria). *it is the prettiest v.[illain]* (TRO 3, 2, 33)
(Cressida).

Villain also originated as a class term for servants, but despite the fact that this
meaning component is still present in Shakespeare's plays, the reproachful connotations dominate, as e.g. in (2)–(4); cf. also Stoll (1989:213–216).

Regardless of the weight of the reproach, pronoun usage is very clear, as there
are 77 instances of addresses involving *thou* and only 5 involving *you* (see Table 39);
the overall frequency of *villain* being 250 tokens (173 verse; 77 prose).

Table 39. T and Y pronouns co-occurring with *villain*

	T pronoun	Y pronoun	combined
Comedies	27*	3	30
Histories	17	2	19
Tragedies	33	–	33
Total	**77**	**5**	**82**

* There is one further case in a letter (TN 3, 4, 163).

Since pronoun usage is so unambiguous, the emotive force, that is to say the
seriousness of the reproach, must be inferred from other linguistic devices, as e.g.
the sentence type and type of adjective. Roused emotions are very often indicated
by (short) exclamatory sentences of the type *O, villain* [...]!

(1) Iago [to Rodrigo]: O murd'rous slave! O villain! (OTH 5, 1, 62)

Furthermore, *villain* is frequently found in usually short and often verbless imperatives,
which adds to the peremptoriness of the order. In this often less opprobrious use it is

given to servants and persons who are regarded as menials, probably as a repercussion of the older sense of "originally, a low-born base-minded rustic; a man of ignoble ideas or instincts; in later use, an unprincipled or depraved scoundrel" (OED):

(2)   Launce: Master, shall I strike?
       Proteus: Who wouldst thou strike?
       Launce: Nothing.
       Proteus: Villain, forbear. (TGV 3, 1, 199–202)

(3)   Speed: Master, be one of them; / It's an honorable kind of thievery.
       Sir Valentine: Peace, villain. (TGV 4, 1, 38–39)

(4)   Petruchio [to Grumio, his manservant]: Villain, I say, knock me at his gate, [...].
       (SHR 1, 2, 11)

In many cases the selection of adjective(s) adds to the abusive force, e.g. *abominable, bloody, brutish, detested, dissembling, dull, hateful, monstrous, notorious, senseless, whoreson* etc. Possibly the strongest accusation in the entire corpus is to be found in MAC:

(5)   Macduff [to Macbeth]: I have no words, / My voice is in my sword, thou bloodier villain / Than terms can give thee out! (MAC 5, 8, 6–8)

Apart from the few cases of endearing use, indicated e.g. by such adjectives as *sweet*, and a mock-polite (?) *you* given in appreciation from a "mistress to her valiant knight" in (7), there are ironic uses of *fine* and *gentle*:

(6)   Queen Margaret [to Gloucester]: Ah, gentle villain, do not turn away!
       (R3 1, 3, 162)

(7)   Doll Tearsheet [to Falstaff]: I pray thee, Jack, be quiet, the rascal's gone. Ah, you whoreson little valiant villain, you! [...] Ah, you sweet little rogue, you! Alas, poor ape, how thou sweat'st! Come let me wipe thy face. Come on, you whoreson chops. Ah, rogue! i' faith, I love thee. Thou art as valorous as Hector of Troy, worth five of Agamemnon, and ten times better than the Nine Worthies. Ah, villain! (2H4 2, 4, 208–209; 216–221)

The few other occurrences of *you* deviating from the majority use can be accounted for by intersocial and circumstantial factors such as the social position of Benedick and Claudio as lords and the situation of aside (= no listener) in (8), the pronoun switching in (9) and (10) as rising anger. In (11) the immediate vicinity of *sir* seems to forbid the use of *thou*:

(8)   Benedick [Aside to Claudio.]: You are a villain. I jest not; [...].
       (ADO 5, 1, 145–146)

(9)   Vincentio: Come hither, you rogue. What, have you forgot me?
       Biondello: Forgot you? no, sir. I could not forget you, for I never saw you before in all my life.

Vincentio: What, you notorious villain, didst thou never see thy [master's] father, Vincentio? (SHR 5, 1, 48–53)

(10) Cloten [to Pisanio]: What, are you packing, sirrah? Come hither. Ah, you precious pandar! Villain, Where is thy lady? In a word, or else / Thou art straightway with the fiends. (CYM 3, 5, 80–83)

(11) Gower: How now, sir? you villain!
Williams: Do you think I'll be forsworn? (H5 4, 8, 11–12)

6.3.6.8 *Witch*
According to Schmidt and Sarrazin, *witch* is used in two different senses:

1. a woman who practises sorcery
    – Term of reproach for an old and ugly woman
2. a male sorcerer

Although *witch* with 40 tokens (26 verse; 14 prose) is much more frequent than *hag*, its use as an abusive term is similar to that of *hag*, as it is not used very often in direct address. There are 5 instances where *witch* co-occurs with *thou*, and 2 (in WIV) with *you* (see Table 40).

Table 40. T and Y pronouns co-occurring with *witch*

	T pronoun	Y pronoun	combined
Comedies	1	2	3
Histories	2	–	2
Tragedies	2	–	2
Total	5	2	7

The contexts show a good deal of overlap between the two terms because both occur next to each other as address to the same persons, often in a whole barrage of insults as in (1). However, *hag* does not overtly cover the meaning of 'sorceress'. Two occurrences of *witch* account for this meaning: "Aroint thee, witch!" (MAC 1, 3, 6 and LR 3, 4, 124):

(1) Ford [to Falstaff disguised as Mother Pratt]: Come down, you witch, you hag you, come down, I say!
[…]
Out of my door, you witch, you rag, you baggage, you poulcat, you runnion! out, out! I'll conjure you, I'll fortune-tell you! (WIV 4, 2, 178–186)

(2) Antipholus of Syracuse [to Courtezan]: Avaunt, thou witch! (ERR 4, 3, 78)

(3) Gloucester [to Queen Margaret]: Foul wrinkled witch, what mak'st thou in my sight? (R3 1, 3, 163)

6.3.6.9   *Summary: Terms of abuse*

In comparison to the terms of endearment, the abusive vocatives are much more frequent. However, if the female terms are contrasted with the male ones, then the latter are again far more numerous.[49]

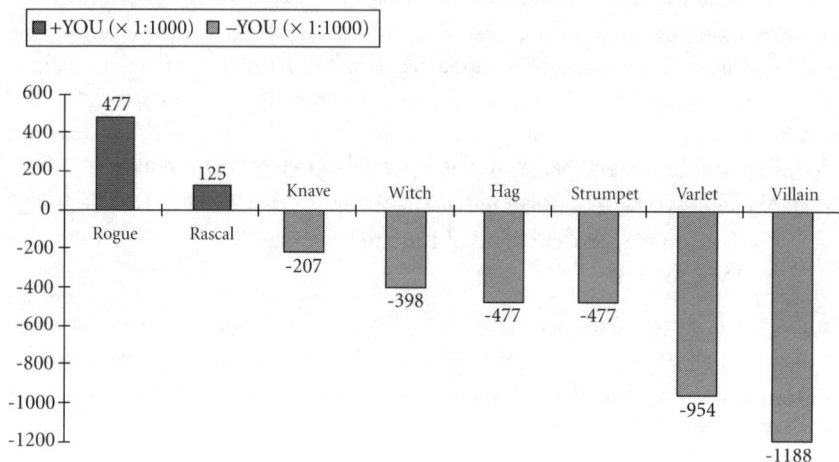

Graph 6. Terms of abuse.

Hag is very infrequent as an abusive address for a woman. The term is used exclusively by male speakers for women who are viewed as vicious or malicious. Apart from WIV, where *you* is the majority form (165 T pronouns:773 Y pronouns), the co-occurring *thou* indicates deep contempt. The same also holds true for *witch*, except that in the sense of 'sorceress' the three witches in MAC address each other as *witch*, but otherwise it is only used by male speakers. With *hag* it has in common that both terms are used extremely contemptibly, which is confirmed by pronoun usage. *Strumpet* is even more marginal than *hag* and *witch*. Practically the only play in which the term plays a role is OTH. There are more T pronouns than Y pronouns, but due to its general infrequency no further conclusions should be drawn from that.

As far as the male terms of abuse are concerned, *villain* is the most frequent one and seems to have been prototypical. In contrast to *rascal* and *rogue*, which are both often used by Falstaff, he never uses *villain*. Concerning pronoun use, *villain* is a typical "*thou* word". The few cases of *you* can be relegated to intersocial and/or situational factors.

Varlet is the most clear-cut case of pronoun use, as it co-occurs exclusively with *thou*. Compared to the other terms of reproof for men it is usually applied less opprobriously and is the least frequent of all.

Knave, rascal and *rogue* show similarities, for all three can also be used less abusively or even as terms of endearment. When used endearingly or compassionately, *thou* appears more often. In the case of *knave* its functions of abuse or endearment are signalled by either negative or positive adjectives and only less obviously by pronouns, because in both cases *thou* appears, although it has to be interpreted differently as either a sign of compassion or reproof. However, when masters chide their servants as *knaves*, they usually address them by *you*. Abbott ([1870] 1972: 155) is of the opinion that in this case the use of the more distant pronoun *you* instead of *thou* reinforces the criticism.

Regarding pronoun use, *rascal* presents a mixed picture, as the overall ratio is almost balanced. On closer inspection, it becomes apparent that it can also be applied less seriously, yet as a contemptive term of serious reproach *thou* is always the co-occurring pronoun. In the other cases pronoun use varies while the discourse participants remain the same. This implies that it depends on the situation.

The same basically also holds true for *rogue*, with the only difference being that the ratio of *you* is even higher. This is mainly due to its being used in the Comedies as an abusive vocative for servants who do not carry out services in accord to their masters' wants and are reproved as *you (negative adj.) rogue.*

6.4 Summary and conclusion

Although the six categories of nominal address and their use of co-occurring second person pronouns have each been summarised in turn, it is necessary after this extensive presentation of data to give an overall summary to put the individual results into perspective and to answer the questions raised in the introduction.

In my opinion the preceding study has basically proved two points: the co-occurrence of second person pronouns and nominal forms of address in Shakespeare's plays can be handled in a fairly consistent numerical approach supplemented by a socio-pragmatic framework. Numerical evidence from the use of address pronouns and co-occurring nominal forms of address tells us that there is indeed a strong correlation between the two, because a log-linear regression can be established. Graph 7 below shows all the groups of vocatives together in order of decreasing use of *you*.

This is to say that the address nouns can be placed along a scale of politeness ranging from negative politeness or deference at the one end, as represented (in declining order of "*you*fulness") by the titles of honour and courtesy, occupational titles and expressions of family relationship, which all co-occur with much more Y forms than T forms, to the generic terms of address, the terms of abuse and, at the far end of positive politeness, the terms of endearment as the most "*thou*ful" ones.

From a bird's-eye view, these results are in accord with Brown and Gilman's "power and solidarity semantics" and also with the claim of politeness theory that most address nouns can be placed at various points along the politeness scale.[50]

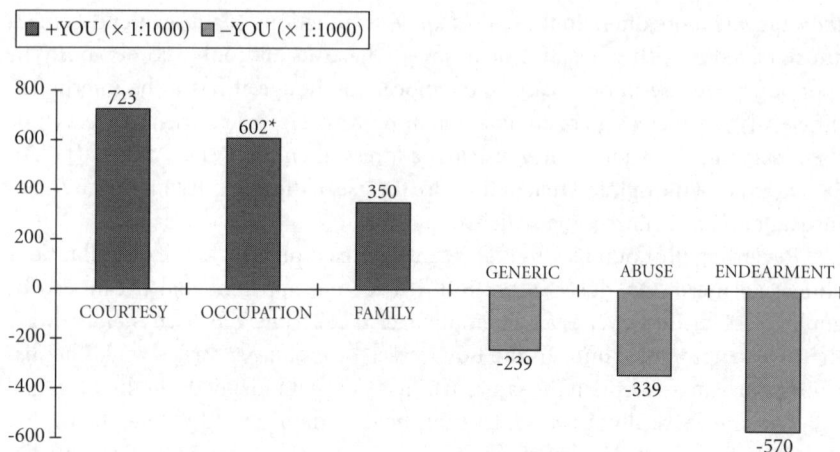

Graph 7. Vocative categories ranked according to co-occurring pronouns considered in the aggregate.

* This column gives the score for all terms excepting *nurse*. If *nurse* — the only form to make use of T pronouns — is considered alongside the others, the score drops to 176.

Thus far Brown and Gilman (1989) and also Kopytko (1993a), who have largely omitted the address pronouns from their studies, seem to be justified in doing so.

However, on closer inspection, there are quite a number of cases and not only a small residue, as Brown and Gilman claim, which run counter to the rules power and solidarity semantics, as, for instance, when masters chide their servants as *you rascal* or *you rogue*. These cases can be regarded as the odd ones out, as Brown and Gilman (1989:178) do, but to assign "complications to context" (ibid.) in my opinion and also in that of Nevalainen and Raumolin-Brunberg means to miss an important factor, because "it seems to us that the variability of placement needs special emphasis, since the interpretation of the use of a given term depends on the context" (Nevalainen and Raumolin-Brunberg 1995:557). Mazzon is also of the opinion that the "hasty dismissal of the issue [of pronoun use] is oversimplistic" for the reasons that "precisely because the pronoun is 'an obligatory aspect of speech', its politeness value can never be overlooked; the choice of a pronoun rather than another could in itself constitute an FTA [...]" (1995:25).

In assuming a constellation of factors that apply or do not apply, Brown and Gilman's model is too rigid, because, in my opinion, for meaningful pronoun choices there is an overlap and often also a clash of permanent, or relatively stable social factors, temporary attitudes, shifts in feeling, etc. In addition to that, those vocatives which showed a mixed pronoun use, illustrate that there is ample room for "social negotiation", as Calvo (1992a) put it.

Furthermore, in addition to these socio-pragmatic constraints the study has revealed that the literary genre also affects pronoun use to a statistically significant degree. Table 41 gives the aggregate data for co-occurring pronouns of all the 36 forms analysed and proves that in the Comedies the ratio of *you* to *thou* is 2:1 as compared to 1:1.15 for the Histories and almost 1: 1 for the Tragedies. Thus, on the corpus level, irrespective of the six vocative categories, it is the genre of Comedy that exhibits the highest degree of Y forms with a ratio of 31.40% T forms and 68.60% Y forms. Compared to this, the Histories and Tragedies show a much higher incidence of T forms with 46.40% T forms and 53.60% Y forms in the Histories, and 48.50% T forms and 51.50% Y forms in the Tragedies. Graph 8 illustrates the distribution of pronouns according to genre.

Table 41. Aggregate data for T and Y pronouns co-occurring with vocatives

	T pronoun	Y pronoun	combined
Comedies	151	330	481
Histories	156	180	336
Tragedies	208	221	429
Total	515	731	1246

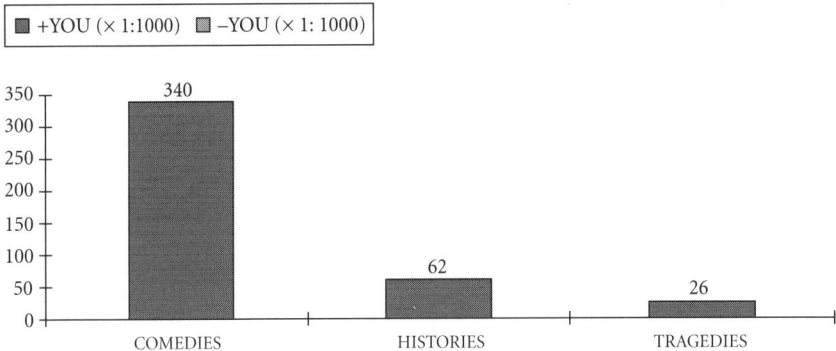

Graph 8. Aggregate pronoun score for the Comedies, Histories and Tragedies.

Although we should not believe that Shakespeare had any reason to present inauthentic language, it must be emphasised that we are dealing with a literary corpus. So some of the pronoun choices may have been made for the sake of rhyme and metre, the requirements of genre, plot or a particular scene, to achieve a certain dramatic effect, etc. In addition to this, with reference to the Histories, Replogle points out that Shakespeare in his later years became more skilful in his artistic ability to depict the address forms used by the nobility:

> It seems evident that Shakespeare's knowledge of the usage of the forms of address among the nobility increased after the writing of the early history plays. In the *Henry VI* plays the English *nobiles majores* use an unwonted degree of familiarity [...]. Since such inappropriate forms are not used in Shakespeare's later history plays, for example *I* and *II Henry IV*, it would seem that in the intervening years the dramatist acquired a better knowledge of the usages of noblemen. (Replogle 1967: 145f.)

This chapter has shown how Shakespeare used both nominal and pronominal address in his plays and that a correlation between these categories in terms of variable rules can be established. However, it has also proved that pronoun use is not fully predictable, because on the micro level of analysis, apart from intersocial relationships other factors have to be taken into account. Beside the factors arising out of rank, affection and context we have to be aware of even more constraints. Other important parameters not to be neglected are either ironic, mock-polite and flattering uses of language, where the nominally polite form is employed to convey the opposite and also cases that do not seek to minimise an FTA, but rather to maximize it.

Obviously, Shakespeare must have been well aware of the social conventions of the day, and he surely exploited them skilfully for dramatic purposes. Nonetheless, on the basis of this investigation we can only construct a "social grammar" of Shakespeare, but we should not assume that the language of drama, with its carefully constructed speeches, bore any close resemblance to real people talking, because it is not always possible to take such renditions at their face value (cf. Chapter 2.5).

CHAPTER 7

"Prithee no more" vs. "Pray you, chuck, come hither"

Prithee and *pray you* as discourse markers

7.1 Introduction and objectives[1]

Within the framework of historical pragmatics the study of discourse markers has received much attention in recent years (cf. Brinton 1996). By taking a look at how the verb *to pray* and the form *prithee* are used in the context of Shakespearean drama it will be investigated what their textual and interpersonal functions are and which factors determine their selection. The two imperatives quoted in the title, said by Othello to Desdemona, clearly indicate that the forms differ in politeness.

The analysis of the two discourse markers will focus mainly on five related aspects:

1. The objective of the first part of the study is to look for corpus-internal variation of the respective forms. Lexico-statistical analyses will be applied in order to elucidate whether a change of usage can be identified during the some 25 years of Shakespeare's writing career, or whether any differences in distribution exist between the dramatic genres.

2. In a second step the forms will be scrutinised in terms of politeness. The co-occurrence of the two forms with vocatives will be investigated to find out whether the politeness expressed by them is different in degree or rather in principle. In this respect the illocutionary force of polite requests will be analysed to check if the results of Brown and Gilman (1989) on collocates with names, honorifics, etc. obtained in a random sample hold, or, if in terms of politeness theory varying degrees and strategies of politeness can be observed between the different genres as Kopytko (1993a) has found out to exist between Tragedies and Comedies.

3. The textual and intersocial discourse functions of *pray* and *prithee* and their interplay with interjections and other pragmatic particles will be highlighted by extensive samples of dialogue from various plays and an in-depth study of WIV and 1H4.

4. Once the discourse functions of *pray* and *prithee* have been established, their syntactic and pragmatic functions will be accounted for in terms of grammaticalization.

5. Finally, the discussion of grammaticalization will be concluded by making a comparison of *pray/prithee* and *please* as discourse markers in polite requests.

7.2   The treatment of the forms in reference works

Quite surprisingly, information on the two forms in the standard Shakespeare dictionaries and -grammars is scanty. Franz ([1939] 1986:276f.) mentions that with recurring everyday expressions like *beseech you, prithee, pray you* and *would (= I wish)* the first-person pronominal subject is often omitted and that the second-person pronoun is often left out in questions because of the characteristic inflectional verb ending. Apart from this, a short remark on the pragmatic function of *prithee* is made. Franz says that in former times it fulfilled the role of modern English *please* and that even in Shakespeare's time it was in the process of being reduced to a particle, as was in fact *pray*.

In contrast to this, Schmidt and Sarrazin ([1875] 1962:s.v. *pray*) offer an abundance of citations for the verb *pray*, yet they do not give any frequencies for the respective constructions. According to them the meaning and syntactic functions of *to pray* in the Shakespeare Corpus can be represented as follows:[2]

1. **to ask earnestly, to entreat:**
    a. absolutely: *I pray now keep below,* (TMP 1, 1, 11)
    b. with *for: A conqueror that will pray in aid for kindness / Where he for grace is kneel'd to,* (ANT 5, 2, 27–28)
    c. with a clause: *and prays that you will hie you home* (ERR 1, 2, 90)
    d. elliptically: *to what, I pray?* (MM 1, 2, 48)
    e. transitively: *I pray thee mark me* (TMP 1, 2, 67)
    f. *I* omitted: *no, pray thee* (TMP 1, 2, 371)
    g. elliptically: *I pray you, is Signior Mountanto return'd?* (ADO 1, 1, 30)
    h. a clause following: *the poor fool prays her that he may depart,* (VEN 578)
    i. an infinitive following with *to: and so I pray you all to think yourselves,* (SHR 2, 1, 113)
    j. an infinitive following without *to: your father prays you leave your books,* (SHR 3, 1, 82)
    k. with an accusative and *to: and pray her to a fault for which I chid her,* (TGV 1, 2, 52)
    l. with an accusative denoting the thing asked: *I know not how to pray your patience,* (ADO 5, 1, 271)

2. **to make petitions to heaven:**
    a. absolutely: *you must pray* (WIV 4, 2, 156)
    b. with a clause (almost = to wish): *he heartily prays some occasion may detain us longer* (ADO 1, 1, 149–150)

c. *I* omitted: *pray heartily he be at' palace* (WT 4, 4, 711)
d. with *to*: *I think and pray / To several subjects* (MM 2, 4, 1–2)
e. with an accusative: *I pray the gods she may* (SHR 4, 4, 67)
f. *I* omitted: *pray heav'n he prove so* (TGV 2, 7, 79)

Prithee, on the other hand, is only described as "a corruption of *pray thee*" with the addition that the pronoun *I* is often omitted and that there is some vacillation between *prithee* and *pray thee* between the First Folio and the different Quarto editions.

7.3 Numerical distribution of the forms in the Shakespeare Corpus

7.3.1 *(I) pray (you/thee*, etc.)

The verb *pray* has an absolute frequency of 778 tokens in the complete works of Shakespeare, 498 (64%) of which occur in verse, and 280 (36%) in prose. A comparison between the verse and prose-proportions of both forms does not yield any statistically significant deviance on the corpus level. Table 1 below shows the combinations of the verb *pray* for Shakespeare's plays in decreasing frequencies. The left-hand column provides the figures for the 38 plays, and the right-hand column those for the plays that were written by Shakespeare alone (minus the dubious plays PER, H8, and TNK).

Table 1 proves that *I pray you* is the most frequent form in the corpus; *pray you* is only about half as frequent. To find out whether the above forms show any corpus-internal variation, the sum total will be broken up according to genres and dates of composition. For this reason the individual genres will first be analysed separately. Since the individual figures for the forms are often rather small they mostly defy a thorough-going statistical approach. Nonetheless, before socio-linguistic and pragmatic tools are applied, the numerical development might in the diachronic perspective of some 25 years hint at changes in usage over time.

The Histories constitute the earliest set of plays. According to the chronology provided in the *Riverside Shakespeare* ([2]1997: 77–87), they were composed between 1589 and 1599, with the exception of H8, which is considered a collaboration of Shakespeare and Fletcher and is usually dated 1612–13. As a consequence of this, the figures from this play have not been added up, but will be investigated separately.

Table 2 shows that the largest group of tokens in the Histories is made up of *I prithee*, yet the overall image is slightly distorted by the fact that 15 forms are used in 1H4 alone. *I pray you* is the second largest category. All the others follow far behind. In comparison to the other genres, the Histories exhibit the lowest number of all *pray* and *prithee* forms. In addition to this, the group "*pray (other)*" in Table 2 shows that the largest number of *pray* tokens do not act as parenthetical particles,

Table 1. The number of *pray* and *prithee* tokens

	38 plays		35 plays	
	tokens	per cent	tokens	per cent
pray total	773	100.00	682	100.00
I pray you	253	32.72	233	34.17
pray you	134	17.33	122	17.89
[pray (other)]	132	17.10	119	17.45
pray	101	13.10	71	10.41
I pray thee	71	9.18	67	9.82
I pray	54	6.98	52	7.62
pray thee	21	2.71	18	2.64
pray ye	3	0.38		
we pray you	3	0.38		
I pray them	1	0.12		
prithee total	228	100.00	211	100.00
I prithee	122	53.51	119	56.40
prithee	106	46.49	92	43.60

Table 2. History Plays (1589–1599; [1612–1613])

	1H6	2H6	3H6	R3	JN	R2	1H4	2H4	H5	[H8]
[pray (other)]	2	6	3	6	5	5	8	4	13	42
I pray you	–	3	–	3	1	1	2	8	6	26
Pray you	–	–	–	1	–	–	–	–	3	3
I pray	3	4	1	1	–	–	–	1	1	10
Pray	1	1	–	–	–	2	1	1	20	6
I pray thee	–	2	–	–	–	1	2	5	–	13
Pray thee	–	–	–	–	–	–	–	4	–	6
I prithee	4	4	2	6	1	–	15	–	–	32
Prithee	–	–	–	–	–	–	5	–	7	7
Total	10	20	6	17	7	9	33	23	50	145

but are used in the sense of 'to make petitions to heaven'. The following examples illustrate this category:

(1)   King Richard: Pray God we may make haste and come too late! (R2 1, 4, 64)

(2)   Hostess: But I pray God the fruit of her womb miscarry. (2H4 5, 4, 12–13)

(3)   Cranmer: Pray heaven he sound not my disgrace! (H8 5, 2, 13)

Although examples of this kind, which belong to the original religious domain of the verb, are to be found throughout the corpus, they are far less numerous in the other genres (cf. the category *"pray (other)"* in Tables 3–6). Among these examples in the other genres are predominantly utterances like: *pray God, pray heaven,* etc.

Table 3. Comedies (1592–1602)

	ERR	SHR	TGV	LLL	MND	WIV	ADO	AYL	TN	
[*pray (other)*)]	2	3	4	3	1	5	2	3	4	27
I pray you	11	10	5	2	6	21	15	15	8	93
Pray you	–	1	1	4	2	15	1	4	2	30
I pray	2	12	2	–	–	4	–	–	–	20
Pray	1	5	1	–	1	1	1	1	1	12
I pray thee	1	3	5	1	3	3	8	2	–	26
Pray thee	–	1	–	–	–	–	4	1	–	6
I prithee	1	4	–	–	–	–	–	14	10	29
Prithee	–	2	–	–	–	2	–	3	4	11
Total	**18**	**41**	**18**	**10**	**13**	**51**	**31**	**43**	**29**	**254**

The Comedies (1592–1601/02), as featured in Table 3, have been written at nearly the same time as the Histories (1589–1599). This fact not withstanding, the overall number of *pray* forms and their distribution are quite different. *I pray you* is the most productive form in the Comedies, followed by a wide margin by *pray you, I prithee,* and *I pray thee.* Within this genre quite considerable vacillation is to be observed between individual plays. With the only exception of SHR, where *I pray* is used 12 times, it is very infrequent otherwise. The same basically also holds true for *(I) pray thee* and *(I) prithee,* all of which are absent from many plays. The first plays to show a higher incidence of *I prithee* are AYL (1599) and TN (1601–02).

This result corroborates the findings of Chapter 3 on the distribution of *thou* and *you* in the Shakespeare Corpus, where, quite contrary to my initial hypothesis, the *you* forms proved to be more frequent in the Comedies than the *thou* forms.

Because Shakespeare critics often divide the genre of Tragedy into the subgenres of Tragedy and Roman Plays (cf. Chapter 3.4), owing to their setting in ancient Greece and Rome, the figures for this study have also been presented in two different tables (4 and 5), but in fact, due to their overriding similarities they will be interpreted as a whole. In the Roman Plays, the forms *I pray you* and *pray you* are the most numerous category, followed by *(I) prithee,* and at a greater distance *I pray* and *pray,* which is only numerous in COR. In the Tragedies the line-up of forms is similar. In both subgenres *I pray thee* and *pray thee* are the forms with the lowest numbers of occurrences; they are absent from the majority of plays under scrutiny and do not feature at all in any play written after 1601/02; i.e. after HAM and TRO.

Table 4. Roman Plays (1593–1608)

	TIT	JC	TRO	ANT	COR	TIM	
[*pray (other)*]	3	3	1	3	4	1	15
I pray you	2	4	5	4	6	2	23
Pray you	–	–	4	10	13	3	30
I pray	–	–	1	1	4	2	8
Pray	1	–	–	1	14	6	22
I pray thee	1	–	2	–	–	–	3
Pray thee	1	–	1	–	–	–	2
I prithee	–	3	5	3	5	5	21
Prithee	–	1	3	7	6	5	22
Total	**8**	**10**	**22**	**29**	**52**	**24**	**146**

Table 5. Tragedies (1596–1606)

	ROM	HAM	OTH	LR	MAC	
[*pray (other)*]	1	2	5	2	3	13
I pray you	3	12	14	5	7	41
Pray you	2	6	5	8	2	23
I pray	4	2	1	2	1	10
Pray	–	3	–	8	–	11
I pray thee	7	2	–	–	–	9
Pray thee	–	–	–	–	–	–
I prithee	–	3	6	5	1	15
Prithee	–	3	11	7	3	24
Total	**17**	**33**	**42**	**37**	**17**	**146**

In the heterogeneous group of Late/Problem Plays the forms *I pray you* and *pray you* are again the most frequent ones, followed by *(I) prithee*. Again, *I pray thee* and *pray thee* are absent from most plays written after 1596/97; i.e. after MV.

The quantitative analysis of all *pray-* and *prithee* tokens in the five genres has yielded the following results:

1. The Histories as the earliest group display the lowest overall level of all *pray* forms in the function of a pragmatic particle. The largest category is made up of the more literal meanings of the verb *to pray* (category "*pray (other)*"). However, the Comedies — having been written in the same period — show a much higher incidence of *pray* forms than the Histories. *I pray you* is by far the most numerous form, and with the only exception of the later plays AYL and TN, *(I) prithee* is used very infrequently or not at all.

Table 6. Late/Problem Plays (1596–1611; [1613])

	MV	AWW	MM	[PER]	CYM	WT	TMP	[TNK]	
[*pray (other)*]	4	4	9	1	2	2	–	5	21
I pray you	21	14	6	6	4	3	2	2	50
Pray you	3	7	5	6	9	9	3	5	46
I pray	–	–	2	2	1	2	1	–	6
Pray	–	1	3	2	8	5	3	18	20
I pray thee	12	–	1	–	–	1	2	–	16
Pray thee	2	–	1	–	–	–	1	1	4
I prithee	–	2	4	1	5	4	7	2	22
Prithee	–	3	–	4	8	9	8	3	28
Total	42	31	31	22	37	35	27	36	203

2. For the forms *I pray thee* and *pray thee* a corpus-internal development can be established, since in all genres they are marginally productive only until 1600, and almost completely absent from the second half of the corpus.

3. As regards the contracted forms *I pray* and *pray* it can be stated that in the Shakespeare Corpus they still lag far behind in frequency in comparison to the full form *I pray you/thee*. Compared to the evidence given in the OED, this means that *I pray you* is not yet obsolescent and that the rise of *(I) pray* has not picked up yet (cf. also 7.7).

4. For reasons of dubious authorship the three plays PER, H8 and TNK have been left out of the discussion so far. Their figures in Tables 2 and 6 were not added up for the totals. PER does not show any marked difference in comparison to the other plays, but as in many other aspects the two plays H8 and TNK feature an exceptional usage of forms. The discourse particle *pray* is another case in point; with 20 instances in H8 and 18 in TNK these figures are the highest in the entire corpus, unmatched by any other play (cf. Chapters 3.5; 10.3.8). The only play to come near these numbers is COR with 14 instances. Whether the high number of tokens in H8 and TNK has to be attributed to the hand of Fletcher or to a change in usage over time cannot be established for certain. An indication for the latter interpretation can be seen in the fact that the only plays in the corpus to show a considerable number of *pray* tokens as a discourse particle are LR (1605) with 8 tokens, CYM (1609–10) also with 8 tokens and COR (1607–08) with 14 tokens, all of which are late plays.

7.3.2   *Prithee*

As evidenced by Table 1, the form *prithee* has an absolute frequency of 228 tokens in the Shakespeare Corpus, 141 (61.84%) of which occur in verse lines and only 87 (38.16%) in prose. This ratio is almost identical to that of *pray*.

The distribution of the form over genres and individual plays and characters is uneven. An overriding pattern or principle cannot easily be established. However, out of the 38 plays in the corpus, *prithee* is used in only 23 of them, and *I prithee* in 28. The plays which do not feature any, or only very few tokens, are the early plays from the first half of the corpus up to 1600. This seems to be the corollary of the development of *(I) pray thee*, which showed declining figures in the later plays. With regard to this, it can be assumed that in the second half of the corpus *(I) prithee* had already largely encroached on the former territory of *(I) pray thee*. Owing to this, it is almost impossible to investigate whether the two forms differ in their degree of colloquialism or politeness because no minimally contrasting discourse dyads can be matched.

7.4   *Pray* and *prithee* in terms of politeness

Having found some indication for changes of usage over time in the case of *(I) pray thee* vs. *prithee*, the collocations of *pray* and *prithee* should be analysed next.

Among other topics, Brown and Gilman (1989) investigate directive speech acts. By means of a formula they calculate the politeness or deference of requests in terms of address forms and honorific titles that co-occur with verbs such as *beseech*, *pray*, *prithee*, etc. by making use of the first one hundred random entries in Spevack's *Harvard Concordance to Shakespeare* (1973). Their results are shown in Table 7. They conclude that *I beseech you* is more deferential than *I pray you*. In respect to *prithee*, the authors initially thought that this form "would be on a continuum with *pray you* but less deferential" (1989: 183). However, concordance evidence has convinced them that *prithee* functions as an in-group identity term. For this reason its use was not counted as a substrategy of negative politeness but as a strategy of positive politeness instead.

By comparing my corpus evidence with Brown and Gilman's findings, I tried to find out whether their conclusions hold and therefore investigated the co-occurrence of *pray* and *prithee* with the following eight types of address:

1. titles of courtesy: *master, mistress, sir, my lord*, etc.,
2. last name (+ adorning adjective),
3. adjective + first name,
4. first name only,
5. terms of endearment: *chuck, coz, love, sweet, wag*, etc.,
6. terms of relationship: *wife/husband, father/daughter*, etc.,
7. generic terms of address: *friend, old man, sweet youth*, etc.,
8. terms indicating occupation: *corporal, master lieutenant, nurse, shepherd*, etc.

Table 7. The politeness values of *beseech*, *pray* and *prithee*

Verb	Politeness value	Examples
to beseech	40% entries with honorific titles	*your Majesty, your Grace, your Highness, your lordship, my lord, sir, madam* (not lower)
	60% entries no form of address	
	96% entries with *you*	
to pray	10% entries with honorific titles	*sir* (not higher)
	17% entries with *thee*	
prithee	co-occurring address forms	*boy, my son, daughter, good friend, fellow student, shepherd*, Christian names, no honorific titles

(Table mine, based on the data of Brown and Gilman 1989: 183 f.)

Co-occurring vocatives show no difference in formality or politeness between *I pray you*, *pray you*, *I pray*, and single *pray*. This confirms Brown and Gilman's statement that "a comparison of 'I pray you' and abbreviated 'pray you' reveals no difference" (1989: 183) for the entire corpus. The above four forms basically all share the same characteristics, i.e. the category that most often co-occurs with them is *titles of courtesy*. All the other categories, except perhaps *terms of relationship* and *generic terms of address*, are of no or only minor importance. My investigation has shown, however, that the array of titles and vocatives is larger and covers a social spectrum that is broader than the one given by Brown and Gilman, including titles and styles used for the nobility. Especially in the History Plays, the title *my lord* is used deferentially in polite requests by speakers of lower social rank, but also by social equals where the address is a sign of decorum and etiquette.

I pray thee and *pray thee* are far less frequent than the above categories. Characteristically, no *sir* (used by itself) occurs as a title of courtesy; there is only *good my liege*. Brown and Gilman state that *prithee* is used most often in conjunction with "*boy, my son, daughter, good friend, fellow student, shepherd*, and various Christian names — not honorific forms at all but terms of friendship, affection, and intimacy" (1989: 183 f.). Evidence from the entire corpus is as follows: there are 25 tokens of *(adjective +) first name*, but with 16 examples the category of *generic terms of address* follows, and there are also nine examples in which *prithee* co-occurs with a title of courtesy. In eight cases *prithee* is used together with a term of relationship. With only two tokens, the smallest category is made up by terms of endearment.

Not all these address forms are "terms of friendship, affection, and intimacy" as Brown and Gilman claim, since the following two contrastive examples both show a certain amount of restraint and condescension towards strangers and/or supposed social inferiors:

(4)   3. Servant [to Coriolanus]: What have you to do here, *fellow*? *Pray you* avoid the house. (COR 4, 5, 22–23)[3]

(5)   Menenius [to 1. Watch]: *Prithee, fellow*, remember my name is Menenius, always factionary on the party of your general. (COR 5, 2, 28–30)

In marked contrast to the vocatives used with *pray you*, which are mostly unadorned, the terms of address that accompany *prithee* are often introduced by positively connotated adjectives; in particular the generic terms of address and to a lesser degree the *titles of courtesy* and *adjective + first name* are preceded by *fair, gentle, good, honest, pretty, sweet* and *valiant*, with *good* being the most frequent adjective:

(6)   King [to Queen]: *I prithee* peace, / *Good queen*, and whet not on these furious peers, [...]. (2H6 2, 1, 32–33)

(7)   Othello [to Iago]: *I prithee, good Iago,* / Go to the bay and disembark my coffers. (OTH 2, 1, 207–208)

(8)   Arcite [to Palamon]: *Prithee* take mine, *good cousin*. (TNK 3, 6, 65)

(9)   Gloucester [to Kent]: *Good friend, I prithee* take him in thy arms; / I have o'erheard a plot of death upon him. (LR 3, 6, 88–89)

(10) Lucio [to Vincentio, the Duke of Vienna disguised as Friar Lodowick]: Farewell, *good friar, I prithee* pray for me. (MM 3, 2, 180)

(11) Caliban [to Stephano]: *Prithee, my king*, be quiet. Seest thou here, / This is the mouth o' th' cell. (TMP 4, 1, 215–216)

(12) Falstaff [to Prince Henry]: *I prithee, good prince* — Hal! — help me to my horse, good king's son. (1H4 2, 2, 40–41)

(13) Old Athenian [to Timon]: This man of thine / Attempts her love. *I prithee, noble lord,* / Join with me to forbid him her resort, [...]. (TIM 1, 1, 125–127)

These examples illustrate again that *prithee* is not *per se* to be interpreted as an in-group identity marker, because in some cases *prithee* and the title of courtesy are deferential, whereas in other cases the forms are used by friends, couples, etc.

The only category to furnish examples from one genre exclusively is *last name (+ adorning adjective)*, which contains only tokens from the History Plays. These address forms are exchanged among nobles with perhaps only a small social difference from sovereign to noble, noble parent to noble son, etc.:

(14) Queen [to Sir William Vaux]: Whither goes *Vaux* so fast? What news, *I prithee*? (2H6 3, 2, 367)

(15) Duke of York [to Duke of Buckingham]: *Buckingham, I prithee* pardon me, [...]. (2H6 5, 1, 32)

(16) Duchess of York [to young Duke of York]: How, *my young York*? *I prithee* let me hear it.
[...]
I prithee, pretty York, who told thee this? (R3, 2, 4, 26; 31)

(17)   King [to Archbishop Cranmer]: *My learn'd and well-beloved servant, Cranmer, /*
       Prithee return; with thy approach, I know, / My comfort comes along.
       (H 8 2, 4, 239–241)

The instances of *prithee* and *pray* involving vocatives usually represent a high degree of politeness. Co-occurrence with terms of endearment is equally rare for both forms:

(18)   Falstaff [to Prince]: But *I prithee, sweet wag,* shall there be gallows standing in
       England when thou art king? (1H4 1, 2, 58–60)

(19)   King Henry [to Katherine]: Speak, *my fair,* and fairly, *I pray thee.*
       (H5 5, 2, 167–168)

(20)   Ophelia [to Laertes]: [...] pray you, love, remember. (HAM 4, 5, 176)

(21)   Timon [to Caphis]: *Mine honest friend, / I prithee* but repair to me next morning.
       (TIM 2, 2, 24–25)

(22)   Othello [to Desdemona]: *Pray you, chuck,* come hither. (OTH 4, 2, 24)

Apart from polite requests, *pray* and *prithee* are also, though less frequently, used in connection with interrogatives and verbless imperatives. The verbless imperatives are characterised by little or no politeness at all, but they are redressed by *pray* or *prithee*:

(23)   Othello [to Desdemona]: Prithee no more [...]. (OTH 3, 3, 75)

(23′)   Portia [to Messenger]: No more, I pray thee. (MV 2, 9, 96)

(24)   Macbeth [to Lady Macbeth]: Prithee peace! (MAC 1, 7, 45)

(24′)   Evans [to Mistress Quickly]: I pray you peace. (WIV 4, 1, 30–31)

(24″)   Mistress Quickly [to Caius]: Peace, I pray you. (WIV 1, 4, 80)

(25)   Lear [to Kent]: Prithee away. (LR 5, 3, 269)

(25′)   Edmund [to Edgar]: Pray you away. (LR 1, 2, 175–176)

The above examples (23)–(25) illustrate the influence of the factor *affect* since the utterances are made in agitated states of mind, reveal impatience or have to be made as effectively as possible, because there is danger pending.

The preceding discussion of titles and honorifics has shown that *pray* and *prithee* differ indeed in their degrees of politeness and deference. However, contrary to Brown and Gilman's (1989: 183 f.) interpretation of *pray you* as a sign of deference and *prithee* as an in-group identity marker, the analysis of the whole corpus has proved that there is a certain overlap between the forms and their functions and not a clear-cut dichotomy.

The strongest factor to condition the choice between these forms is the vertical and horizontal social distance between the interlocutors. In addition to the factors *power* and *distance*, the ranked extremity of a face-threatening act has to be accounted for. In order to test this claim of Brown and Gilman's politeness theory, the verbs that co-occur with the forms were scrutinised. The verbs that are most often used in requests involving *prithee* are in decreasing order of frequency: *tell* (17 tokens), *let* (13), *go* (10), *be* (9), *do* (8), *call* (7), *speak* (6), *say* (6), *dispatch* (4) and *come* (4); but the sequence of verbs for *(I) pray (you)/ (thee)* is almost identical, so that in this respect no difference could be made out. It can be argued from this finding that the weight of the imposition is not an important factor for the choice of either *pray* or *prithee*.

7.5   The discourse functions of *pray* and *prithee*

Corpus evidence has also revealed that *pray* and *prithee* both often follow interjections and other pragmatic markers. The interjection that is most commonly used in conjunction with the two is *o*. Either with or without a noun of address it is usually prefixed to exclamatory sentences, polite requests and optatives, and may be used in mild swearing, but can also express consent. On the one hand, the *o* conveys the emotive state of mind of the speaker, but on the other hand, it also has a conative meaning in that it signals a reaction to what has been said or done before. Together with *pray/prithee* it emphasises the speaker's sincere wish that the action be performed:

(26)   [Enter Puck, and Bottom with an ass's head.]
Bottom: "If I were fair, Thisby, I were only thine."
Quince: *O* monstrous! *O* strange! We are haunted. / *Pray*, masters, fly, masters! Help! (MND 3, 1, 103–105)[4]

(27)   Viola: Madam, I come to whet your gentle thoughts / On his behalf.
Olivia: *O,* by your leave, *I pray you*: / I bade you never speak again of him; […]. (TN 3, 1, 105–107)

(28)   Prince: What, stands thou idle here? Lend me thy sword. / Many a nobleman lies stark and stiff / Under the hoofs of vaunting enemies, / Whose deaths are yet unreveng'd. I prithee lend me thy sword.
Falstaff: *O Hal, I prithee* give me leave to breathe a while. (1H4 5, 3, 39–45)

(29)   Jeweller: I have a jewel here —
Merchant: *O, pray* let's see't. For the Lord Timon, sir? (TIM 1, 1, 12–13)

The interjection *ah* often adds an emotional tone to the address. In the quotation below it is followed by an emotive adjective, the style *my liege* and the pronoun *thou*:

(30)   Berowne: *Ah,* good my liege, *I pray thee* pardon me! / Good heart, what grace hast thou thus to reprove / These worms for loving, that art most in love? (LLL 4, 3, 150–152)

Other quite frequently used interjections are *alas* to mark regret and lamentation (cf. Salmon 1967, Taavitsainen 1995) and *lo,* which has a deictic function or expresses surprise:

(31) Ferdinand: I must remove / Some thousands of these logs, and pile them up, / Upon a sore injunction. [...]
Miranda: *Alas, now pray you* / Work not so hard. I would the lightning had / Burnt up those logs that you are enjoin'd to pile! / *Pray* set it down, and rest you. (TMP (3, 1, 9–11; 15–18)

(32) Caliban: *Lo,* how he mocks me! Wilt thou let him, my lord?
Trinculo: "Lord", quoth he? That a monster should be such a natural!
Caliban: *Lo, lo* again. Bite him to death, *I prithee.* (TMP 3, 2, 30–34)

Besides the tendency of *pray/prithee* to be employed together with interjections, they are also, and to an even greater extent, used with other pragmatic particles. In alphabetical order, with absolute frequencies added in brackets, the following pragmatic particles appear in utterances alongside *pray/prithee*: *ay* (3), *but* (18), *look you* (1), *marry* (1), *nay* (22), *now* (2), *well* (7), *why* (1), *yea* (1).

Even though there are differences between interjections and pragmatic particles, there is also some overlap between these categories. In her account on the use of interjections in the Helsinki Corpus, Taavitsainen treats interjections as a subgroup of pragmatic markers and defines them as linguistic gestures that express a speaker's mental state, action or attitude, or reaction to a situation (cf. 1995: 439). With reference to Ameka (1992: 113f.) she establishes the three communicative functions of interjections in EModE as shown in Table 8.[5]

Taavitsainen has found out that the primary interjections, as listed in Table 8, are a reliable means to differentiate between different genres. Depending on their degree of orality, the different genres can be graded according to their use of interjections. Of all genres under investigation in her material from the period of 1570 to 1640, Comedies show the broadest use of interjections, followed by narrative fiction.

Table 8. The communicative functions of interjections in EModE

1. **Focus on the speaker's/narrator's/author's mind:**
   a. Emotive level: *Ah! Alas! Fy! O! Oh! Pshaw! Tush! Tut! Welaway!*
   b. Cognitive function reflecting the speaker's mental processes: *Ah! Ah ha! Eh! Ha! O! Oh!*
2. **Focus on the addressee/reader/audience:**
   a. Vocative: *Ah! Alas! O! Oh!*
   b. Conative: focuses on the interaction between the participants of the speaking situation. Such interjections are directed at an auditor, and they demand an action or response in return: *Ha! Ho! Hoa! Hush! Lo!*
3. **Textual function:**
   a. Reader involvement: *Alas!*
   b. Turning points in the plot: *Alas! Fy, for shame, fly!*
   c. Topic shift: *Alas! oh!*

(Combination of tables in Taavitsainen 1995: 441, 462)

This is basically also corroborated for the Shakespeare Corpus, because especially the Comedies and 1H4 show a high degree of interjections and other pragmatic particles that are used alongside *pray* and *prithee*. Especially two plays make particular use of them, namely WIV and 1H4. For this reason the use of pragmatic particles in these two plays shall be discussed in greater detail and be analysed in terms of discourse functions as outlined in detail by Salmon (1967) and Brinton (1996):[6]

7.5.1   Discourse samples from WIV

(33)   Sir Hugh Evans, a Welsh parson: Give ear to his motions: Master Slender, I will description the matter to you, if you be capacity of it.
Slender, cousin to Shallow: *Nay*, I will do as my cousin Shallow says. *I pray you* pardon me; he's a Justice of Peace in his country, simple though I stand here. (WIV 1, 1, 214–219)

(34)   Page: *By cock and pie*, you shall not choose, sir! come, come.
Slender: *Nay, pray* you lead the way.
Page: Come on, sir.
Slender: Mistress Anne, yourself shall go first.
Anne: Not I, sir, *pray you* keep on.
Slender: Truly I will not go first; truly *la!*[7] I will not do you that wrong.
Anne: *I pray you*, sir.
Slender: I'll rather be unmannerly than troublesome. You do yourself wrong indeed *la!* (WIV 1, 1, 303–313)

(35)   Mistress Page: You are come to see my daughter Anne?
Mistress Quickly: *Ay, forsooth*; and *I pray*, how does good Mistress Anne?
Mistress Page: Go in with us and see. (WIV 2, 1, 162–166)

(36)   Falstaff: Not I, I assure thee. Setting the attraction of my good parts aside, I have no other charms.
Mistress Quickly: Blessing on your heart for't!
Falstaff: *But I pray thee* tell me this: has Ford's wife and Page's wife acquainted each other how they love me? (WIV 2, 2, 105–110)

(37)   Evans: *I pray you now*, good Master Slender's servingman, and friend Simple by your name, which way have you look'd for Master Caius, that calls himself Doctor of Physic?
Simple: *Marry*, sir, the pittie-ward, the park-ward — every way; Old Windsor way, and every way but the town way. (WIV 3, 1, 1–7)

(38)   Caius: *By gar*, with all my heart. He promise to bring me where is Anne Page; *by gar*, he deceive me too.
Evans: *Well*, I will smite his noddles. *Pray you* follow. (WIV 3, 1, 122–126)

(39)   Caius: *By gar*, I see 'tis an honest woman.
Ford: *Well*, I promis'd you a dinner. Come, come, walk in the park. *I pray you*

pardon me; I will hereafter make known to you why I have done this. Come, wife, come, Mistress Page, *I pray you* pardon me; *pray* heartily pardon me. (WIV 3, 3, 222–227)

7.5.2 Discourse samples from 1H4

(40) Falstaff: Indeed you come near me now, Hal, for we take that purses go by the moon and the seven stars, and not by Phoebus, he, "that wand'ring knight so fair." And *I prithee*, sweet wag, when thou art a king, as, God save thy Grace — Majesty I should say, for grace thou wilt have none —
[…]
Marry, then sweet wag, when thou art king, let not us that are squires of the night's body be call'd thieves of the day's beauty. (1H4 1, 2, 13–18; 23–25)

(41) Falstaff: *Yea*, and so us'd it that, were it not here apparent that thou art heir apparent — But *I prithee*, sweet wag, shall there be gallows standing in England when thou art king? (1H4 1, 2, 57–60)

(42) Worcester: And for whose death we in the world's wide mouth / Live scandaliz'd and foully spoken of.
Hotspur: *But* soft, *I pray you*, did King Richard then / Proclaim my brother Edmund Mortimer / Heir to the crown?
Northumberland: He did, myself did hear it.
Hotspur: *Nay*, then I cannot blame his cousin king, / That wish'd him on the barren mountains starve. (1H4 1, 3, 153–159)

(43) Prince: "Anon, anon, sir! Score a pint of bastard in the Halfmoon", or so. *But*, Ned, to drive away the time till Falstaff come, *I prithee* do thou stand in some by-room, […]. (1H4 2, 4, 27–30)

(44) Francis: Anon, sir. *Pray* stay a little, my lord.
Prince: *Nay, but* hark you, Francis: for the sugar thou gavest me, 'twas a pennyworth, was't not?
Francis: O Lord, I would it had been two!
Prince: I will give thee for it a thousand pound. Ask me when thou wilt, and thou shalt have it. (1H4 2, 4, 57–62)

(45) Falstaff: Hostess, I forgive thee. Go make ready breakfast; love thy husband, look to thy servants, cherish thy guesse. Thou shalt find me tractable to any honest reason; thou seest I am pacified still. *Nay, prithee* be gone. (1H4 3, 3, 170–174)

7.5.3 Analysis of the discourse samples from WIV and 1H4

In the passages above nearly all the speakers often begin their utterances with pragmatic particles such as *ay, but, nay,* and *well.* These particles are clearly context-bound. They qualify a reaction of the speaker to the preceding facts or situation. Adding to this, they usually occur outside the syntactic structure of the sentence. In their function as introductory or resumptive words they are semantically weakened and thus belong to the textual mode of language.

On the other hand, the pragmatic particles not only serve as indicators of turn-taking, to initiate discourse, etc., but they also function on the interpersonal level as pause-fillers to indicate thinking and hesitation. For instance, *well* holds back the proposition, and *hark you* calls for the attention of the listener, or tries to retain it.

It does not come by pure chance that these two plays abound with examples of interjections and pragmatic particles. Concerning the dramatic medium, these plays are characterised by a high proportion of prose (WIV 88% prose lines, 1H4 56% prose lines). For this reason, it can be positively excluded that the particles have been added for metrical purposes. Moreover, they can be taken as instantiations of colloquialism in spoken language. The sheer abundance of these particles in WIV may be explained with reference to the tradition in which this play stands: "it is a *fabliau*, a merry tale dealing with sexual misadventure [...]" (Barton 1997: 321). This draws in with Taavitsainen's findings on the use of interjections as manifestations of emotional involvement, "especially in fiction, and echoes of earlier writings in the fabliaux tradition" (1995: 463).

In her account of "Elizabethan colloquial English in the Falstaff plays" [1H4, 2H4, H5 and WIF], Salmon uses the term *colloquialism* "to denote the language *spoken* in everyday situations" (1967: 68). Sociolinguistically, this kind of language can be characterised as "the speech of London and the shires around, which Puttenham regarded as the standard; socially, it is probably middle-class with lower class lexical deviations derived from the language of the criminal classes" (1967: 39). Regional deviations from this norm occur in the speech of Welsh, Irish and Scottish characters, e.g. Sir Hugh Evans, the Welsh parson, "one that makes fritters of English" (WIV 5, 5, 143), or foreigners such as the French physician Dr. Caius.

In her introduction to the play in the *Riverside Shakespeare*, Barton says that WIV "presents a vivid and detailed picture of small-town society which, if it does not exactly invite the term *realism*, nonetheless cannot be dismissed as farce" (1997: 322). For this reason we may subscribe to Taavitsainen's opinion that "the discourse form of comedy is based on dialogue, and the characters in these plays represent the middle layers of society; thus the language imitates the normal speech of common people. This is the nearest approximation to everyday spoken language in historical texts." (1995: 460).

In some respects, especially in its use of colloquial language, 1H4 can be likened to the comedy WIV, because especially its prose passages are linked to the petit bourgeois milieu. In her description of "Sentence structures in colloquial English" Salmon states that "apart from deliberately rhetorical passages such as the dialogue between Falstaff and Prince Henry in *1 Henry IV* II, iv, Shakespeare's colloquial speech gives an impression of verisimilitude" (1965: 107). Among other things, this is brought about by the discourse markers *pray* and *prithee* used in connection with interjections, both of which help to render the immediacy of language spoken in a certain situation. On the one hand, they express orientation towards the addressee, and on the other hand, their frequent occurrence in exclamations and asseverations signals the speaker's emotional involvement in the message and/or situation.

7.6   *Pray* and *prithee* in terms of grammaticalization

7.6.1   *Prithee* in the context of *you*

The analysis of *pray* and *prithee* in terms of politeness has revealed that their selection is partly determined by social rank and/or degree of intimacy between the interlocutors. If these were the only parameters, then the choice of the pragmatic particles should be dependent on the co-occurrence with a second person pronoun or title. In other words, *(I) pray you* should appear in the context of *you* and/or honorific nominal forms of address, and *(I) pray thee/prithee* in the context of *thou* and/or nominal in-group identity markers.

As was to be expected, the most frequent pronoun to collocate with *prithee* is a T pronoun, with 102 (44.74%) out of 228 cases. In 104 cases (45.61%) no address pronoun is used in the utterance under discussion, and in 22 instances (9.65%) *you* is used by the speaker in the preceding and following utterances which are "interrupted" by a single *prithee* or *prithee* followed by a single *thou*; as for example in:

(46)   Ulysses: *You* are moved, Prince, let us depart, I pray, […]. I beseech *you* go.
       Troilus: Behold, I *pray you.*
       Ulysses: Now, good my lord, go off; / *You* flow to great [distraction]. Come, my lord.
       Troilus: I *prithee* stay.
       Ulysses: *You* have not patience, come.
       Troilus: I *pray you* stay. By hell and all hell's torments, / I will not speak a word. (TRO 5, 2, 36–44)

(47)   Cressida: Here, Diomed keep this sleeve.
       […]
       Diomedes: Whose was't?
       Cressida: It is no matter now I ha't again. / I will not meet with *you* to-morrow night. I *prithee*, Diomed, visit me no more. (TRO 5, 2, 66; 71–74)

(48)   Lady Macbeth: When all's done, / *You* look but on a stool.
       Macbeth: *Prithee* see there! / Behold! look! lo! how say *you*? / Why, what care I? if *thou* canst nod, speak too. (MAC 3, 4, 66–69)

(49)   Hamlet [to 1. Player]: It shall to the barber's with *your* beard. *Prithee* say on, he's for a jig or a tale of bawdry, or he sleeps. Say on, come to Hecuba. (HAM 2, 2, 499–501)

(50)   Hamlet: Now get *you* to my lady's [chamber], and tell her, let her paint an inch thick, to this favor she must come; make her laugh at that. *Prithee*, Horatio, tell me one thing.
Horatio: What's that, my lord?
Hamlet: Dost *thou* think Alexander look'd a' this fashion i' th' earth?
(HAM 5, 1, 192–198)

(51)   Belarius [to Arviragus]: Well, 'tis done. / We'll hunt no more today, nor seek for danger / Where there's no profit. I *prithee* to our rock, / *You* and Fidele play the cooks. (CYM 4, 2, 161–164)

(52)   Cominius: I think 'twill serve, if he / Can thereto frame his spirit.
Volumnia: He must, and will. / *Prithee* now say *you* will, and go about it.
Coriolanus: Must I go show them my unbarb'd sconce? (COR 3, 2, 96–99)

(53)   Stephano [to Caliban]: Now forward with *your* tale. — *Prithee* stand further off. (TMP 3, 2, 83–84)

(54)   Duke [to Friar Thomas]: And to behold his sway, / I will, as 'twere a brother of *your* order, / Visit both prince and people; therefore I *prithee* / Supply me with the habit, and instruct me / How I may formally in person bear / Like a true friar. Moe reasons for this action / At our more leisure shall I render *you*; [...]. (MM 1, 3, 43–49)

These examples prove that *prithee* is used to make a request to a person who is addressed either with *thou* or *you*. On the one hand, such cases of switching between the form of pronominal address and *prithee* could be regarded as unexceptional, because in EModE switching between address pronouns in utterances to one and the same interlocutor was very common (cf. Chapter 2.7) and is usually interpreted sociolinguistically in terms of changes in intimacy, affect, etc. But, on the other hand, in the examples above (46 excepted) *prithee* and *you* occur in the same utterance. These utterances could be interpreted as instances of requests in which the number of the pronoun (2nd pers. pl.) does not correspond to that used in the form *prithee* (2nd pers. sg.). That is to say that the use of the form *prithee* has been extended beyond the domain of the pronoun *thou* as address form.

The above examples of *prithee* in the context of *you* suggest that the distribution of the full form *I pray thee* and the contracted one-word form was no longer consistent. The first component was phonemically reduced, and -*thee* lost its morpheme status and became an enclitic part of a mono-morphemic word.[8] This use of *prithee* outside the *thee/thou* context points toward its grammaticalization with semantic bleaching from a full verb to a discourse particle.

7.6.2   Syntactic analysis of *pray* and *prithee*

So far the function of the forms under discussion has mostly been elaborated with reference to polite requests, but apart from performing this communicative function, they are also used in other sentence types, though to a lesser degree. The following sentence patterns and examples are to illustrate the range of syntactic and pragmatic variation.

The present tense tokens of *pray* as a discourse marker in all of Shakespeare's plays (minus PER, H8 and TNK) amount to 682 (see Table 1). In comparison to this, the other verb forms are of only negligible quantities: *pray'd* (14 tokens), *praying* (7), *prays* (19) and *pray'st* (1).

119 (17.45%) out of the 682 tokens have been excluded from the following syntactic analysis because they refer to religious use, to the act of praying to God, heaven, etc., and thus belong to the category "*pray (other)*". The remaining 570 tokens (81.55%) are parenthetical in the sense of ModE *please*. They can be broken down into two main categories, requests (68.68%) and interrogatives (12.87%), which in turn can be subdivided as follows:

1. REQUESTS (including optatives) of the type:
    a. *(I) pray (you/thee)* + VERB [+ OBJ. + OBJ.]

    (55) I pray you pardon me; [...]. (WIV 1, 1, 218)

    (56) Pray thee go down. (2H4 2, 4, 155)

    (57) Pray be content. (COR 3, 2, 130)

    (58) I pray you show my youth old Shylock's house. (MV 4, 2, 11)

This category accounts for the vast majority of all cases, i.e. 384 tokens (54.94%).

    b. VERB + SUBJ./OBJ. + *(I) pray (you/thee)*

    (59) Grant me two things, I pray you, [...]. (MV 4, 1, 423)

    (60) Let us go see your son I pray you. (AWW 4, 5, 102)

    (61) Arm you, I pray you, [...]. (HAM 3, 3, 24)

This category contains 51 tokens (7.30%).

    c. verbless imperatives

    (62) *Pray you away*, [...]. (CYM 4, 2, 69)

    (63) *Pray now, no more.* (COR 2, 1, 169)

This category contains 45 tokens (6.44%).

2. INTERROGATIVES:
    a. *(I) pray (you/thee)* + *wh*-word/inversion

    (64) *I pray you, what thinks he of our estate?* (H5 4, 1, 96)

    (65) *But I pray, sir, why am I beaten?* (ERR 2, 2, 39)

    (66) *I pray you, is my master yet return'd?* (MV 5, 1, 34)

This category contains 66 tokens (9.44%).

b.   *wh*-word/inversion + [VERB + SUBJ.] + *(I) pray (you/thee)*

(67)   *And what says she, I pray, sir?* (WIV 4, 5, 35)

(68)   *Comes the King forth, I pray you?* (MAC 4, 3, 140)

(69)   *What, I pray you?* (ANT 2, 6, 69)

This category accounts for 24 tokens (3.43%).

This categorisation reveals that despite the abundance of different grammatical constructions listed in Schmidt and Sarrazin (1962; cf. 7.2), the syntactic patterning of *pray* has become quite restricted in Shakespeare's plays. The examples (55)–(69) amply illustrate that *pray* is mostly used parenthetically. Its initial or final position sets it apart from the syntax of the sentence.[9] Intermediate position of *pray* is only a marginal category:

(70)   *Bring it, I pray you, to the Porpentine* […]. (ERR 3, 1, 116)

In this respect it behaves similarly to sentence adverbials and comment clauses,[10] for it no longer acts like a main clause *I pray you/thee* introducing an infinitival subclause or a *that*-clause, but moves freely like an adverbial, thus losing its verbal qualities. Although, due to the transmission of the texts not a very reliable criterion, the separation by comma, and, moreover, the intonation pattern with *(I) pray (you/ thee)* as a separate tone group are further indicators for its parenthetical use. In this respect, the construction *(I) pray (you/thee)* resembles ModE contact clauses, for it expresses the sincerity of the speaker that the thing he/she demands be done, and it also appeals to the willingness of the listener to perform the task.

7.7   *Pray* vs. *please* as discourse markers

The reasons why eventually *(I) pray thee, prithee* and also all the other forms of *pray* have fallen into disuse may have been sociological or sociolinguistic ones in connection with the disappearance of the pronoun *thou* and its function as a shibboleth of the stigmatised Quaker usage (cf. Finkenstaedt 1963: 174–213; Baumann 1970). However, the ensuing stigmatisation of *thou/thee* does not really explain the loss of single *pray* as a discourse particle.

The interesting development of this verb has lately attracted the attention of a number of scholars. For instance, Akimoto has accounted for it in terms of grammaticalization. He suggests that *pray* and *prithee* were both given up in favour of *please* for the reasons that this verb was devoid of the religious connotations of *pray* and possibly also for phonæsthetic reasons, because *please* with its long vowel might have been more effective in earnest appeals (2000: 80).

Kryk-Kastovsky in her analysis of EModE court trials attributes the gradual loss of *pray* mostly to socio-political reasons, in particular to "the secularization of public life at the end of the nineteenth century that made *pray* obsolete as carrying too much religious connotation." In a footnote she offers as an alternative explanation (suggested by Hans-Jürgen Diller) that, quite to the contrary, "*pray* might have been ruled out for reasons of piety" (1998:52).

Fries has investigated it among other items in his study of dialogue in instructional texts (1500–1800). The early texts, as e.g. Coote, *The English School-Maister* (1596), feature the older construction with or without object, i.e. *I pray (you)*. The earliest examples of subjectless *pray* in his corpus are to be found in Brown, *The English School Reformed* (1700). In contrast to this, "*please* is hardly used at all" (1998:94).

Further diachronic evidence for the use of *prithee* can be gathered from Bock's (1938) corpus of British drama (1497–1779) [cf. 10.3.3.1], in which *prithee* does not occur as a discourse marker in any play written before 1600. In marked contrast to this, the use of *prithee* picks up in the next century. Throughout the 17th century all dramatists make quite extensive use of it. In the last plays of his corpus, representing the second half of the 18th century, this development slowly comes to an end, e.g. in Sheridan's play *The Rivals* (1775) there are only two tokens and in his *School for Scandal* (1775/79) there are three as opposed to the most extreme example of Wycherly's *The Plain Dealer* (1677), written a hundred years earlier, which contains no less than 38 instances.

Most recently, Traugott (2000) has compared *promise* and *pray*-parentheticals. She neatly summarizes the development of the verb *pray* as follows: as a performative verb it replaced Old English *biddan*, which could be used both performatively and also parenthetically. As a lexical verb in Middle English *preie-* introduced a subordinate clause. As a performative verb its position is sentence-initial. In its function as a polite parenthetical subjunct its position is more flexible in that it can occur sentence-initially, medially or finally (see examples (55)–(70)). This can lead to functional overlap and ambiguity in sentence-initial position when *I pray you* precedes an imperative.

In short, the life cycle from the performative lexical verb *to pray* to a parenthetical indicating that the speaker/writer pays attention to the listener's or reader's face wants by expressing deference can be summarized as follows:

content > content/procedural > procedural
(Traugott and Dasher 2002: 281)

In order to elucidate further reasons why eventually both *pray* and *prithee* were given up as discourse markers in polite requests, *pray* and *please* shall be investigated together diachronically by making use of the evidence given in the OED.

The transitive use *pray* with a personal object is attested in the OED from 1290 onwards in the sense of:

> To ask earnestly, humbly, or supplicatingly, to beseech; to make devout petition to; to ask (a person) for something as a favour or act of grace; esp. in religious use, to make devout and humble supplication to (God, or an object of worship). *arch[aic]*.

Phrases and idiomatic uses are documented from the beginning of the 16th century.

> †a. I pray you (thee): used parenthetically to add instance or deference to a question or request. So
> b. pray you, pray thee, etc. (Cf. prithee.)
> c. I pray. *Obs[olete]*.

Parenthetical use of *I pray you/thee* is illustrated with quotations ranging from 1519 to 1601. The citations for *pray you/thee* range from 1524 to 1676; those for *I pray* from 1591 to 1704. Only contracted *pray* is documented until the late 19th century. Its last citation stems from 1875.

Prithee basically performs the same functions and is described as an archaic intransitive phrase and an "archaic colloquialism for '(I) pray thee'" (OED 1992: s.v. *prithee*). The citations range from 1522 to 1875.

The documentation of the verb *please* in the OED reveals that the longer impersonal constructions (3.) have died out. The last attestations date from the 19th century.

> *Please*:
> 3. *Impersonally*, with formal subject *it* (the real subject being a following infinitive or clause, expressed or understood): To seem good to one; to be one's will or pleasure. (Equivalent in sense to 'will', 'choose', 'think proper', etc., with the person as subject: cf. 4 b.)
> Formerly usual in deferential phrases of address or request, as *and, an, if it please you*, etc., *may it, will it please you, your honour*, etc.; ellipt. *please it* (corruptly *pleaseth*) *you*, etc.; also (with omission of *it*), *so please you, please you*, and still in *please your honour, please God, please the pigs*, etc.
>
> c. With omission of *it*, in † *please you*, † *so please you*, may it (so) please you; *please your honour, please God*, etc.

Besides this, the commentary under definition 6 illustrates that the case of the pronoun became increasingly ambiguous:

> [6] b. *if († and, an) you please*: if it please you, if you like, if it is your will or pleasure: a courteous qualification to a request, the acceptance of an offer, etc.; also (parenthetically), a sarcastic way of emphasizing any surprising statement, as if asking leave to make it. (So F. *s'il vous plaît*. Cf. *by your leave*: see <u>leave</u> *n.*[1] 1.)

Here *you* may have been originally dative, as in 3 b (i.e. if (it) please you, = L. *si vobis placet,* F. *s'il vous plaît,* Ger. *wenn es Ihnen gefällt*), as in quot. 1483 in 2 [= c. **1483** <u>Caxton</u> *Dialogues* 5/6 *Mais sil vous plaist aulcune chose Que ie puisse fayre*: But if you plaise ony thyng That I may doo.]; but it is now taken as nominative (i.e. if you are pleased, if you like, if it is your will or pleasure): cf. *if he pleases*; *if they please,* above (in 6); and 'if ye please' here in 1530. Shakspere has both *if you be pleased* (4 b), and *if you please.*

c. *please!* (imperative or optative) was app. originally short for *please you* (3 c) = 'may it (or let it) please you'; but it is now usually taken as = 'Be pleased' (imperative of 6), or as short for 'if you please' (6 b).

Görlach (1994: 84f.) explains the development of *please* as follows: with the loss of inflectional endings, constructions of the type *the king liketh the crown* 'dem König gefällt die Krone' have become ambiguous, or, moreover, the increase of SVO sentence structure in declarative sentences has had the effect that *the king* came to be interpreted as subject instead of object. In the course of the 16th century the unambiguous pronominal sentences of the type *me thinketh* were adapted to the SVO pattern. This resulted in the fact that impersonal constructions of the verbs *ail, chance, like, list, please* and *think* left over around 1600 sounded more and more archaic.[11] This explanation, first expressed by Jespersen (1909–1949; Vol. 3: 1927: §11.2, 209), is challenged by Allen (1995).

Kopytko raises the idea that synchronically the various constructions involving *please* express different degrees of politeness: "the unreduced forms are, as a rule, used in a polite address of the inferior to the superior member of speech interaction (i.e. *it please(s), if it please, so it please*); on the other hand, the reduced form *pleaseth* is used in the conversation between equals" (1988: 50).

Chen in his investigation of the addressee-satisfaction conditionals *please, like, will* and *list* notes that with the loss of the sense of conditionality reduced forms such as *(an't) please you* become possible. However, "not all uses of *if you please* in indirect conditional sentences underwent formal reduction. It seems that when it is used in a metalinguistic function, it is resistant to formal reduction" (1998: 27f.). For this he gives the following example:

(71)   We may terme him the Loue-burden, following the originall, or *if it please you,* the long repeat. (1589 Puttenham, Eng. Poesie, iii, xix. (Arb.) 233)

The use of single *please,* which was not yet known to Shakespeare, is documented with only two quotations from the 17th century in the OED. In contrast to this, *I pray you (thee)* used parenthetically (sense 8.a) seems to have become archaic at the same time. With some time lag this also holds true for the shorter forms *pray you (thee), I pray* and *pray* (senses 8.b–d).

This diachronic comparison of the two verbs leads to the hypothesis that for polite requests *please* has replaced *(I) pray (you/thee)* and *prithee* as a discourse particle signalling politeness or urgency. But some EModE examples also show an overlap of both forms:

(72)   *Pray*, sir, put your sword up, *if you please.* (TN 3, 4, 321)

In their analysis of politeness strategies in Shakespeare's tragedies, Brown and Gilman (1989) focus on two types of polite requests which on the basis of Searle's (1969) felicity conditions can be categorised as follows:

1.   Speaker sincerely wants hearer to do X.

> Requests of this type assert the speaker's sincere wish that the hearer do X and thus assert a felicity condition on the part of the speaker. In Shakespearean drama they are often accompanied by constructions like "*I beseech you, I pray you, Prithee, I would that, I require that*, and so on".
> (Brown and Gilman 1989: 181)

2.   Speaker asks hearer whether hearer is willing, sees fit, or is pleased to do X.

> This type concerning a felicity condition in the hearer makes use of constructions like *if it please you* or *may it please you.*

Brown and Gilman find it interesting that "the modern parent's magic word *please* did not exist in the 17th century" (1989: 182), only the afore-mentioned phrases, but they do not offer an explanation for this phenomenon. However, the preceding comparative diachronic investigation of *pray* and *please* seems to suggest a pragmatic interpretation in that type 1) requests involving *pray* or a similar verb have been supplanted by type 2) requests with *please*.

In ModE, requests are mostly realised by routinized constructions like:

(73)   *Pass the salt, please!*

(74)   *Can/could you pass the salt, please?*

(75)   *? I beseech/(I) pray/I would that/I require that, etc. you [to] pass the salt!*

In (73) and (74) *please* acts as a courtesy subjunct and expresses politeness "to tone down the abruptness of a command" (Quirk et al. 1985: 571). The second example, although interrogative in form, is not uttered with the intention of asking a question but rather of making a polite request. A plain *yes* or *no* as an answer to this would clearly violate Grice's (1975) conversational maxims and the principle of co-operativeness.

Pragmatically, the redressed command and the question have in common that they ask for the willingness of the listener to do X (willingness on the part of the hearer being a felicity condition for imperatives to be successful). Yet requests with *pray/prithee* put the focus on the speaker and assert his/her sincerity: Speaker sincerely wants X to be done.

Although I cannot provide numerical evidence, I assume that in present-day English the first category (examples (73)–(74)) is more productive than my made-up example (75), which sounds rather stilted and concocted. The truth of this assumption provided, this could in turn serve as an additional pragmatic explanation why, at least in colloquial speech, requests like *I beseech you, I pray you/prithee, I would that, I require that,* etc. that were numerous in Shakespeare's time, and all of which assert speaker sincerity, have become rarer in comparison to those asking for the listener's willingness to perform X.[12]

7.8 Conclusion

1. In terms of numerical distribution *I pray you* is still the most frequent form with the function of a pragmatic particle in the Shakespeare Corpus. It accounts for approximately one third of all cases. The abbreviated forms are used more sparingly. In comparison to all the *pray* forms, *(I) prithee* is much less numerous and is not used at all in a number of plays. A clear-cut rise or decline of forms, excepting *(I) pray thee,* which is almost absent from the second half of the corpus after 1600 and the subsequent rise of *(I) prithee* at the expense of the former expression(s) could not be established for certain; but in any case, the Histories, as the earliest plays, exhibit the lowest number of all *pray* forms as parenthetical pragmatic particles in the corpus and feature a large number of syntactic constructions like *pray God, pray heaven,* etc.
2. In terms of politeness *pray* and *prithee* differ clearly in their co-occurrence with the respectful title *sir,* which is only used with *pray.* The category *titles of courtesy* occurs most often in connection with *pray* but also with *prithee.* Contrary to Brown and Gilman's interpretation of *(I) pray you* as deferential and *prithee* as an in-group identity marker, corpus evidence has proved that a good deal of overlap exists between the forms and their communicative functions. The almost identical sequence of co-occurring verbs in polite requests has shown that the weight of the imposition is not a relevant factor to determine the choice of the particles.
3. The investigation of the discourse functions of *pray/prithee* has revealed that both fulfil textual and interpersonal functions and that especially in the Comedies they co-occur with interjections and other pragmatic particles to express colloquiality and verisimilitude. They are thus an artistic means to render the normal speech of common people.
4. Both the numerical study and the analysis in terms of politeness have unanimously proved that the different syntactic patterns described in Schmidt and Sarrazin (1962) have already been significantly reduced in Shakespeare's plays when compared to earlier stages of the English language. In comparison to the

function of *I pray you* as a main clause introducing an infinitival or a *that*-sub-clause, *pray* is mostly used parenthetically, often sentence-initially, as a sentence adverbial or comment clause. This grammatical recategorisation from verb- to adverb-like qualities together with semantic bleaching resulting in a pragmatic strengthening can be interpreted in terms of ongoing grammaticalization. In addition to this, *prithee* sometimes occurs in the context of *you*, which can also be described as the routinization of a discourse function.

5. The comparison of requests with *pray* to those with *please* has led me to the assumption that at least in colloquial speech a shift in polite requests has taken place from requests that assert the sincerity of the speaker (*I pray you*) to those that question the willingness of the listener to perform the request (*please*).[13] The confirmation or refutation of this hypothesis would, however, require a new and more detailed diachronic study because it could not be established for certain whether this shift is due to a socio-pragmatic change in politeness strategies, or has, moreover, language internal reasons brought about by a grammatical reanalysis of impersonal constructions with the rise of SVO declarative sentence structure.

CHAPTER 8

The role of grammar
in the selection of *thou* or *you*

8.1 Introduction and objectives

In the previous chapters a number of extralinguistic factors, in particular socio-linguistic variables and pragmatic constraints, were found to be of importance for the selection of second person pronouns. However, over the years some scholars have also maintained that the choice of the pronouns can, at least to a certain extent, be influenced by intralinguistic factors such as the co-occurrence of the second person pronouns with different types of verbs and different sentence types. For this reason it shall next be investigated whether this claim can be corroborated.

8.2 Previous research

The first scholar to hint at the importance of grammatical factors for the selection of second person pronouns is Abbott ([1870] 1972:158). In §234 of his grammar he says: "*thou* is often used in statements and requests, while *you* is used in conditional and other sentences where there is no direct appeal to the person addressed." However, at close inspection this dictum does not really claim intralinguistic reasons, but reference to the presence or absence of an addressee does rather point towards the pragmatic aspects and the social motivations of the pronoun choice (cf. also Kiełkiewicz-Janoviak 1994:52).

In his comment upon pronoun irregularities Abbott makes a further remark in §205 that "for reasons of euphony also the ponderous *thou* is often ungrammatically replaced by *thee*, or inconsistently by *you*. This is particularly the case in questions and requests, where, the pronoun being especially unemphatic, *thou* is especially objectionable" ([1870] 1972:139).

Mulholland (1967) has, among other aspects, also investigated whether the use of second person pronouns in ADO and in LR is influenced to a certain degree by the grammatical system rather than by social reasons alone. On the basis of positional and functional criteria the T and Y pronouns were placed in 11 categories. The basic distinction underlying these categories is whether the pronoun occurs as subject together with a lexical or a closed-class verb. The category of closed-class verbs comprises the primary auxiliaries *be, have, do,* the modal auxiliaries *shall, will, should, could, would, may, might, must* and *ought,* and also the non-auxiliary uses of *be* and *have.*

More recently, Kiełkiewicz-Janoviak (1994) has cast doubt on the incorporation of the non-auxiliary uses of *be* and *have,* although her analysis of AYL did not yield a great discrepancy between the two groups of auxiliary *be* and *have* and non-auxiliary use of the two verbs. Another possible flaw in Mulholland's categorisation is the uncommented incorporation of *do* (cf. Stein 1985, 1990a). These objections not withstanding, her analysis has borne out that in ADO and in LR, though to different extents, there is a marked tendency for *thou* to occur more often with closed-class verbs in statements and questions and, as a corollary of this, for *you* to co-occur more often with lexical verbs in these categories.

Barber has supplemented Mulholland's data on possible grammatical conditioning of the address pronouns by investigating R3. While he finds that her evidence from ADO and LR "does not on the whole suppor[t] the view that the grammatical construction used has any considerable influence on the selection of *YOU* and *THOU*" (1981:285), he acknowledges that the data from R3 support her claim that *thou* is generally selected as subject of closed-class verbs in statements and in questions and, correspondingly, *you* as the subject of a lexical verb in these categories.[1]

Despite some differences about the status of *thou* and *you* as the majority form, the two studies of Mulholland (1967) and Barber (1981) tie in to the interesting observation that the two types of verbs favour co-occurring pronouns to different degrees, from which they infer that this could possibly pre-determine the selection of *you* and *thou* for purely grammatical reasons. In the second edition of his book on EModE, Barber repeats the claim that the choice of either *thou* or *you* may have been influenced by the grammatical construction used in that "*thou* tended to be favoured before auxiliaries, and *you* before lexical verbs" (1997:155), but he does not give an explanation for this tendency.

This observation, however, does not necessarily imply that grammar governs the choice of the pronoun, but that it could, more likely, also be the other way around: "*you* or *thou* might be chosen on social or emotional grounds, and this choice might then influence the grammatical construction used" (Barber 1981:286).

Kiełkiewicz-Janoviak takes up the ideas of Mulholland and Barber not only to look for extralinguistic factors that condition the pronoun choice, but also for intralinguistic ones. She has analysed AYL accordingly and found some contradictory evidence to the earlier studies. For reasons of comparability she has also adopted the major categories chosen by Mulholland and Barber, namely the distinction between closed-class verbs and lexical verbs in the sentence types of statements, interrogatives and imperatives. However, her analysis of the ratio of T to Y forms according to sentence types and also co-occurrence with lexical or closed-class verbs in AYL does not on the whole support the earlier findings. Whereas for questions there is a slight preponderance of *you* in connection with lexical verbs, the difference is not statistically significant, and in fact for statements the opposite is true (see Tables 2 and 3). The data for imperatives were too small to yield any basis for comparison. From her rather limited textual data from AYL she comes to the conclusion that the data "present little evidence for the claim that the variable occurrence of the TH- and Y-pronouns is linguistically conditioned" (1994: 53).

8.3   Pilot study

On the basis of this mixed state of affairs the objective of this chapter will be to carry out a pilot study along these lines in order to find out whether different types of verbs as well as different sentence types have any impact on the selection of the address pronouns at all, or if the choice of pronouns is rather determined the other way around. This is to say that a T or a Y-pronoun is chosen first and foremost for social, affective, metrical, discoursal or other reasons, and that the grammatical construction (verb class, sentence type) plays only a secondary role.

The earlier investigations by Mulholland, Barber and Kiełkiewicz-Janoviak shall be incorporated into a pilot study and be supplemented by the relevant data from four further plays, viz. 3H6, WIV, TN and MAC. These plays have been chosen because they differ widely in such factors as date of composition, *you* or *thou* as the most frequent form and also in the amount of verse and prose, all of which having been found earlier on to be of importance for the choice of either *thou* or *you*.

For reasons of comparability, the grammatical categories to be investigated for the four plays shall be taken over from those of the previous studies. The categories to be analysed for *thou* and singular *you* are given in Table 1.

Table 1. *Thou* and *you* according to verb- and sentence types

Category	Examples
1. subject before closed-class verbs in statements	*you shall pardon me*
	thou wilt be like a lover presently
2. subject before lexical verbs in statements	*when you went onward*
	say that thou over-heardst us
3. subject after closed-class verbs in questions	*are you sure*
	dost thou looke up
4. subject after lexical verbs in questions	*know you anie, Hero*
	what thinkst thou
5. subject after closed-class verbs in imperatives	*be thou constant*
6. subject after lexical verbs in imperatives	*thinke you of a worse title*
	runne thee to the parlour

(Table mine, based on the data in Mulholland 1967: 36f.)

8.3.1   The co-occurrence of second person pronouns and verb types in statements

The figures shown in Table 2 demonstrate that for statements in seven out of the eight plays in the sample *thou* does indeed occur more often as subject of closed-class verbs and *you* as a subject of lexical verbs. The play which shows the most marked difference in this respect is R3, the one investigated by Barber, with a difference of 10.5%, followed by WIV with 8.4%. For TN and MAC the distribution of the two pronouns between closed-class verbs and lexical verbs is almost even. The only play to counteract this tendency is AYL. However, in terms of statistical significance the observed differences for each play and the table as a whole are below the 90% level of confidence ($p < 0.10$), so that the null-hypothesis cannot firmly be rejected. Hence the results have to be regarded as a product of chance, and should not be further interpreted in any direction.

Table 2. *Thou* and *you* in statements

| Play | Statements | | | | | |
| | S before closed verbs | | | S before lexical verbs | | |
	Thou	You	T:Y	THOU	YOU	T:Y
3H6	91	37	2.46	40	21	1.91
1590/91	71.1%	28.9%		65.6%	34.4%	
R3	73	63	1.16	35	46	0.76
1592/93	53.7%	46.3%		43.2%	56.8%	
WIV	28	127	0.22	6	56	0.11
1597	18.1%	81.9%		9.7%	90.3%	
ADO	38	115	0.33	16	74	0.22
1598/99	24.8%	75.2%		17.8%	82.2%	
AYL	61	121	0.50	30	51	0.59
1599	33.5%	66.5%		37.0%	63%	
TN	63	131	0.48	30	64	0.47
1601/02	32.5%	67.5%		31.9%	68.1%	
LR	94	86	1.09	35	37	0.95
1605	52.2%	47.8%		48.6%	51.4%	
MAC	46	40	1.15	19	17	1.12
1606	53.5%	46.5%		52.8%	47.2%	
Total	494	720	0.69	211	366	0.58
	40.7%	59.3%		36.6%	63.4%	

8.3.2   The co-occurrence of second person pronouns and verb types in questions

The data for questions as laid out in Table 3 also present no clear-cut results. The working hypothesis that T forms would correlate predominantly with closed-class verbs and Y forms with lexical verbs holds good for five of the eight sample plays. But again, apart from the two History Plays 3H6 and R3 the differences are not very pronounced, and in fact for WIV, TN and MAC the reverse is true.

Table 3. *Thou* and *you* in questions

Play	Questions					
	S after closed verbs			S after lexical verbs		
	Thou	You	T:Y	Thou	You	T:Y
3H6	31	9	3.44	14	13	1.08
1590/91	77.5%	22.5%		51.9%	48.1%	
R3	31	15	2.07	16	19	0.84
1592/93	67.4%	32.6%		45.7%	54.3%	
WIV	14	51	0.27	7	19	0.37
1597	21.5%	78.5%		26.9%	73.1%	
ADO	20	43	0.47	5	17	0.29
1598/99	31.7%	68.3%		22.7%	77.3%	
AYL	19	58	0.33	8	29	0.28
1599	24.7%	75.3%		21.6%	78.4%	
TN	20	42	0.48	9	9	1.00
1601/02	32.3%	67.7%		50.0%	50.0%	
LR	37	43	0.86	11	17	0.65
1605	46.3%	53.7%		39.3%	60.7%	
MAC	10	24	0.42	4	7	0.57
1606	29.4%	70.6%		36.4%	63.6%	
Total	182	285	0.64	74	130	0.57
	39.0%	61%		36.3%	63.7%	

These findings contradict Abbott's statement mentioned in Chapter 8.2 that especially in questions and requests ponderous *thou* is often ungrammatically replaced by either *thee* or *you*.

Especially for questions it also has to be borne in mind that in EModE loss of the pronoun *thou* was quite common. Salmon (1967:48), for instance, points this out for Shakespeare's plays with the following two examples from 2H4. Regular loss is, however, often confined to *thou* forms in questions.

(1)   Falstaff: What stuff wilt [Ø] have a kirtle of? (*Folio*: wilt thou) (2H4 2, 4, 274)

(2)   Falstaff: [...] shalt [Ø] have a cap to-morrow (*Folio*: Thou shalt) (2H4 2, 4, 275)

With reference to this, Mazzon also draws a connection between the loss of *thou* in questions and a simplified verbal inflection but argues the other way around when she notes "that T is often deleted in questions, i.e. in post-verbal position, possibly because of assimilation between its initial consonant and the final -*t* of the verb ending. This in turn could have encouraged the loss of a distinctive second person verb ending through lack of pronominal 'reinforcement' in the surface structure" (1995: 22, footnote).

Unlike this, Stein (1974: 74) comes to the different conclusion that there does not exist a causal relationship between the choice of pronoun and simplified verbal inflection (*thou* verb + *st* vs. *you* verb + Ø). Moreover, he is of the opinion that the loss of the second person singular pronoun has sociological reasons and that co-occurrence of verb endings with the singular pronoun is a matter of phonology, taking place within the first process but being independent from it (cf. also Finkenstaedt 1963: 220f.).

Görlach puts the relationship between these two processes this way: "the loss of *thou* left English without the possibility of making the vital number distinction in the second person (the -*st* ending was of course lost together with *thou*)" (1999a: 10). Thus he also emphasises the extralinguistic reasons for the pronoun replacement, which then resulted in a simplification of verbal inflection.

8.3.3   Second person pronouns in imperatives

The data for *thou* and *you* as subjects after closed-class or lexical verbs in imperatives proved to be too small in the sample of plays to provide a serious basis for comparison. In some of the plays there were no examples at all. But Millward comes to the following conclusions on pronominal use with second person imperatives.[2] The pronoun may be in the subjective or objective case (for *thee/thou*) or it may be absent. No case distinction is observed between *ye* and *you*. In all of Shakespeare's plays there are 35 imperatives with *ye* and more than 500 involving *you*. On the other hand, there are more than 200 imperatives with *thou*, involving 77 different verbs. "Approximately the same number of imperatives with *thee* occurs, and 56 different verbs are used. Only 17 verbs appear with both *thou* and *thee*, [...] the use of *thou* or *thee* is, in almost all instances, conditioned by other factors in the sentence" (1966: 11).

She further assumes that *thou* as the subject of an imperative "is employed to provide a mildly emphatic tone to the imperative. In verse, it is useful for metrical purposes. Its use (as is the use of *you*) seems to be optional" (ibid.). Quirk confirms her interpretation of *thou* as emphatic beside an unmarked imperative without any pronoun, adding that the oblique form *thee* seeks the "personal involvement of the addressee" (1974: 53):

(3)   Polonius: Farewell, my blessing season this in *thee*!
      Laertes: Most humbly do I take my leave, my lord.
      (HAM 1, 3, 81–82, my emphasis)

Quirk sums up his argument by saying that we today have general difficulty responding to the distinction between *thou/you* and that this is particularly true for their distribution in imperatives. For this an example where four possibilities co-occur with the same verb can be given:

(4)   Come *thou* on my side [...]. (R3 1, 4, 265)

(4′)   Come *thee* on. (ANT 4, 7, 16)

(4″)   Come Ø   on my right hand [...]. (JC 1, 2, 213)

(4‴)   And, Montague, come *you* this afternoon [...]. (ROM 1, 1, 100; (4)–(4″) are taken from Quirk)

8.3.4   Analysis of discourse samples from 3H6

As the bare statistical figures of Tables 2 and 3 do not give us any qualitative information on the direction of influence, i.e. whether the type of verb influences the pronoun choice, or vice versa, an analysis of the most common pronoun-verb-combinations in 3H6 — the play with the most pronounced deviation — will be made.

A look at the closed-class verbs used in 3H6 shows that the figures are not distorted by the verb *do*, as the verbforms *do*, *dost* and *didst* are infrequent. The verbs that occur most often in conjunction with *you* are *are* and *shall*, and *art*, *hast* and *shalt* with *thou*. In questions there are only nine tokens of closed-class verbs used together with *you*, of which *are*, *will* and *should* occur more than once. In comparison to this, *art*, *hast* and *wilt* are the most frequent ones in connection with *thou*. In the following discourse dyads involving the verb *will*, which has proved to be most frequent closed-class verb in interrogatives shall be provided, and interpreted later on:

(5)   York: Will you we show our title to the crown? / If not, our swords shall plead it in the field.
      King Henry: What title hast thou, traitor, to the crown? [Thy] father was, as thou art, Duke of York, / Thy grandfather, Roger Mortimer, Earl of March: / I am the son of Henry the Fift, [...]. (3H6 1, 1, 102–107)

(6)   Edward: Now, perjur'd Henry, wilt thou kneel for grace, / And set thy diadem upon my head, / Or bide the mortal fortune of the field?
      Queen Margaret: Go rate thy minions, proud insulting boy! / Becomes it thee to be thus bold in terms / Before thy sovereign and thy lawful king?

Edward: I am his king, and he should bow his knee. / I was adopted heir by his consent. (3H6 2, 2, 81–88)

(7)   King Edward: Then get your husband's lands, to do them good.
      Lady Grey: Therefore I came unto your Majesty.
      King Edward: I'll tell you how these lands are to be got.
      Lady Grey: So shall you bind me to your Highness' service.
      King Edward: What service wilt thou do me if I give them?
      Lady Grey: What you command that rests in me to do.
      King Edward: But you will take exceptions to my boon.
      Lady Grey: No, gracious lord, except I cannot do it.
      King Edward: Ay, but thou canst do what I mean to ask.
      Lady Grey: Why then I will do what your Grace commands. (3H6 3, 2, 40–49)

(8)   King Edward: Now, brother Richard, will you stand by us?
      Gloucester: Ay, in despite of all that shall withstand you. (3H6 4, 1, 145–146)

(9)   King Edward: Huntsman, what say'st thou? Wilt thou go along?
      Huntsman: Better do so than tarry and be hang'd. (3H6 4, 5, 25–26)

(10) King Edward: Now, Warwick, wilt thou ope the city-gates, / Speak gentle words and humbly bend thy knee, / Call Edward king and at his hands beg mercy? / And he shall pardon thee these outrages.
      Warrick: Nay rather, wilt thou draw thy forces hence, / Confess who set thee up and pluck'd thee down, / Call Warwick patron, and be penitent? / And thou shalt still remain the Duke of York. (3H6 5, 1, 21–28)

The instances of *will* and *wilt* clearly show that the conditioning or, to put it more carefully, the influence does not work in the direction that grammar determines the choice of the pronoun, but rather the other way around in that the pronouns are chosen for social (as in example (5)), for attitudinal, especially emotional grounds (examples (5), (6), (8) and (10)), or for pragmatic reasons (cf. the pronoun switching of the King in (7) when he promises Lady Grey a favour and asks what she would do in return) and that the verb form follows automatically.

Ronberg has provided a detailed analysis of the complete scene, in which Lady Grey after her husband's murder is desperately trying to reclaim land from King Edward the Fourth. Ronberg concentrates on the implications of King Edward's subtle pronoun switching from *you* to *thou*: "the switch to *thou* in the question *What service wilt thou do me....?* tells us at once that the question is deliberately ambiguous, that the King is hinting at the more intimate, sexual sense of 'service'" (1992:86ff.). Despite this innuendo, and primarily because of the king's exalted social position Lady Grey sticks to *you* throughout their conversation. In summary, pronoun use in this passage can be put down to the social and interpersonal functions of the pronouns and also to their textual function as discourse markers that signal personal or topical shifts rather than to the verbs involved in the exchange.

8.4   Conclusion

If the selection of eight plays from different genres and from different periods of Shakespeare's writing career as presented in this pilot study is representative for the corpus as a whole, then the claim made by scholars such as Mulholland (1967) and Barber (1981) that co-occurrence with closed- or open-class verbs and syntactic distribution could perhaps influence the choice of pronouns to a certain degree is not strongly corroborated for statements and to an even lesser degree for interrogatives, as this category provides counter-evidence.

The fact that the tendency is most clearly pronounced in the early History Plays 3H6 and R3 could possibly be attributed to the fact that these plays have a high overall score of T forms anyway (cf. Chapter 3.4, Table 5). Adding to this, Replogle (1967: 145f.) has found out that the early History Plays also differ in terms of nominal forms of address from the later ones.

The numerical development and the discourse samples bring me to the conclusion that in this case no indicators could be found in support of an intralinguistic conditioning of the pronoun choice, or, as Mühlhäusler and Harré have put it: "'closed-class' verbs are much more likely to appear in intimate and informal, than in polite and public, speech [...]. When the markedness principle calls for *thou*, the social situation also calls — though in a less peremptory manner — for a closed-class verb" (1990: 153).

Due to their emotional, subjective nature, modals seem to be more appropriate in intimate and informal situations, because by means of modal auxiliaries the speakers need not commit themselves to factual assertions but can make subtle qualifications. Intuitively it sounds convincing that the modal verbs, which express modality or states of mind, go together well with the more affective of the two pronouns, however, this could not be proved empirically.

CHAPTER 9

"In thine own person answer thy abuse"
The use of *thy* vs. *thine*

9.1 Introduction

In his article on "Morphological variation and change in Early Modern English: *my/mine, thy/thine*", Schendl mentions that "Shakespeare's inconsistent use of these variants has frequently been mentioned, though not really systematically studied" (1997: 180). This statement has sparked my motivation to investigate the case. More importantly, though, for matters of internal consistency, these variants round off my comprehensive study of morpho-syntactic variation of second person pronouns in the Shakespeare Corpus.

This analysis of meaningful choices has so far dealt with the use of the personal pronoun alternatives *thou/you* and the discourse particles *pray you/prithee*. It should thus also include the variants of the second person possessive pronoun and pronoun-determiner *thy/thine*, which, on the one hand, show a morphological relationship to the reflexives, and, on the other hand, to the personal pronouns, from which they stem historically.

The factors governing the distribution of the above-mentioned competing forms differ of course. But it could be shown that in principle the variation of *thou* and *you* including that of the discourse markers *pray you* and *prithee* is largely determined by extralinguistic factors. Intralinguistic factors such as verb- or sentence types were not found to be of any major importance. In contrast to this, it has often been postulated that *thy* and *thine* in their use as determiners, i.e. as attributive possessives or noun-adjuncts, pattern according to phonological criteria in EModE, with *thine* prevailing before vowels, and to a lesser degree before words beginning with ⟨h⟩, and *thy* occurring before words beginning with a consonant. However, Barber (1997: 152) goes so far as to say that by 1600 *my/mine* and *thy/thine* are in free variation before vowels.

By adopting the variationist approach (cf. Chapter 1.2.1), Schendl rejects the traditional concept of free variation, as it is not a sufficient explanation for corpus-internal variation and accuses most of the earlier accounts of the distribution of *thy/thine* before vowels and ⟨h⟩ of resorting to factors such as "euphony, stress patterns or simply 'free variation'" (1997: 181). He concludes his survey by saying that "on the whole, the factors influencing the choice of a given variant are not discussed in any detail in the existing literature. The distribution and development of the variants of the two possessives thus still wait for detailed investigation" (ibid.). The Shakespeare Corpus does not feature in his article, even though it was originally analysed in his search for corpus-internal variation. As no suitable explanation for the obvious variation, which is neither clearly related to date of composition and/or types of plays, was found, it was omitted from his study.

The following specimens from my corpus investigation underline this seemingly random patterning of the variants within a single line of text, as they defy the neat distribution usually given in reference works:

(1)   In *thine* own person answer *thy* abuse. (2H6 2, 1, 40)

(2)   Throw *thy* glove, / or any token of *thine* honor else, [...]. (TIM 5, 4, 49–50)

(3)   I'll take *thy* word for faith, not ask *thine* oath: [...]. (PER 1, 2, 120)

For this reason, the objective of this chapter will be to look for factors which can help to bridge the contradiction between the theoretical claim that free variation is not a viable concept to account for the distribution of *thy/thine* and the obvious irregularities found in the corpus.

Furthermore, the outcome of the empirical corpus study shall be compared to other corpora of EModE so as to evaluate and categorise Shakespeare's usage of the two forms in comparison to that of fellow dramatists and writings in other genres.

However, before we embark on the corpus study, a short glance at reference works such as standard textbooks and grammars shall be taken in order to outline the historical development that has led to the distribution of forms to be encountered in Shakespeare's works, and, more generally, in the period of EModE as a whole, because the distinction between the two variants was not established until early ME. It did not exist in OE, and was finally dismantled in the course of the 18th century (cf. Sweet 1900: 343–346, Brunner 1951: 114f., Poutsma 1916: 782, Strang 1970: 139, Pyles 1971: 199, Faiß 1989: 166f., Görlach 1994: 69, Blake 1996: 219, Wales 1996: 166–179, and Barber 1997: 148–164).[1]

9.2   The history of *thy* and *thine* from Old to Modern English

In OE the possessive pronouns are the genitives of the corresponding personal pronouns. As in other Germanic languages, only the possessive pronouns of the first and second person — *min, þin, ure, eower* — are declined like strong adjectives; the possessives of the third person — *his, hire, hira* — being indeclinable (e.g.: *mid minum freondum* vs. *mid his freondum* 'with my/his friends').[2] There are no separate forms for the two different functions, *min, þin*, etc. being used conjointly as well as absolutely, or in other words, "both determiner and nominal functions are found together in the Old English genitive case of the personal pronoun from which the possessives derive" (Wales 1996: 173).[3]

In early ME a phonetic contrast is introduced, parallel to that of the indefinite article *a/an*. In their function as determiners, *min* and *þin* lose their final *-n* before a noun beginning with a consonant (e.g.: ME *mi fader* instead of OE *min fæder*), with the *-n* being retained only before a vowel or ⟨h⟩ + vowel (e.g.: *min arm, þin herte*).

According to Faiß, the inclusion of words beginning with ⟨h⟩ can be taken as an indicator that the ⟨h⟩ was not pronounced at all, or with only weak articulation.[4] The split of adjectival *min/þin* into *mi/min* and *þi/þin* goes back to the second half of the 12th century. The *-n* is regularly kept when the pronouns are used absolutely, or when followed by a noun (e.g.: *hit is min, broþer min!*). Towards the end of the ME period the *-n* is frequently dropped before a vowel as well. This mixed distribution of the pronouns when followed by a vowel or ⟨h⟩ + vowel, continues into EModE, but the shortened forms soon become the rule, especially in prose. "Very common were *mine* and *thine* before *own*, and *mine host*, a reminiscence of CHAUCER'S *mine host (of the Tabard)*, became a standing expression" (Poutsma 1916:782f.). Sweet says that "the ME distinction between conjoint *mine, thine* and *my, thy* was frequently kept up in Early MnE, but the shorter forms were frequently used before vowels: *mine eyes, my eyes*" (1900:345). Brunner (1951:114f.) states that in some cases the forms ending in *-n* are used before consonants, and also, the other way around, those without *-n* before vowels.

This unsettled state of affairs continues until the early 17th century, when the forms without *-n* (*my/thy*) are generalised in their function as determiners (i.e. in attributive use). Pyles mentions that the distinction *mine/thine* before a vowel or ⟨h⟩, and *my/thy* before consonants, which had been established in the 13th century, continued to be made right down to the 18th century, "when *my* came to be the only regular first person possessive modifier" (1971:199). He gives a few examples of nouns beginning with ⟨n⟩ such as *Ned, Nelly,* and *Noll* which obviously result from a misunderstanding of *mine* + noun, where the *-n* was falsely separated from the pronoun and added to the beginning of the following noun, as in the Fool's *nuncle* in LR (*mine uncle* > *my nuncle*) which is used as a "familiar form of address from Fool to master" (*Riverside Shakespeare* [2]1997:1310, footnote). Faiß is also of the opinion that the distinction of *my/mine* and *thy/thine* is finally given up in the 18th century in favour of *my* and *thy*, but according to Graband (1965:254) *mine* and *thine* in adjectival function are already regarded as dated or archaic at the end of the 17th century. They continue, however, to be used in poetic language well into the 19th century, especially in connection with *own* (cf. Jespersen 1909–49, vol. 2: 401). Sweet also states that the distinction is kept up in the higher literary registers, as in examples like *mine eyes* and *mine host*. "But many modern poets drop the *n* before sounded (h), as in *my heart* = EarlyMnE *mine heart*, keeping it only before vowels and silent *h* + vowel, as in *mine honour*" (1900:345).

The reasons which in Modern Standard English eventually led to the demise of *thy* and *thine*, are the same sociological or sociolinguistic ones that brought about the substitution of *thou* and *thee* by *you* (cf. Graband 1965:255). Nevertheless, Wales includes *thy* and *thine* in the pronoun paradigm of present standard and non-standard English(es) "because they are still known and used by native standard English speakers as part of a general 'elevated' register'" (1996:167f). Yet, due to these usage restrictions they are treated as marked forms.

Having shown that the two forms have a complex and intertwined history, for which once again the period of EModE has proved to be the decisive point in time with the two forms being still in use and showing an overlap in attributive/determiner function, it is necessary to have a closer look at this period as a whole in order to evaluate Shakespeare's usage against this background.

For the development of the two forms in EModE Barber (1997:152) gives a more detailed account by making three synchronic cuts in 1500, 1600 and 1700 and by comparing these subsequent stages of the language to one another (cf. Chapter 1, Table 2).

At the beginning of the period in 1500, the distinction between *thy/thine* is as laid down earlier on. Similarly to *a/an*, *my* and *thy* are used before consonants, and *mine/thine* before a vowel, or sometimes ⟨h⟩ + vowel. In case of silent word-initial ⟨h⟩ as in *honour, host, habit* we find *mine/thine*. This usage changes in the 16th century, and in the 17th century *my*, *thy* and *a* are normal in this position: "in Shakespeare, the word *heart* occurs frequently, but almost without exception he uses *a heart, my heart, thy heart*" (Barber 1997:152). In the course of the period, *my* and *thy* spread at the expense of *mine* and *thine*, so that

> by 1600, *my* and *thy* are almost without exception the forms used before consonants, while before vowels *my* and *mine* are in free variation, as are *thy* and *thine*: Shakespeare has both *thine eyes* and *thy eye*, both *mine own* and *my own*. During the seventeenth century, *mine* and *thine* continue to recede, and by 1700 *my* and *thy* are the normal forms in standard literary prose (though the older forms continue to be used as poetic archaisms). (Barber 1997:152)

Görlach (1994:69) sums up the usage rules for the two variants in EModE as follows: the forms *mine* and *thine* are restricted to positions before vocalic word-initial sounds (as ModE *an*) and before a pause. In the 17th century, attributive use of the *n*-forms becomes more and more seldom. In predicative use, the *n*-forms are characterised by greater intonational emphasis and their possibility to occur before a pause or sentence boundary. Owing to this, the *-n* is generally retained. Thus, in the 17th century the ME phonetic distinction is understood grammatically. Görlach also points out that it is obvious that the *-n* could also be interpreted as a weakened form of *one*, as in *such one, this one*, which had become usual in this position after pronouns. Whether this really was the case, however, cannot be proved.

Strang argues along the same line: "since the use in final position was pronominal, the distribution could serve as matrix for a new, grammatical, distinction. The now familiar difference of use, +/n/ pronominal, −/n/ attributive, develops from this matrix at the end of the 16c; though in attributive use the old phonological distinction continued in use for a time" (1970: 139).

9.2.1   *Thy/thine* in EModE grammars

The grammar books that appeared in the EModE period also mention the two variants. The earliest of these, Bullokar, comments that "[…] we say sometimes *yours* […] used proprietarily without any substantive expressed […] [as well as] *thine* [which is] used only before a substantive beginning with a vowel" (1586: 19f.).
Miege (1688: 47f.) gives the following declension paradigm:

	Singular	Plural
[Subjective]	*thou*	*you*
Possessive	*thy, thine*	*your, yours*
Objective	*thee*	–

to which he adds the comments that *thine* and *yours* are "used at the end of a sentence", and that to the second person pronouns "are frequently added *Own* and *Self*":

thy own   your own
{thy self   {yourselves[5]
{thouself   {you selves

In contrast to this, Aitken's grammar explains the use of *thy/thine* in the following way: "when a vowel follows, we say […] *thine*, for […] *thy*" (1693: 9).
Greenwood mentions that *thine* is normally used when the noun is omitted, but that it appears sometimes when the noun begins with a vowel, "but not else" (1711: 105). Examples like *thy oath* and *thine oath* testify that both variants could be used before vowels.

9.2.2   *Thy/thine* in Shakespeare grammars

In §237, Abbott describes the use of the possessives *mine/my* and *thine/thy* in the following way:

> The two forms, which are interchangeable in E.[arly] E.[nglish] both before vowels and consonants, are both used by Shakespeare with little distinction before vowels. Though there are probably many exceptions, yet the rule appears to be that *mine* and *thine* are used where the possessive adjective is to be unemphatic, *my* and *thy* in other cases. (Abbott [1870] 1972: 160)

Apart from this difference in emphasis, Abbott further mentions stylistic reasons such as antithesis for the choice of *my* and *thy*:

(4)   *My* ear should catch your voice, *my* eye your eye, [...]. (MND 1, 1, 188)

and phonotactic reasons, especially euphony:

(5)   To follow *me* and praise *my* eyes and face? (MND 3, 2, 223)

"The pause which we are obliged to make between *my, thy,* and a following vowel, serves for a kind of emphasis. On the other hand, *mine,* pronounced 'min', glides easily and unemphatically on to the following vowel" (ibid.).

Franz ([1939] 1986:292f.) in §§326–332 gives the following rather general comment on the use of *mine* and *thine* in Shakespeare. With reference to Spies he states that *mine/thine* appear before vowels and ⟨h⟩. From the first half of the 16th century they are no longer used before consonants; *my* and *thy,* on the other hand, are being used adjectivally. In comparison to the *n*-forms, *my/thy* are much more numerous. *Mine own honesty, mine own people* and *my host* are given as examples for highly frequent combinations. As far as metre is concerned, *mine* is used both in accented and in unaccented syllables. The different Quarto editions and especially the later Folio edition show a certain amount of vacillation. *Mine/thine* are often replaced by *my/thy,* and in some cases also the other way around. He further remarks that cases like:

(6)   *Mine* and your mistress! (CYM 5, 5, 230)

are not exceptional, because in Shakespeare's time a strict differentiation between *my/thy* and *mine/thine* had not yet taken place. From present-day usage, however, it is remarkable that other possessives are used absolutely, and not adjectivally:

(7)   In *yours* and my discharge (TMP 2, 1, 254)

(8)   in *theirs* and in the common's ears (COR 5, 6, 4)

(9)   By *hers* and *mine* adultery (CYM 5, 5, 186)

Schmidt and Sarrazin ([1875] 1962:1208f., s.v. *thine* and 1226 s.v. *thy*) give the following rules for the use of the two variants and exemplify them with a number of illustrative quotations which, unfortunately, reveal nothing about the frequency of the different syntactic constructions:

> Thine, possessive pronoun of the second pers. sing.,[6]
> 1) **adjectivally before vowels:** *Wipe thou thine eyes, have comfort.* (TMP 1, 2, 25)
> – a) before *h*: *It is thine host, thine Ephesian, calls.* (WIV 4, 5, 17–18)
> – b) with *own*: *I will, out of thine own confession,* [...]. (MM 1, 2, 37–38)
> Perhaps throughout unemphatical, *thy,* not *thine,* being used, where some stress is laid on the pronoun: *Why, Suffolk, England knows thine insolence. / And thy ambition, Gloucester.* (2H6 2, 1, 31–32)
>
> 2) **without a noun, but with reference to one preceding:** *be subject / to no sight but thine and mine,* [...]. (TMP 1, 2, 301–302)

– a) with *own*: *which may make this island / Thine own for ever,* [...].
(TMP 4, 1, 217–218)
– b) following a noun, not only = one of those which whom or which thou
hast: *and misbegotten blood I spill of thine,* [...]. (1H6 4, 6, 22)
but as often = of thee, thy: *Come, I will fasten on this sleeve of thine,* [...].
(ERR 2, 2, 173)

3) **substantively,** =
– a) thy property: *put up this — 'twill be thine another day.* (LLL 4, 1, 107)
– b) thy relations, thy children, thy family: *To thee and thine hereditary ever /
Remain this ample third of our fair kingdom.* (LR 1, 1, 79–80)

Thy, possessive pronoun of the second pers. sing.,
– Before vowels: *and art thou not asham'd / To wrong him with thy importu-
nacy?* (TGV 4, 2, 110–111).
More emphatical, in this case, than *thine*: *"So sweet a kiss the golden sun gives
not* [...] */ As thy eye-beams,* [...]. (LLL 4, 3, 25–27)

Scheler (1982:40) mentions Shakespeare's use of the possessives only in a footnote,
saying that *my* and *thy* clearly outweigh *mine* and *thine,* which alongside *my/thy* are
used before vowels and ⟨h⟩.

9.3   The Shakespeare Corpus

9.3.1   Quantitative analysis

On the basis of the *Riverside Shakespeare* (^{2}1997) and the Spevack concordances
(1968–1980) the breakdown for the two forms of the second person singular
possessives is as shown in Tables 1 and 2.

Table 1. *Thine* in the Shakespeare Corpus

		Frequency	Verse	Prose
38 plays:	*thine*	418	353	65
	/*thine**	4	4	0
	thine + /*thine*	422 (100%)	357 (84.60%)	65 (15.40%)
Non-dramatic Works:	*thine*	76 (100%)	76 (100%)	0 (0%)
Complete Shakespeare:	*thine*	494	429	65
	thine + /*thine*	498 (100%)	433 (86.95%)	65 (13.05%)

* For the slash-tokens see Chapter 3, note 1.

Table 2. *Thy* in the Shakespeare Corpus

		Frequency	Verse	Prose
38 plays:	*thy*	3,839	3,222	617
	/*thy*	54	51	3
	thy + /*thy*	3,893 (100%)	3,273 (84.07%)	620 (15.93%)
Non-dramatic Works:	*thy*	452	451	1
	/*thy*	15	15	0
	thy + /*thy*	467 (100%)	466 (99.79%)	1 (0.21%)
Complete Shakespeare:	*thy*	4,291	3,673	618
	thy + /*thy*	4,360 (100%)	3,739 (85.76%)	621 (14.24%)

The comparison of tokens makes evident that *thy*, with its 3,893 instances, is about nine times as frequent as *thine*, with only 422 instances. Despite this huge discrepancy, the distribution of the two forms in verse and prose is strikingly similar, in that both forms, with ca. 84% verse and 16% prose show almost exactly the same percentages for the two dramatic media, so that in this respect no preference in usage can be established.

Apart from these similarities there are also important differences between the two variants. Whereas *thy* in all of its 3,893 occurrences acts as a determiner, the functions of *thine* are more varied, as only 249 (59.00%) out of the 422 *thine* tokens function adjectivally as a determiner, and merely 173 (41.00%) absolutely. That is to say, in about 60% of all cases in which *thine* works attributively, there is a functional overlap, and — theoretically speaking — a choice between *thine* and *thy*.

9.3.1.1   *Thy* and *thine* before vowel and before ⟨h⟩

As far as the phonological environment of *thine* as a determiner is concerned, the instances of *thine* before a vowel (including the cases with *own*) amount to 230 (54.50%), and those before ⟨h⟩ to 19 (4.50%).

In comparison to this, Table 3 indicates that *thy* by and large follows the rules of the grammarians, because in the vast majority of cases it is used before consonants (84.38%), but also, though to a far lesser extent, before vowels (6.68%) and before ⟨h⟩. In this case, the 8.71% of *thy* before ⟨h⟩ almost double the figure of *thine* before ⟨h⟩ with only 4.50%. This usage runs contrary to the descriptions of the grammarians and language historians.

9.3.2   Corpus-internal variation in the Shakespeare Corpus?

As shown in Table 4, there is a considerable difference between the plays and the non-dramatic works in their use of *thy* and *thine* in the environment of vowels. In

Table 3. Syntactic and phonological distribution of *thine* and *thy*

			thine		*thy*	
1.	a.	adjectivally before vowels:	157	37.20%	260	6.68%
	b.	with *own*	73	17.30%	9	0.23%
		1.a) + 1.b)	230	54.50%	269	6.91%
	c.	before ⟨h⟩	19	4.50%	339	8.71%
		with consonant	–	–	3,285	84.38%
2.	a.	without a noun, but with reference to one preceding:	66	15.64%		
	b.	following a noun:	32	7.58%		
3.		substantively:				
	a.	thy property	63	14.93%		
	b.	thy relations, children, family:	12	2.84%		
		Total	**422**	100%	**3,893**	100%

the plays, *thy* is used to a larger extent (ca. 54%) than in the non-dramatic works (ca. 43%). In terms of statistical significance the deviation between the plays and the non-dramatic works is significant beyond the 0.10 level of confidence.[7]

If these text types are grouped according to degrees of formality, then drama can best be described as a written speech-based genre that is less formal and more

Table 4. *Thy* and *thine* before vowels and before ⟨h⟩

38 plays:	*thine* + vowel		*thy* + vowel		combined
	abs.	per cent	abs.	per cent	
	73 *own*	89.02%	9 *own*	10.98%	82 *own*
	157 other	37.65%	260 other	62.35%	417 other
	= 230 total	46.09%	= 269 total	53.91%	= 499 total
	thine + ⟨h⟩		*thy* + ⟨h⟩		combined
	19	5.31%	339	94.69%	358
non-dramatic works:	*thine* + vowel		*thy* + vowel		combined
	12 *own*	92.31%	1 *own*	7.69%	13 *own*
	28 other	49.12%	29 other	50.88%	57 other
	= 40 total	57.14%	= 30 total	42.86%	= 70 total
	thine + ⟨h⟩		*thy* + ⟨h⟩		combined
	3	8.33%	33	91.67%	36

colloquial than poetry, which exhibits more written and formal traits. This result corroborates Schendl's hypothesis (cf. 9.4.2) that the *n*-less forms (*my/thy*) first gained ground in less formal text types.

In the introduction it was mentioned that Schendl could not find an explanation for the variation in the Shakespeare Corpus, because "it is not clearly related to chronology nor to types of plays" (1997:189). However, Table 5 demonstrates that for the plays there are differences between genres, but with $p < 0.10$ they are not large enough in terms of statistical significance, so that the null hypothesis that there is no correlation between pronoun usage and genre cannot be firmly rejected. Nonetheless, the figures below support Schendl's claim that around 1600 *thine* is preferred in the more formal text types only in part, because only the Tragedies and not the Histories show a larger number of *thines*.

Table 5. *Thy* and *thine* before vowels according to genres

	thy + vowel	*thine* + vowel
Histories	90 (57.69%)	66 (42.31%)
Tragedies	96 (49.23%)	99 (50.77%)
Comedies	83 (56.08%)	65 (43.92%)
DRAMA total	269 (53.91%)	230 (46.09%)
Non-dramatic Works	30 (42.86%)	40 (57.14%)

9.3.3   Lexical associations

Now it is necessary to investigate the overlap between *thy* and *thine* qualitatively, and to have a look at all the words that begin with either a vowel or ⟨h⟩, because this analysis of lexical associates of the two forms proves that even if the great discrepancy in frequency between *thy* and *thine* is taken into account, certain words co-occur more often with one form than with the other.[8]

9.3.3.1   *Thy and thine + vowel*

The comparison of the lexical associates of *thy/thine* beginning with a vowel (as featured in Table 6) yields the following results: the total instances of *thine* amount to 230, and those of *thy* to 269. As was to be expected on the basis of the reference works cited in Chapter 9.2 the strongest lexical association exists between *thine* and *own*; these cases alone make up 73 instances as opposed to only nine with *thy*. Furthermore, the 230 instances of *thine* + vowel contain only 45 different words. In contrast to this, the 269 cases in which *thy* co-occurs with a vowel consist of 162 different words. But these are not the only differences to be found, because apart from *thine + own*, there are two other high frequency pairs: *eye(s)* (61 times) and *ear(s)* (23 times). Such a strong lexical association does not exist with any of the associates of *thy*. The fact that *thine* mostly co-occurs in high frequency, quasi lexicalised or fossilised combinations can be seen as an indicator of its markedness. If the ten most frequent associates shown in Table 6 are compared to each other, certain disparities in distribution become apparent: *age* (3 *thine* :2 *thy*), *arm(s)* (2:8), *ear(s)* (23:5), *enemy* (17:2), *eye(s)* (61:12), *oath* (3:9), *office* (2:6), *old* (2:9), *own* (73:9), *uncle* (4:6).

When, in addition to this, the non-dramatic works are also taken into account, the above result is strongly corroborated by the data. In the non-dramatic works *thine* has an absolute frequency of 76 tokens, 40 of which occur before vowels (see Table 4). These 40 instances make use of only nine different words. The most frequent combinations are *thine eye(s)* with 18 cases, *thine own* with 12 tokens and *thine ear* with two; all the other associates occurring only once.

For *thy* + vowel the data from the non-dramatic works are as follows: out of the total of 467 occurrences 30 pertain to the phonological environment of *thy* + vowel. In marked contrast to the low number of lexical associates of *thine*, *thy* is found in combination with 25 different words, out of which *own* occurs just once, and with the exception of *outward* with four occurrences, and *eye(s)* with two, all of the other words used in conjunction with *thy* occur only once.

In order to find out whether there is a pattern underlying this distribution, a number of these minimally contrasting dyads in which the same noun is used with either of the possessives shall be investigated next.

9.3.3.1.1 *Selected discourse samples of thy/thine + vowel.* Abbott, Franz and Schmidt and Sarrazin (cf. 9.2.2) postulate the following principles, or rather tendencies, concerning the choice of *thy/thine* before vowels: the two forms differ in emphasis, with *thy* being recognised as the more emphatic pronoun. In addition to this, stylistic considerations such as antithesis and euphony are given as factors governing the choice of pronoun. In order to test these claims, the following 'collocate pairs' of high frequency nouns used in conjunction with both variants shall be examined: *thine age* vs. *thy age*, *thine arm(s)* vs. *thy arm(s)*, *thine ear(s)* vs. *thy ear(s)*, *thine eye(s)* vs. *thy eye(s)*, *thine oath* vs. *thy oath* and *thine uncle* vs. *thy uncle*:

(10) Prospero [to Gonzalo]: First, noble friend, / Let me embrace *thine age*, whose honor cannot / Be measur'd or confin'd. (TMP 5, 1, 120–121)

(11) Gloucester [to himself]: Mine eyes are full of tears, my heart of grief. / Ah, Humphrey, this dishonor in *thine age* / Will bring thy head with sorrow to the ground! (2H6 2, 3, 17–19)

(12) Marcus: Titus, prepare thy aged eyes to weep, / Or if not so, thy noble heart to break: / I bring consuming sorrow to *thine age*. (TIT 3, 1, 59–61)

Table 6. Lexical associates after *thy/thine* beginning with a vowel (38 plays)

	thine	thy		thine	thy		thine	thy		thine	thy
abhorr'd	–	1	artillery	–	1	established	–	1	intention	–	1
abode	–	1	asking	–	1	estate	–	3	intercepter	–	1
abortive	–	1	ass	1	1	estimation	–	1	interest	–	1
absense	–	3	assailant	–	1	eternal	1	–	invention	1	–
abundant	–	1	assault	–	1	Europa	–	1	inward	–	1
abuse	–	1	assistance	–	1	every	–	1	iron	1	–
abused	–	1	assistant	–	1	evidence	–	1	o'ernight's	–	1
act*	1	2	Athenian	–	1	evil	–	1	oath	3	9
addition	–	1	attaint	–	1	excellence	–	1	offense	–	3
admiring	–	1	attempt	–	1	excuse	–	1	office	2	6
adultery	–	1	audacious	–	1	executioner	–	2	old	2	9
advanced	–	1	auld	–	1	exercise	–	1	only	2	–
adversary	–	2	aunt	1	1	exile	–	1	opinion	–	2
adverse	–	1	auspicious	–	1	exit	–	1	opposer	–	1
advice	–	4	avail	1	–	experiment	–	1	oracle	1	–
affair	1	2	eagle	1	–	exquisite	–	1	orison	–	1
affection	–	4	ear(s)	23	5	extorsions	–	1	other	–	9
after-love	–	1	earliness	–	1	eye(s)	61	12	outside	–	1
age	3	2	ecstacy	–	1	eye-ball	–	1	outward	–	1
aged	1	1	edgeless	–	2	eyebeams	–	1	overflow	–	1
agony	–	1	edict	–	1	eyelid	–	1	overthrow	1	1
ague	1	–	Edward	–	2	ignominy	–	1	overview	–	1
allegiance	1	1	effect	–	1	ignorance	1	–	own	73	9
almost	–	1	elbow	–	2	ill-uttering	–	1	uncle	4	6
alms-deed	–	1	elder	1	1	image	2	2	uncover'd	–	1
altar	–	1	eldest	–	2	impatience	–	1	undaunted	–	1
ambition	–	3	element	–	1	impatient	–	1	understanding	–	1
amiable	–	1	eloquence	–	1	impediment	–	1	unhallowed	–	2
ancestor	–	1	embassage	–	1	imperial	–	1	union	–	1
ancient	–	2	embracement	–	1	importunacy	–	1	unkindness	–	3
angel	1	1	embraces	–	1	inch	–	1	unnatural	–	1
angry	–	3	end	–	2	indenture	–	1	unprepared	–	1
annoy	–	1	endless	–	1	indignation	1	1	unrest	–	1
anointed	–	1	enemy	17	2	infancy	–	1	unreverent	–	1
answer	2	2	English	–	1	inference	–	1	unrivall'd	–	1
Antony	–	1	enmity	1	–	infirmity	1	–	unthankfulness	1	–
apperil	1	–	enterprise	1	–	ingratitude	–	1	unworthiness	–	1
approach	–	2	entertainment	–	1	inheritance	1	–	upbraidings	–	1
approof	–	1	entrails	1	–	ink	–	1	uprightness	–	1
arm(s)	2	8	entrance	–	1	insolence	2	1	uprise	–	1
armor	–	2	Ephesian	1	–	instinct	–	1	upward	–	1
arms	–	2	epitaph	1	1	instrument	–	3	usage	–	1
arrand	–	1	errand	–	2	insulting	–	1	use	–	1
arrival	–	1	error	–	1	integrity	–	2	usurping	–	2
art	1	–	escape	–	1	intellect	1	–			
articles	–	1	especial	1	–	intent	–	2			

* Highlighting of lexemes indicates that the items are used in conjunction with both pronouns.

(13)   Duke [to Antipholus of Ephesus]: I see *thy age* and dangers make thee dote. (ERR 5, 1, 330)

(14)   Duchess of York [to King Richard]: A grievous burthen was thy birth to me, / Tetchy and wayward was thy infancy; / Thy schooldays frightful, desp'rate, wild, and furious, / Thy prime of manhood daring, bold, and venturous; / *Thy age* confirm'd, proud, subtle, sly, and bloody, [...]. (R3 4, 4, 168–172)

(15)   Bastard [to Hubert de Burgh]: Go, bear him in *thine arms*. (JN 4, 3, 139)

(16)   Ulysses [to Diomedes]: Fam'd be thy tutor, and thy parts of nature / Thrice fam'd beyond, [beyond] all erudition; / But he that disciplin'd *thine arms* to fight, [...]. (TRO 2, 3, 242–244)

(17)   Lafew [to Parolles]: The devil it is that's thy master. Why dost thou garter up *thy arms* a' this fashion? Dost make hose of thy sleeves? (AWW 2, 3, 249–251)

(18)   King Henry: O God, *thy arm* was here; / And not to us, but to *thy arm* alone, / Ascribe we all! (H5 4, 8, 106–108)

(19)   Aaron [to the Nurse]: Why, what a caterwauling dost thou keep! / What dost thou wrap and fumble in *thy arms*? (TIT 4, 2, 57–58)

(20)   Gloucester [to Kent]: Good friend, I prithee take him in *thy arms*; / I have o'erheard a plot of death upon him. (LR 3, 6, 88–89)

(21)   Edgar [to Gloucester]: Give me *thy arm*; / Poor Tom shall lead thee. (LR 4, 1, 78–79)

(22)   Edgar [to Edmund]: Draw thy sword, / That if my speech offend a noble heart, / *Thy arm* may do thee justice; here is mine: [...]. (LR 5, 3, 126–128)

(23)   2. Queen: Honored Hippolyta, / Most dreaded Amazonian, that hast slain / The scythe-tusk'd boar; that with *thy arm*, as strong [...]. (TNK 1, 1, 77–79)

(24)   King Richard [to Tyrrel]: Hark, come hither, Tyrrel. / Go, by this token. Rise, and lend *thine ear*. (R3 4, 2, 78–79)

(25)   Queen Elizabeth [to King Richard]: But that still use of grief makes wild grief tame, / My tongue should to *thy ears* not name my boys / Till that my nails were anchor'd in thine eyes; [...]. (R3 4, 4, 230–232)

(26)   Juliet [to Romeo]: It was the nightingale, and not the lark, / That pierc'd the fearful hollow of *thine ear*; [...]. (ROM 3, 5, 2–3)

(27)   Paris [to his Page]: Under yond [yew] trees lay thee all along, / Holding *thy ear* close to the hollow ground, [...]. (ROM 5, 3, 3–4)

(28)   Pericles [to Helicanus]: Her face was to mine eye beyond all wonder; / The rest (hark in *thine ear*) as black as incest, [...]. (PER 1, 2, 75–76)

(29)   Marina [to Boult]: To the choleric fisting of every rogue / *Thy ear* is liable; thy food is such / As hath been belch'd on by infected lungs. (PER 4, 6, 167–169)

(30)   Adriana [to Antipholus]: The time was once, when thou unurg'd wouldst vow / That never words were music to *thine ear*, / That never object pleasing in thine

eye, / That never touch well welcome to thy hand, / That never meat sweet-savor'd in thy taste, [...]. (ERR 2, 2, 113–117)

(31) Grumio: Lend *thine ear.* Curtis: Here. Grumio: There. (SHR 4, 1, 60–62)

(32) Polonius [to Laertes]: Beware / Of entrance to a quarrel, but being in, / Bear't that th' opposed may beware of thee. / Give every man *thy ear,* but few thy voice, [...]. (HAM 1, 3, 65–68)

(33) Pisanio: O master, what a strange infection / Is fall'n into *thy ear!* (CYM 3, 2, 3–4)

(34) Demetrius: [Awaking.] O Helen, goddess, nymph, perfect, divine! / To what, my love, shall I compare *thine eyne?* (MND 3, 2, 137–138)

(35) Hermia [to Helena]: I am not yet so low / But that my nails can reach unto *thine eyes.* (MND 3, 2, 297–298)

(36) Oberon [to Titania]: Be it ounce, or cat, or bear, / Pard, or boar with bristled hair, / In *thy eyes* that shall appear / When thou wak'st, it is thy dear: / Wake when some vile thing is near. (MND 2, 2, 30–34)

(37) Puck [to Lysander]: Churl, upon *thy eyes* I throw / All the power this charm doth owe. / When thou wak'st, let love forbid / Sleep his seat on thy eyelid. / So awake when I am gone, / For I must now to Oberon. (MND 2, 2, 78–83)

(38) Lucentio [to Baptista]: Here's Lucentio, / Right son to the right Vincentio, / That have by marriage made thy daughter mine, / While counterfeit supposes blear'd *thine eyne.* (SHR 5, 1, 114–117)

(39) Romeo: O, teach me how I should forget to think.
      Benvolio: By giving liberty unto *thine eyes*: / Examine other beauties. (ROM 1, 1, 226–228)

(40) Juliet: If they do see thee, they will murther thee.
      Romeo: Alack, there lies more peril in *thine eye* / Than twenty of their swords! (ROM 2, 2, 70–72)

(41) Romeo [to Juliet]: Sleep dwell upon *thine eyes*, peace in thy breast! / Would I were sleep and peace, so sweet to rest! (ROM 2, 2, 186–187)

(42) Benvolio [to Romeo]: Take thou some new infection to *thy eye*, / And the rank poison of the old will die. (ROM 1, 2, 49–50)

(43) Capulet [to Juliet]: In one little body / Thou counterfeits a bark, a sea, a wind: / For still *thy eyes*, which I may call the sea, / Do ebb and flow with tears; the bark thy body is, / Sailing in this salt flood; the winds, thy sighs, / Who, raging with thy tears, and they with them, / Without a sudden calm, will overset / Thy tempest-tossed body. (ROM 3, 5, 130–137)

(44) Friar Lawrence [to Juliet]: The roses in thy lips and cheeks shall fade / To [wanny] ashes, *thy eyes'* windows fall, [...]. (ROM 4, 1, 99–100)

(45) Romeo [to the Apothecary]: Famine is in thy cheeks, / Need and oppression starveth in *thy eyes*, / Contempt and beggary hangs upon thy back; / The world is not thy friend, [...]. (ROM 5, 1, 69–72)

(46) Antigonus: [...] anon / Did this break from her: "Good Antigonus, / Since fate (against thy better disposition) / Hath made thy person for the thrower-out / Of my poor babe, according to *thine oath*, / Places remote enough are in Bohemia, [...]." (WT 3, 3, 26–31)

(47) Cassius [to Pindarus]: Come now, keep *thine oath*; / Now be a freeman, and with this good sword, / That ran through Caesar's bowels, search this bosom. (JC 5, 3, 40–42)

(48) Pericles [to Helicanus]: The care I had and have of subjects' good / On thee I lay, whose wisdom's strength can bear it. / I'll take thy word for faith, not ask *thine oath*: [...]. (PER 1, 2, 118–120)

(49) Julia [to Proteus]: Behold her that gave aim to all *thy oaths*, / And entertain'd 'em deeply in her heart. (TGV 5, 4, 101–102)

(50) Duke [to Friar Peter and Mariana]: Thou foolish friar, and thou pernicious woman, / Compact with her that's gone, think'st thou *thy oaths*, / Though they would swear down each particular saint, [...]. (MM 5, 1, 241–243)

(51) Mopsa: [Song] It becomes *thy oath* full well, / Thou to me thy secrets tell. (WT 4, 4, 300–301)

(52) King Richard [to John of Gaunt]: Old John of Gaunt, time-honored Lancaster, / Hast thou, according to *thy oath* and band, / Brought hither Henry Herford, thy bold son, [...]. (R2 1, 1, 1–2)

(53) Lord Marshal [to Mowbray]: Speak truly on thy knighthood and *thy oath*, / As so defend thee heaven and thy valor! (R2 1, 3, 14–15)

(54) Hotspur [to Lady Percy]: Heart, you swear like a comfit-maker's wife: [...] / And givest such sarcenet surety for *thy oaths* / As if thou never walk'st further than Finsbury. (1H4 3, 1, 247–252)

(55) Buckingham [to York]: Or why thou, being a subject as I am, / Against *thy oath* and true allegiance sworn, / Should raise so great a power without his leave, / Or dare to bring thy force so near the court. (2H6 5, 1, 19–22)

(56) Aaron [to Lucius]: Therefore I urge *thy oath*; for that I know / An idiot holds his bauble for a god, [...]. (TIT 5, 1, 78–79)

(57) Dionyza [to Leonine]: *Thy oath* remember, thou hast sworn to do't. / 'Tis but a blow, which never shall be known. (PER 4, 1, 1–2)

(58) Constance [to Arthur]: But Fortune, O, / She is corrupted, chang'd, and won from thee; / Sh' adulterates hourly with *thine uncle* John, [...]. (JN 3, 1, 54–56)

(59) Hubert [to Arthur]: Well, see to live; I will not touch thine eye / For all the treasure that *thine uncle* owes. (JN 4, 1, 121–122)

(60) King Edward [to the young Prince]: Young Ned, for thee, *thine uncles* and myself / Have in our armors watch'd the winter's night, [...]. (3H6 5, 7, 16–17)

(61) Lucius [to Cymbeline]: [...] Cassibelan, *thine uncle* [...], for him / And his succession granted Rome a tribute [...]. (CYM 3, 1, 5–8)

(62) Prospero [to Miranda]: My brother and *thy uncle*, call'd Antonio — / I pray thee mark me — that a brother should / Be so perfidious! (TMP 1, 2, 66–68)

(63)   Benedick [to Beatrice]: I will live in thy heart, die in thy lap, and be buried in thy eyes; and moreover I will go with thee to *thy uncle's*. (ADO 5, 2, 102–104)

(64)   Celia [to Rosalind]: If my uncle, thy banish'd father, had banish'd *thy uncle*, the Duke my father, so thou hadst been still with me, [...]. (AYL 1, 2, 9–11)

(65)   King John [to Arthur]: Cousin, look not sad, / Thy grandame loves thee, and *thy uncle* will / As dear be to thee as thy father was. (JN 3, 3, 2–4)

(66)   Mortimer [to Richard Plantagenet]: With silence, nephew, be thou politic. / Strong fixed is the house of Lancaster, / And like a mountain, not to be remov'd. / But now *thy uncle* is removing hence, [...]. (1H6 2, 5, 101–104)

(67)   Ghost [to Hamlet]: Sleeping within my orchard, / My custom always of the afternoon, / Upon my secure hour *thy uncle* stole, [...]. (HAM 1, 5, 59–61)

The above 'collocate' pairs seem to resist rigid categorisation at first sight. In my opinion an overriding structural pattern does indeed not exist. This is, however, not to say that the two possessives are in free variation before vowels as Barber (1997: 152) claims. To my mind an investigation of the context reveals that a meaningful choice between the two pronouns is being made primarily for stylistic reasons.

For example, rhyme is an important factor constraining the choice of pronouns. Examples (31), (34) and (38) testify to this. In example (31) *thine ear* fully rhymes with *here*, and both provide a half rhyme for *there*. In (34) and (38) the combination of *thine* with the weak plural *eyne* results in an internal rhyme which rhymes with previous *divine* (34) and *mine* (38). Adding to this, the two names in (38) *Lucentio* and *Vincentio* also rhyme.

Parallelism is also an important stylistic device. The emotive speech of the Duchess of York (14) is a good example for this. Her inner tension is revealed through the passionate diction of symmetric asyndetic constructions of equal length that leave out the verbs. The pronoun *thy* is reiterated five times; twice at or towards the end of a sentence as an epiphora, and three times anaphorically. This heightened compact expression could not have been achieved with the use of *thine* in connection with *infancy* and *age*.

Repetition of the same pronoun for means of emphasis is illustrated in quotations (43) and (45). In the speech of Capulet, Juliet's body is compared to "a bark, a sea, a wind". This parallel structure is resumed in the repetition of the same pronoun *thy* (thy eyes = the sea, thy body = the bark, thy sighs = the wind). The speech of Romeo (45) consists of four syntactically parallel sentences (Subject + Verb + Adverbial Complement/Object). The repetition of *thy* in each of the sentences reinforces this effect.

On the other hand, a complete parallelism can be countered by chiasm, as exemplified in (11), where *mine eye* is juxtaposed to *my heart* in the first sentence; this structure being resumed in the next sentence: *thine age* followed by *thy head*; or in example (30), where the same anaphora "that never ..." introduces four consecutive sentences. The first two run parallel to each other in that both end in "thine ear", "thine eye", whereas the final pair terminates in "thy hand", and "thy taste", respectively.

Antithesis of two juxtaposed words or phrases that can nonetheless be grouped together under a usually unexpressed hyperonym, is also often expressed by means of a parallel construction. Citations (62) and (64) testify to this: "My brother and thy uncle" lay the main stress on the head words, and furthermore provide a verse-internal rhyme with *my* and *thy*. Logical antithesis is even more strongly expressed through the parallelism in pronoun use in (64): "If *my* uncle, *thy* banished father, had banish'd *thy* uncle, the Duke *my* father, [...]."

Admittedly, there are also examples that give counter-evidence: "Alack, there lies more peril in *thine* eye / Than twenty of their swords!" (40), in which antithesis is expressed by the "unemphatic" pronoun *thine*. Even so, on the whole, the instances of variation before vowels confirm the tendency that *thy* is indeed the more emphatic pronoun.

9.3.3.2 *Thy and thine* + ⟨h⟩

Table 7 shows that the 19 instances of *thine* before ⟨h⟩ are restricted to only eight different words. In addition to this, four of these words belong to the same root *hon(or)*. Furthermore, all of them are Romance loanwords with Old French, or, in case of *hereditary*, Latin etymology (cf. OED). In marked opposition to this, these words do not play a significant role as associates of *thy*, because in comparison to the overall number of *thy* tokens they are rather infrequent.

Thy, on the other hand, appears 339 times before ⟨h⟩ in the corpus in 71 different words. While most of the co-occurring words turn up only once, twice or three times, a few lexical associates exhibit extraordinarily high frequencies. The five most frequent are: *hand* (93 instances), *head* (53), *heart* (44), *husband* (25) and *heels* (8). In stark contrast to the associates of *thine*, all the above words stem from OE and have Germanic etymologies. This result also holds by and large when the etymologies for all ⟨h⟩ words are taken into account. Apart from the Romance, mostly Old French, words: *heir, honest, honesty, honor* and *honorable* (13 tokens, 18.31%), which appear also in conjunction with *thine*, the only other Latinate or Old French words used together with *thy* are: *habit, harness, hasty, heinous, heroical, history, hour, humble* and *humor* (19 tokens, 26.76%). This distribution proves that words of Germanic origin clearly predominate (39 tokens, 54.93%) as lexical associates of *thy*.

As in the case of *thy/thine* + vowel, evidence from the non-dramatic works confirms this distribution. There are only three instances of *thine* + ⟨h⟩ to be found: *thine honor* (2) and *thine heir*. On the other hand, there are 33 cases of *thy* + ⟨h⟩ which make use of 16 different words. Again, most of the words are only used once; *thy heart* (10 tokens) being the most frequent combination. In contrast to the plays, *thy hand* (3) and *thy head* (1) are far less frequent.

Table 7. Lexical associates after *thy/thine* beginning with ⟨h⟩ (38 plays)

	thine	*thy*		*thine*	*thy*		*thine*	*thy*
habit	–	2	hearth	–	1	honey	–	1
hair	–	3	heaven	–	2	**honor**	**9**	**5**
Halbert	–	1	heavenly	–	2	honor'd	–	1
half	–	1	heaviness	–	1	**honorable**	**1**	**2**
hand	–	93	heavy	–	5	hook	–	1
handkerchief	–	1	heels	–	8	hope	–	3
hap	–	1	heinous	–	2	hopeful	–	1
happiness	–	1	**heir(s)**	**2**	**1**	horn(s)	–	5
happy	–	3	hell	–	1	horse(s)	–	4
hard	–	1	helm	–	1	host	2	–
harm	–	1	help	–	4	hostess	1	–
harmless	–	1	here-approach	–	1	hot	–	1
harness	–	1	hereditary	1	–	hound	–	1
Harry	–	2	Hermia	–	1	hour	–	3
harsh	–	2	heroical	–	1	house	–	5
hasty	–	1	hest	–	1	house-keeping	–	1
hate	–	1	hide	–	1	household	–	2
hated	–	2	high	–	1	hue	–	1
hateful	–	2	hire	–	2	humble	–	5
head	–	53	history	–	1	humor	–	2
health	–	3	hold	–	1	hungry-starved	–	1
health-giving	–	1	Holland	–	1	hunter	–	1
hearer	–	1	home	–	1	huntress	–	1
heart	–	44	**honest**	**1**	**4**	husband	–	25
heart-blood	–	1	**honesty**	**2**	**1**			

Concerning the etymology of the associates, the same picture as for *thy* + ⟨h⟩ in the plays emerges, in that the vast majority (27 tokens, 82%) stem from OE and ultimately have a common Teutonic origin, and only six (18%): *hasty, heinous, honor* (2), *hour* (2) and *humor* go back to Latin or Old French sources.

In contrast to this, Schendl comes in part to a different conclusion from his data, which is not borne out by my investigation:

> The analysis of lexemes with initial ⟨h⟩ in the corpus has shown that the overall frequency of the *n*-variants before ⟨h⟩ never remotely approximated that before vowels, and became increasingly restricted to a small number of lexemes of French origin such as *honour(able), honesty, hour, heir*. The rare occurrence of words of Germanic origin such as *hand, heart, horse* in some of the texts does not allow one to establish any pattern or to draw conclusions on the pronunciation of initial ⟨h⟩ in the corpus. (Schendl 1997: 189, footnote 2)

The first part of his statement also holds for the Shakespeare Corpus. When one compares the number of *thine* + vowel tokens (230 tokens, 54.50%), the mere 19 tokens (4.50%) of *thine* + ⟨h⟩ are indeed only a small fraction. In this case, the reference books quoted should be more precise in saying that out of the two environments favouring *thine*, i.e. vowels and ⟨h⟩, the vowels are far more frequent. In the Shakespeare Corpus, *thy* plays a more important role before ⟨h⟩ than *thine*.

Schendl's next statement that in the context of ⟨h⟩ *thine* is restricted to a limited number of French loanwords is also borne out by my material. However, in my opinion the total absence of any Germanic words in the context of *thine* + ⟨h⟩ and their high prevalence (see above) in conjunction with *thy* seem to be evidence for a pattern of *thine* + ⟨h⟩ in case of Romance loans with little or no word-initial articulation of the /h/, and *thy* + ⟨h⟩ in conjunction with Germanic words with a pronounced /h/. Barber (1997:152) is also of the opinion that in such words as *honour, host* and *habit* the ⟨h⟩ in the spelling was not pronounced and that they are often used together with *mine* and *thine*. (cf. also Faiß 1989:166 and Sweet 1900:345).

9.3.3.2.1 *Complete discourse samples of thy/thine + honor.* In contrast to the situation of *thy/thine* + vowel that provides considerable overlap in usage between the two forms, the environment of *thy/thine* + ⟨h⟩ is different. Table 7 and the preceding discussion of etymology have shown that the two possessives are in a state of contrastive, or almost complementary distribution, with *thine* occurring before Romanisms, and *thy* predominantly before words of Germanic origin. The only word group that is used in connection with both variants is *honest, honesty, honor, honorable,* out of which *honor* is the only one yielding enough examples for juxtaposition. The following discourse samples of *thy/thine honor* make up the complete set of forms in the corpus:

(68) King [to Bertram]: We poising us in her defective scale, / Shall weigh thee to the beam; that wilt not know / It is in us to plant *thine honor* where / We please to have it grow. (AWW 2, 3, 154–157)

(69) Lady Constance [to Lewis, the Dolphin]: That which upholdeth him that thee upholds, / His honor. O, *thine honor*, Lewis, *thine honor!* (JN 3, 1, 315–316)

(70) Buckingham: That is too much presumption on thy part; / But if thy arms be to no other end, / The King hath yielded unto thy demand: / The Duke of Somerset is in the Tower.
York: Upon *thine honor*, is he prisoner?
Buckingham: Upon mine honor, he is prisoner. (2H6 5, 1, 38–43)

(71) Queen Margaret [to King Henry]: But thou prefer'st thy life before *thine honor*; / And seeing thou dost, I here divorce myself / Both from thy table, Henry, and thy bed, […]. (3H6 1, 1, 246–248)

(72) Cominius [to Martius]: And gladly quak'd, hear more; where the dull tribunes, /
That with the fusty plebeians hate *thine honors*, / Shall say against their hearts,
"We thank the gods / Our Rome hath such a soldier." (COR 1, 9, 6–9)

(73) 2. Senator [to Alcibiades]: Throw thy glove, / Or any token of *thine honor* else, /
That thou wilt use the wars as thy redress / And not as our confusion, all thy
powers / Shall make their habor in our town till we / Have seal'd thy full desire.
(TIM 5, 4, 49–54)

(74) Goneril [to Albany]: Milk-liver'd man, / That bear'st a cheek for blows, a head
for wrongs, / Who hast not in thy brows an eye discerning / *Thine honor* from
thy suffering, […]. (LR 4, 2, 50–53)

(75) Caesar [to Antony]: (It wounds *thine honor* that I speak it now) […].
(ANT 1, 4, 69)

(76) Caliban [to Stephano]: How does *thy honor*? Let me lick thy shoe. I'll not serve
him, he is not valiant. (TMP 3, 2, 23–24)

(77) Ford [to his wife]: I rather will suspect the sun with [cold] / Than thee with
wantonness. Now doth *thy honor* stand, / In him that was of late an heretic, / As
firm as faith. (WIV 4, 4, 7–10)

(78) Suffolk [to Reignier, Duke of Anjou]: Yes, there is remedy enough, my lord. /
Consent, and for *thy honor* give consent, / Thy daughter shall be wedded to my
king, […]. (1H6 5, 3, 135–137)

(79) Queen Margaret: [Aside.] And less'ned be that small, God I beseech him! / *Thy
honor*, state, and seat is due to me. (R3 1, 3, 110–111)

(80) Aufidius: [Aside.] I am glad thou hast set thy mercy and *thy honor* / At difference
in thee. (COR 5, 3, 200–201)

(81) Lucrece [to Collatinus]: "Yet am I guilty of *thy honor's* wrack, / Yet for *thy honor*
did I entertain him; / Coming from thee, I could not put him back, / For it had
been dishonor to disdain him. (LUC 841–844)

A clear preference of usage is not to be discerned. Impressionistically speaking
though, cases of *thine* like (69) and (70) are given a prominent position marked by
stress, conclusion of the argument or in the case of (70) change of turn taking. In
contrast to this, *thy* in examples (79) and (80) occurs in an aside that is not intended for
the other participants to be overheard. This would contradict such sweeping statements that *thy* is throughout the emphatic form (cf. Schmidt and Sarrazin).

9.4 Comparison to other corpora

9.4.1 *Thy/thine* in Mitchell's Corpus of British Drama (1580–1780)

Mitchell's corpus study spans the two-hundred years from 1580 to 1780 and covers 62
plays by 29 different dramatists. As regards the distribution of the two possessives,
Mitchell has come to the results that are shown in Tables 8 and 9.

Table 8. Distribution of *thy*/*thine* according to phonological environment in Mitchell's corpus

	Before a consonant (semi-vowel *y*)	Before a vowel (*a, e, i, o, u*)	Before *h*	Totals
thy	2,881 (81.78%)	343 (9.74%)	299 (8.48%)	3,523 (100%)
thine	–	129 (96.99%)	4 (3.01%)	133 (100%)
Total	2,881 (78.80%)	472 (12.91%)	303 (8.29%)	3,656 (100%)

(Table from Mitchell 1971:82; percentages added)

The figures in Table 8 clearly illustrate that the distribution of the two variants is fairly unbalanced, as *thy* with its 3,523 instances compares to only 133 instances of *thine* (92.85% vs. 7.15%). These proportions are fairly similar to those of the Shakespeare Corpus. In the Shakespeare Corpus there are 3,893 cases of *thy* (93.99%) and 249 cases of *thine* before vowel and ⟨h⟩ (6.01%). When compared to the statements of contemporary EModE grammarians and modern language historians, the data from Table 8 confirm the "rule" that *thine* is used exclusively before vowels (96.99%) and to a small degree before ⟨h⟩ (3.01%). However, the distribution of *thy* with 81.78% of its occurrences before consonants, 9.74% before vowels, and 8.48% before ⟨h⟩ runs counter to the descriptions of many grammarians and shows the futility of attempts to prescribe usage in a living language. For the Shakespeare Corpus the corresponding figures for *thy* are almost similar: 84.38% before consonants, 6.61% before vowels, and 8.81% before ⟨h⟩.

Despite its infrequency, *thine* covers more syntactic functions than *thy*, which in all of its 3,523 occurrences functions exclusively as a determiner.

Table 9 illustrates that *thine* appears as determiner 133 times (49%) and 138 times in other positions, which makes 271 instances altogether (51%). In the Shakespeare Corpus the instances of *thine* as determiner amount to 249 tokens (59%) and 173 tokens (41%) in other positions.

The figures in Table 9 point to a clear regression of *thine* over time, because they illustrate neatly that *thine* is about to disappear as a determiner around the turn to the 18th century. The rise in period IV (1730–1780) as a determiner is due to John Home's play *Douglas*, which accounts for all of the six instances, and also for twelve of the total 22 occurrences of *thine*.

As regards *thy*, the data in Table 9 also demonstrate a clear decline over time. This development becomes clearly visible in Diagram 1. The first period (1580–1630) alone accounts for almost half of the instances. In the next period (1630–1680) the numbers are halved. Period III (1680–1730) shows a stagnation, with again a drastic reduction by more than half in the final period (1730–1780). When the figures for *thine* in determiner function and *thy* are compared to each

Table 9. Syntactic function of *thy/thine* in Mitchell's Corpus of British Drama (1580–1780)

	thine	*thine*	*thy*	*yours*	*your*
	total	det.	total	total	total
Period I (1580–1630) 16 plays	174 (64.21%)	113 (84.96%)	1,671 (47.43%)	100 (21.74%)	2,953 (22.44%)
Period II (1630–1680) 15 plays	47 (17.34%)	13 (9.77%)	811 (23.02%)	126 (27.39%)	3,969 (30.16%)
Period III (1680–1730) 15 plays	28 (10.33%)	1 (0.75%)	727 (20.64%)	124 (26.96%)	3,525 (26.79%)
Period IV (1730–1780) 16 plays	22 (8.12%)	6 (4.52%)	314 (8.91%)	110 (23.91%)	2,711 (20.60%)
Total	271 (100%)	133 (100%)	3,523 (100%)	460 (100%)	13,158 (100%)

(Table mine, based on the data given in Mitchell 1971:83f. and 124–152)

other over time, it becomes apparent that *thy* first replaces *thine* in the determiner position before it is finally superseded by *your* in that position. Syntactically, *yours*

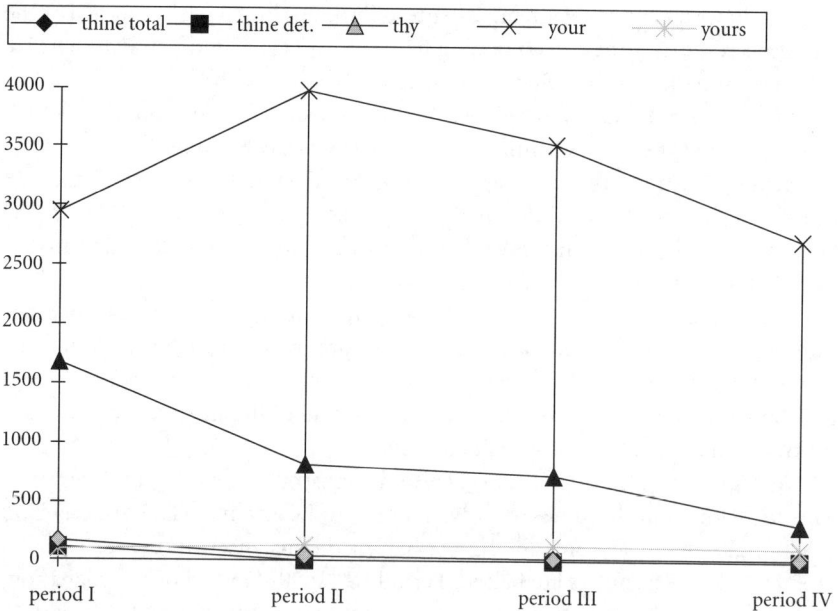

Diagram 1. Distribution of *thy/thine* (and *your/yours*) in Mitchell's drama corpus (1580–1780).

and *thine* do not cover the same ground; thus they can only be compared to each other when the determiner function, which they do not have in common, is omitted: "while *yours* appears 460 times [...], *thine* occurs 138 times (excluding 133 instances as determiner), or at a ratio of about three instances of *yours* to one of *thine*" (Mitchell 1971: 89).

The line for *thy* in Diagram 1 manifests the typical S-curve of linguistic change with an incipient stage, an exponential decrease, a period of stabilisation, and finally a further drastic decline. On the other hand, the figures for *your* do not exhibit a symmetrical mirror image of this development, because the figures first present a rise and then a drop. The numbers for *yours* remain largely constant throughout.

9.4.2 *Thy/thine* in Schendl's corpus of EModE (1500–1649)

In order to test his hypothesis that both "the synchronic and diachronic variation in the forms of the possessives might correlate with levels of formality and that the *n*-less variants entered the emerging written standard from the spoken language", Schendl (1997: 181) first resorted to the Helsinki Corpus. The analysis of the data in the Helsinki Corpus corroborates his claim, if the individual text types are arranged into the two basic types of *formal* vs. *informal*. Schendl concedes that this categorisation is rather a cline than a clear-cut dichotomy, but there are reasons to treat the (more) formal text types (Bible, handbooks, science, philosophy, history, education, sermons, biography and official letters) together, and, at the other end of the scale, the (more) informal ones (autobiography, travelogue, fiction, drama (comedies) diaries and private letters). Table 11 shows the result of this grouping of texts.

Table 11. *Mine, thine* before vowels according to levels of formality

Text Type	*mine/thine* before vowel					
	Period 1: 1500–1570		Period 2: 1570–1640		Period 3: 1640–1710	
	Abs.	%	Abs.	%	Abs.	%
Formal	30/37	81	29/37	78	1/25	4
Informal	39/48	81	15/83	18	1/59	2
Drama (Comedies)	12/12	100	8/19	42	0/21	0
Shakespeare's Plays*			230/499	46		
Non-dramatic Works*			40/70	57		

(Table from Schendl 1997: 182, 183, with my additions for the Shakespeare Corpus)

* In contrast to Schendl's figures, which include *mine* and *thine*, the figures for the Shakespeare Corpus refer only to *thine*.

In Schendl's opinion, the numbers of Table 11 indicate strongly that *my* and *thy* spread from the less formal text types to the more formal ones "from the third quarter of the 16th century at the latest" (1997: 183).

To confirm these results on a broader data base, Schendl compiled an ancillary corpus. His guidelines in corpus creation were the following parameters: shorter periods that span only 50 years, complete texts rather than excerpts, emphasis on informal text types, and different text types by one and the same author.[9] In short, his findings from the subcorpus can be summarised as follows: in period 1 (1500–1549) the occurrence of *my* and *thy* in the phonological environment of vowels is not restricted to specific lexemes. This shows that "the *n*-variants were the stylistically unmarked forms before vowels" (1997: 185).

In period 2 (1550–1599) the distribution of the *n*-variants is less homogeneous, but basically the more formal text types make more use of the *n*-variants before vowels, as opposed to the more informal texts that favour *my* and *thy* in this phonological environment. From this development Schendl assumes "that the *n*-less variants before vowels acquired a stylistic marking as informal in the second half of the 16th century" (1997: 187). In addition to this, the distribution of *mine/thine* becomes limited to certain lexemes.

This process is continued in period 3 (1600–1649), which exhibits a further decline of the *n*-variants *mine* and *thine* before vowels.

From this quantitative and qualitative analysis, Schendl concludes that from the first half of the 16th century to the first half of the 17th century the stylistic value of the forms *my/thy* vs. *mine/thine* resulted in a reversal of markedness. At the first stage the distribution is basically phonologically determined, then *my/thy* are marked as informal, and finally these forms are unmarked, which leads to the marking of *mine/thine* as poetic.

9.5   Conclusion

On the one hand, the preceding study of the variation of *thy/thine* in the Shakespeare Corpus has confirmed many of the well-known facts to be found in standard reference works, but on the other hand, the systematic investigation of real frequencies of usage has brought the factors governing the variation into a clearer perspective. The relevant factors can be summarised as follows:

1.   In a purely quantitative account of sheer numbers the ratio between the two possessives *thine* and *thy* is 1:9. Contrary to this large disparity in numbers, their distribution in verse and prose is strikingly similar. While *thy* always functions attributively as a determiner, the syntactic functions of *thine* are more varied: 59% of all cases are in determiner function before vowels and ⟨h⟩. This usage of Shakespeare is well in accord with that of his contemporaries,

because Mitchell's diachronic corpus study on drama reveals that in the 200-years-span of EModE this function amounts to 49%. Out of the 59% in the Shakespeare Corpus, the use of *thine* before ⟨h⟩ makes up only a very small fraction, with 4.50%. *Thy* occurs in this position twice as often (8.71%). In this respect the statements of language historians and grammarians need to be made more precise.

2. In terms of corpus-internal variation, no tendency of a rise of one form at the expense of the other can be made out. Yet, there are usage differences between genres, which are, however, below the 0.10 level of statistical significance, viz. *thine* is preferred in the more elevated and formal genre of Tragedy. If the plays are contrasted with the poems, then a significant difference can be established, because *thine* shows a preponderance in the more formal text type of Shakespeare's non-dramatic works. This synchronic variation largely validates Schendl's hypothesis that for the period from 1570 to 1640 *thy* (and *my*) prevail in less formal genres.

3. The lexemes that co-occur with *thy* and *thine* clearly point out that the strongest lexical association exists between *thine* and *own*. The 230 tokens of *thine* + vowel consist of only 45 different types; as opposed to the 269 *thy* tokens with 162 types. Furthermore, among the lexical associates of *thine* are a few high frequency words; with *own* and *eye* being the most numerous. Again, this stands in marked contrast to the lexical associates of *thy*. In the case of *thine* + ⟨h⟩ the collocates are even more restricted to a small number of Romance loanwords with supposedly no or only little articulation of the word-initial /h/. *Thy*, on the other hand, is used mostly together with Germanic words, of which *hand* (in the plays) and *heart* (in the non-dramatic works) are the most frequent items; so that before ⟨h⟩ the two possessives are in contrastive, or almost complementary distribution.

4. Schendl's observation that the *n*-variants (*mine/thine*) become lexically restricted in the period ranging from 1550 to 1599 is well in keeping with my findings in the Shakespeare Corpus. Thus, the reasons that eventually led to a rearrangement of the paradigm in the case of *thy/thine* move from more purely intra-linguistically conditioned ones, i.e. phonological environment, to more extra-linguistic factors such as level of formality, text type, etc. This development is accompanied by overall decreasing frequencies of usage of the marked form *thine* with simultaneous restriction to quasi-fixed lexicalised or "frozen" combinations such as *mine/thine host, thine own, thine eyes/eyne* and a relegation to more formal, poetic or archaic registers.

5. Synchronically, Barber's claim that by 1600 *thy* and *thine* were in free variation before vowels is not tenable, because the analysis of "minimal pairs" of discourse samples has revealed that a meaningful choice was made on grounds of intra-textual constraints, in particular, for stylistic reasons. Euphony, emphasis,

antithesis, parallelism and other rhetorical figures are not simply hocus-pocus categories that literary scholars resort to for want of better evidence, but are categories that have to be incorporated into a qualitative empirical investigation of language use in drama. Although not statistically significant, there are also differences between text types, which according to different levels of formality constrain the choice of the variants.

CHAPTER 10

"Stand, sir, and throw us that you have about ye"

The syntactic, pragmatic and social implications of the pronoun *ye*

10.1 Introduction[1]

Whereas there is no dearth of studies analysing the socio-affective dimensions of the pronominal choice between *thou* and *you*, little attention has so far been paid to the use and function of the two variants *ye* and *you* in the Shakespeare Corpus. The dissertation by Bock (1938) investigates, among others, three Shakespeare plays, namely ERR, WIV and ADO, in which, unfortunately, only a single token of *ye* occurs. For the other plays he concludes that unlike in the case of *thou/you* no social or psychological factors play any part in the variation of *ye* and *you* and that, moreover, their distribution has grammatical reasons (cf. 1938:51). With the investigation of ten Shakespeare plays, Mitchell (1971) makes a step forward, but as her main objective is the diachronic development of all the second person pronouns in the two-hundred-year period ranging from 1580 to 1780, Shakespeare's plays only form part of a larger computer-assisted corpus study of 62 plays. She gives both a numerical account and a syntactic analysis for each of the pronouns.

The quotation from TGV used in the title to this chapter shows that Shakespeare does not pay attention any more to the case distinction between nominative *ye* and oblique *you* that was still functional in ME, as the following examples from Chaucer show:[2]

(1)   But ye loveres, that bathen in gladnesse, / If any drope of pyte in yow be, /
        Remembreth yow on passed hevynesse / That ye han felt, [...].
        (*Troilus and Criseyde* 1, 22–25)

In unstressed position, however, Chaucer also uses *ye* in the oblique case:

(1′)   Fro wo to wele, and after out of joie,
        My purpos is, er that I parte fro ye. (*Troilus and Criseyde* 1, 4–5)

On the basis of reference works on the history of English, EModE grammars and Shakespeare grammars, statements about the use of the two variant forms *ye* and *you* will be gathered in order to match and test them in the following against the findings of a corpus analysis of all of Shakespeare's plays. The occurrences of the pronoun *ye* will be accounted for in a number of different ways, beginning with the most obvious questions of:

- syntax, i.e. case and number,
- sociolinguistic variables,
- formal sentence types and discourse functions,
- *ye* as a tool for authorship studies.

Furthermore, by making use of other corpora, the findings on Shakespeare's usage will be put into a broader perspective; first synchronically, by comparing it to that of other contemporary playwrights, and secondly, diachronically, so as to make some more generalisable observations on the factors that have contributed to linguistic change in the case of the two variants *ye* and *you*. This functional approach to one aspect of pronominal variation in the Shakespeare Corpus will serve to highlight the multifariousness of language internal- and external factors that can have an influence on variation ranging from phonology, syntax, pragmatics, sociolinguistics to issues of textlinguistics or stylistics.

10.2 The treatment of *ye* and *you* in reference works

Barber (1997) describes the development of the two forms in EModE in three isolectal stages (cf. Chapter 1, Table 2) as follows (cf. also Brunner 1951:II, 97, Mustanoja 1960:124–128; Faiß 1989:155; Baugh and Cable 1993:237, Lutz 1998):

> In the plural, the nominative is *ye* and the accusative *you*. In the course of the Early Modern period, however, *you* became the normal form for both nominative and accusative, and *ye* became just a minor variant. […] The first examples of nominative *you* go back to the fourteenth century, but in the standard literary language its encroachment was not rapid until the 1540s. In the early sixteenth century, the *ye/you* distinction was preserved by many writers. […] In the course of the sixteenth century, however, *you* was increasingly used as a nominative. […] By Shakespeare's time, *you* was the normal form for both nominative and accusative, and *ye* was a less common variant. […] In the seventeenth century, *ye* is just as likely to be used for the accusative as for the nominative, but is much rarer than *you* in both functions, and in the course of the century becomes increasingly archaic and literary. (Barber 1997:149)

The OED provides the following citations illustrating early replacements of *ye* by *you* in the nominative, saying that "in early use sometimes app.[arently] for emphasis, as opposed to *ye* unemphatic; but often beside *ye* as a mere alternative":

(2)   13.. *Cursor M.* 23160 (Gött.) Vnto mi blis haf ȝue na right.

(3) c. 1400 *Destr. Troy* 7600 And, as yo [sc. Æneas and Hector] counsell in the cas, I comaund be done.

(4) 1526 *Pilgr. Perf.* (W. de W. 1531) 8 b, What ye rede, se you practise it in lyfe and dede.

Brunner (1951:II, 97) also states that from the 14th century onwards, the oblique form *you* begins to be used as a nominative. However, until the middle of the 16th century *ye* still prevails in the nominative. In the second half of the 16th century the use of *you* as a nominative gains momentum, but the archaising language of the *Authorized Version* of the Bible (1611) maintains *ye* in the nominative:

(5) No doubt but *ye* are the people, and wisdom shall die with *you*. (Job 12, 2)

(6) The Lord deal kindly with *you*, as *ye* have dealt with the dead, and with me. The Lord grant *you* that *ye* may find rest [...]. (Ruth 1, 8f.)

Kenyon (1914) has shown that in the *Authorized Version you* only occurs in 7% of all cases as a nominative. *Ye* is also maintained in Tyndale's translation of the New Testament. Simultaneously, many authors show vacillation in their use of the two variants. Beside the *King James Bible*, as the *Authorized Version* is also known, 16th century authors like Lord Berners and Sir Thomas More clearly differentiated both forms, others like Roger Ascham, Bishop Latimer, Cavendish, Sir Thomas Elyot or Lyly (in *Euphues*) used both forms indiscriminately in the nominative, whereas Queen Elizabeth I used only *you* for both functions (cf. Wyld 1936:330, Pyles 1971:202, Baugh and Cable 1993:237, Blake 1996:260, Barber 1997:149).

The archaising pronoun use in the *King James Bible* (also regarding the use of *thou* and *you*) can be explained by the fact that despite its year of publication (1611) the use of language still largely conforms to that of Tyndale's translation of the New Testament (1525), and thus represents the state of the language of almost a hundred years ago. Finkenstaedt (1963:215) adds that the model of the Hebrew text also plays a role.[3]

> By 1611 the usage of Tyndale would be in these respects not archaic, but decidedly old-fashioned in flavour; for the most part Tyndale had chosen forms as being normal. [...] The great prestige of the AV [Authorized Version] led to a growing gap between the familiar expressions of religion and everyday usage as time went on. (Strang 1970:140)

Beginning in the third quarter of the 16th century and coming to a close in the 18th, the paradigm is reordered with *you* as the usual form regardless of case and *ye* being relegated to elevated literary usage. Language historians largely agree that from the turn of the 16th to the 17th century onwards, or even earlier, *ye* becomes a rare minority form, which also implies that *you* lost its case marking (cf. Graband 1965:236–246, Faiß 1989:154f., Görlach 1994:68f., Blake 1996:219). According to Blake "*you* had gradually taken over from *ye* in the subject form as well and by the middle of the eighteenth century *ye* was restricted to specialised contexts, such as poetic apostrophes" (1996: 260).

While the above statements from reference works prove unanimously that the supplanting of *ye* by *you* has been amply described, it has so far, in the opinion of Lutz (1998), not been fully accounted for. Unlike the replacement of *thou* by *you*, which is socially motivated and has accordingly been explained in sociolinguistic terms, in the case of *ye* and *you* two explanations are given most often, viz. a phonological and a syntactic one, or rather a combination of the two, i.e. a confusion of weak forms in unstressed contexts and a cross-over analogy to the second person singular pronouns *thou* and *thee* (cf. Sweet 1900: 338 ff., Poutsma 1916: 708–720, Brunner 1951: II, 97, Faiß 1989: 155, Baugh and Cable 1993: 237). For example, Barber says that "it is not entirely clear why it was the accusative form which became thus standardised, but it may have been by analogy with *thou*: the two forms usually had the same vowel in late Middle English, and [...] the form [jəu], rhyming with *thou*, still existed in the sixteenth century" (1997: 149). According to Scheler (1982: 40) the three pronunciations [juː], [ju], [jəu] coexisted around 1600. Strang also emphasises this point:

> Phoneticians indicate that in the late 16c the strong form was /jəu/ (=PE* [Present-day English] /jau/), weak /ju/. While the modern weak form is a continuation of the old one, the strong form is a new analogical creation, by lengthening of the weak one [...]. The marked circumstances of use of *thou* have, however, enabled the old strong form to survive, though weak /ðu/ has been lost. (Strang 1970: 140 f.)

Görlach (1994: 68 f.) mentions the following factors: both *ye* and *you* had a common unstressed form [jə], which in addition to the redundancy of case marking led to wrong interpretations. This development received further strengthening through the cross-over analogy of vowels in *thou* and *thee*. He also points out that from the Middle English period onwards, the function of case marking was largely supplanted by a fixed SVO-word order. With the consolidation of word order the personal pronouns with their case marking were "over characterised", which made case shiftings without loss of understanding possible. According to Fries (1940: 201) the case differentiation of subject and object by means of word order rather than inflection made progress during the 14th century, and was more or less fixed to SVO by 1500, although case marking in the pronouns was retained much longer. For the maintenance of this distinction in the pronominal system, Howe gives the following reasons:

> that morphologically the personal pronouns are [...] on the whole portmanteau forms rather than suffixed inflection, and are thus phonologically less likely to lose inflection through the reduction of endings common in the Germanic languages in adjectives, nouns and verbs. Furthermore, the high degree of suppletion in the personal pronouns means that given phonological

reduction, forms which have a suppletive distinction will *tend* to remain formally distinct longer than those with less suppletive distinctions, and this seems to be borne out by examples such as English *ye–you* [...].
(Howe 1996: 70)

Heltveit (1952: 378f.) remarks that *ye* and *you* are the only pronouns to have given up marking for nominative or oblique case, as this development did not take place for *I–me, we–us, he–him, she–her, they–them*. This can be attributed to the morpho-phonological form of *ye* and *you*, which differs only in the vowel. In unstressed position even this distinction gets lost (cf. Jespersen: 1894: 256). Spies (1897: 103) mentions that in stressed position *you* is usually preferred to *ye*. With reference to Spies and Jespersen, Howe (1996: 168f.) also underlines the complementary distribution of the vowels in the pairs of *ye/you* and *thou/thee* in the 15th and 16th centuries:

nom.	*obj.*
thou (þou, thu)	thee (the, þe)
ye, yee	you (yow)

According to Jespersen, the pronunciations *ðu* und *jau* coexisted in the 16th century so that *thou* and *you* and also *thee* and *ye* rhymed. A further reason that could have contributed to the confusion of forms is their spelling, as both *thou* and *you* and *thee* and *ye* could be written with ⟨y⟩. Lass offers the following short description and explanation for the replacement of *ye* by *you*, stressing that the process began in the fourteenth century especially in postverbal position, e.g. as subject of a preposed verb, as in:

(7) to morwe schal *yow* wedded be (*Guy of Warrick* 4192, cited by Mustanoja 1960: 125)

The spelling ⟨ye⟩ for *you* in unstressed positions and its pronunciation as /jə/ may have added to the confusion of the two forms. "Thus (at least in written language) there is an early precedent for confusing the shapes of the two forms. And the post-verbal use of *you*, even as subject, simply reflects the fact that oblique pronoun forms typically appear in this position as objects — a generalisation of linear position over syntactic function" (1999: 154).

Howe (1996: 169) succinctly summarises the historical development of *ye* and *you* and their subsequent merger to the following typological scheme:

– Functional merger of *ye* and *you*
– Functional reinterpretation of *you* as +accent form
– Phonological merger (when unaccented) and no subsequent therapeutic change
– Loss of form in *ye*.

However, Lutz (1998: 197) rightly argues that cross-over analogy, which may have had a partial effect on the switch from *ye* to *you*, cannot have been the decisive factor, because the singular nominative and oblique forms *thou* and *thee* do not show signs of confusion throughout the EModE period (cf. also 10.3.4.1). For this reason, she rather assumes that the selection of the ME plural object form *you* as the only remaining form of direct address in Standard English can be attributed to the following interplay of external and internal factors:

a. frequent alternation between polite and intimate address of individuals in French-influenced courtly speech [*you* vs. *thou*];
b. cross-over analogy between subject and object forms of the singular and plural of the second person [*thou/thee* vs. *you/ye*];
c. possible support by the morphologically and phonologically similar French paradigm [*tu/tei/ti/te* vs. *vous* for subject and object function];
d. the frequent use of impersonal constructions with the object form of the personal pronoun in French-influenced courtly discourse [*you*];
e. the personalization of impersonal constructions in connection with the fixing of SVO-order, which made the object form of the old construction the subject form of the new one [*you*];
f. analogical extension of subjective *you* in such constructions to all other verbs;
g. the generalization of the polite form *you* as the form of addressing individuals of all ranks of society (Lutz 1998: 201).

10.2.1 *Ye/you* in EModE grammars

The above historical outline clearly reveals that the change from *ye* to *you* had culminated before 1600 and was then reaching its final stages. With this clear-cut distribution given, it is interesting to check in how far EModE grammarians reacted to this change; i.e. whether they reflected and prescribed the older state of the language or whether they accepted the changed usage, or at least tacitly sanctioned it. As two examples of grammars which appeared during Shakespeare's lifetime, those by Bullokar (1586) and Greaves (1594) can be mentioned. Bullokar, in his *Bref Grammar of English* (1586: 20) gives the following paradigm:

Singularly, *thou*,
Nominative *yee*, or   Accusative   *thee*, or
& Vocative *you*   *you*

Plurally,   *yee*,
Nominative or   Accusative   *you*
& Vocative *you*

This also goes for Greaves (1594: 12) and for later grammarians like Ben Jonson (1640), who list both forms.[4] The uncommented incorporation of both forms in their paradigms seems to suggest that these grammarians reacted to the change in progress.

Nevalainen and Raumolin-Brunberg have come to the conclusion that the switch from *ye* to *you* in subject position (and other morphological changes) came from below the level of consciousness: "little is known about the way in which most morphological changes were recognized at the time of their diffusion in Tudor England, in other words, we have no knowledge of how socially aware people were of a given change in progress" (1996a: 322f.). At least as far as the grammarians are concerned, their paradigms bear out that they realised the change. Admittedly, their awareness does not really say anything about that of the man or woman in the street, but anyhow, scarce as their paradigms may be, they indicate that these grammarians described the language around them, and did not try to prescribe usage as their later fellow grammarians of the 18th century did, when e.g. Greenwood (1711) states: "When we speak to more than one, we use the word *Ye*", or when Lowth (1762: 33f.) criticises Milton, Addison, Pope, Dryden and others for having written ungrammatically in sentences such as:

(7)   His wrath, which one day will destroy *ye* both. (Milton, *Paradise Lost* II, 734; cf. Mitchell 1971: 23)

This has to be interpreted as an attempt to prescribe usage, or to fix language, but not to record variation which by then had been firmly established in the language.[5]

10.2.2 *Ye/you* in Shakespeare grammars

Abbott presents a number of selected examples on the use of *ye*, from which he draws the following generalisations on its syntactic and discourse functions: "in the original form of the language *ye* is nominative, *you* accusative. This distinction, however, though observed in our version of the Bible, was disregarded by Elizabethan authors, and *ye* seems to be generally used in questions, entreaties, and rhetorical appeals" ([1870] 1972: 159f., §236). In addition to this, he further attributes the use of *ye* to metrical reasons in all those cases in which an unstressed syllable was needed, as e.g. in:

(8)   I never lov'd *you* much; but I ha' prais'd *ye*. (ANT 2, 6, 78)

The other citations given, however, emphasise the confusion and irregularity in the use of *you* and *ye*, so that his generalisations cannot be accepted without reservations.

Franz gives the following "usage rules" for *ye*:

> Bei Sh. [akespeare] ist daher der alte Nominativ *ye* schon sehr stark zurückgedrängt und erscheint in verschiedenen Dramen verschieden häufig: verhältnismäßig oft in Hy VI und Hy IV, in Love's Lab. fünfmal, in M. Wives einmal, in Othello dreimal. [...]. *Ye* in der Funktion eines Obliquus (*I assure ye*) ist für

Sh. durch den Reim gesichert und darf als eine Abschwächung von *you* angesehen werden (vgl. me. *þe* (=*þu*) *wylt*), zumal da es meist an unbetonter oder schwachtoniger Satzstelle erscheint. ([1939] 1986:255, §288)

Scheler (1982:40) merely offers numerical evidence for the two plays MAC [*you* (207 tokens), *ye* (3), *thou* (89) and *thee* (61)] and MV [*you* (449 tokens), *ye* (3), *thou* (103) and *thee* (64)]. In his opinion these figures clearly demonstrate that in Shakespeare's plays — unlike the *Authorized Version* — except for a few residual cases *ye* has abandoned its function as nominative singular in favour of *you*.

10.3 The Shakespeare Corpus

For the Shakespeare Corpus the numerical evidence for *ye* and *you* is as follows (for the complete breakdown of individual variant forms such as *you'd*, *you'll* etc. cf. Chapter 3.3. Table 2). If all these variant forms are included, the following distribution for the 38 plays is arrived at: *you*: 14,405 tokens (including *you'd*, *you'ld* and *you'll*) as opposed to 343 tokens of *ye*. 62 tokens of *y'* and one token of *y'ave* were left unaccounted for, because they could not be classified. These figures amply illustrate that the erosion of *ye* had progressed much further than that of *thou* and *thee*; the ratio of *ye* to *you* being 1:42 and that of *thou/thee* (8,628 tokens) to *you* (14,405 tokens) amounting to 1:1.7 in favour of *you*.

As the figures for *ye* are so tiny, they call for a detailed qualitative analysis, which according to McEnery and Wilson offers "a rich and detailed perspective on the data. In qualitative analyses, rare phenomena receive, or at least ought to receive, the same attention as more frequent phenomena, and, because the aim is complete detailed description rather than quantification, delicate variation in the data is foregrounded" (1996:62). However, some of the plays in the Shakespeare Corpus are laden with problems of authenticity resulting from transmission of copy texts, disputed authorship, etc. Whereas these problems do not affect large quantitative studies, as e.g. the relationship between *you* and *thou*, they become virulent in the case of *ye*, as statistical investigations and their qualitative interpretations heavily depend on the reliability of the units that are to be counted and classified.

Stein (1974:7) in his analysis of inflections in the Shakespeare Corpus rightly stresses that due to its literary nature and its transmission the Shakespeare Corpus differs from "natural" corpora in two respects, resulting in a dialectic process between a purely grammatical description and a literary interpretation. He says that in "natural" corpora the primary data are fully authorised and exceptions can thus be explained by means of one or various subsystems of language history. For the Shakespeare Corpus he claims that exceptions need to be accounted for in terms of editorial and literary subsystems (cf. 1974:104). As regards the inflectional endings he comes to the conclusion that *does/doth* are much more robust against textual influences than are *has/hath* (1974:108). However, in a more recent investigation on the topic (1987:413f.) of variation between *-s/-th* in the third person singular, he finds that there is such a decisive caesura in the corpus which is so systematic that the morphological change between 1590 and 1610 cannot be due to influences of textual transmission.

With respect to this, two different versions of the Shakespeare Corpus shall be compared to each other, because for some of the plays they vary in their choice of copy text. Thus, the *Riverside Shakespeare* (²1997), on which Spevack's concordances are based, shall be compared to Wells and Taylor's (1989) *Oxford Electronic Shakespeare* (OES). For the exact breakdown of tokens for each of the plays in the two editions cf. Table 9 appended at the end of this chapter. The differences between the two concordances can be summarised in the following way: first and foremost, they are in no way dramatic, as for 23 of the plays the number of *ye* tokens is identical. With the inclusion of H8 and TNK there is a discrepancy of only one token for thirteen plays. Excepting 2H6, H8 and TNK, in which it is the other way around, the OES usually provides an additional *ye* token in comparison to Spevack. Considerable differences are only to be found in two plays, namely HAM, for which the OES gives twelve *ye* tokens and Spevack only three, and also, though to a lesser extent, for R3, where the OES has five *ye* tokens, and Spevack only two.

10.3.1 Categorisation of the empirical data

First of all, in order to arrive at complete distributions, the numerical corpus data on the frequency and distribution of the *ye* tokens will be systematically classified according to the syntactic criteria of case and number because despite the merits of Abbott's and Franz' Shakespeare grammars, who base their conclusions on an admittedly large but random sample of citations, no final conclusions on overall distributions can be drawn on the basis of their material alone.

Once the data of the Shakespeare Corpus are fully analysed, it will be possible to correlate the empirical findings on Shakespeare's use of *ye* to other corpora. For this reason the drama corpora of Bock (1938) and Mitchell (1971) serve as ancillary corpora for diachronic evidence. By means of the *Helsinki Corpus of Early English Correspondence*, the results on drama will be compared to the text type of letters.

10.3.2 Syntactic analysis

10.3.2.1 *Case*
The data presented in Table 9 have been categorised according to the following criteria: first of all, the *ye* tokens are classified according to their occurrence in subject- or in object position. Within the subject function three further subcategories

of nominative (NOM), nominative of a vocative (VOC), as e.g. "Peace, ye fat-guts, lie down." (1H4 2, 2, 31) and imperative (IMP) were established. The imperatives were separated and not added up to the number of nominatives because for the pronouns *you* and *ye* no case differentiation can be made (cf. 10.3.4.1). Also for the object function a threefold subdivision was put in operation. In addition to the differentiation in dative (DAT) and accusative (ACC) those objects linked by means of a preposition were considered separately in the column marked PREP, e.g.: "Peradventure I will *with ye to the court.*" (2H4 3, 2, 295).

As it is also important for a diachronic assessment to know whether the pronoun is in the singular (SG) or plural (PL) the tokens were then categorised for number. In addition to these syntactic criteria, two extralinguistic variables were observed, namely whether the pronoun occurs in a verse line (VS) or in a prose line (PR). As there are discrepancies for some of the line divisions between the two text bases, these categories appear twice in the table, viz. for the OES and for Spevack.

The counting of tokens for all of the 36 plays[6] that putatively have been composed by Shakespeare alone show the following distribution: all in all, the OES provides a grand total of 244 *ye* forms, out of which 104 cases are in the nominative, 39 in the nominative immediately preceding a vocative, 33 in imperatives, and for the objective cases: 16 in the dative, 12 in prepositional objects and 40 in the accusative, adding up to a grand total of 68 tokens (see Table 9).

When the above categories of NOM and VOC are taken together, then the instances amount to 58.6%. The imperatives make up 13.5%. In contrast to the 72.1% that these categories taken jointly amount to, the occurrences of *ye* in object position are much rarer, as the three categories of objective (DAT, PREP and ACC) account for only 27.9% of all tokens. That is to say that Shakespeare used the pronoun *ye* in about two thirds of all cases in its older function as subjective and only in about one third of its instances in the oblique case.

Once the two plays of H8 and TNK, which must be viewed as collaborations with Fletcher, are incorporated the percentage for the nominatives drops slightly to 54.4%, and the instances of *ye* in object function rise to 36.5%. Among other possibilities, these differences can be used as a linguistic means in authorship studies for the Shakespeare-Fletcher collaborations (cf. 10.3.8).

10.3.2.2   *Number*

The categorisation of tokens according to case has so far left out the question of number. Historically *ye* is the pronoun for the nominative of the second person plural. Owing to this, the next step in the analysis will account for the question if and in how far Shakespeare adhered to the differentiation for number. As it was not possible to give a definitive answer for that question on the basis of a single concordance line (as in Spevack), in cases of doubt the context of the full text version was used to clarify whether one or more persons were addressed by *ye*.

The data for the 36 plays are like this: there are 167 occurrences (68.4%) of *ye* in the singular, and only 77 instances (31.6%) in the plural. When these percentages are compared to those for case, then a remarkable difference becomes apparent. Whereas for case Shakespeare departed in only one third of all cases from the traditional patterning of forms, he adopted a much more innovative stance for the syntactic category of number, in which the patterning is vice versa with more than two thirds in the 'new' category of singular and only less than one third left in the historical plural function.

As in the previous chapter on case, the handling of singular and plural in the two plays H8 and TNK will be looked at separately. In H8 51 occurrences (70.83%) out of the 72 instances of *ye* are to be interpreted as second person plural pronouns, as they refer to two or more persons. As regards TNK, there is a total of 46 *ye* tokens. In all likelihood, 13 tokens (28.26%) are plural. The status of the eight tokens in the epilogue is difficult to assess, because each reader might be addressed individually or, perhaps more likely, the collective readership altogether.[7] With 65% (or respectively 72% if the tokens in the epilogue to TNK are included) of *ye* in the function of a second person plural pronoun, these two plays in this respect reflect an older, or more conservative state of the language than the rest of the corpus proper.

10.3.3 Shakespeare compared to other playwrights

10.3.3.1 *Ye in Bock's Corpus of British Drama (1497–1779)*

In order to evaluate Shakespeare's grammatical usage of *ye* against the background of EModE usage, the results will now be compared to the use of other (contemporary) dramatists. Bock's corpus (1938) provides valuable statistical information on the numerical development of the personal pronouns from 1497 to 1775/79. For the reason that his doctoral dissertation is unpublished, it is not amiss to present the data in full, even though the general tendencies are widely known and have been used previously; cf. for example Finkenstaedt (1963), who also draws upon Bock's data.

The percentages for the first ten plays of Table 1 clearly indicate that until the 1560s *ye* still persists as the dominant form in the nominative singular and plural. Despite variation between individual plays, the overall tendency is plainly visible. Bock presumes that for the first half of the 16th century the "ungrammatical" use of *you* in the nominative can be attributed to stylistic reasons, as e.g. in *Misogonus*. In the later course of the 16th century this feeling for case differentiation was lost. The turning point in the grammatical distribution of *ye* and *you* lies in the middle of the 16th century. By Shakespeare's time, the paradigm had been rearranged completely with *you* being the unchallenged majority form in the nominative for both singular and plural and *ye* becoming a form of marginal frequency in objective function. The slight rise of *ye* forms in the last quarter of the 17th century can be attributed to the fact that the tokens of *ye* in the nominative singular occur mostly

Table 1. The use of *thou/thee* and *you/ye* in the drama corpus of Bock (1938)

| Play | Date | Singular | | | | | | Plural | |
| | | Nom | | Obj | | | | Nom | |
		you	*ye*	*thou*	*you*	*ye*	*thee*	*you*	*ye*
Fulgens and Lucres	1497	3.2	73.4	23.4	75.9	–	24.1	3.1	96.9
Calisto and Melibaea	1530	5.0	34.6	60.4	34.6	–	65.4	7.7	92.3
Thersites	1537	10.9	20.0	69.1	29.9	–	70.1	29.0	71.0
Play of Wit&Science	1541/47	12.2	65.4	22.4	34.3	44.7	21.0	5.9	94.1
Disobedient Child	1547	4.8	23.0	72.2	23.2	6.1	70.7	14.3	85.7
Nice Wanton	1547/53	14.7	65.3	20.0	70.0	2.0	28.0	15.4	84.6
Ralph Roister Doister	1551	9.2	66.9	23.9	76.8	3.9	19.3	9.7	90.3
Gammer Gurton's N.	1552/53	20.1	31.1	48.8	43.8	2.2	54.0	33.3	66.7
Jacob and Esau	1556	9.4	40.6	50.0	46.2	0.5	53.3	–	100
Misogonus	1560	46.8	9.2	44.0	58.8	6.0	35.2	62.3	37.7
Comedy of Errors	1591	56.8	–	43.2	62.6	–	37.4	100	–
Merry Wives	1598	82.2	–	17.8	77.6	–	22.4	100	–
Much Ado	1598	77.8	–	22.2	67.9	–	32.1	100	–
Club Law	1599	71.1	1.3	27.6	64.9	–	35.1	93.5	6.5
Volpone	1610	78.5	–	21.5	78.0	–	22.0	100	–
Bartholomew Fair	1614	78.1	–	21.9	70.8	1.3	27.9	99.0	1.0
The Gamester	1633	77.7	–	22.3	52.5	–	47.5	100	–
The Witty Fair One	1633	80.8	1.7	17.5	71.2	–	28.8	86.7	13.3
Love in a Tub	1664	87.4	–	12.6	71.6	–	28.4	92.0	8.0
The Man of Mode	1676	95.3	–	4.7	88.2	–	11.8	100	–
The Country Wife	1675	86.8	2.6	10.6	87.0	–	13.0	97.6	2.4
The Plain Dealer	1677	81.3	3.1	15.6	77.7	–	22.3	97.1	2.9
The Old Bachelor	1683	81.8	2.1	16.1	67.3	–	32.7	100	–
Way of the World	1700	84.8	2.1	13.1	90.2	–	9.8	93.7	6.3
Relapse	1697	86.1	0.7	13.2	81.0	–	19.0	96.3	3.7
Love's Last Shift	1696	87.1	3.6	9.3	81.0	1.2	17.8	100	–
Careless Husband	1704	96.8	–	3.2	89.8	–	10.2	100	–
The Lying Lover	1703	90.9	0.7	8.4	87.2	–	12.8	91.7	8.3
The Tender Husband	1705	93.5	1.6	4.9	89.7	–	10.3	100	–
Beggar's Opera	1726	86.2	2.6	11.2	66.4	–	33.6	95.2	4.8
Goodnatur'd Man	1768	98.8	–	1.2	98.7	–	1.3	100	–
She Stoops to ...	1773	98.6	0.5	0.9	99.3	–	0.7	100	–
The West Indian	1771	97.2	0.7	2.1	98.2	–	1.8	88.2	11.8
School for Wives	1773	100	–	–	98.9	–	1.1	100	–
The Rivals	1775	96.1	2.3	1.6	99.2	–	0.8	80.0	20.0
School of Scandal	1775/79	98.1	1.5	0.4	98.5	–	1.5	100	–

(Table from Bock 1938:65, Appendix 2)

in unstressed position after *do* and in fossilised combinations such as *hark ye* and *look ye*. This concentration of *ye* on a narrow set of verbs continues into the 18th century and its use is restricted to the combinations of *d'ye, look ye*, and, though more seldom, *hark ye* and *thank ye* (cf. Bock 1938:51–72).

10.3.3.2 *Ye in Mitchell's Corpus of British Drama (1580–1780)*
In her computer-assisted study of form changes in the address pronouns as reflected in British Drama from 1580 to 1780 (cf. Chapters 3.6 and 9.4.1)[8] Mitchell has subdivided this two-hundred-year period into four subperiods of fifty years each. The first period (1580–1630), which is of particular interest because it deals with Shakespeare and his immediate contemporaries, comprises 16 plays. Whereas for all the other periods, playwrights are usually represented by only one or two plays, Shakespeare is included with ten of his plays, and Marlowe, Jonson and Ford with only two plays each. Numerical evidence on the syntactic use of *ye* for Shakespeare and his contemporaries is given in Table 2.

Table 2. Shakespeare's syntactic use of *ye/you* compared to that of his contemporaries

		S*	P	N	DO	IO	OP	Total
Marlowe	ye	10			1	1		12
	you	225	1	10	55	9	42	342
Shakespeare	ye	50		19	13		4	86
	you	2,183	4	98	706	93	370	3,454
Jonson	ye				1			1
	you	805	3	33	299	74	115	1,329
Ford	ye	33		1	39	5	23	101
	you	266	1	2	35	8	22	334

(Table accumulated from the data in Mitchell 1971: 124–127)

* Abbreviations: S: Subject; P: Predicate; N: Nominative of address; DO: Direct Object; IO: Indirect Object; OP: Object of a preposition.

The investigation of Shakespeare and his contemporaries reveals that there are considerable differences in usage, as Jonson uses *you* almost exclusively. At the other end of the spectrum, Ford employs the two pronouns at a ratio of 1:3 in favour of *you*, with Marlowe and Shakespeare occupying an intermediate position, displaying a ratio of *ye* to *you* at 1:29 (Marlowe) and 1:40 (Shakespeare). My investigation of the complete corpus confirms this ratio for Shakespeare (1:42).

When the absolute figures are relativized to percentages, the differences in usage between Shakespeare and Marlowe are marginal, for both use *ye* in about three quarters of all cases in subject position. For Ford, the preference is the other way around. In his plays *ye* occurs in 34% in subject function and in 66% in object function.

The exceptional non-use of *ye* by Jonson in his two plays *Every Man in His Humour* (1598) and *Volpone* (c. 1605/06) corroborates the earlier findings of Bock, who has also investigated *Volpone*, and additionally *Bartholomew Fair* (c. 1614), and who also reports on an isolated token of *ye* in the nominative plural and five tokens in objective singular function. Bock (1938:67) ascribes the complete neglect of *ye* to the fact that Jonson (and also Shakespeare) represent colloquial speech in their dramatic dialogue and that by 1600 *ye* had lost its earlier stylistic function, which was still marginally operational in the 16th century. It is obvious that the language of drama may not be taken as a mirror image of authentic colloquial language, yet on the other hand it is also by no means clear in how far the language of literature departs from ordinary language. In any case, Jonson (in his criticism of Spenser's archaising language use) puts it this way: "the true Artificer will not run away from nature, as he were afraid of her; or depart from life, and the likenesse of Truth; but speak to the capacity of his hearers. And though his language differ from the vulgar somewhat; it shall not fly from all humanity, [...]" (Ben Jonson 1640; quoted in Görlach 1994:28).

For the two-hundred-year period as a whole, Mitchell gives the following summary of syntactic functions: "in nominative positions, *ye* appears 565 times to 154 in accusative positions or 79% to 21%, respectively" (1971:86f.). She goes on to say that

> nominative plural *ye* exhibits the most erratic behavior. In 21% or 154 of the total 719 occurrences of *ye*, it appears in accusative positions. However, the most significant point concerning *ye* in this study is that in the plays of the last half of the eighteenth century (1753–1777), *ye* shifts from its original plural function to the singular function, for it appears in its original nominative plural function in only 10% of the total occurrences. (Mitchell 1971:102f.)

When these statements are compared to the data of Bock it is surprising that the shift from *ye* in its original nominative plural function to the singular dated for the second half of the 18th century by Mitchell, takes place much earlier and much more clearly in the material analysed by Bock, as in his data the plural function drastically decreases from the 1560s onwards and does not play any significant role after 1600, except in Sheridan's *Rivals* (1775).

Concerning usage differences between dramatists, Mitchell (1971:86f.) states that more than any other dramatist, John Ford is responsible for most of the shifts to accusative positions. Out of the 154 instances no less than 67 go back to the two plays by Ford. Furthermore, Mitchell has found that throughout this long period, there is quite substantial vacillation in the use of *ye* among different playwrights. She finds that after Ford (c. 1586–c. 1640), Farquhar (1678–1707) is the other playwright to use *ye* more often as an accusative pronoun. On the other hand, there are a number of dramatists belonging to different subperiods who never use *ye* in accusative function, as e.g.: Boyle (1621–1679), Etheridge (1635/6–1691), Dryden (1631–1700), Congreve (1670–1729), Cibber (1671–1757), Southerne (1660–1746), Rowe (1674–1718), Fielding (1704–1754), Lillo (1693–1739), Moore (1711/12–1757), Home (1722–1808) and Cumberland (1732–1811).

10.3.3.3 Ye/you in the Helsinki Corpus of Early English Correspondence

A number of papers report about ongoing sociohistorical research with different pilot versions of the *Helsinki Corpus of Early English Correspondence* (CEEC) (cf. Nevalainen 1996b,c, Nevalainen and Raumolin-Brunberg 1996a,b, Raumolin-Brunberg 1996a,b, Raumolin-Brunberg and Nevalainen 1997a,b). In these studies the authors concentrate on extralinguistic variables that could have influenced the morpho-syntactic change from *ye* to *you*.[9] The variables tested are social stratification, gender and apparent time.

10.3.3.3.1 *Ye/you in terms of the sociolinguistic variables in the CEEC.* The 1994/95 pilot versions of the CEEC contain about "1.5 million running words, representing over 400 writers from the 15th to the 17th centuries" (Nevalainen and Raumolin-Brunberg 1996a: 309). For the investigation two subperiods were chosen: Period I (1520–1550) und II (1590–1610). The first period comprises the correspondence of 64 writers (278,426 words) and the second period contains 44 writers (201,399 words).[10] The following conclusions can be drawn from the investigations: dialectal factors do not play a role in the change from *ye* to *you* in subject position. However, social stratification has proved an important factor, as it is the upper gentry that leads the change from *ye* to *you* in subject position with 48% of all incidences, followed by the lower gentry with 36%. While this difference is not statistically significant, the upper gentry differs markedly from the two lowest social ranks of the merchants and the non-gentry. Together with the social climbers they use *you* from 25% to 29%. The nobility deviates most sharply from all other social ranks with an incidence of only 8% of *you*. Although the figures for the upper clergy are small, they suggest the same tendency (16%). An important factor that both ranks share is "their frequent use of secretaries to draft and copy their letters" (Nevalainen 1996b: 65). The work of professional clerks could, at least partly, reflect their linguistic conservatism. A counter argument to this is the high percentage (49%) of exclusive *you* usage among the royalty in an earlier pilot study (cf. Nevalainen and Raumolin-Brunberg 1996a: 313), which showed no difference to that of the upper gentry (48%).

When the variables are graded in terms of salience or density (i.e. their frequency per 1,000 words), then some differences to the above results from the social distribution become apparent as "it is now the lower gentry and the merchants who favour this form [you]" (Nevalainen 1996b: 70). This result could be attributed to "the requirements of etiquette, which would show their use of the appropriate titles such as *your Grace* instead of pronominal forms when addressing their peers and social superiors" (Nevalainen 1996b: 70).

In another study (Raumolin-Brunberg and Nevalainen 1997a), seven letter-writers from the first half of the 16th century are selected and scrutinised for the extralinguistic variables of social status, date, genre of writing and the sex of the writer. All of the writers are southerners. As was to be expected, there are considerable differences between the writers, as the replacing of *ye* was still in full swing in this period. Concerning the use of *you* (and also *are*) it is the upper gentry that lead the way in using these two incoming forms. "As regards the use of *you* versus *ye*, it appears that *you* is more frequent in private letters" (Raumolin-Brunberg and Nevalainen 1997a: 711). Out of the factors assessed, the relationship between the writer and the recipient seems to be the strongest factor to condition the choice of variants. This result is confirmed by studies in historical pragmatics, cf. for example Jacobs and Jucker (1995: 8), finding that private letters contain more intimate and colloquial elements than other types of text.

In a newer study (Nevalainen 1996c), one female letter writer, Sabine Johnson, the wife of a 16th century wool-merchant has been added, to investigate gender differences in usage against the background of the two Labovian principles: "1) that men use a higher frequency of non-standard forms than women in stable situations, and 2) that women are generally innovators in linguistic change" (ibid.: 77). As regards the variant forms *ye* and *you*, the investigation has proved that it was indeed Sabine Johnson, who led the spoken-language change from below while at the same time being more conservative in her use of *be* than most of her male contemporaries. However, it is still too early to draw far-reaching sociolinguistic conclusions from this scanty evidence.

Raumolin-Brunberg (1996a) and Raumolin-Brunberg and Nevalainen (1997b) have also carried out two apparent-time investigations with the material of the CEEC. They have analysed the letters (1472–1488) of the Cely family, a late medieval London wool merchant family, in order to "focus on the varying rates of diffusion of Late Middle English pronominal changes in the language of two generations of the Celys" (Raumolin-Brunberg and Nevalainen 1997b: 489). The letters exchanged between the father, probably born about 1420, and his three sons, born in the 1450s, reflect age differences within the Cely family, as far as the shift from *you* as the object form to the subject form and the replacement of the former subject form *ye* are concerned, yielding a Labovian type of apparent time pattern. "Richard Cely the elder represents the old system, whereas all the three sons mix the forms, but not necessarily in the same way" (Raumolin-Brunberg and Nevalainen 1997b: 499). After the discussion of a number of examples showing vacillation of forms among the three sons, the authors sum up their data as follows: "in most instances the earlier system prevails, but as far as the younger Celys are concerned, the data seem to suggest an early stage of an on-going change, in which the brothers participate in different ways" (ibid.: 500). Earlier on, it was reported that due to their similar pronunciations *thou/thee* and *ye/you* could have been mixed up or be accounted for as wrong interpretations of their spellings, but this does not apply to the letters of the Cely family, since the forms "appear in letters to their father or to each other, where no 'thouing' is found at all" (ibid.).

A supplementary corpus of non-family members, but also persons involved in the wool trade, shows that other young people are more advanced in their use of *you* as subject than the Cely brothers, but there is a large range of variation. The study of Raumolin-Brunberg (1996b) has added a corpus with the Johnson's, an Early modern wool merchant family (1542–1553) and a supplementary corpus. This diachronic dimension has given rise to the idea of age-grading, as there is only a very small increase in the use of *you* with the younger generation of the first period and the older generation of the second: "on the whole, this change could be characterized as a change from below, its origin being based on a phonological confusion in spoken language. It seems to progress generationally" (ibid.: 99).

Apart from their interesting social patterning of usage in the first subperiod (1520–1550) of the CEEC, the most striking result is that there are no instances whatsoever of *ye* in subject position in the second subperiod (1590–1620), "indicating that all the differences between the ranks observed some half a century earlier have been levelled out" (Nevalainen 1996b: 66).

When these results are compared to the Shakespeare Corpus and to the two drama corpora of Bock and Mitchell two assumptions are possible. On the one hand, Bock's data also suggest that a decisive change in the relationship between *ye* and *you* took place in the latter half of the 16th century, having been completed (except for a few fossilised cases) in Shakespeare's time. On the other hand, Mitchell's data do not indicate any decisive drop or shift in the use of *ye* for the entire period (1580–1780) before the end of the 18th century. Thus, one conclusion to be drawn is that the diffusion of the incoming form *you* has been different for the text types of drama and letters and that drama is a more conservative text type in which archaic forms persist in formulaic expressions for more than 250 years longer than in letter writing, or if one is sceptical about corpus linguistics and numerical evidence, one could say that even these corpora are not large or consistent enough to allow for generalisations.

10.3.4 The occurrence of *ye* in different sentence types in the Shakespeare Corpus

Apart from an investigation of the distribution of *ye* tokens in terms of case and number it is necessary to analyse their occurrence in certain sentence types (and their discourse functions), because the classification of occurrences has proved that *ye* is predominantly employed in imperatives and exclamatives. For this reason, each of these syntactic categories will be scrutinised.

10.3.4.1 *Ye in imperatives*
Millward (1966) has devoted a special study to the treatment of pronominal case in Shakespearean imperatives. In contrast to ModE, imperatives in Shakespeare's time

were often followed by a second person pronoun. According to Millward, this usage cannot be attributed to sociolinguistic variables such as age, sex, socio-economic status etc. However, unlike imperatives followed by *thou* or *thee*, which are marked for case, those followed by *ye* or *you* are not distinguished for case.

As an explanation of why some verbs in the imperative demand *thee* instead of *thou*, Abbott ([1870] 1972:141) assumes a reflexive use for some verbs of motion, such as *haste*, but forms like *look thee* and *hark thee* are believed to have been chosen for phonotactic reasons: "for reasons of euphony also the ponderous *thou* is often ungrammatically replaced by *thee*, or inconsistently by *you*. This is particularly the case in questions and requests, where, the pronoun being especially unemphatic, *thou* is especially objectionable" (Abbott [1870] 1972:139). Thus, *thou* and *you* are being interpreted as emphatic, and *ye* as unemphatic.

Franz makes a similar statement on the non-emphatic use of the pronouns: "Der nicht emphatische Gebrauch des Pronomens, wie er früher üblich war, hat in der modernen Sprache Spuren hinterlassen; z.B. in dem familiären *lookee!*, *harkee!*; *praise ye the Lord* (Liturgie) [...]" ([1939] 1986:535). He also states that the imperatives of reflexive verbs like *retire thee* have favoured the use of *thee* in other verbs. His further explanation (cf. 1986:249) that plural forms like *go we* (= *let us go*) and *look ye* with their phonetic similarity to *thee* have also contributed to this development seems a bit far fetched in respect to the small number of tokens in the corpus, with only 244 *ye* forms, out of which only 35 occur in imperatives. Put the other way around, by assuming an influence of *thee* on *ye* it seems a little bit more plausible to say so. Yet Mitchell (1971:78) reports for the entire period from 1580 to 1780 of only 49 instances out of a total of 3,469 occurrences in which *thee* appears in subject function. The same evidence can also be gathered from Bock's tables. In his corpus (1497–1779) there are 1,795 occurrences of *thee* in accusative position, and only 22 in the nominative. Thus, unlike the development of *ye*, for which case distinctions became blurred in the course of the 16th century, the distinction between *thou* and *thee* was maintained until the very end of the EModE period.

Poutsma gives a pragmatic explanation for imperatives of the type *look thee*, suggesting that the pronoun "softens the imperiousness of the request" (1926:201). With reference to *thee*, Quirk characterises the function of imperatives with a pronoun in the objective, which according to his opinion should rather be interpreted as an unstressed form of the subject pronoun serving "to seek the personal involvement of the addressee" (1974:53). These imperatives are especially frequent with "verbs used to summon attention, such as *look* and *hark*".

Yamakawa (1966) provides a convincing explanation of the process. He has shown that in Elizabethan colloquial English imperatives followed by pronouns were very fashionable and that this type largely supplanted poetical late ME SV imperatives. "The remarkable feature [...] is that the postposed pronoun often appears in the dative *thee* or *you*, instead of the nominative *thou* or *ye*. This shows that at this stage the type 'imperative + reflexive dative', [...] had been intermingled with the VS type and exerted a considerable influence upon it" (1966:17). Four types of verb are particularly associated with reflexive datives, namely: verbs of motion, verbs of state or posture, verbs of emotion and verbs of attention. So that the frequent use of *thee* instead of *thou* in this position might, together with the unemphatic nature of enclitic *ye*, have served as cross-over analogy.

Nevalainen and Raumolin-Brunberg also report that imperatives involving second person subjects are prone to variation, because "ambiguous syntactic environments [...] are natural loci for this change. One of them is the infinitival structure, such as appears in requests *I pray you do something* and *I pray ye do something* [...] and optative sentences, where the subject follows the verb" (1996a:312f.) as in:

(9)   And this hertely fare *ye* well ... (Thomas Cromwell, social climber)

(10)   ... and so in hast fare *you* well. (Otwell Johnson, merchant; cf. Nevalainen and Raumolin-Brunberg 1996a:312)

In the Shakespeare Corpus the distribution of second person pronouns in imperatives is very heterogeneous. According to Millward (1966:10f.) the 35 plays of the *First Folio* Edition (1623) — *Pericles* was not included — contain only 35 imperatives followed by *ye*, which co-occur with only 13 different verbs, ten of which are also frequently used in conjunction with *you*. The pronoun *you*, on the other hand, occurs more than 500 times with 92 different verbs, and *thou* is employed more than 200 times with 77 different verbs, and about the same number of *thee* tokens are attested with 56 different verbs. For only 17 verbs there is an overlap between *thou* and *thee*. Millward also interprets *ye* in imperatives as a reduced form of *you* that can be used either as nominative or accusative. Owing to this, the imperatives have been considered separately in the numerical corpus analysis. Mitchell (1971:104) comes to the same conclusion, namely that *ye* and *you* following as subjects in imperatives do not show differentiation for case because both forms are used regardless after the same verbs, with the only exception of *haste*.[11]

Millward provides data for all those verbs that co-occur more than four times with *you*. Her results are shown in Table 3. The second figures indicate the number of *ye* tokens.

As the imperatives that are followed by *ye* are not further analysed in Millward's study, this will now be done, because the inventory of co-occurring verbs is very informative. The overview below lists all the occurrences of imperatives followed by *ye* in the corpus with a minimal context and the source of the citation (including the differences between the OES and Spevack). Due to the fact the Millward based her analysis on Kökeritz' (1954) facsimile edition of the *First Folio* and that I have taken the OES and Spevack as reference points in the list below, slight differences in numbers can occur:[12]

Table 3. Verbs in the Shakespeare Corpus that co-occur with *you* and *ye* in imperatives

be	(24, 1)	go	(34)	rest	(9)
bear	(4)	**hark**	(18, 8)	sit	(7)
bethink	(5)	**hear**	(14, 2)	speak	(5)
do, full verb	(7)	hie	(9)	stand	(6)
do, periphrastic	(15)	hold	(7)	take	(12, 1)
fare	(73, 10)	look	(73, 3)	tell	(4)
fear	(11)	mark	(9, 1)		
get	(58, 2)	prepare	(4)		

(Table from Millward 1966: 11, emphasis added)

be (1)
Or be ye not henceforth call'd my children. (TIT 2, 3, 115)

case (1)
Case ye, case ye, on with your vizards. (1H4 2, 2, 53)

fare (12 [11])
Fare ye well (AWW 4, 3, 328), (COR 4, 1, 44), (H5 5, 1, 79), (HAM 1, 2, 250;[13] 2, 1, 66), (LR 4, 6, 32), (MM 4, 3, 163), (MND 3, 2, 243), (MV 1, 1, 58; 103), (TN 2, 1, 39), (TRO 1, 2, 276; 3, 3, 299)

get (3 [2])
Therefore get ye gone. (2H6 4, 2, 153)
Get ye therefore hence (H5 2, 2, 177)[14]
Get ye all three into the box-tree (TN 2, 5, 15)

hang (1)
Hang ye, gorbellied knaves (1H4 2, 2, 88)

hark (8)
Hark ye, not so (1H6 3, 4, 37)
And hark ye, sirs. (1H6 5, 4, 55)
But hark ye (1H4 2, 4, 89)
Hark ye, your Romeo will be here at night. (ROM 3, 2, 140)
Why, hark ye, hark ye, and are you such fools (TIT 2, 1, 99)
Hark ye, lords (TIT 4, 2, 162)
Hark ye, master (WIV 3, 4, 29)
Hark ye, the Queen your mother rounds apace (WT 2, 1, 15)

hear (1)
Hear, ye, Yedward (1H4 1, 2, 134)

look (3)
Look ye how they change (H5 2, 2, 73)
Here is a water, look ye. (TIM 1, 1, 18)
Look ye draw home enough (TIT 4, 3, 3)

mark (1)
Mark ye me (1H4 3, 1, 137)

perish (1)
And perish ye with your audacious prate (1H6 4, 1, 124)

take (1)
In witness, take ye that (1H6 3, 4, 37)

Considering the fact that *you* occurs more than 500 times in imperatives, and *ye* only 33 times, then some of the verbs above show a marked concentration of *ye* tokens. Most conspicuous in this respect is the verb *fare*, which only appears in the formulaic greeting *fare + 2. Person Pronoun + well*. Etymologically it belongs to the class of motion verbs which according to Millward constitute a closed class and demand (in the singular) the oblique pronoun *thee*. In the OES twelve instances with *ye* are attested. The absolute frequency for the 126 pronouns in this formula is as follows:

fare you well	(73)
fare thee well	(40)
fare ye well	(12)
fare thou well	(1)

Get, make, seek, seize and *take* belong to the class of reflexive verbs. They also form a closed class and take an indirect object in imperatives. *Get* is also used together with *ye*.

The so-called verbs of attention that take *thee* in the imperative also constitute a closed class, as only four verbs are involved, viz. *hark, hear, look* and *mark*, all of which also frequently co-occur with *ye*. The 33 incidences of all second person pronouns for *hark* show the following distribution:

hark you	(20)
hark ye	(8)
hark thee	(5)

This plainly recognisable concentration of the pronoun *ye* in the imperative on a very limited set of verbs, and especially, the greeting formula *fare + 2. Person Pronoun + well* can be interpreted as a further sign of its markedness. In addition to this, *ye* is also commonly used in other greeting formulae which are optative subjunctives such as:[15]

(11) God ye good ev'n, William. (AYL 5, 1, 14)

(12) God buy ye. (HAM 2, 1, 66)

(13) God ye good morrow, gentlemen. (ROM 2, 4, 109)

(14) God ye good den, fair gentlewoman. (ROM 2, 4, 110),

(15) O, give ye good ev'n! (TGV 2, 1, 98)

10.3.4.2 *Shakespeare's use of ye in imperatives compared to that of other dramatists*

This result on Shakespeare's use of *ye* in imperatives can, by means of Mitchell's data (1971:90–94), also be compared to that of other dramatists.

Table 4. Pronouns in imperatives

	thou	thee	ye	you	Verbs*	Total
Period I (1580–1630)	19	3	9	42	32	73
Period II (1630–1680)	7	15	5	62	23	89
Period III (1680–1730)	5	12	72	95	21	184
Period IV (1730–1780)	4	0	56	26	9	86
Total	35	30	142	225		432

(Table from Mitchell: 1971:94)

* This column has been added on the basis of the data in Mitchell (1971:92f.)

The diachronic analysis presented in Table 4 demands further explanation. Once again, *you* has proved the dominant form, with the only exception being the 18th century. The numerical rise of *ye* in the 18th century rather disguises the fact that the pronoun becomes increasingly limited to certain verbs. The column for the different verbs indicates a steady, and finally a drastic decline of verbs, e.g. in period III *look* (89) und *hark* (52) alone account for 141 out of 184 imperatives, and in the last period *hark* (41) and *look* (32) together amount to 73 instances out of 86 imperatives. Furthermore, these verbs only occur in such formulaic expressions as: *hark ye, hark'ee, hark'e* and *look ye, look'ee* oder *look'e* (cf. Mitchell: 1971:93). This tendency is also corroborated by Bock's data for the 18th century, which show a number of incidences of *look y'/ee* and *hark y'/ee*.[16]

The diachronic perspective of these four consecutive periods clearly manifests that *ye* in imperatives underlies the process of fossilization. In a first stage it loses its function as a subjective case marker, then its syntactic distribution gets increasingly limited to ambiguous post-verbal positions until it is finally reduced to certain verbs of attention in the imperative and (optative) subjunctive which constitute formulaic expressions. This process goes hand in hand with the loss of morphological independence: as *ye* becomes a phonetically (and also orthographically) reduced unstressed form it becomes an enclitic form *-(e)e* that is added to the verb. In standard English these forms are no longer in use, but they have survived in some dialectal registers.[17]

10.3.4.3 *Ye in exclamations*[18]

Among the sentence types in which *ye* occurs predominantly, the exclamatives deserve special attention because they show concentration of *ye* forms, i.e. out of a total of 77 plural *ye* tokens in the 36 plays there are no less than 38 exclamations. Table 5 lists the occurrences of *ye* in exclamations according to genre, play, context, medium, speaker and source. It reveals that they are divided unequally among the plays and also among the media of verse and prose.

Table 5 also shows that the exclamations are concentrated in the two genres of History and Tragedy. Excepting ADO, they are completely absent from the Comedies; and in MND the only occurrence takes place in the play within the play in Bottom's role as Pyramus, where unwittingly the lay players in the interlude provide a pastiche of Tragedy. In the Romances, there are only three examples. This unequivocal distribution can be explained by the dramatic function of the summonings of real or only imagined supernatural bodies such as gods, spirits, etc. in apostrophe, which have a higher frequency in History and Tragedy than in Comedy. Furthermore, these cases imply that in this register *ye* is used as a plural analogue to the singular *thou*. The table also demonstrates that the occurrence of *ye* in the plural is clearly linked to exclamations, because out of the total of 42 *ye* forms, 30 are plural and only 12 singular. In this respect the use of number in exclamations with a ratio of 72% for the plural reverses the overall ratio in the corpus with 68.4% for the singular.[19]

Finkenstaedt (1963: 156f.) makes the following remarks on the use of *thou* in apostrophe (cf. also Chapter 2.8): the singular is used in all those cases in which no reply is possible, i.e. in address to God(s), imaginary persons (including the address of oneself), to animals and inanimate objects. Unfortunately, Yong-Lin (1991) restricts his investigation "How to talk to the supernatural in Shakespeare" to the use of *thou* to individual supernatural creatures such as ghosts, witches, spirits, etc. and thus leaves out *ye*.

What these uses of *thou* in the singular and those attested for *ye* in the plural in apostrophe have in common are their highly affective connotations, which are reinforced by either honorific or abusive vocatives. A glance at the vocatives co-occurring with *ye* (as listed in Table 5) immediately proves a correlation with terms expressing extreme states of emotion of both a positive (*charming spells, choice spirits, gods, elves*, etc.) and a negative nature (*cuckoo, devil, rascal, rogue, whore*, etc.). The vast majority of syntactically incomplete exclamatives show the following sentence structure:

[[[ADV./INTERJECTION] + (VERB)], *YE* + VOCATIVE, ...]!

10.3.5   *Ye* as a means for characterisation?

The above investigation of exclamatives and especially Table 5 reveal that some characters seem to be using *ye* more often than others. However, Millward (1966), in her analysis of pronominal usage in Shakespearean imperatives, has come to the

Table 5. *Ye* exclamatives in the Shakespeare Corpus

Genre/ Play	Nr	Context	V/P	Speaker	Source
Histories					
1H6	(1)	*Now help, ye charming spells and periapts*	Verse	Joan	5, 3, 2
	(2)	*And ye choice spirits*	Verse	Joan	5, 3, 3
	(3)	*Now, ye familiar spirits*	Verse	Joan	5, 3, 10
	(4)	*I am with child, ye bloody homicides*	Verse	Joan	5, 4, 62
2H6	(–)				
3H6	(–)				
R3	(–)				
JN	(–)				
R2	(5)	*Ye favourites of a king*	Verse	Richard	3, 2, 88
1H4	(6)	*Peace, ye fat-kidneyed rascal*	Prose	Harry	2, 2, 5
	(7)	*Peace, ye fat-guts*	Verse	Harry	2, 2, 31
	(8)	*Out, ye rogue*	Prose	Harry	2, 2, 42
	(9)	*You lie, ye rogue*	Prose	John	2, 2, 56
	(10)	*No, ye fat chuffs*	Prose	John	2, 2, 89
	(11)	*What, ye knaves*	Prose	John	2, 2, 90
	(12)	*Zounds, ye fat paunch*	Prose	Poins	2, 4, 144
	(13)	*A horseback, ye cuckoo*	Prose	John	2, 4, 353
	(14)	*Out, ye rogue*	Prose	John	2, 4, 484
	(15)	*Go, ye giddy goose*	Verse	Lady Percy	3, 1, 137
	(16)	*Lie still, ye thief*	Verse	Lady Percy	3, 1, 234
2H4	(–)				
H5	(–)				
Tragedies					
TIT	(17)	*Zounds, ye whore*	Verse	Aaron	4, 2, 71
	(18)	*What, what, ye sanguine, shallow-hearted boys*	Verse	Aaron	4, 2, 97
	(19)	*Ye white-lim'd walls*	Verse	Aaron	4, 2, 98
	(20)	*ye alehouse painted signs*	Verse	Aaron	4, 2, 98
	(21)	*Welcome, ye warlike Goths*	Verse	Titus	5, 3, 27
ROM	(–)				
JC	(22)	*Ye gods, it doth amaze me*	Verse	Cassius	1, 2, 128
	(23)	*Therein, ye gods, you make the weak most strong*	Verse	Cassius	1, 3, 91
	(24)	*Therein, ye gods, you tyrants do defeat.*	Verse	Cassius	1, 3, 92
	(25)	*O ye gods, render me worthy*	Verse	Brutus	2, 1, 302
	(26)	*O ye gods, ye gods, must I endure all this?*	Verse	Cassius	4, 3, 41
	(27)	*O ye immortal gods!*	Verse	Cassius	4, 3, 157
HAM	(–)				
OTH	(28)	*Whip me, ye devils*	Verse	Othello	5, 2, 277

Table 5. *Ye* exclamatives in the Shakespeare Corpus *(continued)*

Genre/ Nr Play		Context	V/P	Speaker	Source
LR	(29)	*Ye jewels of our father**	Verse	Cordelia	1, 1, 268
MAC		(–)			
ANT		(–)			
COR	(30)	*Help, ye citizens!*	Verse	Sicinius	3, 1, 179
	(31)	*Draw near, ye people.*	Verse	Sicinius	3, 3, 39
TIM	(32)	*You came for gold, ye slaves.*	Verse	Flavius	5, 1, 112
Comedies					
ERR		(–)			
SHR		(–)			
TGV		(–)			
LLL		(–)			
MND	(33)	*Approach, ye furies fell!*	Verse	Bottom	5, 1, 284
MV		(–)			
WIV		(–)			
ADO	(34)	*Ye light a'love with your heels*	Prose	Beatrice	3, 3, 47
AYL		(–)			
TN		(–)			
TRO		(–)			
AWW		(–)			
MM		(–)			
Romances					
PER		(–)			
CYM	(35)	*Displace our heads where — thanks, ye gods — they grow***	Verse	Guiderius	4, 2, 122
WT		(–)			
TMP	(36)	*Ye elves of hills, brooks, standing lakes*	Verse	Caliban	5, 1, 33
	(37)	*And ye that on the sands with printless foot*	Verse	Caliban	5, 1, 34
Shakespeare/Fletcher plays					
H8	(38)	*Anon, ye rascals*	Verse	Porter	5, 3, 1
	(39)	*ye rude slaves*	Verse	Porter	5, 3, 2
	(40)	*ye rogue*	Verse	Porter	5, 3, 6
TNK	(41)	*ye jane judgments*	Verse	Schoolmaster	3, 5, 8
	(42)	*O all ye gods, despise me then*	Verse	Palamon	3, 6, 258

* Only in the OES, Spevack: "*The* jewels of our father."
** Only in the OES, Spevack: "(thanks, [*ye*] gods!)"

conclusion that the pronouns do not show sociolinguistic patterning. The small number of all *ye* tokens rather forbids a thorough sociolinguistic interpretation, but as at least some of the plays investigated show a concentration of *ye* tokens for certain speakers, some tentative conclusions can be drawn.

Out of the 30 forms to be found in 1H4 (see Table 9 in the appendix), it is Sir John Falstaff who uses *ye* most frequently (16 times). In addition to this, most of the abusive vocatives are related to him either as a speaker or addressee (cf. Table 5).

In 1H6 Joan de Pucelle is the character to use *ye* quite frequently (eight out of 23 tokens) mostly in connection with vocatives laden with emotion. In 2H6 the 19 instances of *ye* are divided between a number of characters; Jack Cade uses it five times. In HAM the protagonist employs *ye* six times (out of twelve occurrences).[20]

The forms in JC are mostly restricted to Cassius' vocatives (six out of ten). TIT presents a similar distribution, as Aaron accounts for ten of the 22 tokens. The two instances occurring in OTH are used by Othello. In TMP, Caliban and Prospero are the only characters to use *ye*; in TRO it is Pandarus, with four out of seven forms. In H8 many of the characters make use of this form, but two characters in particular, namely Queen Katherine (23 tokens) and King Henry (15 tokens).

As indicated above, the paucity of material rather forbids a further-going interpretation in the sense of McIntosh's (1963a) famous article "'As You Like It': A grammatical clue to character", but, this not withstanding, the list of characters brings to mind the following sociolinguistic variables: despite all differences in estate, the characters have in common that they are situated at the two extremes of the social scale, as they are rulers, belong to the nobility, or are at least persons of some social standing, e.g. Hamlet, Prospero, King Henry VIII, Queen Katherine and Sir John Falstaff, or are outsiders such as foreigners (Joan), rebels (Jack Cade), conspirators (Cassius), Moors (Othello and Aaron) or, as Caliban, a "savage and deformed slave".

This social patterning of the predominant *ye*-users in the Shakespeare Corpus ties in with the findings for the CEEC of Nevalainen and Raumolin Brunberg (cf. 10.3.3.3.1), as it was the nobility together with the lowest social orders who made the least use of the incoming form *you* in subject position.

Bock (1938: 56f.) states that in earlier plays such as *Fulgens and Lucres* (1497) and also in *Calisto and Melibaea* (c. 1530) the grammatically wrong use of *you* in the nominative and *ye* in the oblique case could be identified as a stylistic means to characterise the language of the lower social orders. However, Carstensen (1959: 192), in his corpus study of the *Paston Letters*, is of the opinion that mixing of pronominal case forms cannot be regarded as a sign of uneducated language. In his corpus the first example of *you* in subject function stems from 1426. As an example he refers to Walter, the youngest of the third generation of Pastons, who took an academic degree at Oxford and who uses *you* in his letters eight times in the nominative as opposed to five instances of *ye*. He goes on to say that this kind of case shifting became "modern" at the beginning of the 15th century so that by the end of the century both forms could be used interchangeably.

Obviously, the feeling of right and wrong had disappeared even more strongly by Shakespeare's time, for when the instances in the Shakespeare Corpus are scrutinised not only in terms of frequency, but also in terms of grammatical "correctness", no clear-cut correlation can be worked out as to those characters who use *ye* in the subjective case and those using it in the objective case, as the instances for *ye* in object position are very rare in any given play.

On the other hand, a weak connection between case and date of composition could be drawn. The plays that show the highest incidence of *ye* in the nominative are 1H6, 2H6, 3H6 and TIT, all of which are very early plays, and which might still reflect the older state of the language, or a more cautious use of the incoming form by the emerging playwright at the beginning of his career (cf. 10.3.7).

10.3.6 The distribution of *ye* in verse and prose

Table 9 (see appendix) illustrates that the *ye* tokens for the 36 plays are divided between blank verse and prose as follows: 64.3% in the OES and 65.9% in Spevack respectively account for blank verse and only 35.7% or 34.1% for prose. This distribution constitutes a clear correlation between the pronoun *ye* and the medium of blank verse. The *ye* tokens in vocatives behave similarly. Excepting the isolated occurrence of *ye* in a prose line in ADO and those in 1H4 all the other cases appear in the context of a verse line.[21] Thus, depending on which count one wishes to follow, 34 or 31 *ye* tokens occur in a verse line as opposed to nine or twelve in prose lines.

In this respect the occurrences of *ye* confirm the close relationship between marked forms and their occurrence in marked linguistic categories. In Chapter 4 the same correlation could be proved to hold between the pronoun *thou* and its predominant appearance in blank verse by taking recourse to the theory of drift as propounded by Andersen (1990: 10f.). Andersen has investigated a large number of different linguistic categories ranging from grammar to pragmatics and stylistics and their openness towards linguistic change, and has revealed that there is a strong tendency for marked forms to occur predominantly in marked linguistic categories (cf. Chapter 5, Table 1). The extreme distribution of *ye* as the marked pronoun in the dyad and blank verse as the marked category in comparison to prose, which according to Andersen are both less open to linguistic innovation, gives additional support to the theory.

10.3.7 The importance of date of composition and genre

In his computer linguistic study of pronominal use in Shakespeare's plays Brainerd (1979) has shown that a correlation holds between the factors date of composition and genre (cf. Chapter 3.2). His data do not explicitly show which pronouns are to be understood as second person singular, or plural, respectively. Despite this he concludes that in the course of Shakespeare's writing career the tokens for the second person singular diminish over time, and as a corollary of this, the tokens for the second person plural show a higher incidence. There are, however, considerable differences to be observed for the genres.

The numerical analysis of Chapter 3 has revealed that such a correlation does indeed hold for the distribution of *you* and *thou*. As far as the variants *ye* and *you* are concerned, the tendency is less clear, but also seems to apply, at least to a certain extent. Accumulations of *ye* tokens occur in the following plays:[22] 1H6 (date of composition 1589/90: 23 tokens), 2H6 (1590/91: 19), 1H4 (1596/97: 30), ROM (1595/96: 12), HAM (1600/01: 12),[23] JC (1599: 10), TIT (1593/94: 22). As regards dates of composition the list of plays shows that "high" numbers of *ye* only occur in plays that belong to the period up to 1600, whereas none of the later plays, excepting the special cases of H8 and TNK (cf. 10.3.8), shows *ye* tokens in large numbers. This corpus-internal development ties in with that of some of the other variants under observation, as for *thou/you* and *pray thee/prithee* a divide in the corpus around 1600 is also to be observed.

Concerning their distribution over the genres, again a quite remarkable concentration on History and Tragedy becomes apparent. In the enumeration above, there is no Comedy to be found whatsoever. The Comedies exhibit the lowest turn-out of *ye* tokens for all genres ranging from a single token in WIV to seven in TGV.

This state of affairs, which despite vacillation between individual plays, shows a declining number of tokens from the genres of History to Tragedy and Comedy can be interpreted in the following way: the *ye* tokens are most numerous in plays of a historical and/or tragic character, which in turn can be attributed to the use of apostrophe and the overproportional representation of *ye* in this literary device. Chapter 3 has shown that the same correlation also holds for *thou*. This patterning indicates that in the Shakespeare Corpus *ye* is clearly limited to the higher literary register. As the literary device of apostrophe does not play such an important part in Comedy, it does not come as a surprise that the Comedies, and especially those having been written at about the same time as the Histories and Tragedies listed above, have fewer *ye* tokens. For the second half of the corpus after 1600 these differences between genres are levelled out, as the numbers of *ye* become less and less frequent.

10.3.8   *Ye* as evidence of authorship in H8 and TNK?

The only plays that seemingly run counter to the tendency described above are H8 and TNK, which despite their late dates of composition, 1612/13 for H8 and 1613 for TNK, show a considerable number of *ye* tokens, namely 72 for H8 and 46 for TNK. This apparent contradiction can be resolved once these plays due to their dubious authorship are taken out of the Shakespeare Corpus proper and are considered separately in their own right. The question then arising is whether *ye*, among other linguistic factors, can serve as intralinguistic evidence for the hand of another playwright.

Hope (1994b: 81 ff.) in his authorship study of the dubious Shakespeare plays draws attention to the fact that H8 shows an unusual ratio of *thou* and *you*. Although he argues that the pronoun choice between *thou* and *you* is not a good means for linguistic evidence of authorship, he interprets the dominance of *you* over *thou* on the background of the collaboration between Shakespeare and Fletcher, but does not say anything on the remarkable and "unusual" use of *ye*. However, once not only the ratio of *thou* to *you* with 25:429 tokens is considered, but also the ratio of *ye* and *you* with 73:429 tokens is incorporated, this play is outside the normal line of pronoun usage in the canon. Despite the fact that Hope refers to Hoy's authorship studies (1956–1962), "The shares of Fletcher and his collaborators in the Beaumont and Fletcher canon", he does not note that Hoy regards the high frequency of *ye* as the most significant intralinguistic evidence for his share in the play: "Hoy [1956] discovered that Fletcher exhibited a linguistic preference for *ye* far beyond any of the other Jacobean dramatists in question" (Mitchell 1971: 76 footnote). Table 6 illustrates Graband's (1965) findings on second person pronoun forms in the works of Beaumont and Fletcher.

Table 6. Second person pronouns in the works of Beaumont and Fletcher

sg subject	*thou*	363	object	*thee*	193
	you	1,183		*you*	596
	ye	42		*ye*	46
pl subject	*you*	136	object	*you*	95
	ye	7		*ye*	0

(Table from Graband 1965: 243)

The sum of all *you* tokens in the works of Beaumont and Fletcher amounts to 2,010 and that of all *ye* tokens to 95 (4.73%). If the numbers for the two plays written in collaboration with Fletcher are subtracted from the grand total of pronoun use in the Shakespeare Corpus then there are 13,591 instances (out of 14,405) of *you* in the remaining 36 plays, and 223 (out of 343) instances of *ye* (1.34%). Thus, Shakespeare uses the two pronouns at a ratio of 1:61 (*ye/you*) and Beaumont and Fletcher at a ratio of 1:21.

As regards TNK there is, following Hope "less controversy about the division of the play than *Henry VIII*" (1994b: 83). The extraordinary ratio for the two pronouns *ye* and *you* (45:385 tokens) could thus serve as a further indicator for the collaboration of Fletcher. The table provided in Hope (1994b: 84) shows the main divisions for acts and scenes between Shakespeare and Fletcher, as established by critics from 1833 to 1989 by employing different types of evidence. These differences notwithstanding, the table shows that for most scenes the critics have reached consensus as to whom they shall be ascribed. Having found earlier that the *thou/you* choice did not prove a reliable criterion in authorship studies, Hope does not pursue this topic any further. However, the distribution of the *ye* tokens exhibits concentrations in the following passages of the play, i.e. act 2, scenes 2, 3; act 3, scenes 5, 6, which alone accounts for 19 items; act 4, scene 1; act 5, scenes 1, 2 and the epilogue. When these data are matched to the division between Shakespeare and Fletcher as laid down in Hope, then the critics almost unanimously agree that these scenes were provided by Fletcher. Total consensus exists for act 3, scenes 5, 6; act 4, scene 1 and also act 5, scene 2. Concerning act 2, scenes 2 and 3 the majority of critics ascribe them to Fletcher, and the epilogue has so far been scrutinised in this respect by only one critic who assumes that it was written by Fletcher. For this coincidence it seems highly unlikely that it is a product of mere chance. Thus, the use of *ye* could serve as a further sign of intralinguistic evidence for the division of the play between Shakespeare and Fletcher.

This claim is underlined by my previous findings on the handling of the grammatical category *number* in the Shakespeare Corpus (cf. 10.3.2.2). In this respect, the two plays clearly differ from the rest of the corpus, because they show a much higher incidence for the plural (e.g. 70.83% in H8 as opposed to 31.6% in the 36 plays).

The tendency for the *ye* forms to appear, apart from some of the Tragedies, mostly in the History Plays, in particular in the three parts of H6 and in the two parts of H4, all of which centre on real monarchs of English Medieval history could, apart from aspects such as early date of composition or *ye* as a possible means of characterisation, be interpreted in yet another direction. The exposition of data has shown that the pronoun had an archaising air about it by Shakespeare's time, at least in some text types, as e.g. letters, and could thus have served as a linguistic means of distancing and back shifting which helped to settle the plays firmly in the past, despite or perhaps because of their many allusions to contemporary politics. It is interesting to note that probably due to political circumspection the Tudor era is not topicalised in any of the Histories in Elizabeth's I lifetime. H8, dated around 1612/13, appeared after the death of the Queen. As shown earlier, the high rate of *ye* can serve as internal evidence for the hand of Fletcher in this play. On the other hand, resuming the above argumentation, the pronoun could also have been employed to mitigate the political implications by resorting to an old-fashioned linguistic form. However, Barber provides a completely different explanation when he says that "the way it [*ye*] is used in the plays of John Fletcher (d. 1625) suggests that in the Jacobean period it may have been considered more refined and courtly than everyday *you*" (1997: 149).

10.4 Conclusion

The foregoing analysis of the use and function of *ye* in the Shakespeare Corpus has revealed a number of interesting facts. First of all, in terms of sheer frequency *ye* is outnumbered by *you* at a ratio of 1:42 if all the 38 plays are taken together. When the two plays H8 and TNK are left out, the ratio drops significantly to 1:61 in favour of *you*. As regards its syntax, *ye* is employed by Shakespeare in more than 70% of its instances as a pronoun in subject position (if the categories nominative, vocative and imperative are taken together) and only in less than 30% in object function. On the other hand, its former position as second person plural pronoun is retained only in 30% of all cases, the majority of which occur in exclamations, where the pronoun in analogy to singular *thou/thee* acts as a form of direct address to invoke supernatural beings in apostrophe. In contrast to this are the two plays TNK and H8, both collaborations with Fletcher, that show a much higher degree of 'ordinary' plural usages.

In relation to sentence types, it is the imperatives that present a high density of *ye* tokens. However, the pronoun co-occurs with only a very limited number of closed-class verbs that seek the attention of the addressee, in particular *hark ye* and *look ye*. It thus shows tendencies of fossilization which become stronger in the 17th and 18th centuries and which, with the disappearance of this type of imperative (verb + pronoun) in standard English, may have contributed to the final loss of the form.

The frequent occurrence of *ye* in post-verbal position in imperatives and in sentences containing the optative subjunctive, in particular in greeting formulae as *fare ye well*, can have added to the confusion of subject and object forms, because with SVO-word order having becoming fixed around 1500, this position is reserved for the object, and also cross-over analogy with the singular construction *fare thee well* (or similar optatives) may, in the long run, have contributed to the final supplanting of the form by *you*.

As concerns its discourse functions, *ye* is clearly marked as the affective pronoun in the dyad, because it frequently occurs in exclamatives, which are mostly found as apostrophes in connection with abstract nouns together with either honorific or abusive vocatives. This shows that the use of *ye* is limited to elevated registers. Further restrictions in terms of register and medium can be observed, as *ye* occurs predominantly in blank verse and not in prose and also in the genres of Tragedy and History, and only to a far lesser extent in Comedy. All of these factors support the correlation of the occurrence of marked forms in marked genres, media, etc.

Again, the date of 1600 suggests a caesura within the corpus, because from then on the *ye* tokens become less "frequent". However, their use in the late plays of TNK and H8 can, among other factors, serve as a linguistic indicator for the collaboration between Shakespeare and Fletcher in authorship studies, as these plays display Fletcher's predilection for *ye* rather than *you*.

Appendix

Table 9. The overall distribution of *ye* tokens in the Shakespeare Corpus

| | OXFORD ELECTRONIC SHAKESPEARE | | | | | | | | | | | SPEVACK | | |
| | SUBJECT | | | OBJECT | | | NUMBER | | | | | | | |
PLAY	NOM	VOC	IMP	DAT	PREP	ACC	SG	PL	Total	VS	PR	Total	VS	PR
1H6	13	4	5	1			11	12	23	23		23	23	
2H6	14					5	13	6	19	12	7	20	13	7
3H6	5	1				2	6	2	8		8	8	8	
R3	2	1		1		1	4	1	5	5		2	2	
ERR														
TIT	13	5	2			2	13	9	22	22		21	21	
SHR	1					3	3	1	4	4		4	4	
TGV	2			1	2	2	6	1	7	5	2	7	5	2
LLL	2			2			4		4	1	3	3	1	2
ROM	4		1	4	1	2	11	1	12	6	6	12	6	6
R2		1					1		1	1		1	1	
MND	1		1				1	1	2	2		2	2	
JN	1						1		1	1		1	1	
MV	1		2				2	1	3	3		3	3	
1H4	8	11	5	1		5	22	8	30	7	23	29	2	27
2H4	2				2	1	5		5	1	4	5	1	4
ADO						1	1		1	1		1		1
H5			3				1	2	3	2	1	2	1	1
JC	2	7				1	3	7	10	10		10	10	
AYL	1			2			3		3	1	2	2	1	1
TN	3	1	1				2	3	5		5	5		5
HAM	6		2	4			9	3	12	6	6	3	2	1

	SUBJECT			OBJECT			NUMBER		Total	VS	PR	Total	VS	PR
PLAY	NOM	VOC	IMP	DAT	PREP	ACC	SG	PL						
WIV			1				1		1	1		1		1
TRO	4		3				7		7	1	6	7	1	6
AWW	3		1				4		4	1	3	3		3
MM			1				1		1		1	1		1
OTH	1	1					1	1	2	2		1	1	
LR		1	1			6	6	2	8	5	3	7	4	3
MAC	3							3	3	3		3	3	
ANT				1		3	3	1	4	4		4	3	1
COR	2	2	2	1		1	6	2	8	8		8	8	
TIM	3	1	1			1	5	1	6	6		6	6	
PER	6						6		6	3	3	5	2	3
CYM	1	1		2		2	2	4	6	6		5	5	
WT			1		1	1	3		3	2	1	3	2	
TMP	1	2			1	1	1	4	5	5	1	5	5	1
Total	104	39	33	16	12	40	167	77	244	157	87	223	147	76
%	42.6	16.0	13.5	6.6	4.9	16.4	68.4	31.6	100	64.3	35.7	100	65.9	34.1
+														
H8	32	3		7	12	18	21	51	72	72		73	70	3
TNK	17	2		7	10	10	33	13	46	44	2	47	47	
Total	153	44	33	30	34	68	221	141	362	273	89	343	264	79
%	42.3	12.1	9.1	8.3	9.4	18.8	61.0	39.0	100	75.4	24.6	100	76.9	23.1

CHAPTER 11

Summary and conclusion

11.1 The development of *thou* and *you*

Even though the individual chapters have each been summarised in turn, the presentation of about three hundred pages of data on different specimens of variation calls for a final evaluation of results, which in its wider perspective of hindsight, brings the different strands together again.

In the 38 plays of the Shakespeare Corpus there is a total of 13,186 T forms and 22,400 Y forms. When these absolute figures are relativized into percentages then the T pronouns have a relative frequency of 1.578% and the Y pronouns 2.681%, the margin being 1.103%. The ratio of the two variants is 0.59:1. However, this evidence from the concordances still needs to be adjusted because it includes the plural Y forms. By means of a control corpus of nine plays from different genres and different dates of composition it can be established that about 20% of the Y tokens are plural. This leaves about 18,000 singular Y forms, and reduces their relative frequency to ca. 2%. With these corrected figures the ratio of the two variants drops to 0.70:1. Nevertheless, in terms of frequency one can still say that Y is, statistically speaking, the (unmarked) majority form and T the (marked) minority form.

Once the corpus has been subcategorised into genres, it becomes apparent that the two variants are being used with differing frequencies. The T forms have the highest incidence in the History Plays and show the lowest turn-out in the Comedies. The Comedies make up the largest category of plays. They stretch over almost the entire writing career of Shakespeare and are hence a fairly heterogeneous genre. Owing to this, they are often further subdivided into Early Comedies, Mature Comedies, Problem Plays and Romances (cf. Suerbaum 1996). With the exception of Romance, which comprises only later plays, all the other subgenres show a regression of T forms over time. In terms of second person pronouns the genre of Romance has affinities to Tragedy. The differences in pronoun use between Roman Plays and Tragedies are not highly significant. However, the different approaches to account for genre in the Shakespeare Corpus confirm unanimously that the Histories, as early plays (1590–1599, excepting H8), feature the highest numbers of T forms as opposed to the Comedies. The correlation of the two factors of genre and date of composition (cf. Brainerd 1979) points toward a divide within the corpus with an earlier part leading up to 1600, or more precisely to 1598, and a later part.

The only plays that show more T than Y forms after this date are TIM and TMP. The 'abnormal' pronoun distribution in H8 (77 T forms and 803 Y forms) could possibly be attributed to the share of Fletcher in this play.

When Shakespeare's use of the second person pronouns is compared to that of his fellow-dramatists, it becomes apparent that Jonson is the one who predominantly uses *you* (82%). The differences between Marlowe, Shakespeare and Ford are not large, as their usage ranges between 44% and 57%.

The surprisingly high frequency of Y forms in Shakespeare's comedies is not an idiosyncratic feature of personal style, but rather a phenomenon that is typical of that genre. A diachronic investigation of the two variants in relation to text types on the basis of Mitchell (1971) has revealed that from 1580 to 1780 the T forms, despite a general decline over time, always have a higher incidence in Tragedy than in Comedy. This can be explained by the primary function of *thou* as a marker of affect and, in particular, by its conventional use in apostrophe in the Tragedies.

This result is also interesting in terms of evaluation (cf. Weinreich et al. 1968), which discusses the level of social awareness related to a change in progress. Brainerd has simply linked the decrease of T forms and the rise of Y forms in the course of Shakespeare's writing career to linguistic change, viz.: "this accords with the gradual replacement, as Shakespeare grew older, of second person singular forms by second plural" (1979:7). However, the consistency with which Shakespearean Comedy and the genre in general display a preponderance of Y forms over an extended period of time (200 years), most likely rather points towards the fact that this development was not an invisible hand process but a change from "above", i.e. one from above the level of consciousness that was actively and quite purposefully employed by Shakespeare and other authors and not only passively taken in and used subconsciously.

Sociolinguistically, the high incidence of Y forms in Comedy can be interpreted as an indicator that *you* was the 'normal' pronoun of rapport between middle and also lower-class characters from 1600 onwards. In terms of transition and embedding, which both deal with the circumstances that lead to the diffusion of innovations from speaker to speaker and the linguistic and social structures in which innovations emerge, the findings from Johnson's (1966) corpus of 17th century drama and prose provide valuable information that support the claim above. She has shown that in the first half of the 17th century the middle and lower class speakers are in the lead as *you* users (81–83%) and that the upper class lags behind with only 64%. Within the next fifty years these differences are levelled out, as all classes predominantly use *you*; the range varying from 81–88%.

Having found so far that for the use of *thou* and *you* in Shakespeare's plays the factors date of composition, genre, or more specifically, their combination are of importance and that the Y forms predominate in Comedy, which makes more use of prose than of blank verse, the next factor examined was the distribution of the two variants in a verse or prose context. The quantitative corpus analysis has revealed that for a great many of plays there is a statistically significant deviation in the distribution with *thou* dominating in blank verse and *you* being the majority form in prose. However, on the corpus level the difference amounts to less than 10%. For the corpus as a whole, the ratio between words occurring in a verse or prose context is 75.73% verse and 23.27% prose. Again, Histories and Tragedies show a fairly similar proportion of verse ranging from 83–86% and the Comedies exhibit the highest ratio of prose (43%). As concerns *you* and *thou*, there are 10,473 T forms (79.44%) occurring in verse and only 2,711 (20.56%) in prose, as opposed 15,731 Y forms (70.23%) in verse and 6,669 (29.77%) in prose. This distribution supports the working hypothesis that there is a correlation between pronoun use and dramatic medium. However, the preponderance of *you* in the genre of Comedy and its higher incidence in the medium of prose do not necessarily support the claim that prose is an indicator of social inferiority in Shakespeare's plays. Quite to the contrary, in ADO and in MND it is the dominant medium of discourse, and even in the clowns' prose as represented by the constables in ADO and by the mechanicals in MND *you* is their pronoun of rapport. This usage proves two things: if it is true that prose is the primary medium of discourse, especially of the lower classes, then it can no longer be maintained that among them *thou* is the normal pronoun. It seems to be rather the other way around in that by 1600 *you* is the ordinary pronoun of address even among the lower social orders (as depicted in Shakespearean comedy).

This interpretation gains additional support from the theory of drift and the concept of markedness as put forward by Andersen (1990, 2001). He establishes a correlation between marked and unmarked linguistic categories and their respective openness towards language change. For example, he describes prose as being more compatible with innovation than poetry. In light of this explanation it is no longer surprising to find that *you* dominates in prose rather than in verse.

In order to substantiate this explanation, a control corpus of poetry consisting primarily of Shakespearean and other Elizabethan sonnets was investigated to check whether all, or at least some of the factors analysed so far for Shakespeare's plays, could also be attributed to the use of *thou* and *you* in his non-dramatic works.

The difference between the plays, viz.: 13,186 T forms (42%) and ca. 18,000 singular Y forms (58%) and his non-dramatic works, viz.: 1,094 T forms (74.12%) and 382 singular Y forms (25.88%), tells us that the two pronouns have a very different status in drama and in poetry. Unlike the drama corpus, no corpus-internal development can be detected in the sonnets and Shakespeare's other non-dramatic works. A further contrast to drama is pronominal consistency in the sonnets, as there are only a few sonnets showing a mixed pronoun use (sonnets no. 24, 100, 105, 116). The pronoun switches in the sonnets addressed to the Young Man have to be attributed to changes in the relationship between speaker and addressee, shifting personae, real and/or imagined social contexts, etc. In the sonnets to the Dark Mistress, Shakespeare uses the conventional pronoun *thou*.

Once Shakespeare's usage is compared to that of other Elizabethan sonneteers it becomes apparent that Shakespeare's contemporaries prefer indirect address by means of the third person pronoun *she*, and often switch to direct address only in the couplet.

Evidence from poems other than sonnets points toward another factor that is important, namely the cline that leads from literate/formal 'truly written' text types to more speech based 'oral' text types and the difference in privacy that results from this. Thus, the avoidance of *you* in the sonnet sequences could then be attributed to their more private nature as opposed to more overtly public poems such as odes, epistles and epigrams, all of which feature *you* more prominently. So, within the genre of poetry a cline can be discerned from the more overtly public, colloquial 'written orality', preferring *you*, to the more private, conventionalised and formal 'truly written' kind of writing, preferring *thou* "in the higher poetic style" (Abbott [1870] 1972: 154), giving proof to Andersen's description of poetry as a marked genre category in contrast to prose and *thou* as the marked pronoun in the dyad.

In the introduction it was stated that one objective of the study should be to describe and explain the pronoun choices, and, if possible, to delimit the number of constraints, and to rank them in terms of importance. Applied to the variation of *thou* and *you* it seems that the socio-pragmatic factors have the greatest impact on the pronoun choice. Evidence from the use of second person pronouns and co-occurring nominal forms of address tells us that there is indeed a strong correlation between the nominal form of address and the address pronoun, because a log-linear regression can be established. The social impact implied in address nouns such as *(my) liege, sir* and other titles indicating deference has become so strong that these respectful titles almost automatically trigger the use of *you*, even if they are being used ironically, mock-politely or in a flippant mood. The correlation between respectful titles and *you* as the polite pronoun is indeed so strong that in a context where *thou* is used between the interlocutors, the occurrence of a respectful title necessitates pronoun switching to a momentary *you* (cf. also Williams 1992: 92).

The address nouns can be placed along a scale of politeness ranging from negative politeness or deference at the one end, as represented (in declining order of '*you*fulness') by the titles of honour and courtesy, occupational titles and expressions of family relationship, which all co-occur with more Y forms than T forms, to the generic terms of address, the terms of abuse and, at the far end of positive politeness, the terms of endearment as the most '*thou*ful' ones. This arrangement of categories shows that out of the factors *power, distance* and *intrinsic extremity* that influence the choice of either *thou* or *you, power* and *distance* are the most important ones.

However, in addition to these socio-pragmatic constraints the statistical findings have further proved that the genre also has a bearing upon the choice of the address pronouns. All in all, 1,246 co-occurrences of address pronouns and address nouns have been analysed. On the corpus level, irrespective of the six vocative categories (as listed above), it is again the genre of Comedy that exhibits the highest degree of Y forms with a ratio of 31.40% T forms and 68.60% Y forms. Compared to this, the Histories and Tragedies show a much higher incidence of T forms with 46.40% T forms and 53.60% Y forms in the Histories, and 48.50% T forms and 51.50% Y forms in the Tragedies, thus underpinning the results on genre difference in pronoun usage as established earlier on (cf. Chapter 3).

While on the one hand it is true that T pronouns hardly ever, if at all, occur in the company of titles such as *sir, my liege,* where the social distance first necessitates the use of the appropriate title, and which in turn almost automatically triggers the polite pronoun, these cases of deference do indeed not add to the politeness of an utterance. However, it is not true to say that the choice of pronoun is totally predictable, as Brown and Gilman (1989) claim it to be, because there are quite a number of cases where there is a meaningful choice to be made, when the pronoun is not dictated by decorum and/or the elevated social position of the addressee. The husband–wife relationship is a good case in point, providing evidence that even in asymmetrical power relationships there is space for social negotiation as expressed by pronouns. Another case that runs counter to power and solidarity semantics is the frequent use of *you* with abusive vocatives, when for instance masters find fault in their servants and address them as *you rascal* or *you knave.* These cases of unequal power relationships (cf. Chapter 2.3, Table 1), which according to Brown and Gilman's theory should result in non-reciprocal T forms, prove that such generalisations on pronoun use are oversimplistic.

As regards the meta-level of methodology, this result strengthens the viewpoint of Mazzon (1995) and others that Brown and Gilman's dismissal of pronouns for the evaluation of the politeness of a speech is not justified, excepting of course the clear-cut cases as outlined above.

A comparison to non-literary text types of the Helsinki Corpus has further shown that, excepting Autobiography, T forms have led only a very marginal existence from as early as 1500 onwards. This reveals that fiction, and especially drama, features forms that have become old-fashioned or archaic elsewhere, thus, supporting Hope's results from his investigation of depositions. He has found that in court records *thou* is clearly the marked form as early as the 1560s and his dictum "that Shakespeare's dramatic usage, if it bears any relation to 'real' Early Modern [English] usage at all, preserves modes of usage which have long disappeared from everyday speech" (1994a: 148) is of considerable importance for the evaluation and interpretation of Shakespearean and other Elizabethan drama.

The difference between historical sociolinguistics and 'modern' sociolinguistics is that in the first discipline the outcome is known but not in the latter, because the phenomena under observation are still going on. Even though the change of the English pronoun paradigm from 1300 to 1700 can be summarised in a few words, the investigation has shown that the concept of markedness can be applied to explain actualization of linguistic change as a diachronic process, but in addition to this, by making a synchronic cut around 1600, the concept can also be brought to fruition in constructing a typology of texts. That is to say by making a link between a statistically more or less probable form (*thou*) and its stylistic value as the marked term in the dyad, the following text typology in terms of '*thou*fulness' can be arrived at:

- In authentic texts (depositions) *thou* is the numerically less frequent and stylistically marked form as early as the 1560s (cf. Hope 1994a). Hope's findings are supported by those of Taavitsainen (1997a). She has found that, excepting Fiction and to a lesser extent also Autobiography, *thou* only plays a marginal role in other non-fictional text types from 1500 onwards.
- In Shakespearean drama the History Plays and the Tragedies are the most '*thou*ful' plays; in the Comedies *you* is more frequent.
- As concerns their distribution in the media of verse and prose, *thou* predominates in verse and *you* in prose.
- This distribution has been confirmed for poetry as an elevated register, which in comparison to drama shows the highest incidence of T forms.
- Within the genre of poetry, there exists a cline from formal 'truly written' and more private poems, preferring *thou* to 'more oral', public poems, which prefer *you*.

In contrast to all the previous extralinguistic factors which were found to be of importance for the variation of *thou* and *you*, no firm evidence for an intralinguistic conditioning of the variation could be proved empirically. The putative influence of grammar on the choice of *thou* and *you* has been upheld repeatedly, as for example by Abbott ([1870] 1972), Mulholland (1967) and Barber (1981), but was refuted by Kiełkiewicz-Janoviak (1994). It could also not be confirmed in a pilot study on the basis of eight Shakespearean plays. If the selection is representative for the corpus as a whole, then the above-mentioned claim of the earlier research that syntactic distribution could perhaps influence the choice of pronouns to a certain degree and that *thou* is used more often as subject of closed-class verbs in statements and questions and, accordingly, *you* for lexical verbs has not been corroborated by the larger set of data. This result has led me, together with Kiełkiewicz-Janoviak, to the conclusion that there is hardly any evidence for an intralinguistic conditioning of the pronoun variation between *thou* and *you*.

11.2   *Prithee* and *pray you* as discourse markers

In addition to *thou* and *you* (including their variants) the cliticised form *prithee* and *(I) pray (you/thee)* have also been investigated in order to scrutinise in how far the process of grammaticalization had progressed around 1600 and which communicative function(s) the variants perform in the Shakespeare Corpus. The second question can be answered straight away, because the forms are primarily used as discourse markers in polite requests, including optatives, and to a lesser degree interrogatives. They carry out textual and interpersonal tasks. Especially in the Comedies, and in some of the History Plays (the Falstaff plays), they are used frequently with interjections and other pragmatic particles to express colloquiality and verisimilitude.

The full form *I pray you* is still the most frequent one in the corpus. The contracted forms *pray you* and *pray*, which, according to the OED, are frequently attested from the 17th to the 19th century are not very numerous. The cliticised forms *prithee* and *I prithee*, on the other hand, are used more often than the full forms *I pray thee* and *pray thee*.

As regards these variants, corpus-internal variation can be observed, as *(I) pray thee* is more frequent in the first half of the corpus up to 1600. Its absence from many of the later plays allows for the conclusion that *prithee* has subsequently taken the place of *(I) pray thee*.

The co-existence of different forms ranging from the full form with subject and object (*I pray you/thee*), to shortened forms featuring either subject or object (*I pray*, *pray you/thee*), to single *pray* and cliticised *prithee* illustrates the process of ongoing grammaticalization. What all of these co-existing forms have in common though is their function as parenthetical disjuncts to signal politeness or urgency, especially in requests and questions. In a number of cases *prithee* occurs next to *you*. This also adds to its routinization as a discourse particle. However, the fact that the original religious meaning of the verb 'to pray' still persists in the corpus proves that the relationship of the grammaticalized forms to their previous history has not yet become opaque by the stage of morphologization.

In terms of politeness the variants *pray* and *prithee* differ in degree rather than in kind, as Brown and Gilman (1989) assume, because the array of co-occurring verbs and, though to a lesser extent, the co-occurring vocatives, show a good deal of overlap.

In the Shakespeare Corpus requests involving *pray/prithee* are less polite than those with *please*. Interestingly enough, *please* used on its own did not exist in Shakespeare's time, it only occurred in longer constructions such as *if it please you* or *if you please*. In the course of the 17th century constructions with *pray* and *prithee* became obsolete and gave way to single *please*. As the loss of *thou* and *thee* cannot explain the loss of single *pray* other explanations must be provided. The comparison of *pray* and *please* has led me to the assumption that a more deep-rooted change in politeness strategies has taken place in the language from requests that assert the sincerity of the speaker *(prithee/(I) pray (you/thee)* to those asking for the willingness of the listener *(please)* to perform the request.

11.3 The development of *thy* and *thine*

The investigation of the factors that govern the distribution of the variants *thy* and *thine* has brought about the following results: in the Shakespeare Corpus *thy* with its 4,360 tokens is much more numerous than *thine* with only 498 tokens. This huge discrepancy of a ratio of 9:1 not withstanding, their distribution in the two dramatic media of verse and prose is almost identical.

The two forms show a functional overlap in their attributive use as determiners before nouns, where 230 tokens of *thine* (54.50%) occur adjectivally before vowels as opposed to only 269 of *thy* (6.91%). The strongest lexical association exists between *thine* and *own*, which has almost become a fixed expression, as there are only nine tokens of *thy own* to be found in the entire corpus.

In contrast to the statement often made in reference works that *thine* is also frequent before ⟨h⟩, my corpus analysis for the plays has revealed that there are only 19 tokens of thine + ⟨h⟩ (5.31%) as opposed to 339 tokens of *thy* + ⟨h⟩ (94.69%). When compared to the total occurrences of the two pronouns, *thy* is about twice as frequent before ⟨h⟩ as *thine*, because the 339 *thy*-tokens make up 8.71% of its total occurrences as opposed to only 4.50% of *thine*. The collocates of *thine* + ⟨h⟩ are restricted to a small number of Romance loanwords like *thine honor*.

With 58% and 56% respectively, the Histories and Comedies feature *thy* + vowel more strongly than the Tragedies with only 49%, but these usage differences between the dramatic genres are not large enough in terms of statistical significance to warrant further investigation. However, if Shakespeare's non-dramatic works are incorporated, *thine* with 57% has a greater frequency in the more formal text type(s) of poems than in drama with only 43%. The finding that drama favours *thy* in comparison to non-dramatic verse could be due to the fact that drama is a speech-based genre that reflects currant usage more accurately than poetry, with its more archaic forms of language. This result ties in with the diachronic findings of Schendl (1997) that *my* and *thy* occur with greater frequency in less formal text types from the second half of the 16th century onwards.

Barber's (1997) statement that by 1600 both forms are in free variation could not be corroborated by the corpus investigation, because a meaningful choice is being made for stylistic reasons, in particular emphasis and rhetorical figures.

As regards the actualization pattern of the change it can be said that the ME phonological distinction between *thy* and *thine* has been reinterpreted in the course of time as a grammatical distinction paralleled by one in terms of formality, which eventually resulted in a markedness reversal with *thine* becoming the statistically less frequent form in 'ordinary' language. In the Shakespeare Corpus *thine* shows clear tendencies of fossilization, as its occurrences become limited to combinations like *thine own* or *thine honour*. In the course of the 17th century this leads to its relegation to the higher literary registers of poetry. Thus, in contrast to the variation between *thou* and *you*, sociolinguistic reasons do not play an important role, but over time intralinguistic factors (phonological patterning) give way to various extra-linguistic ones, for example, textual conventions.

11.4 The development of *ye* and *you*

In comparison to the other variant forms *ye* leads the most marginal existence in the Shakespeare Corpus. When all instances in the 38 plays are taken together, there are — depending on the database — not more than 362 in the OES or 343 in Spevack. Put in relation to the number of 22,400 *you* forms in the corpus this results in a ratio of about 1:61 or 1:64, respectively. This shows that the replacing of *ye* by *you* had peaked earlier on and was nearing its final stages at around 1600. This develop-ment could indeed be proved by a diachronic investigation of ancillary corpora for drama and non-literary text types. In the drama corpus of Bock (1938) the shift from *ye* to *you* in subject position takes place in the 16th century, as *ye* decreases drastically from the 1560s onwards and does not play an important role after 1600. In Mitchell's (1971) drama corpus, however, *ye* tokens occur well into the 18th century, but only in a few fossilised constructions involving the verbs *hark* and *look*.

The importance of text types (and their textual and social conventions) in the diffusion of the change from *ye* to *you* in subject position is underlined by the evidence from the CEEC, as there are no instances of *ye* in this function from the second half of the 16th century onwards. All sociolinguistic differences in usage observed half a century earlier have been levelled out. In terms of sociolinguistic variables the change from *you* to *ye* as subject pronoun has been initiated by the lower gentry and the merchants, who favour *you* in this position while the nobility and the lower classes lag behind in the change.

At least to a certain extent these variable rules also apply to the use of *ye* in the Shakespeare Corpus because there the *ye* users also belong to the two extreme poles of the social scale, as predominantly persons of some social standing or outsiders make use of the form.

Apart from the social patterning, the distribution of the form again seems to be conditioned by genre and medium, because the *ye* tokens have a higher incidence in History and Tragedy than in Comedy and occur predominantly in the context of verse. This distribution validates the correlation between marked forms and marked text types as pronounced earlier on for the distribution of *thou* and *you*. In Tragedy and History *ye* occurs mainly in exclamations, where it serves as a continuation of the singular *thou/thee* in direct address to supernatural beings in apostrophe. Apart from exclamations, *ye* is syntactically frequent in imperatives, that is to say in post-verbal position with verbs to summon attention such as *hark ye* and *look ye*. With the fixation of SVO word order this ambiguous syntactic environment, which in the singular involves either *thou* or *thee* (depending upon the type of verb) is prone to variation and change and might in the long run have added to the confusion of forms. From 1500 onwards this position is reserved for the object. Cross-over analogy to the frequent greeting formula *fare thee well* or other optatives may have added to this.

In summary it can be said that *ye* began to lose ground to *you* in post-verbal position from the fourteenth century onward. So the syntactic position together with pronunciation in unstressed position and cross-over analogy with *thee* may have been responsible for the change from *ye* to *you*. Language use at the turn from the sixteenth to the seventeenth century as represented in the Shakespeare Corpus shows that the few instances in which *ye* still occurs in the language syntactically belong to the domain from where the process started. In exclamatives it is mostly used as a plural pronoun in continuation of single *thou* to address gods or other supernatural beings in apostrophe. Lexically, it becomes more and more restricted as an enclitic in attention-seeking verbs such as *hark* and *look,* and on the discourse level it is affectively marked in comparison to *you* and is thus relegated to elevated registers. In the diachronic perspective this seems to suggest that the primary reason for the change from *ye* to *you* may have been a syntactic one, which once it was almost completed in the Elizabethan period could purposefully be exploited for discourse purposes, as Shakespeare's contemporaries would certainly have sensed the archaising air of the pronoun in the contexts dealt with above.

Appendix
Mitchell's *Corpus of British Drama* (1580–1780)

The corpus comprises the following plays (cf. Mitchell 1971:7–11):

Period I: 1580–1630 (16 plays)
Christopher Marlowe (1563/4–1593)
    The Tragicall History of Dr. Faustus, c. 1589
    The Jew of Malta, c. 1591
William Shakespeare (1564–1616)
    The First Part of King Henry the Sixth, c.1590–92
    The Tragedy of King Richard the Third, c.1593–94
    The Tragedy of King Richard the Second, c.1594–96
    The First Part of King Henry the Fourth, c. 1597–98
    The Life of King Henry the Fifth, c. 1598
    Julius Caesar, c. 1598–99
    Hamlet, 1600
    Twelfth Night, 1602
    King Lear, 1603
    The Tempest, c. 1610–11
Ben Jonson (1572/3–1637)
    Every Man in His Humour, 1598
    Volpone, c. 1605–06
John Ford (c. 1586–c. 1640)
    The Broken Heart, c. 1625
    Perkin Warbeck, c. 1629

Period II: 1630–1680 (15 plays)
James Shirley (1596–1666)
    The Traitor, 1631
    The Cardinal, 1641
William Davenant (D'Avenant) (1606–1668)
    Love and Honour, 1634
    The Wits, 1634
Roger Boyle (1621–1679)
    Mustapha, 1665
    The Black Prince, 1667

John Dryden (1631–1700)
 The Conquest of Granada by the Spaniards, Part I, 1670
 All for Love, 1677
Sir George Etheredge (1635/6–1691)
 She Wou'd if She Cou'd, 1668
 The Man of Mode, 1676
William Wycherley (1640?–1716)
 The Plain Dealer, 1676
Thomas Shadwell (1642?–1692)
 The Sullen Lovers, 1668
 The Virtuoso, 1676
Nathaniel Lee (1652?–1692)
 The Rival Queens, 1677
 Lucius Junius Brutus, 1680

Period III: 1680–1730 (15 plays)
Thomas Otway (1652–1685)
 The Orphan, 1680
 Venice Preserved, 1682
Thomas Southerne (1660–1746)
 Oroonoko, 1696
Sir John Vanbrugh (1664–1726)
 The Relapse, 1696
 The Provok'd Wife, 1697
Wiliam Congreve (1670–1729)
 Love for Love, 1695
 The Way of the World, 1700
Colley Cibber (1671–1757)
 Love's Last Shift, 1669
 The Careless Husband, 1704
Sir Richard Steele (1672–1729)
 The Tender Husband, 1705
 The Conscious Lovers, 1722
Nicholas Rowe (1674–1718)
 The Fair Penitent, 1703
 The Tragedy of Jane Shore, 1714
George Farquhar (1678–1707)
 The Recruiting Officer, 1706
 The Beaux-Stratagem, 1707

Period IV: 1730–1780 (16 plays)
George Lillo (1693–1739)
 The London Merchant, 1731
 Fatal Curiosity, 1736

Henry Fielding (1704–1754)
Tom Thumb, A Tragedy, 1730
The Autor's Farce, 1730
Edward Moore (1711/12–1757)
The Foundling, 1748
The Gamester, 1753
David Garrick (1717–1779)
The Lying Valet, 1741
Harlequin's Invasion, 1759
John Home (1722–1808)
Douglas, 1756
Oliver Goldsmith (1728–1774)
The Good-Natur'd Man, 1768
She Stoops to Conquer, 1773
George Colman, the elder (1732–1794)
The Jealous Wife, 1761
Richard Cumberland (1732–1811)
The Brothers, 1769
The West Indian, 1771
Richard Brinsley Butler Sheridan (1751–1816)
The Rivals, 1775
The School for Scandal, 1777

Notes

Chapter 1: General introduction

1. A detailed outline of the *Helsinki Corpus* can be found in Rissanen et al. (1993), or in Kytö (1996).

2. Cf. Nevalainen and Raumolin-Brunberg (1996b: 39–54).

3. Cf. Schmied (1994: 81–89).

4. Cf. Biber et al. (1994: 1–13).

5. The three EModE subcorpora of the Helsinki Corpus include excerpts of the following six comedies, i.e. Nicolas Udall, *Roister Doister*, William Stevenson (?), *Gammer Gvrton's nedle* (EModE I); William Shakespeare, *The Merry Wives of Windsor*, Thomas Middleton, *A Chaste Maid in Cheapside* (EModE II), John Vanbrugh, *The Relapse*, George Farquhar, *The Beaux Stratagem* (EModE III); cf. Kytö (1996: 14–17).

6. On the basis of this corpus Walker is working on a Ph. D. thesis on the topic of second-person singular pronouns (cf. Walker [1999]).

7. For a more detailed appraisal of the concept for the treatment of personal pronouns in the Shakespeare Corpus see Chapters 2.6 and 2.7.

8. For a discussion of intra- and extralinguistic reasons for this periodisation and also for alternative dates see Görlach (1994: 8f.).

9. The inventory OE, ME and ModE pronoun forms can be looked up in Howe's tables (1996: 131ff., 138, 167).

10. For a concise historical account on the development of the personal pronouns in English, including other Germanic languages as well, see Howe (1996). Finkenstaedt (1963) provides a classic, book-length treatment of the development of the two pronouns from the OE period to the final loss of *thou* from a sociolinguistic perspective with a rich documentation from various primary sources, such as literature, letters, trial records, etc. For present-day English see Wales (1996), who pays attention to "regional, social, generic, stylistic and situational diversity of present-day English pronominal usage, which a conventional grammar-book fails to achieve" (1996: xiii).

11. For the principles of diachronic variation analysis cf. Weinreich et al. (1968), Romaine (1982), Rissanen (1986) and Sankoff (1988).

12. On the use of *me* and *your* in the sense of ethical datives in the Shakespeare Corpus see Gillet (1974).

13. For the sake of readability the abbreviations in the citations from the OED have been replaced by their full forms.

14. The two different functions of *your* have been noted as early as Abbott ([1870] 1972: 148) and Schmidt and Sarrazin ([1874/75] 1962: 1408), who list a number of quotations, as does Leisi (1997: 200f.): "Volkstümlich wird *your* oft gebraucht im Sinne von 'was wir kennen', so'n'; z.B.

your French-crown-colour beard 'so'n goldfarbiger Bart', Mids.N.D. I 2 93." However, Wales is right in concluding that this use has so far been treated rather perfunctorily. For further references see Wales (1985:7).

15. If not mentioned otherwise, all line references to Shakespeare's works in this book are based on *The Riverside Shakespeare* (2nd ed. 1997). Those taken over from quotations of other authors have for the sake of consistency and retrievability been adapted to this standard.

16. Rissanen (1986:107) notes that the concept of the *variant field* is not completely identical with that of the *variable* because it stresses the elements included in it.

17. Sankoff draws the conclusion that if the above-mentioned factors obtain, "then it is appropriate to invoke the statistical notions and methods known [...] as *variable rules*" (1988:984). However, the status of variable rules is by no means undisputed in sociolinguistics: "Many introductory books in sociolinguistics put the variable rule forward as an important concept or device, but it turns out that a handbook of sociolinguistics almost ignores its existence (cf. Coulmas 1997)" (van Hout 1998:1).

18. For more information on the design and use of non-commercial diachronic corpora in the study of English language history cf. Kytö et al. (1994), Hickey et al. (1997) and also several issues of the *ICAME* [International Computer Archive of Modern and Medieval English] *Journal*. For Shakespeare studies there are two commercial corpora available, i.e. *The Oxford Electronic Shakespeare* and H. Joachim Neuhaus' *Shakespeare Database* published at Olms Publishing house, Hildesheim. Chadwick-Healey Publishers also offer large diachronic corpora on drama, poetry, etc.: *literature online: the home of English and American Literature on the World Wide Web*. URL: http://lion.chadwyck.co.uk.

19. When I began this project, H. Joachim Neuhaus' Shakespeare database on CD-ROM announced for April 1996 was not yet available, so that I decided to work with the Spevack concordances and the *Oxford Electronic Shakespeare*, which proved difficult at times: because of textual differences they cannot be used alongside each other.

20. The relationship between the language of EModE drama and 'authentic language' is discussed in Chapter 2.5.

21. For a brief history see Svartvik (1992:7–13) and McEnery and Wilson (1996:1–19).

22. Cf. Hope (1994b), who uses some of these parameters in his sociolinguistic authorship study of Shakespeare's plays. Stein in his analysis of inflections in the Shakespeare Corpus comes to the conclusion that for instance *does/doth* are much less sensitive to influences of textual transmission than are *has/hath* (cf. 1974:108).

23. For a recent and succinct account on socio-historical linguistics (Romaine 1982) or historical sociolinguistics (Milroy 1992) see Raumolin-Brunberg (1996a:11–37). In Nevalainen's opinion (1996a:5) despite Romaine's (1982) programmatic title *Socio-historical linguistics* the weight of her study "was clearly more linguistic than sociohistorical", whereas "the weight in Milroy's falls on sociolinguistics rather than history." Görlach truly emphasises that prior to the studies of Romaine (1982), Tieken-Boon van Ostade (1987) and Devitt (1989), all of which claim the title of *socio-historical linguistics*, "much of the best tradition of historical linguistics has always taken the social and political realities of earlier stages of the language into account. In this respect, books like Wyld (1936), Horn & Lehnert (1954) and Jespersen (1909–49) are relevant to our topic" (1999b:470).

24. For recent sociolinguistic approaches to linguistic variation in post-modern societies see Henn-Memmesheimer (1998:VII–XVII).

Chapter 2: Previous research on the use of personal pronouns in Early Modern English with special reference to Shakespeare's plays

1. For a detailed appreciation and criticism of the various stages of the model of Brown, Gilman and Ford cf. Kendall (1981) and also Braun (1984: 41–72 and 1988: 7–67). Hope (1994b: 58) argues that Brown and Levinson (1987: 45) have found out that singularisation of plural pronouns as a means to express unequal power relationship is a feature common to many unrelated languages and that "this refutes the claim that T/V systems in European languages can be explained by a common Latin source." However, the universality of the phenomenon does not simply rule out the strong likelihood that the English set-up can be explained historically as going back to the cultural and linguistic influence of Latin and courtly French.

2. For more work carried out on the gender variable in the Shakespeare Corpus see Mulholland (1967), Mazzon (1992, 1995) and B. Busse (1997).

3. For a more detailed discussion of the reasons leading to the ultimate loss of *thou* cf. Finkenstaedt (1963: 214–231).

4. For a brief introduction to Brown and Levinson's politeness theory cf. Short (1996: 211–217), Simpson (1997: 155–164) and also Rudanko (1993: 161–167), who additionally draws attention to the differences in substrategies of negative and positive politeness between the theories as expounded by Brown and Levinson (1987) and Brown and Gilman (1989).

5. Kopytko (1995) provides a summary of his monograph (1993a) which leaves out the (meta-) theoretical background on pragmatics and his criticism of Brown and Levinson (1987), but which includes all the major empirical findings of his study.

6. Depending upon the context, *mistress* can be used in the sense of "a term of courtesy used in speaking of or to women (except those of high rank)" or in the sense of "used with some unkindness or contempt of or to women, from whom the affections of the speaker have been estranged" (Schmidt and Sarrazin 1962).

7. Culpeper mentions that "verbal violence is a characteristic of recent twentieth-century drama and film" (1998: 87) due to theatrical censorship beginning in the reign of Henry VIII and which, among other things, has led in the 19th century to "the eponymous Thomas Bowdler's *Family Shakespeare*, a cleaned-up version of Shakespeare's plays fit for the Victorian family" (88). For the Elizabethan stage these restrictions did not apply, as the numerous terms of abuse (cf. Chapter 6) amply illustrate.

8. David Reibel (personal communication) notes that the archaic grammatical usage in the *Authorized Version* of the English Bible of 1611 is not just accidental, but a tribute to the grammatical acumen of its compilers and revisers, as they gave close attention to the solutions of their predecessors in translating Hebrew and Greek idiomatic and grammatical peculiarities into English.

9. For a general discussion of the term *markedness* and its various meanings and usages over the past 150 years cf. Andersen (1989, 2001) and Gvozdanović (1989: 47–66) and also Chapter 4. Stein (forthc.) mentions that the distinction between *marked* and *unmarked* was first applied to *thou* and *you* by Quirk in 1959.

10. For a comment on the subtle shifts in pronominal address in LR 1, 1 cf. also McIntosh (1963b).

11. Calvo (1992a) has provided an interesting re-appraisal of AYL taking McIntosh's (1963a) study as a starting point.

12. For Elizabethan soliloquies and those of Shakespeare in particular cf. Muir (1964), Carson (1976) and Clemen (1987).

13. Spies (1897:114–121) gives an account of pronominal usage to religious figures, people in discourse, abuse, and address to inanimate objects, cf. also Barber (1997:154).

14. Stidson (1917:79) mentions that 14th century texts consistently make use of *thou* in addresses to swords, love, souls and ghosts.

Chapter 3: *Thou* and *you*

1. The concordances are based on the *Riverside Shakespeare* (1974), which generally takes the *First Folio* (1623) as its major copy-text, but includes some readings from the Quarto editions for certain plays. Emendations and additions to the copy-text are added in square brackets. As the computer that produced the concordances was not able to print these square brackets they appear as slashes before the respective word-form. "The slash [in front of a word-form] represents square brackets [...], the indication of an editorial alteration of the basic copy-texts [...]. Words with slashes are listed separately, immediately preceding the same words without slashes, where such cases exist. As far as the statistics are concerned, words with slashes are always added to the total number of words but are added to the number of different words only when the same words without slashes are not present" (Spevack 1968:ix).

2. The two plays H8 and TNK also show an unusual use of the pronoun *ye*, which also points towards a collaboration with Fletcher (cf. Chapter 10.3.8).

3. Hope (1994b) has carried out two pilot studies which are made up of six plays by Shakespeare and also six plays by Fletcher. The results are then compared to the whole of Shakespeare's plays (59–62). In his numerical analysis, which is supplemented by a qualitative assessment of "values for relationship by sex of speaker/addressed" (61), he comes to the conclusion that "the comparison samples overlap in their ranges (38–70 per cent for Shakespeare and 55–78 per cent for Fletcher), [...] [and] that factors other than the social or biographical ones [...] are affecting the choices made by Shakespeare and Fletcher" (59). From this disconcerting evidence he concludes that "any attempt to use T/V choice as evidence for authorship is therefore bound to be highly speculative, because it is impossible to allow for stylistic patterning of the variants. Unfortunately therefore, T/V choice has only a minor role to play in authorship studies" (64). Auxiliary *do* and the relative markers were found to have a much better predictive force for dubious authorship.

4. Due to the fact that Mitchell's dissertation is only available on University microfilms, the authors and plays that constitute her corpus are cited in full in the appendix at the end of the book; cf. pp. 293–295.

5. For a detailed analysis of the considerable vacillation of pronoun use that is to be found between authors in all of the four periods cf. Mitchell's table p. 55.

6. For the full inventory of texts analysed by her, cf. Johnson (1966:263).

7. Labov (1994:78) defines the terms *above* and *below* to "refer here simultaneously to levels of social awareness and positions in the socio-economic hierarchy. *Changes from above* are introduced by the dominant social class, often with full public awareness. [...] *Changes from below* are systematic changes that appear first in the vernacular, and represent the operation of internal, linguistic factors. At the outset, and through most of their development, they are completely below the level of social awareness."

8. For a definition of the terms *genre, text type* and *personal affect* cf. Taavitsainen (1997a: 185–202).

9. For the study the following comedies were analysed: Period I (1560–1600): Peele, *The Old VVives Tale* (1595), Warner, *Menaecmi* (1595), Chapman, *A Humorous Dayes Mirth* (1599). Period II (1680–1720): Manley, *The Lost Lover* (1696), Farquhar, *The Beaux Stratagem* (1707) and Killigrew, *Chit-Chat* (1719).

10. Stein (1987) — or in greater detail (1974) — in his study of *-s/-th* variants for the third person singular inflection has also found a corpus-internal development in the Shakespeare Corpus. He reports a sudden change from *-th* to *-s* between 1590 and 1610 in the Shakespeare Corpus "in such a systematic way that the effect of textual history in creating these patterns can be ruled out" (1987: 414) and assumes that this development, which is not confined to Shakespeare as the impressive data gleaned from Bambas (1947) suggest, is "an abrupt catching up with the state of the spoken language. We must assume that *th* was a feature of the literary written variety only" (429). Stein adds that his findings corroborate research on other aspects of Shakespeare's language, as e.g. Clemen (1951) has marked a change in imagery and Voitl (1969: 152–163) has noted a change in word formation patterns, finding a caesura from the plays H5, TN and JC onwards.

More recently, another study has confirmed this divide. Ilsemann has investigated the kind of reply a character gives according to 29 categories such as length, number of words, etc. (cf. 1998: 263–264) in order to derive a typology of text types and has come to the conclusion that the length of replies in the plays written before 1599 amounts to eight to ten words, and from the opening of the Globe Theatre onwards it decreases to an average of four or five.

The results of these scholars, who report decisive changes in the corpus, confirm Stein's (1987: 429) statement "that the morphological divides within the corpus correlate with changes in other, unrelated areas seems another argument against the role of factors of textual history and rather points to an overall change in the tools of Shakespeare's artistry" or perhaps rather to a growing ability to capture ongoing linguistic change.

11. "Leaving aside *Troilus and Cressida, Julius Caesar* and *Henry IV, Part 2*, we have shown that it is possible to discriminate for genre by means of personal pronouns at all levels of comparison" (Brainerd 1979: 12).

12. In the graphs the disputed plays PER, H8 and TNK have been left out, and also TRO, which does not really fit into either Comedy or Tragedy.

Chapter 4: The distribution of *thou* and *you* and their variants in verse and prose

1. Throughout this chapter, the term *significant* is used in the restricted sense of 'statistically significant'.

2. The complete titles of the two parts in the Quarto editions are as follows (cf. Chambers 1930: 376, 378):

> *The History of Henrie the Fourth;*
> *With the battell at Shrewsburie, betweene the King and Lord*
> *Henry Purcy, surnamed Henrie Hotspur of the North. With*
> *the humorous conceits of Sir Iohn Falstaffe*
> and

The Second part of Henrie the fourth, continuing to his death,
and the coronation of Henrie the fift. With the humours of sir Iohn
Falstaffe, and swaggering Pistoll.

3. With the help of the chi-square test the difference between the theoretical distribution that would obtain if the two categories were spread purely by chance throughout a play and their real frequency can be calculated. The null hypothesis assumes that a given distribution is merely a product of chance. The test tells us something about the probability of a deviation. If there is a high probability the deviation is not significant and the null hypothesis cannot be refuted. If, on the other hand, the result of the test is extremely unlikely, then this cannot be the product of chance and for this reason stylistic etc. conclusions may be drawn with various degrees of confidence. Depending on the degrees of freedom (df), the result of the chi-square test can be looked up in statistical tables. In statistics a result is traditionally said to be significant if there is less than one chance in 20 of obtaining the result given the null hypothesis. One chance in 20 corresponds to a probability of 0.05 and is normally referred to as the 0.05 or 5% level of significance. For example, a result at the 0.02 level of significance means that we stand two chances in 100 to obtain this theoretical result and consequently two chances of error if we refute the null hypothesis and claim that the detected phenomenon is real. In cases like this we may then confidently assume that the result is statistically highly significant. A detailed and instructive description of the chi-square test can be found in Muller (1972:53–55, 114–125) and in Rietveld and van Hout (1993:111–124).

4. In addition to the plural tokens of *you* the tokens of *your* in its indefinite sense of 'that you know of' (1, 2, 93–96 and 3, 1, 32) have also been excluded.

5. For the use and function of verse and prose in ADO see also Morgan (1971) and Barish (1974).

6. Even though Beatrice and Benedick may be said to be at the centre of interest, in terms of textual genesis their story has to be regarded as the subplot.

Chapter 5: "A woman's face with Nature's own hand painted / Hast thou, the master mistress of my passion"

1. For a previous version of this chapter cf. Busse (2001)

2. For the application of the concept of markedness to address pronouns in Shakespeare's plays see Chapter 2.6.

3. The dates of composition have been taken from Evans and Tobin (1997:77–87); cf. also Schabert (1992:641–677). For the sonnets Evans and Tobin say that "the date span here suggested reflects the great range of critical opinion [...]. Minority views would either push the dating back into the middle 1580's for some of the sonnets or see other sonnets as late as 1609 [...]. Some of the sonnets [...] were in existence by 1598" (79). This is also confirmed by Schabert (1992:642).

4. "Wenn der 'Elizabethan Fowler' des *you* und *thou* tatsächlich existiert und Shakespeare verwendet die Pronomen ihm entgegengesetzt, dann muß er das seinen Lesern eindeutig mitteilen. Man wende nicht ein, die Sonette seien selbst diese Mitteilung; sie wäre zumindest arg versteckt, und bis 1958 unentschlüsselt geblieben! [...] Vielleicht greift jemand anders das Problem der Pronomenverteilung im Gedicht noch einmal unabhängig auf?" (Finkenstaedt 1963:167). It should be noted, however, that the prescriptive nature of a Fowler would probably disqualify it as a possible guide to Elizabethan syntax.

5. As the ordering of Shakespeare's sonnets is by no means authoritative, it could also be argued with some justification whether pronoun switching really illustrates a process of change, or whether these sonnets despite being thematically related should rather be regarded as independent entities.

6. In his plays Shakespeare does not use *ye* as an objective very often either. In more than two thirds of all cases (72.1%) he uses *ye* in its older function as subjective and only in less than one third of its instances (27.9%) as an objective (cf. Chapter 10.3.2.1).

Chapter 6: "You beastly knave, know you no reverence?"

1. A very much condensed version of this chapter appears in Taavitsainen and Jucker (eds) (forthc.). While this article provides all the major findings it presents only three specimens for the nominal forms of address.

2. No relation of mine. Beatrix Busse is a doctoral student at Osnabrück University.

3. Nevalainen and Raumolin-Brunberg (1995: 555) use the following categories:

1. Words denoting kinship and family ties,
2. names, both Christian and surnames,
3. words denoting social status,
4. professional titles and
5. "address phrases which contain no nominal headword at all, like the formal *trusty and well-beloved* and the deferential *right worshipful.*"

4. The method employed by Brown and Gilman (1989) to score politeness of verbs such as *beseech, pray* etc. by examining 100 random entries in Spevack's *Harvard Concordance to Shakespeare* (1973) does not capture all pronouns, because in many cases the context provided (one line of text) is not large enough. Thus a number of pronouns are missed. For example, Williams (1992: 92 f.) meets the same problems when he says that "Shakespeare uses the respectful *you* with *sirrah* sixty times in the same line and the seemingly more appropriate *thou* only fifteen times". This is exactly the number of tokens one gets when skimming through concordance lines in Spevack, but in fact there are 74 Y forms and 23 T forms when one looks at more than one concordance line. My approach of taking a single utterance as a starting point avoids this problem, but it does, admittedly, accommodate pronoun switching between interlocutors only as long as the vocative expression remains identical. Nonetheless, it has the advantage of being clearly definable. Otherwise it would by no means be clear how much context should be analysed to arrive at a more reliable result.

5. The assignment of the plays to the genres follows Spevack. If not noted otherwise, the "doubtful" plays have been included. In constrast to Chapter 3 a simpler tripartite model of genres has been adopted, since not all nominal forms of address occur in all plays, and especially with less frequent items a model of four or even five genres would have resulted in empty cells in the contingency tables.

6. *Goodman*: "Title accorded a yeoman, i.e. one below the rank of a gentleman. Hence *goodman boy* is a double-barrelled insult to Tybald" (*Riverside Shakespeare*). The use of *boy* can be regarded as an instance of "positive nastiness", and in particular of the substrategy "use markers denoting lack of identity and emphasizing difference of group" (cf. Rudanko 1993: 168).

7. *Goodman boy*: "A form of address intended to deflate a presumptuous youth" (*Riverside Shakespeare*).

8. "The appellation 'gossip' was appropriate wherever 'goodwife' was, and used in this way it carried none of the pejorative connotations with which we regard the term today, though it seems to indicate slightly more familiarity than 'goodwife'" (Replogle 1967:54).

9. Two additional Y pronouns occur, but have been omitted, because one is plural (HAM 2, 2, 86) and the other is not used for direct address (R3 4, 4, 475). One T pronoun was also left out (3H6 3, 3, 95) for the same reason.

10. On the use of adjectives in connection with vocatives see Stoll (1989:226–232). Breuer (1983:59f.) draws attention to the fact that attributes like *gentle* and *worthy* do not only denote character traits of the persons so described, but also refer or allude to their social rank. For the diachronic aspect of adjectives and participles used as intensifiers cf. Nevalainen and Raumolin-Brunberg (1995:554–558). Regarding their letter corpus they come to the conclusion that "the inventory [...] used as honorifics and terms of endearment is somewhat larger than that of nouns, and it is here that changes also took place during our period [1420–1680]" (556f.).

11. One token of *thou* in a love letter from Falstaff to Mistress Page (WIV 2, 1, 10), one token of *you* in a song (TN 2, 3, 39) and two instances of *thou* in a prayer to Venus (TNK 5, 1, 146; 169) have been left out because they are not given in direct address to an interlocutor.

12. *Minion*: "spoiled child" (*Riverside Shakespeare*).

13. The OED gives the following description: "1.a. A term of address used to men or boys, expressing contempt, reprimand, or assumption of authority on the part of the speaker; sometimes employed less seriously in addressing children. [1526–1855]. b. Used attributively with appellations or proper names. [1588–1860]. †2. Applied to women (seriously or in jest). *Obs.* [1604–1711]."

14. The numbers for the sense divisions have been added.

15. Replogle (1967:62–65) provides a quite detailed discussion of the term. She concludes: "I have found nothing to substantiate the common belief that 'sirrah' was, like 'fellow' proper only for those of the lowest orders. All evidence seems to show, rather, that the form was dependent upon a person's position *relative* to the speaker" (62).

16. The number of *you* forms has been divided through the number of *thou* forms and from the quotient the logarithm has been taken: log (Y:T). An even ratio of *you* and *thou* tokens results in a logarithm of 0. A logarithm of +1 indicates that the *you* forms are ten times more frequent than the *thou* forms, and a logarithm of −1 shows that the T forms are ten times as frequent as the Y forms. For the sake of graphic clearness, these results were then multiplied by 1,000 in graphs 1–8, which show the vocatives arranged in decreasing order of "*you*fulness".

17. The same also holds true for *sir*, which beside *lord* is the most frequent form of address in Shakespeare's plays. It has a total frequency of 2,613 tokens. A sample of 20 plays with 1,233 tokens of *sir* yielded only 28 instances of *thou*. As the case was so clear, a context-based investigation was considered too unwieldy and too poor in result. In this case it is rather more illuminating to investigate the social rank and the circumstances under which a character is addressed as *sir*, either seriously, ironically, etc. (cf. also Grannis 1990:113f.). Rudanko (1993:168) also draws attention to the use of *sir* in terms of nastiness: while it is usually a feature of negative politeness, "indicating deference, it may under certain circumstances become a marker of disrespect, not of respect".

18. The OED gives the following explanation: "[f. sir *n*. The additional syllable had probably no definite origin, though explained by Minsheu as the interj. *ah* or *ha*.]."

19. For a short historical outline of the title cf. Böhm (1936:32–35), the OED and also Replogle (1967:38f.).

20. When Falstaff talks with Bardolph about Shallow he refers somewhat ironically to his full title. "I'll through Gloucestershire, and there will I visit Master Robert Shallow, esquire. I have him already temp'ring between my finger and my thumb, and shortly will I seal with him" (2H4 4, 3, 128–131).

21. For the use of other military ranks as kinds of occupational titles see Stoll (1989: 166f.).

22. For the social position of bastards cf. Replogle (1967: 112–116).

23. The relationship of the younger brother(s) to the elder brother was oftentimes problematical, because the elder brothers were more privileged. "Recountings of the disadvantages of younger sons are legion" (Replogle 1967: 83).

24. Another possible explanation for the use of *thou* could be the early date of its composition.

25. In the Tragedies the exclamation O often introduces emotional imperatives and exclamatives, e.g. TRO 5, 6, 12; TIT 2, 3, 204, 233; 3, 1, 214; ROM 5, 3, 296; JC 4, 3, 233 and TNK 3, 6, 226.

26. If TNK, which was not entirely written by Shakespeare, with its 15 *you* tokens and 8 *thou* tokens is left out of the calculation, the chi-square value rises to 5.098 (2 df; $p > 0.10$).

27. In HAM 1, 2, 64 the King addresses Hamlet as: "But now, my cousin Hamlet, and my son", upon which Hamlet comments punningly in an aside: "A little more than kin, and less than kind." The *Riverside Shakespeare* glosses this passage as: "closer than a nephew, since you are my mother's husband; yet more distant than a son, too (and not well disposed to you)."

28. In the Tragedies TNK with its 53 instances accounts for most of the *cousin* tokens.

29. For the relationship between husband and wife and its linguistic reflexes cf. also Finkenstaedt (1963: 120–128) and Replogle (1967: 75f.)

30. For the use of *cousin* in the *Corpus of Early English Correspondence* cf. Nevalainen and Raumolin-Brunberg (1995: 572f.).

31. Stoll (1989: 206–208) gives practically the same four sense divisions.

32. In two cases *thou* is omitted, but represented in the inflectional ending of the verb: "What canst tell, boy?" and "How dost, my boy?" (LR 1, 5, 17 and 3, 2, 68).

33. *Goodman*: "The insult is most fitting, for Tybalt is acting like a goodman by showing his ignorance of polite behavior in trying to start a fight [...]" (Replogle 1967: 67).

34. Cf. footnote 6.

35. *Compellation*: "Addressing or calling upon any one; an address; the words addressed to any one" (OED).

36. "The prevalence of elaborate ritual formulae in common situations of daily life was a feature of Elizabethan culture [...]" (Salmon 1967: 41).

37. "I.e. in addressing the Hostess and Doll as 'gentlewomen'." (*Riverside Shakespeare*).

38. "An allusion to Sir John Oldcastle, the name that Shakespeare originally intended for Falstaff" (*Riverside Shakespeare*).

39. There is one further instance in TMP: Stefano: "*Coraggio*, bully-monster, *coraggio!*" (5, 1, 258).

40. The OED documents this sense with five quotations ranging from 1590 (MND) to 1876: "[3] b. Used (esp. *dial.*) as a term of endearment for a sweetheart, child, etc.; a darling."

41. Quirk (1974: 51) finds this use of *you* conspicuous: "in indicating a special feeling that Lear has for the girl he calls 'our joy', who has been, as France says, Lear's 'best object', the argument of his praise, the balm of his age, the best, the dearest".

42. The *Riverside Shakespeare* glosses this use as "rogue".

43. The OED is more precise, because it also draws attention to witchcraft: "2. A woman supposed to have dealings with Satan and the infernal world; a witch; sometimes, an infernally wicked woman. Now associated with 3. [...] 3. a. An ugly, repulsive old woman: often with implication of viciousness or maliciousness."

44. In the sense of "3. A low, mean, unprincipled or dishonest fellow; a rogue, knave, scamp", *rascal* is attested in the OED from 1586 onwards. Additionally, the term can be "used without serious implication of bad qualities, or as a mild term of reproof"; with a first citation dating from 1610.

45. Hamlet also calls fortune a strumpet: "Out, out, thou strumpet fortune!" (HAM 2, 2, 493). *Harlot* is even rarer. It occurs only 7 times in the entire corpus and appears once as an abusive vocative, viz.: Antipholus of Ephesus to Adriana, his wife: "Dissembling harlot, thou art false in all." (ERR 4, 4, 101). Leisi (1997:88) mentions that *harlot* can still be used for both sexes in Shakespeare's plays in the sense of "'nichtsnutziger Kerl', 'Lümmel'"; cf. COR 2, 2, 112 and WT 2, 3, 4.

46. *Precious varlet* in CYM 4, 2, 83 is glossed as "arrant knave" in the *Riverside Shakespeare*.

47. For the sake of consistency, the original line numberings have been changed to those given in the *Riverside Shakespeare*.

48. For the use "as a term of opprobrious address" the OED gives a first citation from 1303. b. "In descriptive use (Common from c. 1590)".

49. Stoll simply says that for women and girls *minion, strumpet, harlot, witch* and *hag* are very frequent and gives a number of unassorted citations for them (1989:219). However, corpus evidence reveals that abusive vocatives for females are in fact scanty.

50. Nevala (forthc.; Figure 1) presents a similar continuum based on Raumolin-Brunberg (1996c:171) ranging from negative politeness (*honorific terms* and *endearments*) via *other titles* and *family* to positive politeness represented by *nicknames*.

Chapter 7: "Prithee no more" vs. "Pray you, chuck, come hither"

1. Earlier versions of this chapter were given at the *X. International Conference on English Historical Linguistics*, Manchester, 21–26 August 1998 and at the *Anglistentag*, Erfurt, 1998; cf. Busse 1999. I would like to thank the participants for their valuable comments and remarks. Any remaining errors or oversights are, of course, my own.

2. For the sake of consistency and accessibility, the abbreviations and line references used in Schmidt and Sarrazin have been replaced by those based on Spevack, and the inflected forms of the verb *pray* represented by a dash in the original have been given in full. The letters indicating the different grammatical constructions are my addition.

3. My emphasis in this and all the following quotations.

4. Salmon (1967:62) describes *O monstrous* as an exclamation of annoyance. Exclamations containing "words and phrases with referential meaning, are usually oaths and asseverations. Oaths which name the Deity or his attributes, the Devil, or various diseases, share the vocative characteristic of lack of syntactic relationship to the remainder of the utterance. They are impulsive reactions to the situation or message which are difficult to classify, since they depend so much on context and intonation for their meaning."

5. A comparison to Taavitsainen (1997b) shows that the textual function of marking turn-taking has become obsolete from the Late Middle English Period to the Early Modern English Period. She ascribes this phenomenon to a rise in literacy, and resulting from this, changed reading habits and a wider reading public.

6. For an historical outline of *marry* cf. Fischer (1998), where he shows how *marry* developed from the religious domain to a discourse particle that is often used in asseverations and imprecations. For *well* see Jucker (1997).

7. "*La* is an indication of emphasis by the speaker on the message conveyed; its function is not now easy to understand [...]. The exclamation is characteristic of naive and stupid people, and may be identical with the form which is written *lor'* (= *lord*) in later literature" (Salmon 1967:62).

8. Manfred Görlach (personal communication) argues that it is questionable whether written language accurately represents these reduced forms; cf. e.g. German *bitt(e)schön* < [*ich*] *bitte(e)* [*Sie*] *schön*, which also no longer appears as a form inflected for person.

9. However, there is a clear emotional distinction between initial and final position, just as there is with vocatives. For vocatives Grannis states that "a vocative preceding an imperative indisputably lends it force", and that "a vocative at the end of an imperative or a question adds an intensifying element of appeal" (Grannis 1990: 114).

10. According to Quirk et al. "comment clauses are parenthetical disjuncts. They may occur initially, or medially, and thus generally have a separate tone unit. [...] Comment clauses are either content disjuncts that express the speakers' comments on the content of the matrix clause, or style disjuncts that convey the speakers' views on the way they are speaking" (1985:112f.).

11. For a detailed analysis of *methinks* cf. Palander-Collin (1997), and for the impersonal use of verbs in Shakespeare's plays see Kopytko, who states that "the language of Shakespeare possessed more than thirty verbs that could be used in impersonal constructions" (1988:42). The most frequent of them are *please, stand* and *methink/methought. Please* appears in the following constructions: ...*it please(s)*, conditional ... *if it please* or *so it please*, in a reduced form as *please* or *pleaseth* (cf. 49).

Another interesting point raised by Kopytko is the distribution of impersonal constructions according to genres. Unfortunately, the most frequent verbs such as *please* are not included, but apart from this, he has found that these constructions appear more frequently in the Histories than in the other genres (cf. 50). This ties in with my results on pronoun use (the highest score of T forms) and the use of *pray* in the older sense of 'pray God, heaven, etc.', which show that the genre of History seems to be less open to linguistic innovations than other genres.

12. A study to confirm this hypothesis is presently in preparation; cf. Busse forthc.

13. Although not exactly parallel to my findings, Kopytko (1993a: 110) has also noted a general change in pragmatic strategies from a prevalence of positive politeness strategies in the Elizabethan age to a "negative politeness culture" in modern British society.

Chapter 8: The role of grammar in the selection of *thou* or *you*

1. "In both statements and questions, it will be seen, *you* is more favoured with lexical verbs, and *thou* with closed verbs. The differences, however, are not statistically significant, being below the 90% confidence limit for statements, and below the 95% confidence limit for questions. If the figures for Richard III are added to Mulholland's figures for King Lear and Much Ado, the differences approach the significant level, being between 95% and 97.5% for both statements and questions" (Barber 1991:286). "For all three plays combined, chi-squared is 4.57 for the statements table, and 4.40 for the questions table. In each case there is one degree of freedom." (289, footnote).

2. As first and third person imperatives are not relevant to the choice of *you* and *thou*, I leave these results aside.

Chapter 9: "In thine own person answer thy abuse"

1. Grammatical treatments of possessive pronouns and their two functions are characterised by overlapping terminologies. According to Wales (1996: 169) the possessive pronouns are usually divided by their determiner and nominal functions. Other terms used by 20th century grammarians to characterise this distinction comprise *attributive* vs. *predicative, adjective* vs. *pronoun, dependent* vs. *independent,* or *determinative* vs. *independent.* Görlach, Brunner and others, for example, use the terms *attributive* (= determiner) and *predicative* (= nominal) which are usually used in conjunction with adjective declension.

2. Depending on their syntactic function, most adjectives had two distinctive endings and belonged to the weak or strong declension type.

3. For this reason "in traditional grammars the possessive forms were actually listed as the genitive case forms in tables which also gave the corresponding subjective and objective case forms, now regarded as the 'personal pronouns' proper. In having a 'genitive case', the personal pronouns would appear to confirm their noun-like status [...]. In the three-term case paradigm, however, the personal pronouns resemble the relative pronoun (*who/whom/whose*), which yet lacks a reflexive form" (Wales 1996: 169).

4. For a different opinion on the pronunciation of ⟨h⟩ cf. Luick (1964: §§729, 790f.).

5. The braces indicate optional variants.

6. For the sake of consistency and accessibility the abbreviations and line references used in Schmidt and Sarrazin have been replaced by those based on Spevack. In cases where only line references were given, the quotations have been supplied in full, but usually only one for each sense division. The letters indicating the different grammatical constructions are (mostly) my addition.

7. The tokens of *thine* + ⟨h⟩ constitute too small a sample for any hypothesis on genre differences beyond speculation.

8. For statistical tools to measure the strength of lexical associations see Church and Hanks (1990) and Biber et al. (1998: 265ff.)

9. A complete list of authors' names and titles is to be found in his article (1997: 183–184).

Chapter 10: "Stand, sir, and throw us that you have about ye"

1. This chapter is a revised, enlarged and updated version of a paper originally prepared for the annual conference of the *Gesellschaft für Angewandte Linguistik (GAL)* 1997 in Bielefeld (cf. Busse 1998b).

2. "In the earliest periods of English *ye* was restricted to the nom. pl. In the 13th c. it came to be used as a nom. sing. = 'thou', first as a respectful form addressed to a superior. This use survives in modern dialects, esp. (in the form *ee*) in interrog. and imperative formulæ (e.g. *Dee* = 'do ye'), but also in objective uses = 'thee' (e.g. *Oi tell ee*). When *you* had usurped the place of *ye* as a nom., *ye* came to be used (in the 15th c.), vice versa, as an objective sing. and pl. (='thee' and 'you'')." (OED s.v. *ye*).

"Between 1300 and 1400 it [*you*] began to be used also for the nominative ye, which it had replaced in general use by about 1600. During the 14th century it also appears as a substitute for the singular obj. thee and nom. thou [...]" (OED s.v. *you*).

3. Even the *Prayer Book* of Edward VI (1549) makes a clear-cut distinction between *ye* and *you* only in the "scriptural parts" and otherwise uses *you* frequently in the nominative (cf. Kenyon 1914:461ff., Finkenstaedt 1963:215).

4. Finkenstaedt (1963:215) points out that the two variant forms were recognised as early as Linacre (1525?) in his grammar *Linacri Progymnasmata Grammatices Vulgaria*: "and the words of the vocative in English be *thou, thee, you* and *ye.*"

5. For a more detailed description of grammars see Bock (1938:121–129) and Mitchell (1971:16–25).

6. PER was included because it does not show "abnormal" pronoun use; cf. also Hope (1994b:106–113).

7. For the address to the reader in the 16th and 17th centuries cf. also Finkenstaedt (1963:157f.).

8. For the authors and the plays selected cf. the appendix, page 293.

9. Apart from *ye/you* they report on the variables *the which/which, who/(the)which* and *be/are.* For a description of the CEEC see Nevalainen and Raumolin-Brunberg 1996b:39–54.

10. In an earlier version the numbers of writers for both periods were identical (44), but for the first period writers for the underrepresented ranks of the nobility, upper clergy and the non-gentry were added.

11. Franz ([1939] 1986:255f.) regards *fare ye well, hark ye* and *look ye* as nominatives and *hang ye* as an oblique case. In his opinion, forms like *get thee gone* can be explained in two different ways: "Diese Erscheinung findet ihre Erklärung in einer älteren Sprachgewohnheit, nach welcher zu gewissen intransitiven Verben [...] vielfach ein Dativ des Pronomens trat. Daher hat sich auch im Imperativ die Form mit *thee* und *you* als die übliche festgesetzt: *hie thee, get thee (you) gone.* Es ist jedoch hier eine zweifache Auffassung möglich, *thee* kann z.B. ursprünglich Dativ und Nominativ sein; akkusativische Auffassung liegt andererseits besonders nahe in Ausdrücken wie *get thee away, get thee gone,* die in der älteren Sprache stereotyp waren" (278f.).

12. Here and in the following, spellings and line references refer to the OES. In this chapter, unlike the others, the OES was taken as a database, because it supplies more *ye* tokens than Spevack. In the OES there 362 tokens, and in Spevack only 343. For the differences to Spevack see the respective footnotes and Table 9.

13. Only in the OES, Spevack: *you.*

14. See footnote 13.

15. "8. In phrases expressive of a strong wish, chiefly for the benefit or injury of some person, as *God bless, damn, help, preserve, save,* † *shield,* † *speed,* † *yield* (you, him, etc.); also *God forbid, grant* (that); *God give* (something): for these see the various verbs. Hence occasionally used in participial expressions. Some of these phrases assumed abbreviated or corrupted forms through frequent use, as *God eyld (ild, dild) you, goddilge yee* = God yield you (see yield); *God b'wy (buy) ye* = God be with you (see good-bye); *God (Godge) you good even* = God give you, etc. (also *God dig-you-den, God(g)igoden:* see good-even). In such phrases as have remained current, *God* is often omitted, as *bless you, damn you, preserve us*" (OED s.v. *god*). The first citation stems from 1579.

16. Theoretically, *'ee* could also be a contraction of *thee,* but it is usually explained as a further weakening of the unstressed form [ji]; cf. Sweet (1900:339); Poutsma (1916:720), see also footnote 2.

17. The OED also documents a number of combinations in which *ye* or rather *'ee* occurs proclitically or enclitically with other words such as † *ʒet* = ye it, *yare* = ye are, *y'have; d'ee, dee* = do ye, hark'ee, harkee. An isolated quotation is given for the 13th century: "c. 1200 Ormin 9006 Loc ʒiff ʒet wilenn follʒhenn." The other citations range from 1611 to 1775 (OED s.v. *ye*).

18. In the following the term *exclamation* serves as a portmanteau for such communicative functions as exclamative, (rhetorical) appeal, entreaty, asseveration, abuse, imprecation, etc., which in the broadest sense of the term can be summarised under the heading of *apostrophe*. Pragmatically, all of these instances are characterised by a high degree of emotional involvement on the part of the speaker, and syntactically they normally do not constitute complete sentences. As regards the position of the verb (if present), exclamatives may be formally realised as declarative, interrogative or imperative sentences which are often introduced by means of modal particles or interjections, and prosodically they are characterised by an exclamative intonation.

19. This result is also confirmed by Bock's investigation for the 16th century, for which he finds: "Aus dem Nominativ Pluralis, seinem eigentlichen Ursprung, ist 'ye' fast vollständig verschwunden. Es handelt sich immer nur um vereinzelte Fälle. [...] Verhältnismäßig häufig steht 'ye' vor abstrakten Substantiven. [...] Es dient dem Ausdruck des Pathos, der tiefen Gemütsbewegung, wozu im Singular 'thou' gebraucht wurde. [...] Man kann also sagen, daß der Gebrauch von 'ye' [...] traditionsbedingt ist und eine reguläre Pluralbildung zu 'thou' darstellt" (1938:72f.).

The OED attests that this use "(as the plural of *thou*) in addressing a number of persons (or, rhetorically, of things), in the nominative (or vocative)" has a long-standing tradition in English literature, ranging from *Beowulf* to the beginning of the 20th century.

20. This goes only for the OES, because Spevack accounts for only three tokens altogether: Polonius uses it twice in the parting formulae: "God buy ye, fare ye well" [to Reynaldo] in HAM 2, 1, 66.

21. Within the group of History Plays, 1H4 is the play with the highest proportion (46%) of prose.

22. The figures are based on the OES; the putative dates of composition have been taken from Evans and Tobin (1997:78–87).

23. Cf. footnote 20.

References

1. Primary sources (corpus)

OES 1989 = (Oxford Electronic Shakespeare) Wells, Stanley and Taylor, Gary (eds)
    1989   *William Shakespeare. The complete works.* Electronic edition. Oxford: OUP.
Riverside Shakespeare = G. Blakemore Evans (ed.)
    1997   *The Riverside Shakespeare.* [with the assistance of J.J.M. Tobin] 2nd ed. Boston: Houghton Mifflin.
Arden Shakespeare = Katherine Duncan-Jones
    1997   *The Arden Shakespeare: Shakespeare's Sonnets.* London: Nelson and Sons.

2. EModE grammars

Aitken, Joseph
    1693   *The English grammar* [facsimile repr. 21, 1967, English Linguistics 1500–1800. Menston: Scholar Press].
Bullokar, William
    1586   *Bref grammar of English.* London.
Greaves, Paul
    1594   *Grammatica Anglicana* [facsimile repr. 169, 1969, English Linguistics 1500–1800. Menston: Scholar Press].
Greenwood, James
    1711   *An essay towards a practical English grammar* [facsimile repr. 128, 1968, English Linguistics 1500–1800. Menston: Scholar Press].
Jonson, Ben
    1640   *The English grammar* [repr. 1972, Menston: Scholar Press].
Lowth, Robert
    1762   *A short introduction to English grammar* [facsimile repr. 18, 1967, English Linguistics 1500–1800. Menston].
Miege, Guy
    1688   *The English grammar* [facsimile repr. 152, 1969, English Linguistics 1500–1800. Menston].

3. Secondary sources

Abbott, Edwin A.
    [1870] 1972 *A Shakespearian grammar: An attempt to illustrate some of the differences between Elizabethan and modern English.* London: Macmillan [repr. 1972, New York: Haskell].

Aers, David and Kress, Gunther
  1981   "The language of social order: Individual, society and historical process in *King Lear*".
           In *Literature, language and society in England 1580–1680*. D. Aers, B. Hodge and G.
           Kress, 75–99. Dublin: Gill and Macmillan.
Aitcheson, Jean
  1991   *Language change: Progress or decay?* 2nd ed. Cambridge: CUP.
Akimoto, Minoji
  2000   "The grammaticalization of the verb *pray*". In Fischer et al. (eds), 67–84.
Alexander, Gillian
  1982   "Politics of the pronoun in the literature of the English revolution". In *Language and
           literature*, R. Carter (ed.), 217–235. London: Allen & Unwin.
Allen, Cynthia L.
  1995   "On doing as you please". In A. H. Jucker (ed.), 275–308.
Ameka, Felix
  1992   "Interjections: The universal yet neglected part of speech". *Journal of Pragmatics* 18:
           101–118.
Andersen, Henning
  1989   "Markedness theory — the first 150 years". In O. M. Tomić (ed.), 11–46.
  1990   "The structure of drift". In H. Andersen and K. Koerner (eds), 1–20.
  2001   "Markedness and the theory of linguistic change". In H. Andersen (ed.), 21–57.
Andersen, Henning (ed.)
  2001   *Actualization. Linguistic change in progress.* [Current Issues in Linguistic Theory 219].
           Amsterdam: John Benjamins.
Andersen, Henning and Koerner, Konrad (eds)
  1990   *Historical Linguistics 1987. Papers from the 8th International Conference on Historical
           Linguistics (8. ICHL, Lille, 31 August — 4 September 1987).* [Amsterdam Studies in the
           Theory and History of Linguistic Science 66]. Amsterdam: John Benjamins.
Andreas, James R.
  1993   "The vulgar and the polite: Dialogue in *Hamlet*". *Hamlet Studies* 15: 9–23.
Archer, C.
  1936   "*Thou* and *you* in the Sonnets". *Times Literary Supplement* 27.6.1936: 544.
Auden, Wystan Hugh
  1965   "Introduction" to William Shakespeare *The Sonnets*, xvii-xxxviii. New York: Signet.
Bailey, Charles-James
  1973   *Variation and linguistic theory.* Washington, D. C.: Center for Applied Linguistics.
Bambas, Rudolph C.
  1947   "Verb forms in *-s* and *-th* in Early Modern English prose". *Journal of English and
           Germanic Philology* 46: 183–187.
Barber, Charles
  1976   *Early Modern English.* London: Deutsch.
  1981   "*You* and *thou* in Shakespeare's *Richard III*". *Leeds Studies in English*, New Series 12:
           273–289 [reprinted in V. Salmon and E. Burness (eds), 163–179].
  1997   *Early Modern English.* 2nd ed. Edinburgh: EUP.
Barish, Jonas A.
  1972   "Continuities and discontinuities in Shakespearian prose". In C. Leech and J. M. R.
           Margeson (eds), 59–75.
  1974   "Pattern and purpose in the prose of *Much Ado About Nothing*". *Rice University
           Studies* 60: 19–30.

Barton, Anne
 1997 "Introduction to the *Merry Wives of Windsor*". In *The Riverside Shakespeare*, 320–323.
Battistella, Edwin L.
 1996 *The logic of markedness*. New York and Oxford: OUP.
Baugh, Albert C. and Cable, Thomas
 1993 *A history of the English language*. 4th ed. London: Routledge.
Baumann, Richard
 1970 "Aspects of 17th century Quaker rhetoric". *The Quarterly Journal of Speech* 56: 67–74.
Berry, Francis
 1958a *Poets' grammar: Person, time, and mood in poetry*. London: Routledge and Kegan Paul.
 1958b "*Thou* and *you* in Shakespeare's *Sonnets*". *Essays in Criticism* 8: 138–146.
 1959 "Pronouns in poetry". *Essays in Criticism* 9: 196–197.
Biber, Douglas and Finegan, Edward
 1992 "The linguistic evolution of five written and speech-based English genres from the 17th to the 20th centuries". In *History of Englishes. New Methods and Interpretations in Historical Linguistics*, M. Rissanen et al. (eds), 688–704. Berlin: Mouton de Gruyter.
Biber et al. 1994 = Biber, Douglas, Finegan, Edward and Atkinson, Dwight
 1994 "ARCHER and its challenges: Compiling and exploring a representative corpus of historical English registers". In *Creating and using English language corpora. Papers from the Fourteenth International Conference on English Language Research on Computerized Corpora, Zürich 1993*, U. Fries, G. Tottie and P. Schneider (eds), 1–13. Amsterdam: Rodopi.
Biber et al. 1998 = Biber, Douglas, Conrad, Susan and Reppen, Randi
 1998 *Corpus linguistics: Investigating language structure and use*. Cambridge: CUP.
Blake, Norman F.
 1989 *The language of Shakespeare*. 2nd ed. London: Macmillan.
 1990 "Shakespeare's language: Some recent studies and future directions". *Deutsche Shakespeare-Gesellschaft West, Jahrbuch 1990*: 61–77.
 1996 *A history of the English language*. Houndmills: Macmillan.
 2002a *A grammar of Shakespeare's language*. Houndmills: Palgrave.
 2002b "Forms of address in *Hamlet*". In *Of dyuersitie & chaunge of langage: Essays presented to Manfred Görlach on the occasion of his 65th birthday*, K. Lenz and R. Möhlich (eds), 305–318. Heidelberg: Winter.
Bock, Martin
 1938 *Der stilistische Gebrauch des englischen Personalpronomens der 2. Person im volkstümlichen Dialog der älteren englischen Komödie*. Unpublished Ph. D. thesis, University of Innsbruck.
Böhm, Annemarie
 1936 *Entwicklungsgeschichte der englischen Titel und Anreden seit dem 16. Jahrhundert*. Berlin: Brandenburgische Buchdruckerei und Verlagsanstalt.
Bolton, W. F.
 1992 *Shakespeare's English: Language in the history plays*. Oxford: Blackwell.
Borgmeier et al. (eds) 1998 = Borgmeier, Raimund, Grabes, Herbert and Jucker, Andreas H. (eds)
 1998 *Anglistentag 1997. Giessen. Proceedings*. Trier: WVT.
Bordukat, Gertrud
 1918 *Die Abgrenzung zwischen Vers und Prosa in den Dramen Shakespeares*. Unpublished Ph. D. thesis, University of Königsberg.
Borinski, Ludwig
 1955 "Shakespeare's comic prose". *Shakespeare Survey* 8: 57–68.

1969   "Konstante Stilformen in Shakespeares Prosa". *Deutsche Shakespeare-Gesellschaft West, Jahrbuch 1969*: 81–102.

Brainerd, Barron

1979   "Pronouns and genre in Shakespeare's drama". *Computers and the Humanities* 13: 3–16.

1980   "The chronology of Shakespeare's plays: A statistical study". *Computers and the Humanities* 14: 221–230.

Braun, Friederike

1984   "Die Leistungsfähigkeit der von Brown/Gilman und Brown/Ford eingeführten anredetheoretischen Kategorien bei der praktischen Analyse von Anredesystemen". In W. Winter (ed.), 41–72.

1988   *Terms of address: Problems of patterns and usage in various languages and cultures.* [Contributions to the Sociology of Language 50]. [With a supplement to Braun/ Kohz/Schubert (1986)]. Berlin: Mouton de Gruyter.

Braun, Friederike, Kohz, Armin and Schubert, Klaus

1986   *Anredeforschung: Kommentierte Bibliographie zur Soziolinguistik der Anrede.* Tübingen: Narr.

Breuer, Horst

1983   "Titel und Anreden bei Shakespeare und in der Shakespearezeit". *Anglia* 101: 49–77.

Brinton, Laurel J.

1996   *Pragmatic markers in English: Grammaticalization and discourse functions.* [Topics in English Linguistics 19]. Berlin: Mouton de Gruyter.

Britton, Derek (ed.)

1996   *English Historical Linguistics 1994. Papers from the 8th International Conference on English Historical Linguistics.* (8. ICEHL, Edinburgh, 19–23 September 1994). [Amsterdam Studies in the Theory and History of Linguistic Science 135]. Amsterdam: John Benjamins.

Brook, G. L.

1976   *The language of Shakespeare.* London: Deutsch.

Brown, Gillian and Yule, George

1983   *Discourse analysis.* Cambridge: CUP.

Brown, Penelope and Levinson, Stephen C.

1987   *Politeness: Some universals in language usage.* Cambridge: CUP.

Brown, Roger W. and Gilman, Albert

1960   "The pronouns of power and solidarity". In *Style in language*, T. A. Sebeok (ed.), 253–276. Cambridge, Mass.: MIT Press [repr. in J. Laver and S. Hutcheson (eds) 1972 *Communication in face to face interaction.* 103–127. Harmondsworth: Penguin].

1989   "Politeness theory and Shakespeare's four major tragedies". *Language in Society* 18: 159–212.

Brown, Roger W. and Ford, Marguerite

1961   "Address in American English". *Journal of Abnormal and Social Psychology* 62: 375–385 [repr. in Dell Hymes (ed.) 1964 *Language in culture and society.* 234–244. New York: Harper & Row].

Brunner, Karl

1951   *Die englische Sprache: Ihre geschichtliche Entwicklung.* Vol. 2 *Die Flexionsformen, ihre Verwendung. Das Englische ausserhalb Europas.* Halle: Niemeyer.

Bruti, Silvia

2000   "Address pronouns in Shakespeare's English: A re-appraisal in terms of markedness". In *The history of English in a social context: A contribution to historical sociolinguistics.*

[Trends in Linguistics. Studies and Monographs 129], D. Kastovsky and A. Mettinger (eds), 25–51. Berlin and New York: Mouton de Gruyter.

Burke, Peter
1992 "The language of orders in early modern Europe". In *Social orders and social classes in Europe since 1500: Studies in social stratification*, M. L. Bush (ed.). London: Longman.

Burton, Dolores M.
1973 *Shakespeare's grammatical style*. Austin: University of Texas Press.

Busse, Beatrix
1997 Linguistic indications of attitude in the language of Shakespeare. Unpublished state examination thesis, University of Osnabrück.
(in prep.) Functional analysis of vocative constructions in the language of Shakespeare. Ph. D. thesis, University of Osnabrück.

Busse, Ulrich
1998a "Forms of address in Shakespeare's plays: Problems and findings". In R. Schulze (ed.), 33–60.
1998b "'Stand, sir, and throw us that you have about ye': Zur Grammatik und Pragmatik des Anredepronomens *ye* in Shakespeares Dramen". In *Betrachtungen zum Wort: Lexik im Spannungsfeld von Syntax, Semantik und Pragmatik*, E. Klein and St. J. Schierholz (eds), 85–115. Tübingen: Stauffenburg.
1999 "'Prithee now, say you will, and go about it': *Prithee* vs. *pray you* as discourse markers in the Shakespeare Corpus". In *Anglistentag 1998 Erfurt. Proceedings*, F.-W. Neumann and S. Schülting (eds), 485–500. Trier: WVT.
2001 "The use of address pronouns in Shakespeare's plays and sonnets". In H. Andersen (ed.), 119–142.
forthc. "The co-occurence of nominal and pronominal address forms in the Shakespeare Corpus: Who says *thou* or *you* to whom?" In I. Taavitsainen and A. H. Jucker (eds).
forthc. "Manipulative speech acts in English: A diachronic survey with special emphasis on the rise of *please* and the demise of *pray*". In *Corpus approaches to grammaticalization*, H. Lindquist and C. Mair (eds). Amsterdam: John Benjamins.

Byrne, Geraldine
[1936] 1970 *Shakespeare's use of the pronoun of address; its significance in characterization and motivation*. Ph. D. thesis, Catholic University of America, Washington, D. C. [repr. 1970, New York: Haskell].

Calvo, Clara
1992a "Pronouns of address and social negotiation in *As You Like It*". *Language and Literature* 1: 5–27.
1992b "'Too wise to woo peaceably': The meanings of *thou* in Shakespeare's wooing-scenes". In *Actas del III Congreso International de la Sociedad Española de Estudios Renacentistas Ingleses. Proceedings of the III International Conference of the Spanish Society for English Renayssance* [sic] *Studies*, M. L. Dañobeitia (ed.), 49–59. Granada.

Carson, Neil
1976 "The Elizabethan soliloquy — direct address or monologue?" *Theatre Notebook* 30: 12–18.

Carstensen, Broder
1959 *Studien zur Syntax des Nomens, Pronomens und der Negation in den Paston Letters*. [Beiträge zur Englischen Philologie 42]. Bochum: Pöppinghaus.

Chambers, Edmund K.
1930 *William Shakespeare: A study of facts and problems*. 2 vols. Oxford: Clarendon Press.

Chen, Guohua
  1998   "The degrammaticalization of addressee-satisfaction conditionals in Early Modern English". In J. Fisiak and M. Krygier (eds), 23–32.
Church, Kenneth W. and Hanks, Patrick
  1990   "Word association norms, mutual information, and lexicography". *Computational Linguistics* 16: 22–29.
Clemen, Wolfgang
  1951   *The development of Shakespeare's imagery.* London: Methuen [2nd ed. repr. 1987].
  1969   "Die dramatischen Impulse in Vers und Rhythmus". *Deutsche Shakespeare-Gesellschaft West, Jahrbuch 1969*: 10–23.
  1987   *Shakespeare's soliloquies.* London: Methuen.
Coulmas, Florian (ed.)
  1997   *The handbook of sociolinguistics.* Oxford: Blackwell.
Coulthard, Malcolm and Montgomery, Martin (eds)
  1981   *Studies in discourse analysis.* London: Routledge and Kegan Paul.
Coupland, Nikolas and Jaworski, Adam (eds)
  1997   *Sociolinguistics: A reader and coursebook.* Houndmills: Macmillan.
Craig, D. H.
  1991   "Plural pronouns in Roman Plays by Shakespeare and Jonson". *Literary & Linguistic Computing* 6: 180–186.
Crane, Milton
  1951   *Shakespeare's prose.* Chicago: The University of Chicago Press and Cambridge: The University Press.
Crystal, David
  1988   *The English language.* Harmondsworth: Penguin.
Culpeper, Jonathan
  1996   "Towards an anatomy of impoliteness". *Journal of Pragmatics* 25: 349–367.
  1998   "(Im)politeness in dramatic dialogue". In *Exploring the language of drama: From text to context*, J. Culpeper, M. Short and P. Verdonk (eds), 83–95. London: Routledge.
Delius, Nicolaus
  1870   "Die Prosa in Shakespeare's Dramen". *Shakespeare-Jahrbuch* 5: 227–273.
Devitt, Anny J.
  1989   *Standardizing written English: Diffusion in the case of Scotland 1520–1659.* Cambridge: CUP.
Diller, Hans-Jürgen
  1990   "On first looking into the Electronic Oxford Shakespeare: Some statistical observations on adjectival word formation and genre". *Deutsche Shakespeare-Gesellschaft West, Jahrbuch 1990*: 94–104.
Doran, Madelaine.
  1976   *Shakespeare's dramatic language.* Madison, Wisc. and London: University of Wisconsin Press.
Downes, William
  1988   "Discourse and drama: King Lear's *question* to his daughters". In W. van Peer (ed.), 225–257.
Downing, Bruce T.
  1969   "Vocatives and third-person imperatives in English". *Papers in Linguistics* 1: 570–592.
Drury, Richard
  2000   "Pronouns of address in Early Modern English: The use of oblique forms". In *English Diachonic Pragmatics*, G. di Martino and M. Lima (eds), 159–176. Napoli: CUEN.

Eagleson, Robert D.
 1971 "Propertied as all the tuned spheres: Aspects of Shakespeare's language". *The Teaching of English* 20: 4–15 [repr. in V. Salmon and E. Burness (eds), 133–144].
Eichhorn, Traudl
 1950 "Prosa und Vers im vorshakespeareschen Drama". *Shakespeare-Jahrbuch* 84/86: 140–198.
Evans, G. Blakemore and Tobin, J.J.M.
 1997 "Chronology and sources". In *The Riverside Shakespeare*, 77–87.
Evans, Ifor
 1985 *The language of Shakespeare's plays.* Westport, Conn.: Greenwood Press.
Faiß, Klaus
 1989 *Englische Sprachgeschichte.* Tübingen: Francke.
Feldmann, Doris
 1997 "Multimedia Shakespeares". In Feldmann et al. (eds), 129–143.
Feldmann et al. (eds) 1997 = Feldmann, Doris, Neumann, Fritz-Wilhelm and Rommel, Thomas (eds)
 1997 *Anglistik im Internet: Proceedings of the 1996 Erfurt Conference on computing in the humanities.* Heidelberg: Winter.
Finkenstaedt, Thomas
 1954 "Zur Methodik der Versuntersuchung bei Shakespeare". *Shakespeare-Jahrbuch* 90: 82–107.
 1958 "Pronouns in poetry". *Essays in Criticism* 8: 456–457.
 1963 You *and* Thou: *Studien zur Anrede im Englischen (mit einem Exkurs über die Anrede im Deutschen).* Berlin: de Gruyter.
Fischer, Andreas
 1998 "*Marry*: From religious invocation to discourse marker". In R. Borgmeier et al. (eds), 35–46.
Fischer et al. (eds.) 2000 = Fischer, Olga, Rosenbach, Anette, and Stein, Dieter (eds)
 2000 *Pathways of change: Grammaticalization in English.* [Studies in Language Companion Series 53]. Amsterdam: John Benjamins.
Fish, Stanley E.
 1976 "How to do things with Austin and Searle: Speech act theory and literary criticism". *Modern Language Notes* 91: 983–1025.
Fisiak, Jacek (ed.)
 1990 *Historical linguistics and philology.* [Trends in Linguistics. Studies and Monographs 46]. Berlin: Mouton de Gruyter.
 1997 *Studies in Middle English linguistics.* [Trends in Linguistics. Studies and Monographs 103]. Berlin: Mouton de Gruyter.
Fisiak, Jacek and Krygier, Marcin (eds)
 1998 *Advances in English Historical Linguistics (1996).* [Trends in Linguistics. Studies and Monographs 112]. Berlin: Mouton de Gruyter.
Flatter, Richard
 1951 "The veil of beauty: Some aspects of verse and prose in Shakespeare and Goethe". *Journal of English and Germanic Philology* 50: 437–450.
Fludernik, Monika
 1993 "Second person fiction: Narrative *you* as addressee and/or protagonist". *AAA — Arbeiten aus Anglistik und Amerikanistik* 18: 217–247.
Forchheimer, Paul
 1953 *The category of person in language.* Berlin: de Gruyter.

Franz, Wilhelm
  [1939] 1986 *Die Sprache Shakespeares in Vers und Prosa unter Berücksichtigung des Ameri-*
  kanischen entwicklungsgeschichtlich dargestellt. Shakespeare-Grammatik. 4th ed.
  Tübingen: Niemeyer [1st ed. 1898/99].
Fraser, Bruce and Nolen, William
  1981   "The association of deference with linguistic form". *International Journal of the*
  Sociology of Language 27: 93–109.
Fries, Charles Carpenter
  1940   "On the development of the structural use of word-order in modern English".
  Language 16: 199–208.
Fries, Udo
  1998   "Dialogue in instructional texts". In R. Borgmeier et al. (eds), 85–96.
Gillett, Peter J.
  1974   "Me, U, and non-U: Class connotations of two Shakespearean idioms". *Shakespeare*
  Quarterly 25: 297–309 [reprinted in V. Salmon and E. Burness (eds), 117–129].
Gilman, Albert and Brown, Roger W.
  1958   "Who says *Tu* to *Whom*". *ETC: A Review of General Semantics* 15: 169–174.
Givón, Talmy
  1979   *On understanding grammar.* New York: Academic Press.
  1990   *Syntax: A functional-typological introduction.* Vol. 2. Amsterdam: John Benjamins.
Goffman, Erving
  1956   "The nature of deference and demeanor". *American Anthropologist* 58: 473–502.
Goodenough, W. H.
  1965   "Rethinking *status* and *role*: Toward a general model of the cultural organisation of
  social relationships". In *The relevance of models for social anthropology,* M. Banton
  (ed.), 1–24. London: Tavistock.
Gordon, George
  1928   "Shakespeare's English". In *Society for Pure English. Tract No. 24,* 255–276. Oxford:
  Clarendon Press.
Görlach, Manfred
  1994   *Einführung ins Frühneuenglische.* 2nd ed. Heidelberg: Winter.
  1999a   *Aspects of the history of English.* Heidelberg: Winter.
  1999b   "Regional and social variation". In R. Lass (ed.), 459–538.
Graband, Gerhard
  1965   *Die Entwicklung der frühneuenglischen Nominalflexion. Dargestellt vornehmlich*
  aufgrund von Grammatikerzeugnissen des 17. Jahrhunderts. Tübingen: Niemeyer.
Grannis, Oliver
  1990   "The social relevance of grammatical choice in Shakespeare". *Deutsche Shakespeare-*
  Gesellschaft West, Jahrbuch 1990: 105–118.
Greenberg, Joseph H.
  1966   *Language universals.* The Hague: Mouton.
Greenberg, Joseph H. (ed.)
  1978   *Universals of human language.* Vol. 3: *Word structure.* Stanford: Stanford Univ. Press.
Greiner, Norbert
  1983   *Studien zu "Much Ado About Nothing".* Frankfurt: Peter Lang.
Grice, H. Paul
  1975   "Logic and conversation". In *Syntax and semantics.* Vol. 3: *Speech Acts,* P. Cole and J.
  Morgan (eds), 41–58. New York: Academic Press.

Gurr, Andrew
1982   "*You* and *Thou* in Shakespeare's Sonnets". *Essays in Criticism* 32: 9–25.
Gvozdanović, Jadranka
1989   "Defining markedness". In O.M. Tomić (ed.), 47–66.
Haase, Martin
1994   *Respekt: Die Grammatikalisierung von Höflichkeit.* [Edition Linguistik 03]. München and Newcastle: Lincom Europa.
Halliday, M.A.K.
1978   *Language as a social semiotic: The social interpretation of language and meaning.* London: Arnold.
Harris, Alice and Campbell, Lyle
1995   *Historical syntax in cross-linguistic perspective.* [Cambridge Studies in Linguistics 74]. Cambridge: CUP.
Hatch, Evelyn and Lazaraton, Anne
1991   *The research manual: Design and statistics for applied linguists.* New York: Newbury House.
Head, B.F.
1978   "Respect degrees in pronominal reference". In J.H. Greenberg (ed.), vol. 3, 151–211.
Heltveit, T.
1952   "Notes on the development of the personal pronouns in English". *Norsk Tidsskrift for Sprogvidenskap* 16: 377–386.
Henn-Memmesheimer, Beate
1998   *Sprachliche Varianz als Ergebnis von Handlungswahl.* [Reihe Germanistische Linguistik 198]. Tübingen: Niemeyer.
Hesse, Beatrix
1998   *Shakespeares Komödien aus der Sicht der pragmatischen Kommunikationstheorie.* [Studien zur englischen Literatur 9]. Münster, Hamburg and London: LIT Verlag.
Hibbard, G.R.
1972   "'The forced gait of a shuffling nag'". In C. Leech and J.M.R. Margeson (eds), 76–88.
1977   "*Henry IV* and *Hamlet*". *Shakespeare Survey* 30: 1–12.
Hickey et al. (eds) 1997 = Hickey, Raymond, Kytö, Merja, Lancashire, Ian and Rissanen, Matti (eds)
1997   *Tracing the trail of time: Proceedings from the Second Diachronic Corpora Workshop, New College, University of Toronto, May 1995.* Amsterdam: Rodopi.
Hickey, Raymond and Puppel, Stanisław (eds)
1997   *Language history and linguistic modelling: A festschrift for Jacek Fisiak on his 60th birthday.* Vol. 1: *Language History.* [Trends in Linguistics. Studies and Monographs 101]. Berlin: Mouton de Gruyter.
Holdsworth, Richard
1982   Middleton and Shakespeare: The case for Middleton's hand in *Timon of Athens.* Unpublished Ph. D. thesis, University of Manchester.
Hook, Donald D.
1984   "First names and titles as solidarity and power semantics in English". *IRAL — International Review of Applied Linguistics in Language Teaching* 22: 183–189.
Hope, Jonathan
1993   "Second person singular pronouns in records of Early Modern *spoken* English". *Neuphilologische Mitteilungen* 94: 83–100.
1994a   "The use of *thou* and *you* in Early Modern spoken English: Evidence from depositions in the Durham ecclesiastical court records". In D. Kastovsky (ed.), 141–151.

1994b *The authorship of Shakespeare's plays: A socio-linguistic study.* Cambridge: CUP.
Hopper, Paul J.
1991 "On some principles of grammaticalization". In E. Closs Traugott and B. Heine (eds), vol. 1, 17–35.
Hopper, Paul J. and Traugott, Elizabeth Closs
1993 *Grammaticalization.* Cambridge: CUP.
Horn, Wilhelm and Lehnert, Martin
1954 *Laut und Leben: Englische Lautgeschichte der neueren Zeit (1400–1950).* 2 vols. Berlin: Deutscher Verlag der Wissenschaften.
Hout, Roeland van
1998 Paper distributed at the statistics workshop: "Variable rules, optimality", held at the 10th International Conference on English Historical Linguistics, Manchester, 21–26 August 1998.
Howe, Stephen
1996 *The personal pronouns in the Germanic languages: A study of personal pronoun morphology and change in the Germanic languages from the first records to the present day.* [Studia Linguistica Germanica 43]. Berlin: de Gruyter.
Hoy, Cyrus
1956 "The shares of Fletcher and his collaborators in the Beaumont and Fletcher Canon". *Studies in Bibliography* 8 [repr. in S. P. Zitner (ed.) 1966 *The practice of modern literary scholarship.* 58–73. Glenview, Illinois].
Hulme, Hilda M.
1977 *Explorations in Shakespeare's language: Some problems of word meaning in the dramatic text.* London: Longman.
Hussey, Stanley S.
1982 *The literary language of Shakespeare.* London: Longman.
Ilsemann, Hartmut
1998 *Shakespeare disassembled: Eine quantitative Analyse der Dramen Shakespeares.* [Literarische Studien 5]. Frankfurt/Main: Lang.
Ilson, Robert F.
1971 Forms of address in Shakespeare, with special reference to the use of 'thou' and 'you'. Unpublished Ph. D. thesis, University of London.
Ingram, David
1978 "Typology and universals of personal pronouns". In J. H. Greenberg (ed.), vol. 3, 213–247.
Jacobs, Andreas and Jucker, Andreas H.
1995 "The historical perspective in pragmatics". In A. H. Jucker (ed.), 3–33.
Janssen, Vincent Franz
1897 Die Prosa in Shakespeares Dramen. Ph. D. thesis, Gießen/Straßburg.
Jespersen, Otto
1894 *Progress in language: With special reference to English.* London: Swan, Sonnenschein & Co.
1909–1949 *A modern English grammar on historical principles.* 7 vols. Heidelberg: Winter and Copenhagen: Munksgaard.
[1946] 1972 *Growth and structure of the English language.* 9th ed. Oxford: Blackwell.
Johnson, Anne C.
1966 "The pronoun of direct address in seventeenth-century English". *American Speech* 41: 261–269.

Johnson, Judith A.
1975   "Second person pronouns in Shakespeare's tragedies". *The Michigan Academician* 8/2: 151–156.

Jones, G. P.
1981   "*You, thou, he* or *she*? The master-mistress in Shakespearian and Elizabethan sonnet sequences". *Cahiers Elisabéthains* 19: 73–84.

Jucker, Andreas H. (ed.)
1995   *Historical pragmatics: Pragmatic developments in the history of English.* [Pragmatics & Beyond. New Series 35]. Amsterdam: John Benjamins.

Jucker, Andreas H.
1997   "The discourse marker *well* in the history of English". *English Language and Linguistics* 1: 91–110.

2000   "*Thou* in the history of English: A case for historical semantics or pragmatics?" In *Words: Structure, meaning, function. A festschrift for Dieter Kastovsky*, C. Dalton-Puffer and N. Ritt (eds), 153–163. Berlin: Mouton de Gruyter.

Kastovsky, Dieter (ed.)
1994   *Studies in Early Modern English.* [Topics in English Linguistics 13]. Berlin: Mouton de Gruyter.

Kendall, Martha B.
1981   "Toward a semantic approach to terms of address: A critique of deterministic models in sociolinguistics". *Language and Communication* 1 (2/3): 237–254.

Kennedy, Arthur G.
1915   *The pronoun of address in English literature of the thirteenth century.* Stanford: Stanford University Press.

Kenyon, John S.
1914   "*Ye* and *you* in the King James Version". *PMLA — Proceedings of the Modern Language Association of America* 24, New Series 12: 453–471.

Kiełkiewicz-Janowiak, Agnieszka
1994   "Sociolinguistics and the computer: Pronominal address in Shakespeare". *Studia Anglica Posnaniensia* 29: 49–56.

Klein, Magdalene
1930   "Shakespeares dramatisches Formgcsctz: Bindung von Vers und Prosa von Shakespeare bis zum deutschen Expressionismus". *Wortkunst*, Neue Folge 4.

Kohz, Armin
1982   *Linguistische Aspekte des Anredeverhaltens: Untersuchungen am Deutschen und am Schwedischen.* Tübingen: Narr.

1984   "Markiertheit, Normalität und Natürlichkeit von Anredeformen". In W. Winter (ed.), 25–39.

König, Goswin
1888   *Der Vers in Shakespeares Dramen.* Straßburg and London.

Kopytko, Roman
1988   "The impersonal use of verbs in William Shakespeare's plays". *Studia Anglica Posnaniensia* 21: 41–51.

1993a   *Polite discourse in Shakespeare's English.* [Seria Filologia Angielska 24]. Poznań: Adam Mickiewicz University Press.

1993b   "Linguistic pragmatics and the concept of *face*". VIEWS — *Vienna English Working Papers* 2: 91–103.

1995   "Linguistic politeness strategies in Shakespeare's plays". In A. H. Jucker (ed.), 515–540.

Kryk-Kastovsky, Barbara
    1998   "Pragmatic particles in Early Modern English court trials". In R. Borgmeier et al. (eds), 47–56.
Kytö, Merja (comp.)
    1996   *Manual to the diachronic part of the Helsinki Corpus of English Texts: Coding conventions and lists of source texts.* 3rd ed. Helsinki: Department of English, University of Helsinki.
Kytö, Merja and Rissanen, Matti
    1993   "General introduction" to *Early English in the computer age: Explorations through the Helsinki Corpus* [Topics in English Linguistics 11], M. Rissanen, M. Kytö and M. Palander-Collin (eds), 1–17. Berlin: Mouton de Gruyter.
Kytö et al. (eds) 1994 = Kytö, Merja, Rissanen, Matti and Wright, Susan (eds)
    1994   *Corpora across the centuries: Proceedings of the First International Colloquium on English Diachronic Corpora, St Catherine's College, Cambridge, 25–27 March, 1993.* Amsterdam: Rodopi.
Labov, William
    1966   *The social stratification of English in New York City.* Washington, D.C.: Center for Applied Linguistics.
    1970   "The study of language in its social context". *Studium Generale* 23: 30–87.
    1994   *Principles of linguistic change.* Vol. 1: *Internal factors.* [Language in Society 20]. Oxford and Cambridge, Mass.: Blackwell.
Laslett, Peter
    1983   *The world we have lost further explored.* 3rd ed. London: Methuen.
Lass, Roger
    1987   *The shape of English: Structure and history.* London: Dent & Sons.
    1999   "Phonology and morphology". In R. Lass (ed.), 56–186.
Lass, Roger (ed.)
    1999   *The Cambridge history of the English language.* Vol. 3: *1476–1776.* Cambridge: CUP.
Leech, Clifford and Margeson, J.M.R. (eds)
    1972   *Shakespeare 1971. Proceedings of the World Shakespeare Congress Vancouver, August 1971.* Toronto and Buffalo: University of Toronto Press.
Leech, Geoffrey
    1983   *Principles of pragmatics.* London: Longman.
Leisi, Ernst
    1997   *Problemwörter und Problemstellen in Shakespeares Dramen.* Tübingen: Stauffenburg.
Leith, Dick
    1983   *A social history of English.* London: Routledge & Kegan Paul [and 2nd ed. 1997].
Listen, Paul
    1999   *The emergence of German polite Sie: Cognitive and sociolinguistic parameters.* [Berkeley Insights in Linguistics and Semiotics 32]. Frankfurt/Main: Lang.
Luick, Karl
    1964   *Historische Grammatik der englischen Sprache.* 2 vols. Stuttgart: Tauchnitz. [1st ed. vol. 1: 1914, vol. 2: 1940, Leipzig: Tauchnitz].
Lutz, Angelika
    1998   "The interplay of external and internal factors in morphological restructuring: The case of *you*". In J. Fisiak and M. Krygier (eds), 189–210.
Magnusson, A. Lynne
    1992   "The rhetoric of politeness and *Henry VIII*". *Shakespeare Quarterly* 43: 387–409.

1999   *Shakespeare and social dialogue: Dramatic language and Elizabethan letters.* Cambridge: CUP.

Macdonald, J. F.
1933   "The use of prose in English drama before Shakespeare". *University of Toronto Quarterly: A Canadian Journal of the Humanities* 2: 465–481.

Maguire, Laurie E.
1996   *Shakespearean suspect texts: The bad quartos and their contexts.* Cambridge: CUP.

Mahood, Molly
1957   *Shakespeare's wordplay.* London and New York: Methuen.

Mausch, Hanna
1993   "Democratic *you* and paradigm". *Studia Anglica Posnaniensia* 25–27: 143–153.

Mazzon, Gabriella
1992   "Shakespearean *thou* and *you* revisited, or socio-affective networks on stage". In C. Nocera Avila et al. (eds), 123–136.
1995   "Pronouns and terms of address in Shakespearean English: A socio-affective marking system in transition". *VIEWS — Vienna English Working Papers* 4: 20–42 [A revised version is to appear in I. Taavitsainen and A. H. Jucker (eds)].

McCombie, Frank
1980   "Medium and message in *As You Like It* and *King Lear*". *Shakespeare Survey* 33: 67–80.

McEnery, Tony and Wilson, Andrew
1996   *Corpus linguistics.* Edinburgh: EUP.

McIntosh, Angus
1963a   "*As You Like It*: A grammatical clue to character". *Review of English Literature* 4: 68–81.
1963b   "*King Lear* act I, scene 1: A stylistic note". *Review of English Studies,* New Series 14: 54–56.

McManaway, James G.
1950   "Recent studies in Shakespeare's chronology". *Shakespeare Survey* 3: 22–23.

Millward, Celia
1966   "Pronominal case in Shakespearean imperatives". *Language* 42: 10–17. [repr. in V. Salmon and E. Burness (eds), 301–308].

Milroy, James
1992   *Linguistic variation and change: On the historical sociolinguistics of English.* [Language in Society 19]. Oxford: Blackwell.

Milroy, James and Milroy, Lesley
1985   "Linguistic change, social network and speaker innovation". *Journal of Linguistics* 21: 339–384.

Mitchell, Eleanor R.
1971   Pronouns of address in English, 1580–1780: A study of form changes as reflected in British drama. Ph. D. thesis, Texas Agricultural and Mining University [University Microfilms International].

Morgan, W. W.
1971   "Verse and prose in *Much Ado About Nothing*". *English* 20: 89–92.

Mühlhäusler, Peter and Harré, Rom
1990   *Pronouns and people: The linguistic construction of social and personal identity.* Oxford: Blackwell.

Muir, Kenneth
1964   "Shakespeare's soliloquies". *Ocidente* 67: 45–58.

Mulholland, Joan
  1967   "*Thou* and *you* in Shakespeare: A study in the second person pronoun". *English Studies* 48: 34–43. [repr. in V. Salmon and E. Burness (eds), 153–161].
Muller, Charles
  1972   *Einführung in die Sprachstatistik*. München: Hueber.
Muncaster, Marie
  1919   "The use of prose in Elizabethan drama: A summary sketch". *Modern Language Review* 14: 10–15.
Mustanoja, Tauno F.
  1960   *A middle English syntax*. Vol.1: *Parts of speech*. Helsinki: Société Néophilologique.
Neuhaus, H. Joachim
  1990   "Shakespeare Hypertext". *Deutsche Shakespeare-Gesellschaft West, Jahrbuch 1990*: 78–93.
Nevala, Minna
  2002   "*Youre moder send a letter to the*: Pronouns of address in private correspondence from late Middle to late Modern English". In *Variation past and present: VARIENG studies on English for Terttu Nevalainen*, H. Raumolin-Brunberg, M. Nevala, A. Nurmi and M. Rissanen (eds), 135– 159. Helsinki: Société Neophilologique.
  forthc. "Family first: Address and subscription formulae in English family correspondence from the 15th to the 17th century". In I. Taavitsainen and A. H. Jucker (eds).
Nevalainen, Terttu
  1994   "Ladies and gentlemen: The generalization of titles in Early Modern English". In *Papers from the 7th International Conference on English Historical Linguistics. Valencia, 22–26 September 1992*, F. Fernández, M. Fuster and J. J. Calvo (eds), 317–327. Amsterdam: John Benjamins.
  1996a "Introduction" to T. Nevalainen and H. Raumolin-Brunberg (eds), 3–9.
  1996b "Social stratification". In T. Nevalainen and H. Raumolin-Brunberg (eds), 57–76.
  1996c "Gender difference". In T. Nevalainen and H. Raumolin-Brunberg (eds), 77–91.
  1998   "Migration, mobility and the evolution of Standard English". Paper given at the 10th International Conference on English Historical Linguistics (10. ICEHL, Manchester, 21–26 August 1998).
Nevalainen, Terttu and Raumolin-Brunberg, Helena
  1995   "Constraints on politeness: The pragmatics of address formulae in Early English Correspondence". In A. H. Jucker (ed.), 541–601.
  1996a "Social stratification in Tudor English?" In D. Britton (ed.), 303–326.
  1996b "The Corpus of Early English Correspondence". In T. Nevalainen and H. Raumolin-Brunberg (eds), 39–54.
Nevalainen, Terttu and Raumolin-Brunberg, Helena (eds)
  1996   *Sociolinguistics and language history: Studies based on the Corpus of Early English Correspondence*. Amsterdam: Rodopi.
Nocera Avila, C., Pantaleo, N. and Pezzini, D. (eds)
  1992   *Early Modern English: Trends, forms and texts: Papers read at the IV National Conference of History of English, Catania 2–3 May 1991*. Fasano: Schena.
OED 1992 = *The Oxford English Dictionary on Compact Disc*. J. Simpson and E. S. C. Weiner (eds). 2nd ed. Oxford: OUP.
Ogino, Tsunao
  1986   "Quantification of politeness based on the usage patterns of honorific expressions". *International Journal of the Sociology of Language* 58: 37–58.

Ogura, Mieko and Wang, William S-Y.
   1996   "Snowball effect in lexical diffusion: The development of -s in the third person singular present indicative in English". In D. Britton (ed.), 119–141.
Ostheeren, Klaus
   1990   "Kontextualismus und Kontextualisierung in der Analyse der Sprache Shakespeares". *Deutsche Shakespeare-Gesellschaft West, Jahrbuch 1990*: 119–142.
Palander-Collin, Minna
   1997   "A medieval case of grammaticalization, *methinks*". In M. Rissanen et al. (eds) 1997b, 371–403.
Partridge, A. C.
   1979   "Shakespeare's English: A bibliographical survey". *Poetica*: 46–79.
Peer, Willie van (ed.)
   1988   *The taming of the text: Explorations in language, literature and culture*. London: Routledge.
Poutsma, Hendrik
   1914–1926 *A grammar of late Modern English: For the use of continental, especially Dutch, students*. Part II (1916): *The parts of speech*, Section I, B *Pronouns and numerals*. Section II (1926) *The verb and the particles*. 2nd ed. Groningen: Noordhoff.
Poynton, Cate
   1984   "Names as vocatives: Forms and functions". *Nottingham Linguistics Circular* 13: 1–34.
Pyles, Thomas
   1971   *The origins and development of the English language*. 2nd ed. New York: Harcourt Brace Jovanovich.
Quirk et al. 1985 = Quirk, Randolph, Greenbaum, Sidney, Leech, Geoffrey and Svartvik, Jan
   1985   *A comprehensive grammar of the English language*. London: Longman.
Quirk, Randolph
   1971   "Shakespeare and the English Language". In *A new companion to Shakespeare studies*, K. Muir and S. Schoenbaum (eds), 67–82. London: CUP [repr. with minor alterations in R. Quirk 1974 *The linguist and the English language*. 46–64, London: Arnold, this again repr. in V. Salmon and E. Burness (eds), 3–21].
Ransom, John Crow
   1948   "On Shakespeare's language". *Sewanee Review* 55: 181–198.
Raumolin-Brunberg, Helena
   1996a   "Historical sociolinguistics". In T. Nevalainen and H. Raumolin-Brunberg (eds), 11–37.
   1996b   "Apparent time". In T. Nevalainen and H. Raumolin-Brunberg (eds), 93–109.
   1996c   "Forms of address in early English correspondence". In T. Nevalainen and H. Raumolin-Brunberg (eds), 167–181.
Raumolin-Brunberg, Helena and Nevalainen, Terttu
   1997a   "Social embedding of linguistic changes in Tudor English". In R. Hickey and S. Puppel (eds), vol 1, 701–717.
   1997b   "Like father (un)like son: A sociolinguistic approach to the language of the Cely family". In J. Fisiak (ed.), 489–511.
Replogle, Carol A. H.
   1967   Shakespeare's use of the forms of address. Ph. D. thesis, Brandeis University, Mass. [University Microfilms International].
   1973   "Shakespeare's salutations: A study in stylistic etiquette". *Studies in Philology* 70: 172–186 [repr. in V. Salmon and E. Burness (eds), 101–115].

Rietveld, Toni and van Hout, Roeland
   1993   *Statistical techniques for the study of language and language behaviour.* Berlin: de Gruyter.
Rissanen, Matti
   1986   "Variation and the study of English historical syntax". In D. Sankoff (ed.), 97–109.
   1990   "On the happy reunion of English philology and historical linguistics". In J. Fisiak (ed.), 353–369.
Rissanen et al. (eds) 1993 = Rissanen, Matti, Kytö, Merja and Palander-Collin, Minna (eds)
   1993   *Early English in the computer age: Explorations through the Helsinki Corpus.* Berlin: Mouton de Gruyter.
Rissanen et al. (eds) 1997a = Rissanen, Matti, Kytö, Merja and Heikkonen, Kirsi (eds)
   1997a *English in transition: Corpus-based studies in linguistic variation and genre styles.* [Topics in English Linguistics 23]. Berlin: Mouton de Gruyter.
Rissanen et al. (eds) 1997b = Rissanen, Matti, Kytö, Merja and Heikkonen, Kirsi (eds)
   1997b *Grammaticalization at work: Studies of long-term developments in English.* [Topics in English Linguistics 24]. Berlin: Mouton de Gruyter.
Romaine, Suzanne
   1982   *Socio-historical linguistics: Its status and methodology.* Cambridge: CUP.
Ronberg, Gert
   1992   *A way with words: The language of English Renaissance literature.* London: Arnold.
Rotundo, Barbara
   1979   "Forms of address: Reading between the lines". *Harvard Library Bulletin,* 349–358.
Rudanko, Juhani M.
   1993   *Pragmatic approaches to Shakespeare: Essays on* Othello, Coriolanus *and* Timon of Athens. Lanham: University Press of America.
Ryan, Kiernan
   1988   "The language of tragedy". In W. van Peer (ed.), 106–122.
Salmon, Vivian
   1965   "Sentence structures in colloquial Shakespearian English". *Transactions of the Philological Society:* 105–140 [repr. in V. Salmon and E. Burness (eds), 265–300].
   1967   "Elizabethan colloquial English in the Falstaff Plays". *Leeds Studies in English* 1: 37–70 [repr. in V. Salmon and E. Burness (eds), 37–70].
Salmon, Vivian and Burness, Edwina (eds)
   1987   *A reader in the language of Shakespearean drama.* [Amsterdam Studies in the Theory and History of Linguistic Science 35]. Amsterdam: John Benjamins.
Samuels, M. L.
   1972   *Linguistic evolution, with special reference to English.* Cambridge: CUP.
Sankoff, David (ed.)
   1986   *Diversity and diachrony.* [Amsterdam Studies in the Theory and History of Linguistic Science 53]. Amsterdam: John Benjamins.
Sankoff, David
   1988   "Variable rules". In *An international handbook of the science of language and society,* U. Ammon, N. Dittmar and K. J. Mattheier (eds), 984–997. Berlin: de Gruyter.
Schabert, Ina
   2000   *Shakespeare-Handbuch: Die Zeit, der Mensch, das Werk, die Nachwelt.* 4th ed. Stuttgart: Kröner [and 3rd ed. 1992].
Scheler, Manfred
   1982   *Shakespeares Englisch: Eine sprachwissenschaftliche Einführung.* Berlin: E. Schmidt.

Schendl, Herbert
1996 "The 3rd plural present indicative in Early Modern English: Variation and linguistic contact". In D. Britton (ed.), 143–160.
1997 "Morphological variation and change in Early Modern English: *my/mine, thy/thine*". In R. Hickey and S. Puppel (eds), vol. 1, 179–191.

Scherer, Bernhard
1932 Vers und Prosa bei den jüngeren dramatischen Zeitgenossen Shakespeares. Unpublished Ph. D. thesis, University of Münster.

Schiffrin, Deborah
1987 *Discourse Markers*. Cambridge: CUP.

Schmidt, Alexander and Sarrazin, Gregor
[1874, 1875] 1962 *Shakespeare-Lexicon: A complete dictionary of all the English words, phrases and constructions in the works of the poet*. 2 vols., 5th unchanged ed. Berlin: de Gruyter. [1st ed. vol 1: 1874, vol 2: 1875].

Schmied, Josef
1993 "Qualitative and quantitative research approaches to English relative constructions". In *Corpus based computational linguistics*, C. Souter and E. Atwell (eds), 85–96. Amsterdam: Rodopi.
1994 "The Lampeter Corpus of Early Modern English Tracts". In Kytö et al. (eds), 81–89.
1997 "Networking on corpora". In Feldmann et al. (eds), 113–128.

Schulze, Rainer
1985 *Höflichkeit im Englischen*. Tübingen: Narr.

Schulze, Rainer (ed.)
1998 *Making meaningful choices in English: On dimensions, perspectives, methodology and evidence*. [Language in Performance 16]. Tübingen: Narr.

Searle, John R.
1969 *Speech acts: An essay in the philosophy of language*. London: CUP.

Searle, John R. and Vanderveken, Daniel
1985 *Foundations of illocutionary logic*. Cambridge: CUP.

Seebold, Elmar
1983 "Hat es im Indogermanischen ein Höflichkeitspronomen gegeben?" *Die Sprache* 29: 27–36.

Shapiro, Michael
1983 *The sense of grammar: Language as semiotics*. Bloomington: Indiana University Press.

Sharpe, Henry
1885 "The prose in Shakespeare's plays". *Transactions of the New Shakespeare Society*, First Series 10: 523–562.

Short, Michael
1996 *Exploring the language of poems, plays and prose*. London: Longman.

Simpson, Paul
1997 *Language through literature: An introduction*. London: Routledge.

Simpson, Percy
1955 "Shakespeare's versification: A study of development". In *Studies in Elizabethan drama*, P. Simpson, 64–88. Oxford: Clarendon Press.

Smith, Hallett
1997 "Introduction to the Sonnets". In *Riverside Shakespeare*, 1839–1842.

Smith, Jeremy
1996 *An historical study of English: Function, form and change*. London: Routledge.

Sperber, Dan and Wilson, Deirdree
  1995   *Relevance: Communication and cognition.* Oxford: Blackwell.
Spevack, Marvin
  1968–1980 *A complete and systematic concordance to the works of Shakespeare.* 9 vols. Hildesheim: Olms.
  1972   "Shakespeare's English: The core vocabulary". *Review of National Literatures* 3: 106–122.
  1973   *The Harvard concordance to Shakespeare.* 2nd impr. Cambridge, Mass.: Belknap Press of Harvard University Press.
  1985   "Shakespeare's language". In *William Shakespeare: His world, his work, his influence,* J. Andrews (ed.), 343–361. New York: Charles Scribner's Sons.
  1993   *A Shakespeare thesaurus.* Hildesheim: Olms.
Spies, Heinrich
  1897   *Studien zur Geschichte des englischen Pronomens im XV. und XVI. Jahrhundert.* [Studien zur Englischen Philologie 1]. Halle: Niemeyer.
Stein, Dieter
  1974   *Grammatik und Variation von Flexionsformen in der Sprache des Shakespeare Corpus.* München: Tuduv.
  1985a "Discourse markers in Early Modern English". In *Papers from the 4th International Conference on English Historical Linguistics Amsterdam, 10–13 April, 1985* [Amsterdam Studies in the Theory and History of Linguistic Science 41], R. Eaton, O. Fischer, W. Koopman and F. van der Leek (eds), 283–302. Amsterdam: John Benjamins.
  1985b "Stylistic aspects of syntactic change". *Folia Linguistica Historica* 6: 153–178.
  1987   "At the crossroads of philology, linguistics and semiotics: Notes on the replacement of *th* by *s* in the third person singular in English". *English Studies* 68: 406–432.
  1990a *The semantics of syntactic change: Aspects of the evolution of* do *in English.* [Trends in Linguistics. Studies and Monographs 47]. Berlin: Mouton de Gruyter.
  1990b "Functional differentiation in the emerging English standard language: The evolution of a morphological discourse and style marker". In H. Andersen and K. Koerner (eds), 489–498.
  1992   "Style and grammar". In C. Nocera Avila et al. (eds), 41–57.
  1994   "Sorting out the variants: Standardization and social factors in the English language 1600–1800". In D. Stein and I. Tieken-Boon van Ostade (eds), 1–17.
  forthc. "Pronominal usage in Shakespeare: Between sociolinguistics and conversational analysis". In I. Taavitsainen and A. H. Jucker (eds).
Stein, Dieter and Tieken-Boon van Ostade, Ingrid (eds)
  1994   *Towards a standard English 1600–1800.* [Topics in English Linguistics 12]. Berlin: Mouton de Gruyter.
Stidson, Russell O.
  1917   *The use of* ye *in the function of* thou *in Middle English literature from MS. Auchinleck to MS. Vernon* [revised for publication by A. G. Kennedy]. [Leland Stanford Junior University Publications. University Series 28]. Stanford: Stanford University Press.
Stoll, Rita
  1989   *Die nicht-pronominale Anrede bei Shakespeare.* [Neue Studien zur Anglistik und Amerikanistik 41]. Frankfurt/Main: Lang.
Strang, Barbara M. H.
  1970   *A history of English.* London: Methuen.
Suerbaum, Ulrich
  1996   *Shakespeares Dramen.* 2nd ed. Tübingen: Francke.

Svartvik, Jan
    1992   "Corpus linguistics comes of age". In J. Svartvik (ed.), 7–13.
Svartvik, Jan (ed.)
    1992   *Directions in corpus linguistics: Proceedings of Nobel Symposium 82 Stockholm, 4–8 August 1991.* [Trends in Linguistics. Studies and Monographs 65]. Berlin: Mouton de Gruyter.
Sweet, Henry
    1898–1900   *A new English Grammar: Logical and historical.* 2 vols. Oxford: Clarendon Press.
Taavitsainen, Irma
    1995   "Interjections in Early Modern English: From imitation of spoken to conventions of written language". In A. H. Jucker (ed.), 439–465.
    1997a   "Genre conventions: Personal affect in fiction and non-fiction in Early Modern English". In M. Rissanen et al. (eds) 1997a, 185–266.
    1997b   "Exclamations in late Middle English". In *Studies in Middle English*, J. Fisiak (ed.), 573–607. Berlin: Mouton de Gruyter.
Taavitsainen, Irma and Jucker, Andreas H. (eds)
    forthc.   *Diachronic perspectives in address term systems.* Amsterdam: John Benjamins.
Thompson, Sandra A. and Mulac, Anthony
    1991   "A quantitative perspective on the grammaticalization of epistemic parentheticals in English". In E. Closs Traugott and B. Heine (eds), vol. 2, 313–329.
Tieken-Boon van Ostade, Ingrid
    1987   *The auxiliary* do *in eighteenth-century English: A sociohistorical-linguistic approach.* Dordrecht: Foris.
    1994   "Standard and non-standard pronominal usage in English, with special reference to the eighteenth century". In D. Stein and I. Tieken-Boon van Ostade (eds), 217–242.
Tomić, Olga Miseska (ed.)
    1989   *Markedness in synchrony and diachrony.* [Trends in Linguistics. Studies and Monographs 39]. Berlin: Mouton de Gruyter.
Trask, R. L.
    1993   *A dictionary of grammatical terms in linguistics.* London: Routledge.
    1996   *Historical linguistics.* London: Arnold.
Traugott, Elizabeth Closs
    1982   "From propositional to textual and expressive meanings: Some semantic-pragmatic aspects of grammaticalization". In *Perspectives on historical linguistics*, W. P. Lehmann and Y. Malkiel (eds), 245–271. Amsterdam: John Benjamins.
    1994   "Grammaticalization and lexicalization". In *The encyclopedia of language and linguistics*, R. E. Asher (ed.), vol. 3, 1481–1486. Oxford: Pergamon Press.
    2000   "*Promise* and *pray*-parentheticals." Paper given at the XI. International Conference on English Historical Linguistics (11. ICEHL, Santiago de Compostella, 7–12 September 2000).
Traugott, Elizabeth Closs and Dasher, Richard B.
    2002   *Regularity in semantic change* [Cambridge Studies in Linguistics 96]. Cambridge: CUP.
Traugott, Elizabeth Closs and Heine, Bernd (eds)
    1991   *Approaches to grammaticalization.* 2 vols. Amsterdam: John Benjamins.
Trudgill, Peter
    1974   *Sociolinguistics: An introduction.* Harmondsworth: Penguin.

Tschopp, Elisabeth
  1956   *Zur Verteilung von Vers und Prosa in Shakespeares Dramen.* [Schweizer Anglistische Arbeiten 41]. Bern: Francke.
Uhlig, Claus
  1968   "Zur Chronologie des Shakespeareschen Frühwerks". *Anglia* 86: 437–462.
Vendler, Helen
  1997   *The art of Shakespeare's Sonnets.* Cambridge, Mass.: The Belknap Press of Harvard University Press.
Verschueren, Jef
  1995   "The pragmatic perspective". In *Handbook of pragmatics,* J. Verschueren, J.-O. Östman and J. Blommaert (eds), 1–19. Amsterdam: John Benjamins.
Vickers, Brian
  1968   *The artistry of Shakespeare's prose.* London: Methuen.
Visser, Frederik Theodoor
  1963–1973 *An historical syntax of the English language.* 3 vols. Leiden: Brill.
Voitl, Herbert
  1969   "Shakespeares Komposita: Ein Beitrag zur Stilistik seiner Wortneuprägungen". *Deutsche Shakespeare-Gesellschaft West, Jahrbuch 1969:* 152–173.
Wales, Kathleen M.
  1983   "*Thou* and *you* in Early Modern English: Brown and Gilman re-appraised". *Studia Linguistica* 37: 107–125.
  1985   "Generic *your* and Jacobean drama: The rise and fall of a pronominal usage". *English Studies* 66: 7–24.
Wales, Katie [Kathleen M.]
  1995   "Your average generalisations: A case-study in historical pragmatics". In A. H. Jucker (ed.), 309–328.
  1996   *Personal pronouns in present-day English.* Cambridge: CUP.
Walker, Terry
  1999   Second-person singular pronouns in Early Modern English dialogues: A corpus-based study. Ph. D. thesis proposal, Uppsala University.
  2000   "The choice of second person singular pronouns in authentic and constructed dialogue in late sixteenth-century England". In *Corpus linguistics and linguistic theory,* C. Mair and M. Hundt (eds) [Language and Computers: Studies in Practical Linguistics 33], 375–384. Amsterdam: Rodopi.
  forthc. "*You* and *thou* in Early Modern English dialogues: A pattern of usage". In I. Taavitsainen and A. H. Jucker (eds).
Weidhorn, Manfred
  1969   "The relation of title and name to identity in Shakespearean tragedy". *Studies in English Literature* 9: 303–319.
Weinreich et al. 1968 = Weinreich, Uriel, Labov, William and Herzog, Marvin I.
  1968   "Empirical foundations for a theory of language change". In *Directions for historical linguistics: A symposium,* W. P. Lehmann and Y. Malkiel (eds), 95–195. Austin and London: University of Texas Press.
Wells et al. = Wells, Stanley, Taylor, Gary with Jowett, John and Montgomery, William
  1987   *William Shakespeare: A textual companion.* Oxford: Clarendon Press.
Williams, Charles
  1953   "The use of the second person in *Twelfth Night*". *English* 9: 125–128.

Williams, Joseph M.
1992   "*O! When degree is shak'd*: Sixteenth-century anticipations of some modern attitudes toward usage". In *English in its social contexts: Essays in historical sociolinguistics*, T. W. Machan and C. T. Scott (eds), 69–101. Oxford: OUP.

Williamson, Colin
1963   [Note on McIntosh 1963b]. *Review of English Studies*, New Series 14: 56–58.

Wilson, John Dover
1923   "The copy for *Much Ado About Nothing*". *New Shakespeare*. Cambridge: University Press.

Wischer, Ilse
1997   "Lexikalisierung versus Grammatikalisierung — Gemeinsamkeiten und Unterschiede". *Papiere zur Linguistik der Universität Klagenfurt* 2: 121–134.

2000   "Grammaticalization versus lexicalization: '*Methinks*' there is some confusion". In Fischer et al. (eds), 355–370.

Winter, Werner (ed.)
1984   *Anredeverhalten*. [Ars linguistica 13]. Tübingen: Narr.

Wood, Linda A. and Kroger, Rolf O.
1991   "Politeness and forms of address". *Journal of Language and Social Psychology* 10: 145–168.

Wright, Eugene Patrick
1993   *The structure of Shakespeare's sonnets*. Lewiston, Queenston and Lampeter: Mellen Press.

Wrightson, Keith
1991   "Estates, degrees, and sorts: Changing perceptions of society in Tudor and Stuart England". In *Language, history and class*, P. J. Corfield (ed.), 30–52. Oxford: Blackwell.

Wyld, Henry C.
1936   *A history of modern colloquial English*. Oxford: Blackwell [3rd ed., repr. 1953 Oxford: Blackwell].

Yamakawa, Kikuo
1966   "The imperative accompanied by the second personal pronoun". *Hitotsubashi Journal of Arts and sciences* 7/1: 6–25.

Yong-Lin, Yang
1988   "The English pronoun of address: A matter of self-compensation". *Sociolinguistics* 17: 157–180.

1991   "How to talk to the supernatural in Shakespeare". *Language in Society* 20: 247–261.

Name index*

---

* Italics point out Early English poets, dramatists, etc.

Subject index

In the PRAGMATICS AND BEYOND NEW SERIES the following titles have been published thus far or are scheduled for publication:

1. WALTER, Bettyruth: *The Jury Summation as Speech Genre: An Ethnographic Study of What it Means to Those who Use it.* Amsterdam/Philadelphia, 1988.
2. BARTON, Ellen: *Nonsentential Constituents: A Theory of Grammatical Structure and Pragmatic Interpretation.* Amsterdam/Philadelphia, 1990.
3. OLEKSY, Wieslaw (ed.): *Contrastive Pragmatics.* Amsterdam/Philadelphia, 1989.
4. RAFFLER-ENGEL, Walburga von (ed.): *Doctor-Patient Interaction.* Amsterdam/Philadelphia, 1989.
5. THELIN, Nils B. (ed.): *Verbal Aspect in Discourse.* Amsterdam/Philadelphia, 1990.
6. VERSCHUEREN, Jef (ed.): *Selected Papers from the 1987 International Pragmatics Conference. Vol. I: Pragmatics at Issue. Vol. II: Levels of Linguistic Adaptation. Vol. III: The Pragmatics of Intercultural and International Communication* (ed. with Jan Blommaert). Amsterdam/Philadelphia, 1991.
7. LINDENFELD, Jacqueline: *Speech and Sociability at French Urban Market Places.* Amsterdam/Philadelphia, 1990.
8. YOUNG, Lynne: *Language as Behaviour, Language as Code: A Study of Academic English.* Amsterdam/Philadelphia, 1990.
9. LUKE, Kang-Kwong: *Utterance Particles in Cantonese Conversation.* Amsterdam/Philadelphia, 1990.
10. MURRAY, Denise E.: *Conversation for Action. The computer terminal as medium of communication.* Amsterdam/Philadelphia, 1991.
11. LUONG, Hy V.: *Discursive Practices and Linguistic Meanings. The Vietnamese system of person reference.* Amsterdam/Philadelphia, 1990.
12. ABRAHAM, Werner (ed.): *Discourse Particles. Descriptive and theoretical investigations on the logical, syntactic and pragmatic properties of discourse particles in German.* Amsterdam/Philadelphia, 1991.
13. NUYTS, Jan, A. Machtelt BOLKESTEIN and Co VET (eds): *Layers and Levels of Representation in Language Theory: A functional view.* Amsterdam/Philadelphia, 1990.
14. SCHWARTZ, Ursula: *Young Children's Dyadic Pretend Play.* Amsterdam/Philadelphia, 1991.
15. KOMTER, Martha: *Conflict and Cooperation in Job Interviews.* Amsterdam/Philadelphia, 1991.
16. MANN, William C. and Sandra A. THOMPSON (eds): *Discourse Description: Diverse Linguistic Analyses of a Fund-Raising Text.* Amsterdam/Philadelphia, 1992.
17. PIÉRAUT-LE BONNIEC, Gilberte and Marlene DOLITSKY (eds): *Language Bases ... Discourse Bases.* Amsterdam/Philadelphia, 1991.
18. JOHNSTONE, Barbara: *Repetition in Arabic Discourse. Paradigms, syntagms and the ecology of language.* Amsterdam/Philadelphia, 1991.
19. BAKER, Carolyn D. and Allan LUKE (eds): *Towards a Critical Sociology of Reading Pedagogy. Papers of the XII World Congress on Reading.* Amsterdam/Philadelphia, 1991.
20. NUYTS, Jan: *Aspects of a Cognitive-Pragmatic Theory of Language. On cognition, functionalism, and grammar.* Amsterdam/Philadelphia, 1992.
21. SEARLE, John R. et al.: *(On) Searle on Conversation.* Compiled and introduced by Herman Parret and Jef Verschueren. Amsterdam/Philadelphia, 1992.

22. AUER, Peter and Aldo Di LUZIO (eds): *The Contextualization of Language.* Amsterdam/Philadelphia, 1992.
23. FORTESCUE, Michael, Peter HARDER and Lars KRISTOFFERSEN (eds): *Layered Structure and Reference in a Functional Perspective. Papers from the Functional Grammar Conference, Copenhagen, 1990.* Amsterdam/Philadelphia, 1992.
24. MAYNARD, Senko K.: *Discourse Modality: Subjectivity, Emotion and Voice in the Japanese Language.* Amsterdam/Philadelphia, 1993.
25. COUPER-KUHLEN, Elizabeth: *English Speech Rhythm. Form and function in everyday verbal interaction.* Amsterdam/Philadelphia, 1993.
26. STYGALL, Gail: *Trial Language. A study in differential discourse processing.* Amsterdam/Philadelphia, 1994.
27. SUTER, Hans Jürg: *The Wedding Report: A Prototypical Approach to the Study of Traditional Text Types.* Amsterdam/Philadelphia, 1993.
28. VAN DE WALLE, Lieve: *Pragmatics and Classical Sanskrit.* Amsterdam/Philadelphia, 1993.
29. BARSKY, Robert F.: *Constructing a Productive Other: Discourse theory and the convention refugee hearing.* Amsterdam/Philadelphia, 1994.
30. WORTHAM, Stanton E.F.: *Acting Out Participant Examples in the Classroom.* Amsterdam/Philadelphia, 1994.
31. WILDGEN, Wolfgang: *Process, Image and Meaning. A realistic model of the meanings of sentences and narrative texts.* Amsterdam/Philadelphia, 1994.
32. SHIBATANI, Masayoshi and Sandra A. THOMPSON (eds): *Essays in Semantics and Pragmatics.* Amsterdam/Philadelphia, 1995.
33. GOOSSENS, Louis, Paul PAUWELS, Brygida RUDZKA-OSTYN, Anne-Marie SIMON-VANDENBERGEN and Johan VANPARYS: *By Word of Mouth. Metaphor, metonymy and linguistic action in a cognitive perspective.* Amsterdam/Philadelphia, 1995.
34. BARBE, Katharina: *Irony in Context.* Amsterdam/Philadelphia, 1995.
35. JUCKER, Andreas H. (ed.): *Historical Pragmatics. Pragmatic developments in the history of English.* Amsterdam/Philadelphia, 1995.
36. CHILTON, Paul, Mikhail V. ILYIN and Jacob MEY: *Political Discourse in Transition in Eastern and Western Europe (1989-1991).* Amsterdam/Philadelphia, 1998.
37. CARSTON, Robyn and Seiji UCHIDA (eds): *Relevance Theory. Applications and implications.* Amsterdam/Philadelphia, 1998.
38. FRETHEIM, Thorstein and Jeanette K. GUNDEL (eds): *Reference and Referent Accessibility.* Amsterdam/Philadelphia, 1996.
39. HERRING, Susan (ed.): *Computer-Mediated Communication. Linguistic, social, and cross-cultural perspectives.* Amsterdam/Philadelphia, 1996.
40. DIAMOND, Julie: *Status and Power in Verbal Interaction. A study of discourse in a close-knit social network.* Amsterdam/Philadelphia, 1996.
41. VENTOLA, Eija and Anna MAURANEN, (eds): *Academic Writing. Intercultural and textual issues.* Amsterdam/Philadelphia, 1996.
42. WODAK, Ruth and Helga KOTTHOFF (eds): *Communicating Gender in Context.* Amsterdam/Philadelphia, 1997.
43. JANSSEN, Theo A.J.M. and Wim van der WURFF (eds): *Reported Speech. Forms and functions of the verb.* Amsterdam/Philadelphia, 1996.

44. BARGIELA-CHIAPPINI, Francesca and Sandra J. HARRIS: *Managing Language. The discourse of corporate meetings.* Amsterdam/Philadelphia, 1997.
45. PALTRIDGE, Brian: *Genre, Frames and Writing in Research Settings.* Amsterdam/Philadelphia, 1997.
46. GEORGAKOPOULOU, Alexandra: *Narrative Performances. A study of Modern Greek storytelling.* Amsterdam/Philadelphia, 1997.
47. CHESTERMAN, Andrew: *Contrastive Functional Analysis.* Amsterdam/Philadelphia, 1998.
48. KAMIO, Akio: *Territory of Information.* Amsterdam/Philadelphia, 1997.
49. KURZON, Dennis: *Discourse of Silence.* Amsterdam/Philadelphia, 1998.
50. GRENOBLE, Lenore: *Deixis and Information Packaging in Russian Discourse.* Amsterdam/Philadelphia, 1998.
51. BOULIMA, Jamila: *Negotiated Interaction in Target Language Classroom Discourse.* Amsterdam/Philadelphia, 1999.
52. GILLIS, Steven and Annick DE HOUWER (eds): *The Acquisition of Dutch.* Amsterdam/Philadelphia, 1998.
53. MOSEGAARD HANSEN, Maj-Britt: *The Function of Discourse Particles. A study with special reference to spoken standard French.* Amsterdam/Philadelphia, 1998.
54. HYLAND, Ken: *Hedging in Scientific Research Articles.* Amsterdam/Philadelphia, 1998.
55. ALLWOOD, Jens and Peter Gärdenfors (eds): *Cognitive Semantics. Meaning and cognition.* Amsterdam/Philadelphia, 1999.
56. TANAKA, Hiroko: *Language, Culture and Social Interaction. Turn-taking in Japanese and Anglo-American English.* Amsterdam/Philadelphia, 1999.
57 JUCKER, Andreas H. and Yael ZIV (eds): *Discourse Markers. Descriptions and theory.* Amsterdam/Philadelphia, 1998.
58. ROUCHOTA, Villy and Andreas H. JUCKER (eds): *Current Issues in Relevance Theory.* Amsterdam/Philadelphia, 1998.
59. KAMIO, Akio and Ken-ichi TAKAMI (eds): *Function and Structure. In honor of Susumu Kuno.* 1999.
60. JACOBS, Geert: *Preformulating the News. An analysis of the metapragmatics of press releases.* 1999.
61. MILLS, Margaret H. (ed.): *Slavic Gender Linguistics.* 1999.
62. TZANNE, Angeliki: *Talking at Cross-Purposes. The dynamics of miscommunication.* 2000.
63. BUBLITZ, Wolfram, Uta LENK and Eija VENTOLA (eds.): *Coherence in Spoken and Written Discourse. How to create it and how to describe it.Selected papers from the International Workshop on Coherence, Augsburg, 24-27 April 1997.* 1999.
64. SVENNEVIG, Jan: *Getting Acquainted in Conversation. A study of initial interactions.* 1999.
65. COOREN, François: *The Organizing Dimension of Communication.* 2000.
66. JUCKER, Andreas H., Gerd FRITZ and Franz LEBSANFT (eds.): *Historical Dialogue Analysis.* 1999.
67. TAAVITSAINEN, Irma, Gunnel MELCHERS and Päivi PAHTA (eds.): *Dimensions of Writing in Nonstandard English.* 1999.
68. ARNOVICK, Leslie: *Diachronic Pragmatics. Seven case studies in English illocutionary development.* 1999.

69. NOH, Eun-Ju: *The Semantics and Pragmatics of Metarepresentation in English. A relevance-theoretic account.* 2000.
70. SORJONEN, Marja-Leena: *Responding in Conversation. A study of response particles in Finnish.* 2001.
71. GÓMEZ-GONZÁLEZ, María Ángeles: *The Theme-Topic Interface. Evidence from English.* 2001.
72. MARMARIDOU, Sophia S.A.: *Pragmatic Meaning and Cognition.* 2000.
73. HESTER, Stephen and David FRANCIS (eds.): *Local Educational Order. Ethnomethodological studies of knowledge in action.* 2000.
74. TROSBORG, Anna (ed.): *Analysing Professional Genres.* 2000.
75. PILKINGTON, Adrian: *Poetic Effects. A relevance theory perspective.* 2000.
76. MATSUI, Tomoko: *Bridging and Relevance.* 2000.
77. VANDERVEKEN, Daniel and Susumu KUBO (eds.): *Essays in Speech Act Theory.* 2002.
78. SELL, Roger D. : *Literature as Communication. The foundations of mediating criticism.* 2000.
79. ANDERSEN, Gisle and Thorstein FRETHEIM (eds.): *Pragmatic Markers and Propositional Attitude.* 2000.
80. UNGERER, Friedrich (ed.): *English Media Texts – Past and Present. Language and textual structure.* 2000.
81. DI LUZIO, Aldo, Susanne GÜNTHNER and Franca ORLETTI (eds.): *Culture in Communication. Analyses of intercultural situations.* 2001.
82. KHALIL, Esam N.: *Grounding in English and Arabic News Discourse.* 2000.
83. MÁRQUEZ REITER, Rosina: *Linguistic Politeness in Britain and Uruguay. A contrastive study of requests and apologies.* 2000.
84. ANDERSEN, Gisle: *Pragmatic Markers and Sociolinguistic Variation. A relevance-theoretic approach to the language of adolescents.* 2001.
85. COLLINS, Daniel E.: *Reanimated Voices. Speech reporting in a historical-pragmatic perspective.* 2001.
86. IFANTIDOU, Elly: *Evidentials and Relevance.* 2001.
87. MUSHIN, Ilana: *Evidentiality and Epistemological Stance. Narrative retelling.* 2001.
88. BAYRAKTAROĞLU, Arın and Maria SIFIANOU (eds.): *Linguistic Politeness Across Boundaries. The case of Greek and Turkish.* 2001.
89. ITAKURA, Hiroko: *Conversational Dominance and Gender. A study of Japanese speakers in first and second language contexts.* 2001.
90. KENESEI, István and Robert M. HARNISH (eds.): *Perspectives on Semantics, Pragmatics, and Discourse. A Festschrift for Ferenc Kiefer.* 2001.
91. GROSS, Joan: *Speaking in Other Voices. An ethnography of Walloon puppet theaters.* 2001.
92. GARDNER, Rod: *When Listeners Talk. Response tokens and listener stance.* 2001.
93. BARON, Bettina and Helga KOTTHOFF (eds.): *Gender in Interaction. Perspectives on femininity and masculinity in ethnography and discourse.* 2002
94. McILVENNY, Paul (ed.): *Talking Gender and Sexuality.* 2002.
95. FITZMAURICE, Susan M.: *The Familiar Letter in Early Modern English. A pragmatic approach.* 2002.
96. HAVERKATE, Henk: *The Syntax, Semantics and Pragmatics of Spanish Mood.* 2002.

97. MAYNARD, Senko K.: *Linguistic Emotivity. Centrality of place, the topic-comment dynamic, and an ideology of* pathos *in Japanese discourse*. 2002.
98. DUSZAK, Anna (ed.): *Us and Others. Social identities across languages, discourses and cultures*. 2002.
99. JASZCZOLT, K.M. and Ken TURNER (eds.): *Meaning Through Language Contrast. Volume 1.* n.y.p.
100. JASZCZOLT, K.M. and Ken TURNER (eds.): *Meaning Through Language Contrast. Volume 2.* n.y.p.
101. LUKE, Kang Kwong and Theodossia-Soula PAVLIDOU (eds.): *Telephone Calls. Unity and diversity in conversational structure across languages and cultures.* n.y.p.
102. LEAFGREN, John: *Degrees of Explicitness. Information structure and the packaging of Bulgarian subjects and objects.* 2002.
103. FETZER, Anita and Christiane MEIERKORD (eds.): *Rethinking Sequentiality. Linguistics meets conversational interaction.* 2002.
104. BEECHING, Kate: *Gender, Politeness and Pragmatic Particles in French.* 2002.
105. BLACKWELL, Sarah E.: *Implicatures in Discourse.* n.y.p.
106. BUSSE, Ulrich: *Linguistic Variation in the Shakespeare Corpus.* 2002.
107. TAAVITSAINEN, Irma and Andreas H. JUCKER (eds.): *Diachronic Perspectives on Address Term Systems.* n.y.p.
108. BARRON, Anne: *Acquisition in Interlanguage Pragmatics. How to do things with words in a study abroad context.* n.y.p.
109. MAYES, Patricia: *Language, Social Structure, and Culture. A genre analysis of cooking classes in Japan and America.* n.y.p.
110. ANDROUTSOPOULOS, Jannis K. and Alexandra GEORGAKOPOULOU (eds.): *Discourse Constructions of Youth Identities.* n.y.p.
111. ENSINK, Titus and Christoph SAUER (eds.): *Framing and Perspectivising in Discourse.* n.y.p.